Kaplan Publishing are constantly finding new
difference to your studies and our exciting c
offer something different to students lookir

This book comes with free MyKaplan onlin
study anytime, anywhere. **This free online
separately and is included in the price of the book.**

CW00708689

Having purchased this book, you have access to the following online study materials:

CONTENT	ACCA (including FBT, FMA, FFA)		FIA (excluding FBT, FMA, FFA)	
	Text	Kit	Text	Kit
Electronic version of the book	✓	✓	✓	✓
Knowledge checks with instant answers	✓		✓	
Material updates	✓	✓	✓	✓
Latest official ACCA exam questions*		✓		
Pocket Notes (digital copy)	✓		✓	
Study Planner	✓			
Progress Test including questions and answers	✓		✓	
Syllabus recap Videos		✓		✓
Revision Planner		✓		✓
Question Debrief and Walkthrough Videos		✓		
Mock Exam including questions and answers		✓		

* Excludes BT, MA, FA, FBT, FMA, FFA; for all other papers includes a selection of questions, as released by ACCA

How to access your online resources

Received this book as part of your Kaplan course?
If you have a MyKaplan account, your full online resources will be added automatically, in line with the
information in your course confirmation email. If you've not used MyKaplan before, you'll be sent an activation
email once your resources are ready.

Bought your book from Kaplan?
We'll automatically add your online resources to your MyKaplan account. If you've not used MyKaplan before,
you'll be sent an activation email.

Bought your book from elsewhere?
Go to **www.mykaplan.co.uk/add-online-resources**
Enter the ISBN number found on the title page and back cover of this book.
Add the unique pass key number contained in the scratch panel below.
You may be required to enter additional information during this process to set up or confirm your account
details.

This code can only be used once for the registration of this book online. This registration and your online
content will expire when the examinations covered by this book have taken place. Please allow one hour from
the time you submit your book details for us to process your request.

Please scratch the film to access your unique code.

Please be aware that this code is case-sensitive and you will need
to include the dashes within the passcode, but not when entering
the ISBN.

KAPLAN

PUBLISHING

ACCA

Strategic Professional – Options

Advanced Performance Management (APM)

Study Text

KAPLAN PUBLISHING'S STATEMENT OF PRINCIPLES

LINGUISTIC DIVERSITY, EQUALITY AND INCLUSION

We are committed to diversity, equality and inclusion and strive to deliver content that all users can relate to.

We are here to make a difference to the success of every learner.

Clarity, accessibility and ease of use for our learners are key to our approach.

We will use contemporary examples that are rich, engaging and representative of a diverse workplace.

We will include a representative mix of race and gender at the various levels of seniority within the businesses in our examples to support all our learners in aspiring to achieve their potential within their chosen careers.

Roles played by characters in our examples will demonstrate richness and diversity by the use of different names, backgrounds, ethnicity and gender, with a mix of sexuality, relationships and beliefs where these are relevant to the syllabus.

It must always be obvious who is being referred to in each stage of any example so that we do not detract from clarity and ease of use for each of our learners.

We will actively seek feedback from our learners on our approach and keep our policy under continuous review. If you would like to provide any feedback on our linguistic approach, please use this form (you will need to enter the link below into your browser).

https://docs.google.com/forms/d/1Vc4mltBPrfViy8AhfyKcJMHQKBmLaLPoa_WPqFNf4MI/edit

We will seek to devise simple measures that can be used by independent assessors to randomly check our success in the implementation of our Linguistic Equality, Diversity and Inclusion Policy.

KAPLAN PUBLISHING

British library cataloguing-in-publication data

A catalogue record for this book is available from the British Library.

Published by:

Kaplan Publishing UK
Unit 2 The Business Centre
Molly Millars Lane
Wokingham
Berkshire
RG41 2QZ

ISBN 978-1-83996-672-9

© Kaplan Financial Limited, 2024

Acknowledgements

We are grateful to the Association of Chartered Certified Accountants and the Chartered Institute of Management Accountants for permission to reproduce past examination questions. The answers have been prepared by Kaplan Publishing.

This product contains material that is ©Financial Reporting Council Ltd (FRC). Adapted and reproduced with the kind permission of the Financial Reporting Council. All rights reserved. For further information, please visit www.frc.org.uk or call +44 (0)20 7492 2300.

The coverage of the United Nations' Sustainable Development Goals (SDGs) in Chapter 2 is based on content retrieved on 22 March 2022 from www.un.org/sustainabledevelopment © 2022 United Nations. Used with the permission of the United Nations.

Contents

Introduction

How to Use the Materials

These Kaplan Publishing learning materials have been carefully designed to make your learning experience as easy as possible and to give you the best chances of success in your examinations.

The product range contains a number of features to help you in the study process. They include:

1   Detailed study guide and syllabus objectives

2   Description of the examination

3   Study skills and revision guidance

4   Study text

5   Question practice

The sections on the study guide, the syllabus objectives, the examination and study skills should all be read before you commence your studies. They are designed to familiarise you with the nature and content of the examination and give you tips on how to best to approach your learning.

The **Study Text** comprises the main learning materials and gives guidance as to the importance of topics and where other related resources can be found. Each chapter includes:

- The **learning objectives** contained in each chapter, which have been carefully mapped to the examining body's own syllabus learning objectives or outcomes. You should use these to check you have a clear understanding of all the topics on which you might be assessed in the examination.

- The **chapter diagram** provides a visual reference for the content in the chapter, giving an overview of the topics and how they link together.

- The **content** for each topic area commences with a brief explanation or definition to put the topic into context before covering the topic in detail. You should follow your studying of the content with a review of the illustration/s. These are worked examples which will help you to understand better how to apply the content for the topic.

- **Test your understanding** sections provide an opportunity to assess your understanding of the key topics by applying what you have learned to short questions. Answers can be found at the back of each chapter.

- **Summary diagrams** complete each chapter to show the important links between topics and the overall content of the syllabus. These diagrams should be used to check that you have covered and understood the core topics before moving on.

KAPLAN PUBLISHING

Quality and accuracy are of the utmost importance to us so if you spot an error in any of our products, please send an email to mykaplanreporting@kaplan.com with full details, or follow the link to the feedback form in MyKaplan.

Our Quality Co-ordinator will work with our technical team to verify the error and take action to ensure it is corrected in future editions.

Icon Explanations

 Definition – Key definitions that you will need to learn from the core content.

 Supplementary reading – These sections will help to provide a deeper understanding of core areas. The supplementary reading is **NOT** optional reading. It is vital to provide you with the breadth of knowledge you will need to address the wide range of topics within your syllabus that could feature in an exam question. **Reference to this text is vital when self studying**

 Test your understanding – Exercises for you to complete to ensure that you have understood the topics just learned.

Some of the test your understandings in this material are shorter or more straightforward than questions in the Advanced Performance Management (APM) exam. They are contained in the material for learning purposes and will help you to build your knowledge and confidence so that you are ready to tackle past exam questions during the revision phase.

 Illustration – Worked examples help you understand the core content better.

On-line subscribers

Our on-line resources are designed to increase the flexibility of your learning materials and provide you with immediate feedback on how your studies are progressing.

If you are subscribed to our on-line resources you will find:

1   On-line reference ware: reproduces your Study Text on-line, giving you anytime, anywhere access.

2   On-line testing: provides you with additional on-line objective testing so you can practice what you have learned further.

3   On-line performance management: immediate access to your on-line testing results. Review your performance by key topics and chart your achievement through the course relative to your peer group.

Syllabus

Introduction to the syllabus

The aim of ACCA **Advanced Performance Management (APM)** is to apply relevant knowledge, skills and exercise professional judgement in selecting and applying strategic management accounting techniques in different business contexts, to contribute to the planning, control and evaluation of the performance of an organisation and its strategic and operational development.

Main capabilities

On successful completion of this exam, candidates should be able to:

A Use strategic planning and control models to plan and monitor organisational performance

B Identify and evaluate the design features of effective performance management information and monitoring systems and recognise the impact of developments in technology on performance measurement and management systems

C Apply appropriate strategic performance measurement techniques in evaluating and improving organisational performance

D Advise clients and senior management on strategic business performance evaluation

E Apply a range of professional skills in addressing requirements within the Advanced Performance Management exam, and in preparation for, or to support, current work experience

F Employability and technology skills

ACCA Performance Objectives

In order to become a member of the ACCA, as a trainee accountant you will need to demonstrate that you have achieved nine performance objectives. Performance objectives are indicators of effective performance and set the minimum standard of work that trainees are expected to achieve and demonstrate in the workplace. They are divided into key areas of knowledge which are closely linked to the exam syllabus.

There are five Essential performance objectives, all of which must be achieved.

There is a choice of seventeen Technical performance objectives, grouped under seven headings. Four of these objectives will need to be achieved.

The performance objectives which link to this exam are:

PO1 – Ethics and professionalism (Essential)

PO3 – Strategy and innovation (Essential)

PO5 – Leadership and management (Essential)

PO12 – Evaluating management accounting systems (Technical)

PO13 – Plan and control performance (Technical)

PO14 – Monitor performance (Technical)

PO21 – Business advisory (Technical)

PO22 – Data analysis and decision support (Technical)

The following link provides an in depth insight into all of the performance objectives:

https://www.accaglobal.com/content/dam/ACCA_Global/Students/per/PER-Performance-objectives-achieve.pdf

Progression

There are two elements of progression that we can measure: first how quickly students move through individual topics within a subject; and second how quickly they move from one course to the next. We know that there is an optimum for both, but it can vary from subject to subject and from student to student. However, using data and our experience of student performance over many years, we can make some generalisations.

A fixed period of study set out at the start of a course with key milestones is important. This can be within a subject, for example 'I will finish this topic by 30 June', or for overall achievement, such as 'I want to be qualified by the end of next year'.

Your qualification is cumulative, as earlier exams provide a foundation for your subsequent studies, so do not allow there to be too big a gap between one subject and another. We know that exams encourage techniques that lead to some degree of short-term retention, the result being that you will simply forget much of what you have already learned unless it is refreshed (look up Ebbinghaus Forgetting Curve for more details on this). This makes it more difficult as you move from one subject to another: not only will you have to learn the new subject, you will also have to relearn all the underpinning knowledge as well. This is very inefficient and slows down your overall progression which makes it more likely you may not succeed at all.

In addition, delaying your studies slows your path to qualification which can have negative impacts on your career, postponing the opportunity to apply for higher level positions and therefore higher pay.

You can use the following diagram showing the whole structure of your qualification to help you keep track of your progress.

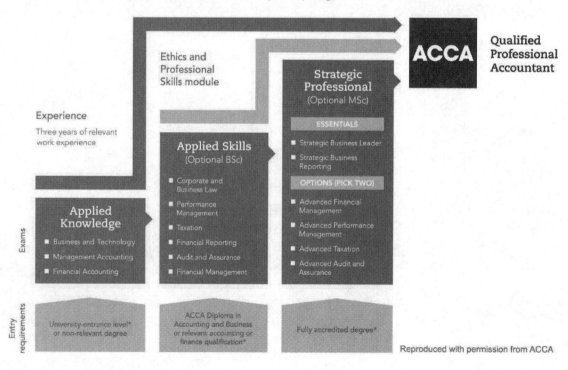

Reproduced with permission from ACCA

Syllabus objectives

We have reproduced the ACCA's syllabus below, showing where the objectives are explored within this book. Within the chapters, we have broken down the extensive information found in the syllabus into easily digestible and relevant sections, called Content Objectives. These correspond to the objectives at the beginning of each chapter.

The superscript numbers in square brackets indicate the intellectual depth at which the subject area could be assessed within the examination. Level 1 (knowledge and comprehension) broadly equates with the Applied Knowledge module, Level 2 (application and analysis) with the Applied Skills module and Level 3 (synthesis and evaluation) to the Strategic Professional level. However, lower level skills can continue to be assessed as you progress through each module and level.

Syllabus learning objective	Chapter reference

A STRATEGIC PLANNING AND CONTROL

1 Strategic management accounting

(a)	Explain the role of strategic performance management in strategic planning and control.[2]	1
(b)	Discuss the role of performance measurement in checking progress towards the corporate objectives.[2]	1
(c)	Compare planning and control between the strategic and operational levels within a business entity.[2]	1
(d)	Discuss the scope for potential conflict between strategic business plans and short-term localised decisions.[2]	1
(e)	Evaluate how models such as SWOT analysis, PEST, Boston Consulting Group, balanced scorecard, Porter's generic strategies and 5 Forces may assist in the performance management process.[3]	2 & 13
(f)	Apply and evaluate the methods of benchmarking performance.[3]	1
(g)	Evaluate how risk and uncertainty play an important role in planning, decision-making and reporting of performance at all levels of an organisation, including the impact of the different risk appetites of stakeholders.[3]	3

2 Performance hierarchy

(a)	Discuss how the purpose, structure and content of a mission statement impacts on performance measurement and management.[2]	1
(b)	Discuss how strategic objectives are cascaded down the organisation via the formulation of subsidiary performance objectives.[2]	1
(c)	Apply critical success factor analysis in developing performance metrics from business objectives.[3]	1
(d)	Identify and discuss the characteristics of operational performance.[2]	1
(e)	Discuss the relative significance of planning as against controlling activities at different levels in the performance hierarchy.[3]	1
(f)	Explain the performance 'planning gap' and evaluate alternative strategies to fill the gap.[3]	2

3 Performance management and control of the organisation

(a) Evaluate the strengths and weaknesses of alternative budgeting models and compare such techniques as fixed and flexible, rolling, activity based, zero based and incremental.[3] 5

(b) Evaluate different types of budget variances and how these relate to issues in planning and controlling organisations.[3] 5

(c) Evaluate the increased use of non-traditional profit-based performance measures in controlling organisations (e.g. beyond budgeting).[3] 5

4 Changes in business structure and management accounting

(a) Identify and discuss the particular information needs of organisations adopting a functional, divisional or network form and the implications for performance management.[2] 6

(b) Assess the changes to management accounting systems to reflect the needs of modern service orientated businesses compared with the needs of a traditional manufacturing industry.[3] 6

(c) Assess the influence of Business Process Re-engineering on systems development and improvements in organisational performance.[3] 6

(d) Analyse the role that performance management systems play in business integration using models such as the value chain and McKinsey's 7S's.[3] 6

(e) Discuss how changing an organisation's structure, culture and strategy will influence the adoption of new performance measurement methods and techniques.[3] 6

(f) Assess the need for businesses to continually refine and develop their management accounting and information systems if they are to maintain or improve their performance in an increasingly competitive and global market.[3] 7

5   Environmental, social and governance factors

(a)   Discuss the ways in which stakeholder groups operate and how they influence an organisation and its performance measurement and performance management systems (e.g. using Mendelow's matrix).[3]   4

(b)   Discuss the social and ethical issues that may impact on strategy formulation and evaluate the role of the management accountant in the collection of data, measurement and reporting of social and environmental factors, such as are used to demonstrate a wider view of performance in reporting, for example, sustainability.[3]   4

(c)   Discuss, evaluate and apply environmental management accounting using for example lifecycle costing, input-output analysis and activity-based costing.[3]   4

B   PERFORMANCE MANAGEMENT INFORMATION SYSTEMS AND DEVELOPMENTS IN TECHNOLOGY

1   Performance management information systems

(a)   Discuss, with reference to performance management, ways in which the information requirements of a management structure are affected by the features of the structure.[2]   7

(b)   Evaluate the compatibility of management accounting objectives and the management accounting information systems.[3]   7

(c)   Discuss the issue of data silos and the problems they present for the accounting function.[2]   7

(d)   Discuss the integration of management accounting information within an overall information system, for example the use of enterprise resource planning systems.[2]   7

(e)   Evaluate whether the management information systems are lean and the value of the information that they provide (e.g. using the 5 Ss).[3]   7 & 14

(f)   Evaluate the external and internal factors (e.g. anticipated human behaviour) which will influence the design and use of a management accounting system.[3]   7

2 Sources of management information

(a) Discuss the principal internal and external sources of management accounting information, their costs and limitations.[2]

7

(b) Demonstrate how the information might be used in planning and controlling activities, e.g. benchmarking against similar activities.[3]

7

3 Recording and processing systems and technologies

(a) Demonstrate how the type of business entity will influence the recording and processing methods.[2]

7

(b) Discuss how IT developments may influence management accounting systems (e.g. unified corporate databases, process automation, the internet of things, RFIDs, cloud and network technology).[3]

7

(c) Explain how information systems provide instant access to previously unavailable data that can be used for benchmarking and control purposes and help improve business performance (e.g. through the use of artificial intelligence (AI), enterprise resource planning, knowledge management and customer relationship management systems and also, data warehouses).[3]

7

(d) Discuss the difficulties associated with recording and processing data of a qualitative nature.[2]

8

4 Data analytics

(a) Discuss the development of big data and its impact on performance measurement and management, including the risks and challenges it presents.[3]

7

(b) Discuss the impact of big data and big data analytics on the role of the management accountant.[3]

7

(c) Demonstrate and evaluate different methods of data analysis (e.g. descriptive, diagnostic and prescriptive analytics).[3]

7

(d) Discuss the use of alternative methods of data analytics (e.g. text, image, video and voice analytics and sentiment analysis) .[2]

7

(e) Discuss the ethical issues associated with information collection and processing (e.g. the use of 'black box' algorithms and large-scale data collection and mining).[2]

7

5   Management reports

(a)   Evaluate the output reports of an information
      system in the light of. [3]   8

      (i)   best practice in presentation

      (ii)   the objectives of the report/organisation

      (iii)   the needs of the readers of the report; and

      (iv)   avoiding the problem of information overload

      (v)   the use of presentation techniques such as
              data visualisation

(b)   Advise on common mistakes and misconceptions
      in the use of numerical data used for performance   8
      measurement.[3]

(c)   Explore the role of the management accountant in
      providing key performance information for   8
      integrated reporting to stakeholders.[2]

C   STRATEGIC PERFORMANCE MEASUREMENT

1   Strategic performance measures in private sector

(a)   Demonstrate why the primary objective of financial
      performance should be primarily concerned with   10
      the benefits to shareholders.[2]

(b)   Discuss the appropriateness of, and apply different
      measures of performance, including:[3]   10 & 11

      (i)   Gross profit and operating profit

      (ii)   Return on Capital Employed (ROCE)

      (iii)   Return on Investment (ROI)

      (iv)   Earnings Per Share (EPS)

      (v)   Earnings Before Interest, Tax, Depreciation
               and Amortisation (EBITDA)

      (vi)   Residual Income (RI)

      (vii)   Net Present Value (NPV)

      (viii)   Internal Rate of Return and Modified Internal
               Rate of Return (IRR, MIRR)

      (ix)   Economic Value Added (EVA™)

(c)   Discuss why indicators of liquidity and gearing
      need to considered in conjunction with   10
      profitability.[3]

(d)   Compare and contrast short and long run financial
      performance and the resulting management   10
      issues.[3]

(e)   Assess the appropriate benchmarks to use in
      assessing performance.[3]   10

2 Divisional performance and transfer pricing issues

3 Strategic performance measures in not-for-profit organisations

4 Non-financial performance indicators

7 Other behavioural aspects of performance measurement

(a)	Discuss the accountability issues that might arise from performance measurement systems.[3]	9
(b)	Assess the statement; 'What gets measured, gets done' in the context of performance management.[3]	1 & 9
(c)	Demonstrate how management style needs to be considered when designing an effective performance measurement system (e.g. Hopwood's management styles).[3]	9

D PERFORMANCE EVALUATION

1 Alternative views of performance measurement and management

(a)	Apply and evaluate the 'balanced scorecard' approach as a way in which to improve the range and linkage between performance measures.[3]	13
(b)	Apply and evaluate the 'performance pyramid' as a way in which to link strategy, operations and performance.[3]	13
(c)	Apply and evaluate the work of Fitzgerald and Moon that considers performance measurement in business services using building blocks for dimensions, standards and rewards.[3]	13
(d)	Discuss and evaluate the application of activity-based management.[3]	5
(e)	Evaluate and apply the value-based management approaches to performance management.[3]	11

2 Strategic performance issues in complex business structures

(a)	Discuss the problems encountered in planning, controlling and measuring performance levels, e.g. productivity, profitability, quality and service levels, in complex business structures.[3]	6 & 11
(b)	Discuss the impact on performance management of the use of business models involving strategic alliances, joint ventures and complex supply chain structures.[3]	6

E PROFESSIONAL SKILLS

1 Communication

(a) Inform concisely, objectively and unambiguously, adopting a suitable style and format, using appropriate technology.[3]   15

(b) Advise using compelling and logical arguments, demonstrating the ability to counter argue where appropriate.[3]   15

(c) Clarify and simplify complex issues to convey relevant information in a way that adopts an appropriate tone and is easily understood and reflects the requirements of the intended audience.[3]   15

2 Analysis and evaluation

(a) Investigate relevant information from a range of sources, using appropriate analytical techniques to establish reasons and causes of issues, assist in decision-making and to identify opportunities or solutions.[3]   15

(b) Consider information, evidence and findings carefully, reflecting on their implications and how they can be used in the interests of the individual, business function, division and the wider organisational goals.[3]   15

(c) Assess and apply appropriate judgement when considering organisational plans, initiatives or issues when making decisions; taking into account the implications of such decisions on the organisation and those affected.[3]   15

(d) Appraise information objectively with a view to balancing costs, risks, benefits and opportunities, before advising on or recommending appropriate solutions or decisions.[3]   15

3 Scepticism

(a) Explore the underlying reasons for key organisational plans, issues and decisions, applying the attitude of an enquiring mind, beyond what is immediately apparent.[3]   15

(b) Question opinions, assertions and assumptions, by seeking justifications and obtaining sufficient evidence for either their support and acceptance or rejection.[3]   15

KAPLAN PUBLISHING

(c) Challenge and critically assess the information presented or decisions made, where this is clearly justified, in the wider professional, ethical, organisational, or public interest. [3] 15

4 Commercial acumen

(a) Demonstrate awareness of organisational and external factors, which will affect the measurement and management of an organisation's strategic objectives and operational activities.[3] 15

(b) Recognise key issues in determining how to address or resolve problems and use judgment in proposing and recommending commercially viable solutions.[3] 15

(c) Show insight and perception in understanding behavioural responses, process and system-related issues and wider organisational matters, demonstrating acumen in offering advice and arriving at appropriate recommendations.[3] 15

F EMPLOYABILITY AND TECHNOLOGY SKILLS

1 Use computer technology to efficiently access and manipulate relevant information. 16

2 Work on relevant response options, using available functions and technology, as would be required in the workplace. 16

3 Navigate windows and computer screens to create and amend responses to exam requirements, using appropriate tools. 16

4 Present data and information effectively, using the appropriate tools. 16

The examination

Approach to examining the syllabus

The Advanced Performance Management (APM) exam builds upon the skills and knowledge examined in the Performance Management (PM) exam. At this stage candidates will be expected to demonstrate an integrated knowledge of the subject and an ability to relate their technical understanding of the subject to issues of strategic importance to the organisation. The study guide specifies the wide range of contextual understanding that is required to achieve a satisfactory standard at this level.

The examination will also focus on the following professional skills and behaviours:

- Communication

- Analysis and Evaluation

- Scepticism

- Commercial Acumen

Examination structure

- The syllabus is assessed by **a 3 hour 15 minutes computer based examination (CBE)**.

- **Total 100 marks.**

- The **pass mark is 50%**.

- Dates will be in the format 20XX, e.g. 20X5. This will make the dates for each exam session generic.

- Candidates will receive a present value table and an annuity table.

Section A

Section A of the exam will always be a single **50-mark case study**, based on an organisation in a particular business context. The 50 marks will **comprise 40 technical marks and 10 professional skills marks** (syllabus section E). **All the professional skills will be examined** in Section A.

It is likely to include the organisation's mission statement and strategic objectives and candidates will be expected to be able to assess the methods by which the organisation is controlling, managing, and measuring performance in order to achieve its objectives. This assessment could include an evaluation of the organisation's performance report, its information systems, new strategies or projects and its performance management and measurement systems. Candidates should understand that they will be expected to undertake calculations, draw comparison against relevant information where appropriate and be prepared to offer alternative recommendations as needed.

Management accountants are required to look across a range of issues which will affect organisational performance, the achievement of objectives and impact on operations and so candidates should expect to see Section A of the exam focus on a **range of issues across technical syllabus sections A, B and C**. These will vary depending of the business context the case study in Section A is based on.

Section A questions will ask candidates to produce a response in a report format, for example a report to the Board of Directors.

Section B

Candidates will be required to answer a further **two 25-mark questions** in Section B of the exam, which will comprise of scenario-based questions. The 25 marks will **comprise 20 technical marks and 5 professional skills marks**. Section B questions will examine a **combination of professional skills appropriate to the question** (syllabus section E). **Each question will examine a minimum of two professional skills from Analysis and Evaluation, Scepticism and Commercial Acumen. Analysis and Evaluation will be included in all questions.**

One of the Section B questions will include technical marks mainly from syllabus section D. The other section B question will include technical marks from any other technical syllabus section(s).

Section B questions will also require candidates to address a range of issues influencing performance of organisations in specific business situations.

Strategic Professional CBE

It is essential that students become familiar with the CBE environment as part of their exam preparation. For additional support, please refer to the Practice Platform on the ACCA Global Website.

Examination tips

In addition to reading the tips contained here, we recommend that you review Chapter 16 of the Study Text and the resources available on the ACCA Global Website before sitting the CBE. Here you will find guidance documents, videos and a link to the CBE question practice platform.

Before the exam starts – You will be given 10 minutes to read the introductory page and the four pages of instructions. These will be the same for each APM exam and therefore it is important that you familiarise yourself with these (using the ACCA practice exams) during your revision. The exam time (3 hours and 15 minutes) will start automatically at the end of the 10 minutes or earlier if actioned by you.

Time allocation – The time allowed for this exam is 3 hours and 15 minutes/ 195 minutes.

Read each question carefully, reviewing the format and content of the requirements so that you understand what you need to do.

There are 80 technical marks and 20 professional skills marks. **Professional skills marks should be achieved as you work through the technical marks**.

If 15 minutes are spent reading the examination requirements (it may be sensible to allocate time to this), your time allocation should be 2.25 minutes per mark (180/80). This gives 90 minutes for section A and 45 minutes for each section B question.

If you do not allow a specific amount of time for reading and planning (a more straightforward approach but the risk is that you run out of time) your time allocation will be 2.4 minutes per mark (195/80). This gives 97 minutes for section A and 49 minutes for each section B question.

If you plan to spend more or less time on reading and planning, your time allocation per mark will be different.

Planning your answers – When the exam starts spend a few minutes skimming through each question to get a feel for what is included.

Once you have done this carry out an initial review of Section A. This will include a number of **exhibits** breaking down the scenario into relevant sections and including the detailed requirement. It will also include a list of the summarised **requirements** and an option to complete your answer in a **word processing** document and/or a **spreadsheet** document.

You can move around and resize the windows that you open to lay the screen out in a format that suits you.

Now copy and paste the specifics of the requirement into your answer document, perhaps highlighting in bold the different parts of the requirement and the verb used. Once complete review the exhibits in detail, highlighting and making notes as you do so and copy and pasting any relevant information to your answer document. These steps will help with your planning and structure but will also enable you to minimise the number of windows you have open.

The procedure will be similar for Section B.

Completing your answers – Start by revisiting the relevant exhibits for each requirement. Remember that the aim is to produce a professional and easy to read answer. For calculations and numerical work, use a logical and well laid out structure in a spreadsheet. Calculations should be labelled and referenced in to any relevant discussion in the word processor. For discursive answers, the word processing format should be used and answers should include bold headings and sub-headings and professional language. Ensure all aspects of the requirement are addressed in a sensible and balanced way. It is vital that you relate your answer to the specific circumstances given. In Section A you will usually be required to produce a report. Head up your answer as a report and use the requirements as a basis for your introduction.

If you get completely stuck with a question return to it later.

If you do not understand what a question is asking, state your assumptions. Even if you do not answer in precisely the way the examiner hoped, you should be given some credit, if your assumptions are reasonable.

Finally, leave enough time to read through the answers, ensuring they are clear and organised, and to make any necessary changes.

KAPLAN PUBLISHING

Study skills and revision guidance

This section aims to give guidance on how to study for your ACCA exams and to give ideas on how to improve your existing study techniques.

Preparing to study

Set your objectives

Before starting to study decide what you want to achieve – the type of pass you wish to obtain. This will decide the level of commitment and time you need to dedicate to your studies.

Devise a study plan

Determine which times of the week you will study.

Split these times into sessions of at least one hour for study of new material. Any shorter periods could be used for revision or practice.

Put the times you plan to study onto a study plan for the weeks from now until the exam and set yourself targets for each period of study – in your sessions make sure you cover the course, course assignments and revision.

If you are studying for more than one exam at a time, try to vary your subjects as this can help you to keep interested and see subjects as part of wider knowledge.

When working through your course, compare your progress with your plan and, if necessary, re-plan your work (perhaps including extra sessions) or, if you are ahead, do some extra revision/practice questions.

Effective studying

Active reading

You are not expected to learn the text by rote, rather, you must understand what you are reading and be able to use it to pass the exam and develop good practice. A good technique to use is SQ3Rs – Survey, Question, Read, Recall, Review:

1   **Survey the chapter** – look at the headings and read the introduction, summary and objectives, so as to get an overview of what the chapter deals with.

2   **Question** – whilst undertaking the survey, ask yourself the questions that you hope the chapter will answer for you.

3   **Read** through the chapter thoroughly, answering the questions and making sure you can meet the objectives. Attempt the exercises and activities in the text, and work through all the examples.

4   **Recall** – at the end of each section and at the end of the chapter, try to recall the main ideas of the section/chapter without referring to the text. This is best done after a short break of a couple of minutes after the reading stage.

5   **Review** – check that your recall notes are correct.

You may also find it helpful to re-read the chapter to try to see the topic(s) it deals with as a whole.

Note-taking

Taking notes is a useful way of learning, but do not simply copy out the text. The notes must:

- be in your own words

- be concise

- cover the key points

- be well-organised

- be modified as you study further chapters in this text or in related ones.

Trying to summarise a chapter without referring to the text can be a useful way of determining which areas you know and which you don't.

Three ways of taking notes:

Summarise the key points of a chapter.

Make linear notes – a list of headings, divided up with subheadings listing the key points. If you use linear notes, you can use different colours to highlight key points and keep topic areas together. Use plenty of space to make your notes easy to use.

Try a diagrammatic form – the most common of which is a mind-map. To make a mind-map, put the main heading in the centre of the paper and put a circle around it. Then draw short lines radiating from this to the main sub-headings, which again have circles around them. Then continue the process from the sub-headings to sub-sub-headings, advantages, disadvantages, etc.

Highlighting and underlining

You may find it useful to underline or highlight key points in your study text – but do be selective. You may also wish to make notes in the margins.

Revision

The best approach to revision is to revise the course as you work through it. Also try to leave four to six weeks before the exam for final revision. Make sure you cover the whole syllabus and pay special attention to those areas where your knowledge is weak. Here are some recommendations:

Read through the text and your notes again and condense your notes into key phrases. It may help to put key revision points onto index cards to look at when you have a few minutes to spare.

Review any assignments you have completed and look at where you lost marks – put more work into those areas where you were weak.

Practise exam standard questions under timed conditions and in the CBE correct format. If you are short of time, list the points that you would cover in your answer and then read the model answer, but do try to complete at least a few questions under exam conditions.

Also practise producing answer plans and comparing them to the model answer.

If you are stuck on a topic find somebody (e.g. your tutor or, where appropriate, a member of Kaplan's Academic Support team) to explain it to you.

Read good newspapers and professional journals, especially ACCA's Student Accountant – this can give you an advantage in the exam.

Ensure you **know the structure of the exam** – how many questions and of what type you will be expected to answer. During your revision attempt all the different styles of questions you may be asked.

Further reading

The following publication may also support your studies for this, and other, ACCA examinations:

A Student's Guide to Writing Business Reports by Zoe Robinson and Stuart Pedley-Smith.

You can find further reading and technical articles under the student section of ACCA's website.

Technical update

This text has been updated to reflect Examinable Documents September 2023 to June 2024 issued by ACCA.

Present value table

Present value of 1, i.e. $(1 + r)^{-n}$

Where   r = discount rate

              n = number of periods until payment

Periods (n)	Discount rate (r)									
	1%	2%	3%	4%	5%	6%	7%	8%	9%	10%
1	0.990	0.980	0.971	0.962	0.952	0.943	0.935	0.926	0.917	0.909
2	0.980	0.961	0.943	0.925	0.907	0.890	0.873	0.857	0.842	0.826
3	0.971	0.942	0.915	0.889	0.864	0.840	0.816	0.794	0.772	0.751
4	0.961	0.924	0.888	0.855	0.823	0.792	0.763	0.735	0.708	0.683
5	0.951	0.906	0.863	0.822	0.784	0.747	0.713	0.681	0.650	0.621
6	0.942	0.888	0.837	0.790	0.746	0.705	0.666	0.630	0.596	0.564
7	0.933	0.871	0.813	0.760	0.711	0.665	0.623	0.583	0.547	0.513
8	0.923	0.853	0.789	0.731	0.677	0.627	0.582	0.540	0.502	0.467
9	0.914	0.837	0.766	0.703	0.645	0.592	0.544	0.500	0.460	0.424
10	0.905	0.820	0.744	0.676	0.614	0.558	0.508	0.463	0.422	0.386
11	0.896	0.804	0.722	0.650	0.585	0.527	0.475	0.429	0.388	0.350
12	0.887	0.788	0.701	0.625	0.557	0.497	0.444	0.397	0.356	0.319
13	0.879	0.773	0.681	0.601	0.530	0.469	0.415	0.368	0.326	0.290
14	0.870	0.758	0.661	0.577	0.505	0.442	0.388	0.340	0.299	0.263
15	0.861	0.743	0.642	0.555	0.481	0.417	0.362	0.315	0.275	0.239

Periods (n)	Discount rate (r)									
	11%	12%	13%	14%	15%	16%	17%	18%	19%	20%
1	0.901	0.893	0.885	0.877	0.870	0.862	0.855	0.847	0.840	0.833
2	0.812	0.797	0.783	0.769	0.756	0.743	0.731	0.718	0.706	0.694
3	0.731	0.712	0.693	0.675	0.658	0.641	0.624	0.609	0.593	0.579
4	0.659	0.636	0.613	0.592	0.572	0.552	0.534	0.516	0.499	0.482
5	0.593	0.567	0.543	0.519	0.497	0.476	0.456	0.437	0.419	0.402
6	0.535	0.507	0.480	0.456	0.432	0.410	0.390	0.370	0.352	0.335
7	0.482	0.452	0.425	0.400	0.376	0.354	0.333	0.314	0.296	0.279
8	0.434	0.404	0.376	0.351	0.327	0.305	0.285	0.266	0.249	0.233
9	0.391	0.361	0.333	0.308	0.284	0.263	0.243	0.225	0.209	0.194
10	0.352	0.322	0.295	0.270	0.247	0.227	0.208	0.191	0.176	0.162
11	0.317	0.287	0.261	0.237	0.215	0.195	0.178	0.162	0.148	0.135
12	0.286	0.257	0.231	0.208	0.187	0.168	0.152	0.137	0.124	0.112
13	0.258	0.229	0.204	0.182	0.163	0.145	0.130	0.116	0.104	0.093
14	0.232	0.205	0.181	0.160	0.141	0.125	0.111	0.099	0.088	0.078
15	0.209	0.183	0.160	0.140	0.123	0.108	0.095	0.084	0.074	0.065

Annuity table

Present value of an annuity of 1, i.e. $\dfrac{1-(1+r)^{-n}}{r}$

Where   r = discount rate

             n = number of periods

Periods (n)	Discount rate (r)									
	1%	2%	3%	4%	5%	6%	7%	8%	9%	10%
1	0.990	0.980	0.971	0.962	0.952	0.943	0.935	0.926	0.917	0.909
2	1.970	1.942	1.913	1.886	1.859	1.833	1.808	1.783	1.759	1.736
3	2.941	2.884	2.829	2.775	2.723	2.673	2.624	2.577	2.531	2.487
4	3.902	3.808	3.717	3.630	3.546	3.465	3.387	3.312	3.240	3.170
5	4.853	4.713	4.580	4.452	4.329	4.212	4.100	3.993	3.890	3.791
6	5.795	5.601	5.417	5.242	5.076	4.917	4.767	4.623	4.486	4.355
7	6.728	6.472	6.230	6.002	5.786	5.582	5.389	5.206	5.033	4.868
8	7.652	7.325	7.020	6.733	6.463	6.210	5.971	5.747	5.535	5.335
9	8.566	8.162	7.786	7.435	7.108	6.802	6.515	6.247	5.995	5.759
10	9.471	8.983	8.530	8.111	7.722	7.360	7.024	6.710	6.418	6.145
11	10.368	9.787	9.253	8.760	8.306	7.887	7.499	7.139	6.805	8.495
12	11.255	10.575	9.954	9.385	8.863	8.384	7.943	7.536	7.161	6.814
13	12.134	11.348	10.635	9.986	9.394	8.853	8.358	7.904	7.487	7.103
14	13.004	12.106	11.296	10.563	9.899	9.295	8.745	8.244	7.786	7.367
15	13.865	12.849	11.938	11.118	10.380	9.712	9.108	8.559	8.061	7.606

Periods (n)	Discount rate (r)									
	11%	12%	13%	14%	15%	16%	17%	18%	19%	20%
1	0.901	0.893	0.885	0.877	0.870	0.862	0.855	0.847	0.840	0.833
2	1.713	1.690	1.668	1.647	1.626	1.605	1.585	1.566	1.547	1.528
3	2.444	2.402	2.361	2.322	2.283	2.246	2.210	2.174	2.140	2.106
4	3.102	3.037	2.974	2.914	2.855	2.798	2.743	2.690	2.639	2.589
5	3.696	3.605	3.517	3.433	3.352	3.274	3.199	3.127	3.058	2.991
6	4.231	4.111	3.998	3.889	3.784	3.685	3.589	3.498	3.410	3.326
7	4.712	4.564	4.423	4.288	4.160	4.039	3.922	3.812	3.706	3.605
8	5.146	4.968	4.799	4.639	4.487	4.344	4.207	4.078	3.954	3.837
9	5.537	5.328	5.132	4.946	4.772	4.607	4.451	4.303	4.163	4.031
10	5.889	5.650	5.426	5.216	5.019	4.833	4.659	4.494	4.339	4.192
11	6.207	5.938	5.687	5.453	5.234	5.029	4.836	4.656	4.486	4.327
12	6.492	6.194	5.918	5.660	5.421	5.197	4.968	4.793	4.611	4.439
13	6.750	6.424	6.122	5.842	5.583	5.342	5.118	4.910	4.715	4.533
14	6.982	6.628	6.302	6.002	5.724	5.468	5.229	5.008	4.802	4.611
15	7.191	6.811	6.462	6.142	5.847	5.575	5.324	5.092	4.876	4.675

Introduction to performance management

Chapter learning objectives

Upon completion of this chapter you will be able to:

- explain the role of strategic performance management in strategic planning and control

- discuss the role of performance measurement in checking progress towards the corporate objectives

- compare planning and control between the strategic and operational levels within a business entity

- discuss the scope for potential conflict between strategic business plans and short-term localised decisions

- apply and evaluate the methods of benchmarking performance

- discuss how the purpose, structure and content of a mission statement impacts on performance measurement and management

- discuss how strategic objectives are cascaded down the organisation via the formulation of subsidiary performance objectives

- apply critical success factor analysis in developing performance metrics from business objectives

- identify and discuss the characteristics of operational performance

- discuss the relative significance of planning activities as against controlling activities at different levels in the performance hierarchy

- assess the statement 'What gets measured, gets done' in the context of performance management.

PER

One of the PER performance objectives (PO1) is to take into account all relevant information and use professional judgement, your personal values and scepticism to evaluate data and make decisions. You should identify right from wrong and escalate anything of concern. You also need to make sure that your skills, knowledge and behaviour are up-to-date and allow you to be effective in you role. Another PER performance objectives (PO5) is to manage yourself and your resources effectively and responsibly. You contribute to the leadership and management of your organisation – delivering what's needed by stakeholders and the business. PER performance objective (PO22) is data analysis and decision support, which involves enabling relevant stakeholders to make decisions. Working through this chapter should help you understand how to demonstrate these objectives.

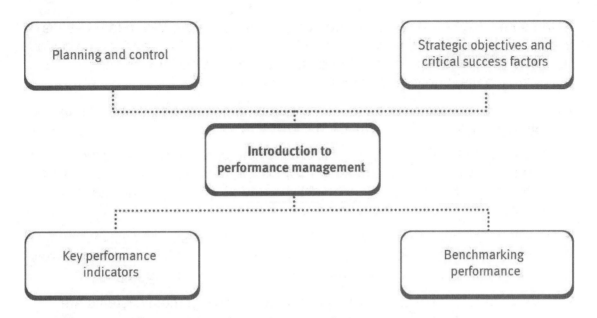

1 Introduction to Advanced Performance Management (APM)

APM will require you to assess different approaches to performance management from a variety of perspectives. This will require you to know what the approaches are and, more importantly, you should be able to compare one with another.

It will focus on the use of strategic management accounting techniques in different organisational contexts to contribute to the planning, control and evaluation of the performance of an organisation and its strategic and operational development.

The technical syllabus content (syllabus sections A to D) is covered in Chapters 1–14. Success in APM will require a good understanding and application of the these syllabus areas. However, this must be underpinned by the demonstration of a range of professional skills (syllabus section E) and employability and technology skills (syllabus section F). These two syllabus sections are covered in Chapters 15 and 16 respectively. It is important that the final two chapters are used in partnership with your technical learning and they should be read and referred to as you work through the technical content.

2 Common knowledge

APM **builds on knowledge gained in Performance Management (PM)**. It also **includes knowledge contained in the Strategic Business Leader (SBL) exam but this it is not a problem if you are yet to study for this exam and there is no expectation that you have any SBL knowledge in place**.

PM tested your knowledge and application of core management accounting techniques. APM develops key aspects introduced at the PM level with a greater focus on linking the syllabus topics together and evaluation of the key topics and techniques. Therefore, you should not expect to be retested in a PM style but need to be aware that all PM knowledge is assumed to be known.

In the same way, APM contains knowledge included in the SBL exam but it is important to draw a distinction between the two exams. You need to approach the common topics from an APM perspective, i.e. how do they influence performance management and measurement.

For example, in terms of strategy planning and choice, a SBL question might look at evaluating a strategic decision. However:

- The focus in APM would look at whether the company has a suitable mission and related key strategic objectives, at what the critical success factors (CSFs) are for these objectives and at what key performance indicators (KPIs) are being used.

- APM very much focuses on that hierarchy and questions revolve around whether the CSFs/KPIs are appropriate for the objectives and why. If they are not, then why not and what could the organisation do better.

- APM thus looks more at what performance management systems are needed and what performance measures are most appropriate.

Chapter 3 builds on your knowledge of risk from PM.

Chapter 2 also covers a number of topics that are also included in SBL. However, as stated there is no expectation that you have any SBL knowledge in place and therefore the topics that are common to both APM and SBL will not be listed in this chapter or any subsequent chapters.

3 Introduction to Chapter 1

This chapter introduces some of the areas discussed and built upon in later chapters and sets the scene to Part A of the syllabus, **'strategic planning and control'**.

It provides an overview to the overall process of **performance management** as a discipline for planning and controlling performance so that the strategic objectives of an organisation can be set, monitored and controlled. We will consider the difference between **planning** and **control** as well as the **different levels of planning and control** within an organisation.

A central part of the performance management process is to understand how the **objectives** of the organisation link to the **critical success factors** (CSFs) and **key performance indicators** (KPIs). This is based on the concept of **'what gets measured, gets done'** which means that an organisation is more likely to achieve improvement in the areas and activities which are being measured. Therefore, it is important to identify appropriate performance measures for all of the activities which need to 'get done' in order to achieve the oganisation's objectives.

Finally, we will move onto benchmarking. An important aspect of strategic planning is to understand how to **benchmark** performance so that areas for performance improvement can be identified.

4 Introduction to performance management

4.1 Performance management

 Performance management is any activity that is designed to improve the organisation's performance and ensure that its goals are met.

The first stage of this process is to identify the organisation's **objectives, goals** and **targets** so that we know how the organisation would like to perform.

Next we need to identify appropriate **performance measures** and put in place **systems** to effectively capture the information required to **report** performance measured to the organisation's management.

The managers must then **evaluate** the performance measures to determine whether targets have been met and whether the organisations objectives are being achieved.

If the objectives have not been met then **corrective** action should be taken. Alternatively if the objectives have been met then the management may wish to consider **rewarding** staff to encourage them to continue this behaviour in the future.

The performance management process

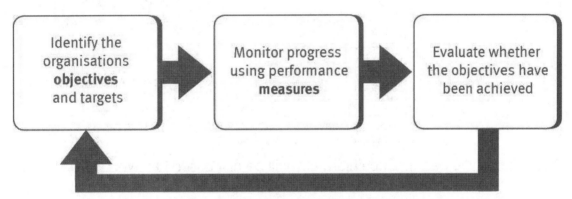

Take **action** to correct or reward performance

Each of the stages of this cycle are reflected in Sections A-D of the syllabus:

A   Use **strategic planning and control models** to plan and monitor organisational performance

B   Identify and evaluate the **design features of effective performance management information and monitoring systems** and recognise the impact of developments in technology on performance measurement and management systems

C   Apply appropriate strategic **performance measurement techniques** in evaluating and improving organisational performance

D   Advise clients and senior management on **strategic business performance evaluation**.

5 Planning and control

5.1 Definitions

 Strategic planning is concerned with:

- where an organisation wants to be (usually expressed in terms of its objectives) and

- how it will get there (strategies, i.e. where and how to compete to gain sustainable competitive advantage).

 Control is concerned with monitoring the achievement of objectives and suggesting corrective action.

5.2 The performance hierarchy

Planning and **control** takes place at different levels within an organisation. This can be illustrated using the performance hierarchy.

The **performance hierarchy** operates in the following order:

Each part of the performance hierarchy will be discussed below.

5.3 Mission

 A **mission statement** outlines the broad direction that an organisation will follow and summarises the reasons and values that underlie that organisation.

Characteristics of a good mission statement

A mission should be **succinct**, **memorable** and **enduring**, i.e. the statement should not change unless, for example, there is a significant change in the organisation's key stakeholders or market. Importantly (particularly in the context of APM), it should be **translated into and aligned with the strategic, tactical and operational plans and objectives**. The mission should act as **a guide for employees to work towards** and should be **addressed to a number of stakeholder groups** (for example, shareholders, employees and customers).

Mission statements and performance management

The purpose, structure and content of a mission forms a key part of performance measurement and management:

- The mission acts as a source of inspiration and ideas for the organisation's detailed plans and objectives at strategic, tactical and operational level. These plans should be aligned with the mission.

- The organisation's mission can be used to assess the suitability of any proposed plans in terms of their fit with the mission, providing a framework within which managerial decisions can be made and assisting in resolving conflict between stakeholder groups.

- The mission can impact the day to day workings of an organisation. For example, assisting in communicating key cultural values and business practices to employees and other stakeholders.

This may be the focus of how mission is examined in APM.

Illustration 1 – Mission statement examples

American Express – famous for their great customer service. They believe that customers will never love a company until the employees love it first. Their mission reads:

'At American Express we have a mission to be the world's most respected service brand. To do this, we have to establish a culture that supports our team members, so they can provide exceptional service to our company.'

IKEA – their mission could have been a promise for beautiful, affordable furniture. Instead IKEA dream big with their mission:

'To create a better everyday life for the many people. Our business ideas support this by offering a wide range of well-designed, functional home furnishing products at prices so low that as many people as possible will be able to afford them.'

Nike – view each customer as an athlete. Their mission is:

'To bring inspiration and innovation to every athlete in the world. If you have a body, you are an athlete.'

The Motor Neurone Disease Association (MNDA) – mission is just as applicable for not-for-profit organisations. This charity's mission is:

'We improve care and support for people with MND, their families and carers. We fund and promote research that leads to new understanding and treatments, and brings us closer to a cure for MND. We campaign and raise awareness so the needs of people with MND and everyone who cares for them are recognised and addressed by wider society.'

5.4 Strategic, tactical and operational planning and control

To enable an organisation to fulfil its mission, it should be translated into strategic, tactical and operational plans and objectives.

Importantly, **each level should be aligned with** and be consistent with **the one above**.

This process will involve moving from general broad aims, to more specific objectives, and ultimately to detailed targets.

	Strategic level	Tactical level	Operational level
Time frame	Focus is on **long-term** planning (3–10 years) by **senior management** since achievement of strategies will influence the achievement of mission.	**Middle management** focuses on **more detailed** and **shorter-term objectives than at strategic level** (perhaps over a quarter of a year).	Focuses on the **day-to-day** management of activities by **operational managers**.
Scope	Considers **whole organisation** as well as individual divisions/ departments and **all stakeholders**.	Considers individual **divisions/ departments** and their **activities and resources**.	Ensures specific **objectives set at tactical level are achieved**.
Information	**Information** has an **external** focus (internal information is also used), will commonly be **qualitative** in nature (i.e. non-numerical, such as customer attitudes).	**Information** has an **internal** focus and is used to ensure that the **strategic objectives are being supported** in the organisation's activities.	**Information** is **detailed, task specific**, mainly **internal** and largely **quantitative**.
Relative significance of planning against controlling activities	Information is mainly used for **planning** (formulating, evaluating and selecting strategies to attain strategic objectives) **rather than controlling** activities.	Information **aids short-term planning at operational level**.	Focus will be on **controlling** the organisation (not planning) **to achieve short-term** (perhaps weekly) **objectives**.

5.5 Potential conflict between strategic plans and operational decisions

Strategic planning is a **long-term**, top-down process. The decisions made can conflict with the **short-term** localised **operational** decisions. For example:

- Divisional managers tend to be rewarded on the short-term results they achieve. Therefore, it will be difficult to motivate managers to achieve long-term strategic objectives.

- Divisional managers need to be able to take advantage of short-term unforeseen opportunities or avoid serious short-term crisis. Strict adherence to a strategy could limit their ability to do this.

Note: The potential for long-term and short-term conflicts will be touched upon again and built on in later chapters.

Long-term and short-term conflicts

The whole concept of strategic planning explored earlier in this chapter implies a certain top-down approach. Even in the era of divisional autonomy and employee empowerment it is difficult to imagine that a rigorous strategic planning regime could be associated with a bottom-up management culture. There is a potential for conflict here.

- The idea of divisional autonomy is that individual managers operate their business units as if they were independent businesses – seeking and exploiting local opportunities as they arise.

- Managers are rewarded in a manner which reflects the results they achieve.

- The pressures on management are for short-term results and ostensibly strategy is concerned with the long-term. Often it is difficult to motivate managers by setting long-term expectations.

- Long-term plans have to be set out in detail long before the period to which they apply. The rigidity of the long-term plan, particularly in regard to the rationing and scheduling of resources, may place the company in a position where it is unable to react to short-term unforeseen opportunities, or serious short-term crisis.

- Strict adherence to a strategy can limit flair and creativity. Operational managers may need to respond to local situations, avert trouble or improve a situation by quick action outside the strategy. If they then have to defend their actions against criticisms of acting 'outside the plan', irrespective of the resultant benefits, they are likely to become apathetic and indifferent.

- The adoption of corporate strategy requires a tacit acceptance by everyone that the interests of departments, activities and individuals are subordinate to the corporate interests. Department managers are required to consider the contribution to corporate profits or the reduction in corporate costs of any decision. They should not allow their decisions to be limited by short-term departmental parameters.

- It is only natural that local managers should seek personal advancement. A problem of strategic planning is identifying those areas where there may be a clash of interests and loyalties, and in assessing where an individual has allowed vested interests to dominate decisions.

6 Strategic objectives and critical success factors

6.1 Strategic objectives

As discussed in section 4, the **mission statement will be translated into a set of strategic objectives**. Achievement of these SMART objectives should ultimately help the organisation to achieve its mission.

6.2 Critical success factors

Once an organisation has established its strategic objectives, it needs to identify the key factors and processes that will enable it to achieve those objectives.

Some aspects of performance are 'nice to have' but others are critical to the organisation if it is to succeed.

 Critical success factors (CSFs) are the vital areas 'where things must go right' for the business in order for them to achieve their strategic objectives.

The achievement of CSFs, through the execution of appropriate strategic plans, should allow the organisation to cope better than its rivals with any changes in the competitive environment and to maximise its performance.

The organisation will need to have in place the **core competencies** that are required to achieve the CSFs, i.e. something that they are able to do that is difficult for competitors to follow.

Classifying CSFs

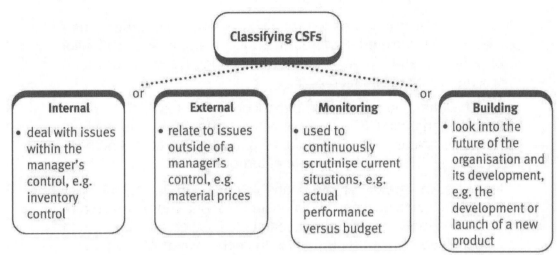

Note: In the APM exam you may be asked to:

- evaluate if the CSFs are aligned to the strategic objectives and mission

- explain the meaning of the different classifications and/or

- classify CSFs correctly

in the context of the given scenario.

Further detail on classifying CSFs

Internal versus external sources of CSFs

Every manager will have internal CSFs relating to the department and the people they manage. These CSFs can range across such diverse interests as human resource development or inventory control. The primary characteristic of such internal CSFs is that they deal with issues that are entirely within the manager's sphere of influence and control.

External CSFs relate to issues that are generally less under the manager's direct control such as the availability or price of a particular critical raw material or source of energy.

Monitoring versus building/adapting CSFs

Managers who are geared to producing short-term operating results invest considerable effort in tracking and guiding their organisation's performance, and therefore employ monitoring CSFs to continuously scrutinise existing situations.

Almost all managers have some monitoring CSFs, which often include financially-oriented CSFs such as actual performance versus budget or the current status of product or service transaction cost. Another monitoring CSF might be personnel turnover rates.

Managers who are either in reasonable control of day-to-day operations, or who are insulated from such concerns, spend more time in a building or adapting mode. These people can be classified as future-oriented planners whose primary purpose is to implement major change programmes aimed at adapting the organisation to the perceived emerging environment.

Typical CSFs in this area might include the successful implementation of major recruitment and training efforts, or new product or service development programmes.

Sources of CSFs

There are **five** prime sources of CSFs:

1. **The structure of the industry** – CSFs will be determined by the characteristics of the industry itself, e.g. in the car industry 'efficient dealer network organisation' will be important where as in the food processing industry 'new product development' will be important.

2. **Competitive strategy, industry position and geographic location**

    -   Competitive strategies such as differentiation or cost leadership will impact CSFs.

    -   Industry position, e.g. a small company's CSFs may be driven by a major competitor's strategy.

    -   Geographical location will impact factors such as distribution costs and hence CSFs.

3. **Environmental factors** – factors such as increasing fuel costs can have an impact on the choice of CSFs.

4. **Temporary factors** – temporary internal factors may drive CSFs, e.g. a supermarket may have been forced to recall certain products due to contamination fears and may therefore generate a short term CSF of ensuring that such contamination does not happen again in the future.

5. **Functional managerial position** – the function will affect the CSFs, e.g. production managers will be concerned with product quality and cost control.

Test your understanding 1

The directors of Dream Ice Cream (DI), a successful ice cream producer, with a reputation as a quality supplier, have decided to enter the frozen yogurt market in its country of operation. It has set up a separate operation under the name of Dream Yogurt (DY). The following information is available:

- DY has recruited a management team but production staff will need to be recruited. There is some concern that there will not be staff available with the required knowledge of food production.

- DY has agreed to supply yogurts to Jacksons, a chain of supermarkets based in the home country. They have stipulated that delivery must take place within 24 hours of an order being sent.

- DY hopes to become a major national producer of frozen yogurts.

- DY produces four varieties of frozen yogurt at present; Mango Tango, Very Berry, Orange Burst and French Vanilla.

Required:

Explain five CSFs on which the directors must focus if DY is to achieve success in the marketplace. **(10 marks)**

Important note of professional skills

In the exam, professional skills marks will be attached to the overall question (10 professional skills marks in each Section A question, 5 professional skills marks in each Section B question). Professional skills marks are earned as you work through the technical marks by providing comprehensive and relevant responses to the technical requirements. Some examples of how professional skills marks may be awarded in this question are as follows:

Communication

- Appropriate structure, e.g. use of headings/sub-headings.

- Effectiveness of communication – content is relevant and tailored to DY.

- Adherence to specific request to provide five CSFs.

Analysis and Evaluation

CSFs clearly explained and supported with evidence from the scenario.

Commercial acumen

Recommendations of CSFs are practical and plausible in the context of DY.

Student accountant article: visit the ACCA website, www.accaglobal.com, to review the article on 'Critical success factors'.

7 Key performance indicators

7.1 The importance of performance measures

It is not enough merely to make plans and implement them. The results of the plans have to be **measured**. Performance measurement is essential to the achievement of objectives since **'what gets measured, gets done'** i.e. things that are measured get done more often than things that are not measured.

Once measured, the results should be **compared** against the organisation's stated objectives to assess the firm's performance.

Action can then be taken to remedy any shortfalls in performance.

Performance measurement is an **ongoing process**, which must react quickly to the changing circumstances of the organisation and of the environment.

Note: The terms performance measures, performance metrics and performance indicators mean the same thing and may be used interchangeably in the exam.

What gets measured, gets done

In some respects the statement 'what gets measured, gets done' seems obvious – measuring something gives you the information you need in order to make sure you actually achieve what you set out to do. Without a standard, there is no logical basis for making a decision or taking action.

However, there can be some problems with this approach:

- It assumes that staff have some motivation to deliver what is measured, whether due to the potential of positive feedback and/or rewards or the consequences of failure. The statement could thus be modified to say 'What gets measured and fed back gets done well. What gets rewarded, gets repeated' (this is discussed further in Chapter 9).

- It assumes that staff have been informed up front that the particular issue would be measured and have thus been able to adapt their behaviour.

- It assumes that the factor being measured can be directly influenced by staff. In many situations factors have elements that are not controllable – for example, sales volume is partly due to the state of the economy.

- It assumes that expectations and targets are seen to be fair and achievable – failure on either of these counts could result in staff giving up and not trying to meet targets.

- A significant potential problem is that a firm will focus on what is easy to measure, such as cost, but ultimately ignore factors that are more difficult to measure, such as customer perception. Albert Einstein reportedly had a sign on his office wall that stated: "Not everything that counts can be counted, and not everything that can be counted counts."

- It implies that "what gets done" is what management wanted – for example, a focus on measuring profit may result in short termism at the expense of long-term shareholder value.

- Measurement may foster unhealthy rivalry whereas before there was cooperation.

7.2 KPIs

Just as critical success factors are more important than other aspects of performance, not all performance indicators are created equal. The performance indicators that measure the most important aspects of strategic performance are the key performance indicators.

Key performance indicators (KPIs) are the measures which indicate whether or not the CSFs are being achieved.

Illustration 2 – CSFs and KPIs

A parcel delivery service, such as DHL, may have a strategic objective to increase revenue by 4% year on year. The business will establish CSFs and KPIs which are aligned to the achievement of this strategic objective, for example:

CSF	KPI
Speedy collection from customers after their request for a parcel to be delivered	Number of collections from customers within 3 hours of orders being received, in any part of the country, for orders received before 2.30pm on a working day.
Rapid and reliable delivery	Number of next day delivery for destinations within the UK or number of deliveries within two days for destinations in Europe.

7.3 KPIs and CSFs

Test your understanding 2
Revisit the CSFs that you identified for Dairy Ice Cream in TYU 1.
Required:
Suggest an appropriate KPI which could be used to measure whether each CSF is being achieved. **(5 marks)**

7.4 Features of good performance measures

Performance measures should be SMART (**s**pecific, **m**easurable, **a**ttainable, **r**elevant and **t**ime-bound).

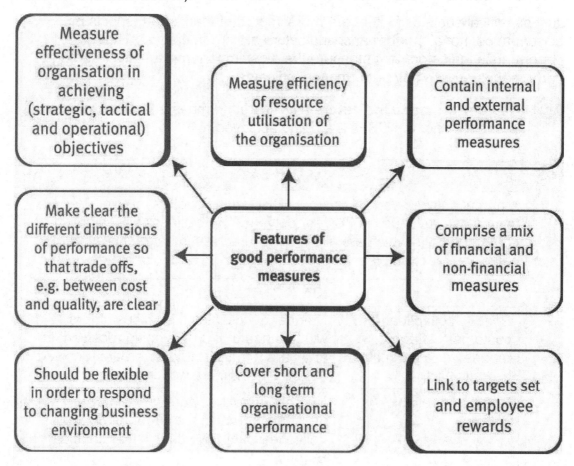

Student accountant article: visit the ACCA website, www.accaglobal.com, to review the article on 'Performance indicators'.

7.5 Longer question

Some of the test your understandings (TYUs) in this material are shorter or more straightforward than questions in the APM exam. They are contained in the material for learning purposes and will help you to build your knowledge and confidence so that you are ready to tackle past exam questions during the revision phase.

However, it is also useful to look at some longer, exam standard questions right from the beginning of this course in order to understand how the areas covered may be tested in the real exam. You need to understand how to interpret the requirements read and understand the scenario and plan and structure your answer. You may not be able to tackle the entire question at this point but you should read and learn from the answer.

Test your understanding 3

Film Productions Co (FP) is a small international company producing films for cinema release and also for sale on DVD or to television companies. FP deals with all areas of the production from casting, directing and managing the artists to negotiating distribution deals with cinema chains and TV channels. The industry is driven by the tastes of its films' audience, which when accurately predicted can lead to high levels of profitability on a successful film.

The company's stated mission is to 'produce fantastic films that have mass appeal'. The company makes around $200 million of sales each year equally split between a share of cinema takings, DVD sales and TV rights. FP has released 32 films in the past five years. Each film costs an average of $18 million and takes 12 months to produce from initial commissioning through to the final version. Production control is important in order to hit certain key holiday periods for releasing films at the cinema or on DVD.

The company's films have been moderately successful in winning industry awards although FP has never won any major award. Its aims have been primarily commercial with artistic considerations secondary.

The company uses a top-down approach to strategy development with objectives leading to critical success factors (CSFs) which must then be measured using performance indicators. Currently, the company has identified a number of critical success factors. The two most important of these are viewed as:

(i)   improve audience satisfaction

(ii)   strengthen profitability in operations.

At the request of the board, the chief executive officer (CEO) has been reviewing this system in particular the role of CSFs. Generally, the CEO is worried that the ones chosen so far fail to capture all the factors affecting the business and wants to understand all possible sources for CSFs and what it means to categorise them into monitoring and building factors.

These CSFs will need to be measured and there must be systems in place to perform that role. The existing information system of the company is based on a fairly basic accounting package. However, the CEO has been considering greater investment in these systems and making more use of the company's website in both driving forward the business' links to its audience and in collecting data on them.

The CEO is planning a report to the board of Film Productions and has asked you to help by drafting certain sections of this report.

Required:

Draft the sections of the CEO's report answering the following questions:

(a) Explain the difference between monitoring CSFs and building CSFs, using examples appropriate to FP. **(4 marks)**

(b) Identify information that FP could use to set its CSFs and explain how it could be used giving two examples that would be appropriate to FP. **(6 marks)**

(c) For each of the two critical success factors given in the question, identify two performance indicators (PIs) that could support measurement of their achievement and explain why each PI is relevant to the CSF. **(10 marks)**

(d) Discuss the implications of your chosen PIs for the design and use of the company's website, its management information system and its executive information system. **(9 marks)**

Professional marks will be awarded for the demonstration of skill in communication, analysis and evaluation, scepticism and commercial acumen in your answer. **(7 marks)**

(Total: 36 marks)

Note: This is not a complete Section A question and therefore only contains 7 professional skills marks. It is useful at this point in your studies to consider an example of the marking guide for the professional skills marks. Do spend time reading through this in the answer. It will help you to start focusing on how you can maximise these marks in the exam to develop good exam technique from the start.

Additional note: Requirement (b) is on information and requirement (d) covers systems design. These areas are covered in Chapter 7 and therefore you may prefer to tackle these requirements once you have completed this chapter. Alternatively, you could attempt the requirements and use the answer provided to understand the areas covered.

8 Benchmarking performance

8.1 What is benchmarking?

 Benchmarking is the process of identifying **best practice** in relation to the products (or services) and the processes by which those products (or services) are created and delivered. The objective of benchmarking is to understand and evaluate the current position of a business or organisation in relation to best practice and to identify areas and means of performance improvement.

8.2 Types of benchmarks

There are **three** basic methods of benchmarking; **internal**, **competitor** and **process/activity**.

In the exam you need to be able to do the following:

- Explain each method; perhaps correctly identifying which type of benchmarking is being used in the given scenario.

- Evaluate each method, for example which method is most appropriate in the context of the given scenario or what are the relative advantages and disadvantages of the different methods?

Each method is discussed in turn below:

Internal

 This is where another function or division of the organisation is used as a benchmark.

Advantages	Disadvantages
• Can share best practice between different parts of the organisation. • Ability to obtain detailed operational data. • It should help to integrate the different functions/divisions. • It can show the different functions/ divisions the advantage of being part of a larger organisation since they can learn from one another.	• Won't necessarily identify world-beating performance improvements or innovative solutions. • No external focus – the organisation may ignore competitor performance. • Often involves non-financial data which can be less robust.

Illustration 3 – Benchmarking success at multinational food manufacturer Kelloggs

Kelloggs' factories all use the same monitoring techniques, so it is possible to compare performance between sites, although there are always some things that are done differently. They can interrogate this information to improve performance across every site. As things have improved, Kelloggs have also had to reassess their baseline figures and develop more sophisticated tools to monitor performance to ensure they continue to make progress. They have seen a 20% increase in productivity in a six year period using this system.

Competitor

This uses a direct competitor in the same industry with the same or similar processes as the benchmark.

Advantages	Disadvantages
• Valuable for identifying where other organisations demonstrate competitive advantage. • Valuable for identifying areas for improvement with a similar business.	• It can be difficult to persuade competitors to share information. • The problem above may mean that only information in the public domain is obtained. This will tend to focus more on strategic (rather than operational) areas for improvement. • If competitors do agree to share information, they may want something in return. • It identifies where competitive advantage exists but will not identify how to gain this competitive advantage.

Performance comparison with the competition

Comparative analysis can be usefully applied to any value activity which underpins the competitive strategy of an organisation, an industry or a nation.

To find out the level of investment in fixed assets of competitors, the business can use physical observation, information from trade press or trade association announcements, supplier press releases as well as their externally published financial statements, to build a clear picture of the relative scale, capacity, age and cost for each competitor.

The method of operating these assets, in terms of hours and shift patterns, can be established by observation, discussions with suppliers and customers or by asking existing or ex-employees of the particular competitor. If the method of operating can be ascertained it should enable a combination of internal personnel management and industrial engineering managers to work out the likely relative differences in labour costs. The rates of pay and conditions can generally be found with reference to nationally negotiated agreements, local and national press advertising for employees, trade and employment associations and recruitment consultants. When this cost is used alongside an intelligent assessment of how many employees would be needed by the competitor in each area, given their equipment and other resources, a good idea of the labour costs can be obtained.

Another difference which should be noted is the nature of the competitors' costs as well as their relative levels. Where a competitor has a lower level of committed fixed costs, such as lower fixed labour costs due to a larger proportion of temporary workers, it may be able to respond more quickly to a downturn in demand by rapidly laying off the temporary staff. Equally, in a tight labour market and with rising sales, it may have to increase its pay levels to attract new workers.

In some industries, one part of the competitor analysis is surprisingly direct. Each new competitive product is purchased on a regular basis and then systematically taken apart, so that each component can be identified as well as the processes used to put the parts together. The respective areas of the business will then assess the costs associated with each element so that a complete product cost can be found for the competitive product.

A comparison of similar value activities between organisations is useful when the strategic context is taken into consideration. For example, a straight comparison of resource deployment between two competitive organisations may reveal quite different situations in the labour cost as a percentage of the total cost. The conclusions drawn from this, however, depend upon circumstances. If the firms are competing largely on the basis of price, then differentials in these costs could be crucial. In contrast, the additional use of labour by one organisation may be an essential support for the special services provided which differentiate that organisation from its competitors.

One danger of inter-firm analysis is that the company may overlook the fact that the whole industry is performing badly, and is losing out competitively to other countries with better resources or even other industries which can satisfy customers' needs in different ways. Therefore, if an industry comparison is performed it should make some assessment of how the resource utilisation compares with other countries and industries. This can be done by obtaining a measurement of stock turnover or yield from raw materials.

Benchmarking against competitors involves the gathering of a range of information about them. For quoted companies financial information will generally be reasonably easy to obtain, from published accounts and the financial press. Some product information may be obtained by acquiring their products and examining them in detail to ascertain the components used and their construction ('reverse engineering'). Literature will also be available, for example in the form of brochures and trade journals.

However, most non-financial information, concerning areas such as competitors' processes, customer and supplier relationships and customer satisfaction will not be so readily available. To overcome this problem, benchmarking exercises are generally carried out with organisations taken from within the same group of companies (intra-group benchmarking) or from similar but non-competing industries (inter-industry benchmarking).

Process/activity

 This focuses on a similar process or activity in another company which is not a direct competitor.

Advantages	Disadvantages
• It can be easier (than competitive benchmarking) to obtain the information from the other organisation since they are not a direct competitor.	• It can be difficult to translate lessons learned from one industry to another. For example, even generic activities such as marketing will differ between different industries.
• Can still find innovative solutions, if not more innovative, compared to the other methods. • If done for generic activities (such as marketing) it can be easier to translate lessons learned from one industry to another.	• Sharing of information may be difficult since, for example, organisations in different industry sectors may use different systems to collect data or connecting with organisations who are not competitors may be more difficult.

Illustration 4 – Process benchmarking at Xerox

Some years ago, Xerox confronted its own unsatisfactory performance in product warehousing and distribution. It did so by identifying the organisation it considered to be the very best at warehousing and distribution, in the hope that 'best practices' could be adapted from this model. The business judged to provide a model of best practice in this area was L L Bean, a catalogue merchant (i.e. it existed in an unrelated sector). Xerox approached Bean with a request that the two engage in a co-operative benchmarking project. The request was granted and the project yielded major insights in inventory arrangement and order processing, resulting in major gains for Xerox when these insights were adapted to its own operations.

8.3 Benchmarking evaluation

Benefits	Drawbacks
• Can help in assessing its current strategic position.	• Identifying best practice is difficult.
• Identifies gaps in performance and sets targets which are challenging but achievable.	• It is not very forward looking; what is best today may not be so tomorrow.
• A method for learning from the success of others and applying best practice.	• Differences, for example in accounting treatment, may make comparisons meaningless.
• Minimises complacency and self-satisfaction with own performance and can provide an early warning of competitive disadvantage.	• Too much attention is paid to the aspects of performance that are measured as a part of the benchmarking process, to the detriment of the organisation's overall performance.
• Encourages continuous improvement; it is not viewed as a one off exercise.	• Potential for lack of commitment by management and staff. To minimise this, staff need to be reassured that their status, remuneration and working conditions will not suffer; this requires supportive leadership and potentially a shift in culture.
• Can help in assessing generic strategy (e.g. will a cost leadership or differentiation strategy best enable the organisation to effectively compete?).	• Costly in terms of time and money.

It is important that you can evaluate benchmarking in the context of the scenario given in the APM exam. The above are suggestions only and your evaluation should be tailored to the specifics of the scenario.

8.4 The benchmarking process

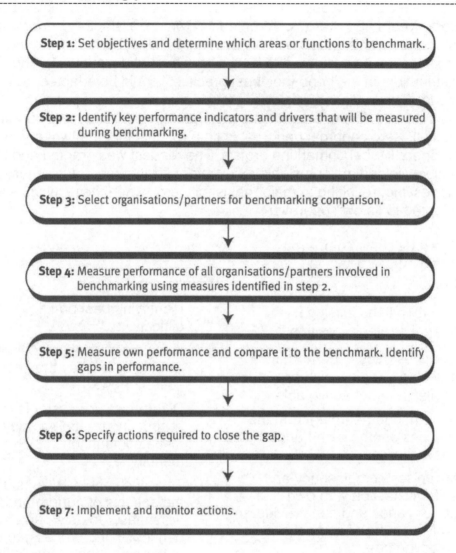

Step 1: Set objectives and determine which areas or functions to benchmark.

Step 2: Identify key performance indicators and drivers that will be measured during benchmarking.

Step 3: Select organisations/partners for benchmarking comparison.

Step 4: Measure performance of all organisations/partners involved in benchmarking using measures identified in step 2.

Step 5: Measure own performance and compare it to the benchmark. Identify gaps in performance.

Step 6: Specify actions required to close the gap.

Step 7: Implement and monitor actions.

Note: An APM question requirement is unlikely to ask you to list the entire process. However, knowledge of the steps is required; for example, you may be asked to complete a benchmarking exercise that has already been started or carry out a particular step or you may be asked to comment on the results of a benchmarking exercise already done.

Question practice

The following question is a longer style question on benchmarking. Make sure that you take the time to attempt this question and to review the recommended answer. Do not be overwhelmed by the numerical information in this question. In the exam, the numbers would be contained in an appendix and are likely to be less detailed than here.

Test your understanding 4

AV is a charitable organisation, the primary objective of which is to meet the accommodation needs of persons within its locality. In an attempt to improve its performance, AV's directors have started to carry out a benchmarking exercise. They have identified a company called BW which is a profit seeking private provider of rented accommodation.

BW has provided some operational and financial data which is summarised below along with the most recent results for AV for the year ended 31 May 20X4.

Income and expenditure accounts for the year ended 31 May 20X4 were as follows:

	AV ($)	BW ($)
Rents received	2,386,852	2,500,000
Less:		
Staff and management costs	450,000	620,000
Major repairs and planned maintenance	682,400	202,200
Day-to-day repairs	478,320	127,600
Sundry operating costs	305,500	235,000
Net interest payable and other similar charges	526,222	750,000
Total costs	2,442,442	1,934,800
Operating (deficit/surplus)	(55,590)	565,200

Operating information in respect of the year ended 31 May 20X4 was as follows:

1   Property and rental information:

AV – size of property	AV – number of properties	AV – rent payable per week ($)	BW – number of properties
1 bedroom	80	40	40
2 bedrooms	160	45	80
3 bedrooms	500	50	280
4 bedrooms	160	70	nil

AV had certain properties that were unoccupied during part of the year. The rents lost as a consequence of unoccupied properties amounted to $36,348. BW did not have any unoccupied properties at any point during the year.

2   Staff salaries were payable as follows:

AV – number of staff	AV – salary per staff member per year	BW – number of staff	BW – salary per staff member per year
	$	$	$
2	35,000	3	50,000
2	25,000	2	35,000
3	20,000	20	20,000
18	15,000	–	–

3   Planned maintenance and major repairs undertaken

Nature of work	AV – number of properties	AV – cost per property ($)	BW – number of properties	BW – cost per property ($)
Miscellaneous construction work	20	1,250	–	–
Fitted kitchen replacements (all are the same size)	90	2,610	10	5,220
Heating upgrades/ replacements	15	1,500	–	–
Replacement sets of windows and doors for 3 bedroomed properties	100	4,000	25	6,000

All expenditure on planned maintenance and major repairs may be regarded as revenue expenditure.

4   Day-to-day repairs information:

Classification of repair	AV – number of repairs undertaken	AV – total cost	BW – number of repairs undertaken
		$	
Emergency	960	134,400	320
Urgent	1,880	225,600	752
Non-urgent	1,020	118,320	204

Each repair undertaken by BW costs the same irrespective of classification of repair.

Required:

(a)   Assess the progress of the benchmarking exercise to date, explaining the actions that have been undertaken and those that are still required. **(7 marks)**

(b)   Evaluate, as far as possible, AV's benchmarked position. **(6 marks)**

(c)   Evaluate the benchmarking technique being used and discuss whether BW is a suitable benchmarking partner for AV to use. **(7 marks)**

Professional marks will be awarded for the demonstration of skill in analysis and evaluation, scepticism and commercial acumen in your answer. **(5 marks)**

(Total: 25 marks)

Note: Do not ignore the professional skills marks. They account for a significant 20% of the overall marks. This Section B question contains all three possible professional skills that could be tested in Section B ('communication' will also be included as a professional skill in Section A questions). In terms of awarding marks, there may be slightly more marks available than the set amount of 5, with each professional skill being awarded either 0, 1 or 2 marks up to a maximum of 5. Do review the sample professional skills marking guide in the answer.

Chapter summary

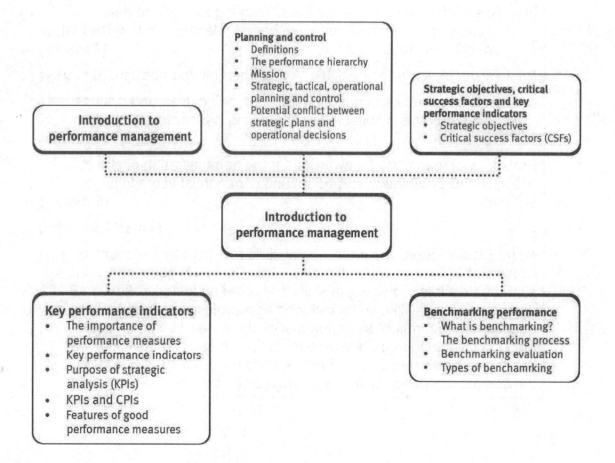

Planning and control
- Definitions
- The performance hierarchy
- Mission
- Strategic, tactical, operational planning and control
- Potential conflict between strategic plans and operational decisions

Introduction to performance management

Strategic objectives, critical success factors and key performance indicators
- Strategic objectives
- Critical success factors (CSFs)

Introduction to performance management

Key performance indicators
- The importance of performance measures
- Key performance indicators
- Purpose of strategic analysis (KPIs)
- KPIs and CPIs
- Features of good performance measures

Benchmarking performance
- What is benchmarking?
- The benchmarking process
- Benchmarking evaluation
- Types of benchamrking

Test your understanding answers

Test your understanding 1

Critical success factors (CSFs) are as follows:

Product quality – the fact that production staff may have no previous experience in a food production environment is likely to prove problematic. It is vital that a comprehensive training programme is put in place at the earliest opportunity. DY need to reach and maintain the highest level of quality as soon as possible.

Reliability – the quality and timeliness of delivery into Jacksons supermarkets assumes critical significance. Hence supply chain management must be extremely robust as there is little scope for error.

Technical quality – compliance with existing regulators regarding food production including all relevant factory health and safety requirements is vital in order to establish and maintain the reputation of DY as a supplier of quality products. The ability to store products at the correct temperature is critical because yogurts are produced for human consumption and in extreme circumstances could cause fatalities.

External credibility – accreditation by relevant trade associations/regulators will be essential if nationwide acceptance of DY as a major producer of frozen yogurts is to be established.

New product development – while DY have produced a range of frozen yogurts it must be recognised that consumer tastes change and that in the face of competition there will always be a need for a continuous focus on new product development.

Margin – while DY need to recognise all other CSFs they should always be mindful that the need to obtain desired levels of gross and net margin remain of the utmost importance.

Note: only five CSFs were required. Alternative relevant discussion and examples would be appropriate.

Test your understanding 2

Key performance indicators (KPIs) which could be used to measure each CSF are as follows:

Product quality – percentage of samples of frozen yoghurt which pass internal quality control checks.

Reliability – number of late deliveries (deliveries which did not arrive within 24 hours of the order being placed) to Jacksons supermarkets.

Technical quality – average number of compliance training days completed per employee each year.

External credibility – number of accreditations obtained/retained.

New product development – total revenue from new products.

Margin – gross profit margin and net profit margin.

Note: This was based on the CSFs identified in the answer for TYU1. Alternative relevant discussion and examples would be appropriate.

Test your understanding 3

(a) **Building and Monitoring critical success factors**

Critical success factors (CSFs) are those areas of business performance where the company must succeed in order to achieve its overall strategic objectives. Monitoring CSFs are those that are used to keep abreast of ongoing operations, for example, comparison of actual results to budgets or industry averages. Building CSFs are those which look to the future of the organisation and its development, for example, the launch of niche products such as music concert films or the use of new distribution methods such as downloadable films.

(b) **Information for establishing CSFs**

The company can use information about the internal and external environment to set its CSFs. Relevant external information would include the structure of the industry and the strategy of FP's competitors. The geographical location of production and the main sales markets may also be relevant. Film is a hit driven industry where word of mouth can lead to success, therefore, recognition of the product and the brand ('Film Productions') by the public would lead to success. For example, the Walt Disney Company has achieved a high level of brand recognition that has enabled it to expand into other entertainment areas using characters from its films.

Relevant internal information would include measures of seasonality on sales which will dictate the timing of film releases and effectiveness of marketing campaigns. By forecasting the size of the market along with likely levels of competition, profit can be optimised. However, these forecasts will be subject to uncertainty and so the information systems will need to be flexible and allow probabilistic analysis. A CSF based on the quality of these forecasts would therefore be appropriate. Other internal sources could include measures of the cost per film and the time taken to produce a film.

Other possible information could include contingent factors (those that depend on specific threats or opportunities facing FP).

KAPLAN PUBLISHING

(c) **Performance indicators linked to the CSFs**

Audience satisfaction – performance indicators are:

- Sales per film – currently the company releases an average of 6.4 films per year and makes about $31.25 million on each one. These figures should be compared to industry averages. Trends on sales per film should be monitored for indications of changes in consumer taste.

- Brand recognition – consumers should be surveyed to identify if the FP name is known and used as an indicator of quality when selecting films. If FP regularly uses certain artists (directors or film stars) then positive consumer recognition of these names will indicate satisfaction.

- Repeat viewings – with TV showings, it will be possible to measure viewers for each showing of the film and monitor the decline in viewing over repetitions. The level of DVD purchases following a cinema release will also indicate customer satisfaction with customers actively wanting to own their own copy of a favourite film.

- Awards won – number of awards won will indicate success. However, the level of recognition of any award must be brought into account as major ones such as those voted on by the public or those whose ceremonies are widely reported have the greatest impact.

- Response of the media – scores by film critics often appear in the media and these give a measure of satisfaction although this category must be treated carefully as critics often look for artistic merit while FP is seeking commercial success and broad audience acceptance.

Profitability in operations – performance indicators are:

- Industry average margin – collect data on competitor companies to set an appropriate benchmark. This will require care to ensure that appropriate comparator companies are chosen, for example, those with a production budget similar to FP's of $18 million per film.

- Time in production – the cost of a film will depend on the length of time it takes to produce. If the film is intended to meet a current customer demand it may require to be produced quickly, in order to meet revenue targets. Therefore, the time in production will affect both sales and cost levels so altering the gross margin. Again, it would be helpful to identify if films meet their production schedule and if these schedules compare favourably to those of other film companies.

– Costs – the costs should be broken down into categories such as those for artists, production technicians and marketing. The cost structure for each film should be compared internally, to others that FP produces and also externally, to available figures for the industry

(d) **Impact on FP's information systems**

The company website can collect audience survey results and comments posted on the site. Consumers can be drawn to the site with clips and trailers from current films and those in production. The site can log the frequency with which films are viewed and if audience members create accounts then further detail on the age, gender and location of the audience can be collected. This will allow a more detailed profile of the customer base for FP to be created and will be used to help in decisions about what films to commission in the future. The account members can be given the opportunity to score each film providing further information about satisfaction.

The company could also consider scanning the websites of its competitors to identify their performance – especially their published results which will provide benchmark information on gross margin levels.

A management information system (MIS) will collate the information from individual transactions recorded in the accounting system to allow middle level management to control the business. This system will allow customer purchases to be summarised into reports to identify both products that sell well and the customers (such as cinema chains and TV networks) who provide the main sources of revenue (indicators of satisfaction). The level of repeat business on a customer account will give an indication of the satisfaction with FP's output. The system will also produce management accounts from which gross margins will be drawn and it should be capable of breaking this down by film and by customer to aid decision-making by targeting FP's output to the most profitable areas. This will aid decision-making about the performance of the production team on a film and can be used to set rewards for each team.

An executive information system (EIS) is one that will supply information to the senior management of the organisation allowing them to drill down into the more detailed transaction reports where necessary. The EIS will provide summarised information, focused on the key performance indicators in order to allow the directors to quickly judge whether the company is meeting its CSFs. It will draw on internal sources such as the MIS and also external sources such as market data on revenues that different films are earning at the box office.

Professional skills marks may be awarded as follows (maximum 7 marks):

Communication:

- Report format and structure – use of headings/sub-headings
- Style, language and clarity – appropriate tone of report response, easy to follow and understand
- Effectiveness of communication – content of the report is relevant and tailored to the question scenario
- Adherence to the specific request to include no more than two examples for the information and two PIs.

Analysis and Evaluation:

- Reasoned assessment of information FP could use and how it could be used
- Comprehensive explanation of why each PI is relevant to the CSF
- Reasoned discussion of impact of PIs on information systems.

Scepticism:

Recognition of the need for the organisation's website, management information system and executive information system to be adapted to support the PIs identified.

Commercial Acumen:

- Effective use of example drawn from across the scenario information and other practical considerations related to the context to illustrate the points being made throughout the report
- Recommendations of PIs are practical and plausible in the context of the company situation.

Test your understanding 4

(a) The benchmarking process can be described using seven steps. These are outlined below, together with AV's current progress against these stages.

   1 **Set objectives and decide areas to benchmark**

   It is not clear exactly what AV's objectives are here, as "improve performance" is too generic. AV must carefully identify what specific areas it is looking to improve upon – for example, reduced repair costs, improved staff productivity, better rental collections.

   2 **Identify key performance drivers and indicators**

   To some extent these can be identified by looking at the expense headings in the Income statement. AV will improve performance by operating more efficiently across its major cost headings. It should be noted here that as a not for profit organisation performance will be measured in a different way from BW. For example, AV will not wish to increase rentals charged in order to report a surplus, so measures of efficiency become much more important so that it can provide good quality accommodation within the cost constraints imposed by the rents received.

   3 **Select organisations for benchmarking comparison**

   AV has selected a profit motivated company, BW, for benchmarking against, so this step has been carried out. However, it is not clear how this partner has been selected. Whilst there may be some examples of best practice to be learned from, it should again be noted that BW is profit motivated and so will have fundamentally different objectives from AV.

   4 **Measure performance of all organisations involved**

   Some basic data has been gathered here.

   5 **Compare performance**

   This is the stage that AV has now reached, as there is as yet no comparison of, or commentary on, the relative performance of the two organisations. Part (b) addresses this area.

   6 **Specify areas for improvement**

   Once the comparisons above are made this should identify areas for improvement. Care should be taken that processes identified at BW can be transferred across to AV. Again, given their widely different objectives, this may not be possible. AV may also need to retrain some staff (or even recruit others) to ensure the requisite skills are in place.

7   **Implement and monitor improvements**

Management must continuously monitor the impact of any changes implemented to make sure that the intended benefits are realised. Without this monitoring, any changes may be short lived because staff may soon revert back to their familiar way of doing things.

So, in conclusion, AV has identified a benchmarking partner (albeit one that may not be wholly suitable), and has collected some basic operational and financial data for comparison. It needs to more clearly define its objectives before it can proceed to specify actions for improvement.

(b)   As discussed in part (c) below, it is not surprising that we see some major differences between the two organisations as they have very different objectives.

1   **Rental income**

AV has average rental income per property of $52 per week compared to $120 per week for BW. This is not surprising, given that AV wants to make cheap housing available to as many people as possible, and BW seeks to charge higher rates for premium properties to tenants who can afford to pay. This should not be seen as an indicator that AV should increase its rents.

It should also be noted that the mix of properties is different. AV has a larger proportion of 3 and 4 bedroomed properties (presumably to cope with large families), whereas BW has no four bedroomed property. Taking this into account, the rentals on a "per room" basis are even higher for BW.

2   **Staff salaries**

The average annual salary per employee in AV is $18000, whereas it is $24800 for BW. Again, this can largely be explained by the differing objectives that will encourage AV to keep costs to a minimum. It should be noted, however, that there may be a trade – off here between cost and productivity. If AV paid higher salaries would it be able to recruit better quality staff who are more productive? Staff numbers (25 in total) are the same for both companies, even though AV has 900 properties compared to only 400 for BW. This may lead to a reduced level of service for AV, which in turn could lead to a delay in dealing with problems such as repairs or collecting overdue rent.

3   **Planned maintenance and repairs**

The major repair and maintenance cost for AV totalled $682,400, which is over three times as much as BW. There are two likely reasons for this. Firstly AV has more than twice as many properties (900 compared to 400), and secondly it may well be that their housing stock is in poorer condition and therefore needs more maintenance. It should also be noted that the repair costs are higher per property for BW (replacement kitchens cost twice as much as for BW for example), which will again reflect their different objectives and the needs of their clients. This should not be interpreted to mean that AV is "more efficient" as it is almost certainly not a like for like comparison. Hence, as noted in part (c) below, benchmarking against other not-for-profits may yield more meaningful comparisons.

One point that should be noted – there is always a possible trade-off between cost and quality. If AV paid more per repair, would the quality be better and therefore the repairs last longer before further expenditure is needed?

4   **Day-to-day repairs**

AV has undertaken a total of 3,860 repairs in the year at an average cost of $124 per repair. BW has carried out 1,276 repairs at a cost of $100 per repair. Whilst there is not a massive difference per repair, a saving of $24 per repair would result in overall cost savings of 3860 × $24 = $92,640.

AV should carry out further research as to how BW has obtained a fixed fee per repair, and see if it can obtain a similar contract as this could produce significant savings.

5   **Sundry operating costs**

Whilst these are 30% higher for AV ($305,500 compared to $235,000), we have no breakdown of the figures and so cannot really comment further. It seems reasonable that, since AV has more than twice as many properties and tenants, it will incur a higher level of costs here.

6   **Net interest and other charges**

Again no analysis is given, so no further comment is possible.

Conclusion

AV clearly operates at the "lower end" of the rental market compared with BW. It has more properties and charges lower rents per property. It is likely that the housing stock is in poorer condition, and so necessitates more ongoing repairs and maintenance. Attention should be given to getting the best possible deals from suppliers on repair work, perhaps negotiating a "fixed fee" in the same way as BW has done. It is surprising that staffing levels are the same for both companies as AW has more than twice as many properties. Overall though, it should be noted that the two organisations have totally different objectives that may well go some way towards explaining these differences.

(c)   AV has chosen to benchmark itself against BW, a profit seeking company operating in the same sector. There are a number of **advantages** to this chosen method of benchmarking. Firstly, it is method of **learning from the success of BW and for learning and applying best practices**. Secondly, it will help AV in **assessing its current positioning and identifying any gaps in performance**.

However, there are a number of **drawbacks**. Firstly, this benchmarking exercise will be **costly in terms of time and money**. Before investing any more funds in the exercise, it is important that AV's directors determine if the cost of the exercise is less than the benefit. Secondly, **BW may not be the best practice organisation**. How was this benchmarking partner chosen? Another drawback is that **too much attention may be paid to the aspects of performance that are measured as a result of the benchmarking exercise**, to the detriment of the organisation's overall performance.

Finally and most importantly, as mentioned previously, **the two organisations differ fundamentally because of their objectives**. The objectives of not-for-profit organisations like AV can vary significantly. AV's primary objective is to "meet the accommodation needs of persons in its locality". So, it is likely to want to keep as many people as possible in accommodation regardless of cost. How can it measure whether or not it has met this non quantitative objective? Could it in fact have provided more properties if it had adopted different policies relating to staff or repairs? BW has a primary objective of maximising profit. This is a clear and measureable objective that will probably lead BW to provide high quality accommodation in desirable areas that will generate high revenues and profits. This will support high rents (the average property rental for BW is $120 per week compared to $52 per week for AV) and will necessitate quality repairs and maintenance and customer service levels. Whilst efficiency will still be important for BW, to some extent it can pass on higher costs to its tenants by increasing rents.

AV on the other hand will seek to maintain low rents, and to provide as much housing as possible within its budgetary constraints. This will necessitate a very high level of efficiency as it will not seek to pass on high costs to its tenants. So, like any not-for-profit the critical measures of economy, efficiency and effectiveness must be considered.

Because of these fundamental differences AV would be better advised to consider benchmarking against other similar charities. This would give it much more meaningful comparisons as the objectives of the organisations would be more closely aligned. In addition, charitable organisations are generally more willing to share information to their mutual benefit, so such benchmarking partners may be readily found.

The use of a benchmarking partner that shares similar objectives would allow AV to obtain a much more objective comparison for its own performance.

Professional skills marks (maximum 5 marks):

Analysis and Evaluation:

- Appropriate use of data to support discussion and draw conclusions on the progress of the benchmarking exercise to date

- Comprehensive evaluation of AV's benchmarking position including recognition of further analysis which could be carried out to enable a full evaluation

- Drawbacks of benchmarking technique clearly supported with examples.

Scepticism:

Recognition of the limitations of benchmarking AV and BW with each other.

Commercial Acumen:

- Effective use of example drawn from across the scenario information and other practical considerations related to the context to illustrate the points being made throughout the answer

- Demonstration of an understanding of the usefulness but also the limitations of the benchmarking exercise carried out.

Strategy and performance

Chapter learning objectives

Upon completion of this chapter you will be able to:

- explain the role of strategic performance management in strategic planning and control

- discuss the role of performance measurement in checking progress towards the corporate objectives

- evaluate how models such as SWOT analysis, PEST, Boston Consulting Group, balanced scorecard, Porter's generic strategies and 5 Forces may assist in the performance management process

- explain the performance 'planning gap' and evaluate alternative strategies to fill that gap.

PER

One of the PER performance objectives (PO1) is to take into account all relevant information and use professional judgement, your personal values and scepticism to evaluate data and make decisions. You should identify right from wrong and escalate anything of concern. You also need to make sure that your skills, knowledge and behaviour are up-to-date and allow you to be effective in you role. Another PER performance objectives (PO5) is to manage yourself and your resources effectively and responsibly. You contribute to the leadership and management of your organisation – delivering what's needed by stakeholders and the business. PER performance objective (PO22) is data analysis and decision support, which involves enabling relevant stakeholders to make decisions. Working through this chapter should help you understand how to demonstrate these objectives.

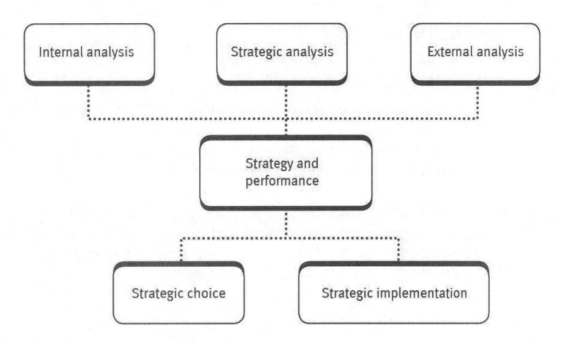

1 Common knowledge

Chapter 2 includes **knowledge contained in the Strategic Business Leader (SBL) exam but this it is not a problem if you are yet to study for this exam and there is no expectation that you have any SBL knowledge in place**.

2 Introduction

In Chapter 1, we learned that an important part of performance management is to identify the organisation's **strategy** and **objectives**. Once the organisation's strategy and objectives has been set, this will determine the **performance measures** that the organisation uses to monitor whether the objectives have been achieved.

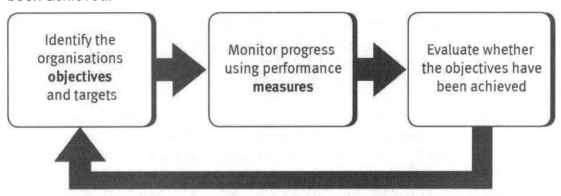

Take **action** to correct or reward performance

In this chapter we will consider how an organisation's strategy and long-term objectives are developed. We will look at the different stages of **strategic planning** and some models which organisations can use during this process. These include **SWOT, Boston Consulting Group** (BCG) **matrix, PEST, Porter's Five Forces, Ansoff's matrix** and **Porter's generic strategies**.

3 Strategic planning

Strategic planning is concerned with:

- where an organisation wants to be (usually expressed in terms of its objectives) and

- how it will get there (strategies, i.e. where and how to compete to gain sustainable competitive advantage).

Illustration 1 – Use of the rational model for strategic planning

This three-stage model of strategic planning is a useful framework for seeing the 'bigger picture' of performance management.

Strategic analysis
- External analysis to identify opportunities and threats
- Internal analysis to identify strengths and weaknesses
- Stakeholder analysis to identify key objectives and to assess power and interest of different groups
- Gap analysis to identify the difference between desired and expected performance.

↓

Strategic choice
- Strategies are required to 'close the gap'
- Competitive strategy – for each business unit
- Directions for growth – which markets/products should be invested in
- Whether expansion should be achieved by organic growth, acquisition or some form of joint arrangement.

↓

Strategic implementation
- Formulation of detailed plans and budgets
- Target setting for KPIs
- Monitoring and control.

Note: Each of the areas will be covered in more detail throughout the course. However, it is worth noting that although strategy is still included in this exam, the main thrust in APM will be looking at where objectives come from, identifying critical success factors, choosing metrics and how to implement strategy. **Strategic theory will be secondary and this model will not be directly examined**.

4 Strategic analysis

4.1 Purpose of strategic analysis

The purpose of **strategic analysis** is to assess the organisation's present situation by identifying the organisation's **internal** strengths and weaknesses and any **external** opportunities and threats.

Therefore, strategic analysis can be split into two main components which are:

- Internal analysis (section 5)

- External analysis (section 6).

Once both of these have been complete, the organisation's **strengths** and **weaknesses** can be compared to any **opportunities** and **threats** as part of an overall **corporate appraisal** using the **SWOT analysis** model.

4.2 SWOT

The purpose of **SWOT analysis** (corporate appraisal) is to provide a summarised analysis of an organisation's:

- internal strengths and weaknesses

- external opportunities and threats.

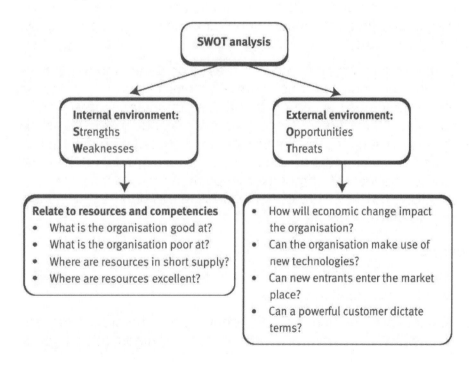

SWOT analysis and the performance management process

- SWOT analysis helps an organisation to understand its environment and its internal capacities and hence to evaluate the potential strategic options it could pursue in its quest to improve organisational performance and to close any performance gaps that exist.

- It can also help an organisation to identify key aspects of performance (CSFs) that need measuring (through the establishment of KPIs).

- Finally, it can help in determining the information needs of the business in relation to measuring and reporting on the KPIs set.

Test your understanding 1

Envie Co owns a chain of retail clothing stores specialising in ladies' designer fashion and accessories. Jane Smith, the original founder, has been pleasantly surprised by the continuing growth in the fashion industry during the last decade. The company was established 12 years ago, originally with one store in the capital city. Jane's design skills and entrepreneurial skills have been the driving force behind the expansion. Due to unique designs and good quality control, the business now has ten stores in various cities.

Each store has a shop manger that is completely responsible for managing the staff and stock levels within each store. They produce monthly reports on sales. Some stores are continually late in supplying their monthly figures.

Envie runs several analysis programmes to enable management information to be collated. The information typically provides statistical data on sales trends between categories of items and stores. The analysis and preparation of these reports are conducted in the marketing department. In some cases the information is out of date in terms of trends and variations. As the business has developed Jane has used the service of a local IT company to implement and develop their systems. She now wants to invest in website development with the view of reaching global markets.

Required:

(a) Construct a SWOT analysis with reference to the proposal of website development.

(b) Explain how the use of SWOT analysis may be of assistance to Envie Co's performance management and measurement process.

Note: The question above requires you to construct a SWOT analysis. It is useful to produce one for Envie Co, for practice of constructing a SWOT. However, in the exam environment it is likely that the SWOT will have been done for you and that the requirements will focus on the performance management and measurement implications of the factors raised by the SWOT.

5 Internal analysis

5.1 The purpose of internal analysis

Internal analysis is used to identify an organisation's strengths and weaknesses which could include any of the following:

- **skills:** management expertise, experience of employees
- **reputation:** strong brand image, relationship with customers
- **resources available:** cash position, manufacturing capacity.

5.2 Boston Consulting Group (BCG)

One area that could be considered as part of internal analysis is the balance of the company's divisions or products.

The BCG matrix classifies an organisation's divisions or products according to:

- **relative market share** (an indicator of competitive strength)
- **market growth** (an indicator of market attractiveness).

	Star	**Problem child**
High	Large share of high-growth market.	Small share of high-growth market. Two choices:
Market growth	• High investment required to hold/build position. • Moderate cash flow. • Future cash cow?	• **Invest** – Large investment required to grow market share to become future star. • **Divest** (quickly or slowly) if investment too high.
	Cash cow	**Dog**
Low	Large share of low-growth market. • Cash generator; used for stars and problem children. • Strategy is minimal investment to keep the product going but avoid it becoming a dog.	Small share of low-growth market. • Moderate or negative cash flow. • Probably divest (quickly or slowly) depending on contribution/other factors.
	High	**Low**

Relative market share

The BCG matrix **shows whether the firm has a balanced portfolio** in terms of the products it offers and the market sectors it operates in. A balanced portfolio means:

- Having cash cows of sufficient size/number to fund stars and problem children

- Stars of sufficient size/number to become future cash cows

- Problem children with reasonable prospects to become future stars

- No dogs or if there are any there would need to be a good reason. For example, the dog may be part of a wider product range and performance would be impacted negatively if the product was removed. Alternatively, the dog may deliver a positive contribution; this may be modest but still contributes to enhanced performance.

Market growth and relative market share

If the relevant information is available, market growth and relative market share can be calculated as follows:

> **Market growth** = the % increase/decrease in annual market revenue

Note: If market revenue is given for a number of successive years the average % increase/decrease in annual market revenue can be calculated:

> $1 + g = $ (most recent market revenue ÷ earliest market revenue)$^{(1/n)}$

g = the average increase/decrease in annual market revenue (as a decimal)

n = the number of periods of growth

(Be guided by the question in the exam. If you have time and the required information then use the method above to calculate the average figure. If you do not have market revenue for a number of successive years or only have a limited amount of time, then it would be acceptable to calculate the market growth based on two consecutive years only.)

As a guide, 10% is often used as the dividing line between high and low growth. However, this is a general guide only – do refer to and use the information given in the scenario.

> **Relative market share** = division's market share ÷ largest competitor's market share

where: division's market share = divisional revenue ÷ market revenue

A relative market share greater than 1 indicates that the division or product is the market leader. As a guide, 1 can be used as the dividing line between high and low market share. However, this is a general guide only – do refer to and use the information given in the scenario.

KAPLAN PUBLISHING

Factors to consider for performance management

When conducting a BCG assessment an organisation should consider the following:

- How to manage the different categories (as per the points included in the matrix above) in order to optimise the performance of the organisation.

- What performance indicators (metrics) are required for each category. For example, performance measures for a cash cow may focus on cash flow or changes in relative market share whereas performance measures for a star may focus on profit or return on investment (ROI).

- The alignment of the performance indicators with the objectives of the organisation (as per the performance hierarchy) and the individuals within it.

BCG evaluation

Benefits	Drawbacks
• Ensures that a balanced portfolio of products or divisions exists. • Can use to manage divisions in different ways, e.g. divisions in a mature market should focus on cost control and cash generation. • Metrics used for each category can be in line with the analysis. • Looks at the portfolio of divisions or products as a whole rather than assessing the performance of each one separately. • Can be used to assess performance, e.g. if an organisation consists mainly of cash cows we would expect to see static or low growth in revenue.	• Too simplistic, considering two variables only. Market growth is just one indicator of industry attractiveness and market share is just one indicator of competitive advantage. Other factors will also be determinants of success. • Designed as a tool for product portfolio analysis rather than performance management. • Downgrades traditional measures such as profit and so may not be aligned with shareholders' objectives. • Determining what 'high' and 'low' growth and share mean in different situations is difficult. • Does not consider links between business units, e.g. a dog may be required to complete a product range. • May encourage organisations to adopt a holding strategy for its cash cows rather than trying to increase share in the market.

Test your understanding 2

Food For Thought (FFT) has been established for over 20 years and has a wide range of food products. The company's objective is the maximisation of shareholder wealth. The organisation has four divisions:

1   Premier

2   Organic

3   Baby

4   Convenience.

The Premier division manufactures a range of very high quality food products, which are sold to a leading supermarket, with stores in every major city in the country. Due to the specialist nature of the ingredients these products have a very short life cycle.

The Organic division manufactures a narrow range of food products for a well-established Organic brand label.

The Baby division manufactures specialist foods for infants, which are sold to the country's largest Baby retail store.

The Convenience division manufactures low fat ready-made meals for the local council.

FFT's board have decided to perform a Boston Consulting Group (BCG) analysis to understand whether they have right mix of businesses.

The following revenue data ($m) has been gathered for the year ended 31st March:

		20X3	20X4	20X5	20X6	20X7
Premier	Market size	180	210	260	275	310
	Sales revenue	10	12	18	25	30
Organic	Market size	18.9	19.3	19.6	19.8	20.4
	Sales revenue	13.5	14	14.5	15	16
Baby	Market size	65	69	78	92	96
	Sales revenue	2.5	2.7	2.8	2.9	3
Convenience	Market size	26	27.2	27.6	28	29
	Sales revenue	0.9	0.9	0.92	0.94	0.9

The management accountant has also collected the following information for 20X7 for comparison purposes.

Largest competitor	% share
Premier	17%
Organic	20%
Baby	25%
Convenience	31%

Each of division's performance is measured using EVA™ (covered in Chapter 11). The divisional manager's remuneration package (remuneration is covered in Chapter 9) contains a bonus element which is based on the achievement of the division's cost budget (this is set at board level).

Required:

(a) Using the BCG matrix assess the competitive position of Food For Thought. **(10 marks)**

(b) Evaluate, the divisional manager's remuneration package in light of the divisional performance system and your BCG analysis. **(5 marks)**

Professional marks will be awarded for the demonstration of skill in analysis and evaluation, scepticism and commercial acumen in your answer. **(4 marks)**

(Total: 19 marks)

Note: This is not a complete Section B question. Section B questions in the exam will include 20 technical marks and 5 professional skills marks.

Further detail on applying the BCG matrix

Star	Problem Child
• Is the high investment being spent effectively?	• **Assuming the strategy is to invest:**
• Is market share being gained, held or eroded?	– Is market share being gained?
• Is customer perception (e.g. brand, quality) improving?	– Effectiveness of advertising spend.
• Are customer CSFs changing as the market grows?	• **Assuming the strategy is to divest:**
• What is the net cash flow?	– Monitor contribution to see whether to exit quickly or divest slowly.
• Is the star becoming a cash cow?	
Cash Cow	**Dog**
• What is the net cash flow?	• Monitor contribution to see whether to exit quickly or divest slowly.
• Is market share being eroded – could the cash cow be moving towards becoming a dog?	• Monitor market growth as an increase in the growth rate could justify retaining the product.

The nature of the four classifications shown above is self-explanatory. An understanding of where given products stand in relation to this matrix can be another essential element in strategic planning. For example, if a product is a cash cow, then it may be very useful, but it should be appreciated that it may be at an advanced stage in its life cycle and the cash it generates should be invested in potential stars.

However, it is not always easy to determine future stars. Many businesses have poured money into the development of products that they believed were potential stars only to find that those products turned into dogs. The Sinclair C5 (a small, battery-powered car) is often quoted as an example of this phenomenon. The promoters of this product in the 1980s proceeded on the basis that there was a market for such a car as a means of urban transport and that the C5 would enjoy a high share of this market. In fact, the only niche it found was as a children's toy and it achieved only a low market share with little growth potential as such.

The general point this model makes is that current period cash flow is not an unambiguous statement on the performance of a product or business sector. To appreciate fully the performance of a product, one has to appreciate where the product stands in terms of the above matrix. A poor current cash flow may be acceptable from a product or service considered to be a 'star'.

Other application issues

Following the advice of the model may lead to unfortunate consequences, such as

- Moving into areas where there is little experience

- Over-milking of cash cows

- Abandonment of potentially healthy businesses labelled as problem children

- Neglect of interrelationships among businesses, and

- Too many problem children within the business portfolio largely as a consequence of incorrect focus of management attention.

6   External analysis

51

6.1   The purpose of external analysis

External analysis is used to identify opportunities and threats which come from the organisation's external environment, including the following:

- **macro environment:** political, economic, social and technological factors

- **industry level:** competition, bargaining power of customers and suppliers.

It is important that an organisation considers the impact of external factors on its performance.

The organisation can use two different models when considering this impact. Each model focuses on a different level in the external environment and is explained in detail in sections 6.2 and 6.3 below.

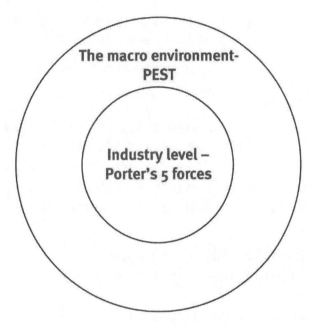

6.2   PEST

The PEST model looks at the macro-environment and its influence on organisational performance, using the following headings:

Heading	Examples
Political factors	<ul><li>Taxation policy</li><li>Government stability</li><li>Foreign trade regulations</li><li>Taxation</li><li>Employment law</li><li>Monopoly legislation</li><li>Environmental protection legislation</li></ul>

Economic factors	• Interest rates • Inflation • Unemployment • Business cycles
Social factors	• Population demographics • Social mobility • Income distribution • Lifestyle changes • Attitudes to work and leisure • Levels of education and consumerism • How to produce goods with minimal environmental damage
Technological factors	• Speed of technological transfer • Rates of obsolescence

(**Note:** This model is sometimes referred to as PESTEL. The additional 'E' is for environmental factors (included as part of social factors in PEST) and the additional 'L' is for legal factors (included as part of political factors in PEST)).

The key issue in APM is to appreciate that, **as well as being used for strategic analysis, this model can be used to help manage and maximise performance:**

- PEST can be used to **identify opportunities** that exist in the external environment. Steps can then be taken to exploit the opportunities in order to improve performance.

- **Threats and risk and uncertainty** in the macro environment can be **identified** and **monitored** and **action** can be taken to manage these.

- PEST analysis can assist in the **identification of relevant CSFs and the development of KPIs** linked to these. For example, an organisation may decide to source supplies from politically stable countries or may adapt its product portfolio to reflect social factors such as a change in consumer tastes.

- Changes in the macro environment may result in the **revision of KPIs and the targets** based around these KPIs.

Illustration 2 – PEST and performance management

PEST can be used to identify key performance management issues. For example:

Identifying CSFs and KPIs

Current trends have indicated that British consumers have moved towards 'one-stop' and 'bulk' shopping which is due to a variety of social changes. As a result, supermarkets such as Tesco (the United Kingdom's (UK's) biggest supermarket) have increased the amount of non-food items for sale. This may be seen as a CSF and necessary to meet the needs of the modern customer. Tesco may develop KPIs around this CSF, for example by measuring the number or proportion of non-food items for sale in each store.

Revising targets

Increasing public concern for the natural environment has resulted in many supermarkets setting targets for say, wastage, recycling and energy efficiency. These targets may need revising if the external environment changes. For example, in the UK it was recently reported that more than two thirds of the bagged salad sold by Tesco ends up being thrown away. As a result of this investigation, Tesco (and a number of other retailers) have put more stringent wastage targets in place, recognising that performance would deteriorate if no action was taken.

PEST analysis and performance measurement

Environmental legislation may have been identified as being particularly important to a chemicals producer, in which case it should set up a series of targets to measure compliance. For example:

- level of fines

- number of environmental prosecutions

- number of environmental enforcement actions

- number of 'notifiable' incidents (local legislation will define what is 'notifiable' and what is not)

- percentage of employees working within an ISO 14001 (a recognised quality standard) compliant Environmental Management System

- the firm's rating in independent benchmarking such as the 'Business in the Environment' Index.

6.3 Porter's 5 forces model

The level of competition in the industry can also affect an organisation's performance.

All businesses in a particular industry are likely to be subject to similar pressures that determine how attractive the sector is.

Industry attractiveness depends on five factors or forces:

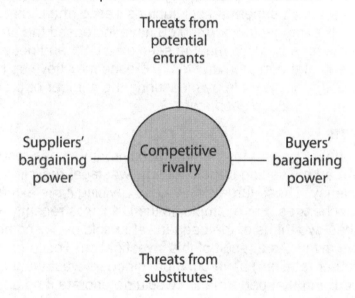

Force	Explanation	Possible metrics to measure the strength of force
Competitive rivalry	There will be a tough environment if there are many competitors but a much easier one if there is a monopoly.	<ul><li>Market share</li><li>Market growth</li><li>Market capacity</li></ul>
Buyer's bargaining power	A few, large customers can exert powerful bargaining power. Many, small customers find it harder to apply pressure.	<ul><li>Number of buyers</li><li>Size of buyers</li><li>Switching costs</li><li>Elasticity of demand</li></ul>
Supplier's bargaining power	A monopoly supplier of a vital component can apply great pressure. Any one of many suppliers of an ordinary component cannot.	<ul><li>Number of suppliers</li><li>Size of suppliers</li><li>Switching costs</li><li>Quality/price of suppliers used</li></ul>

Threats from potential entrants	The key issue here is to assess barriers to entry. For example, high capital costs, know-how and regulation are all barriers to entry which will help to reduce competition.	• Brand value • Customer loyalty • % of revenue protected by patents
Threats from substitutes	The level of the threat is determined by relative price/performance and the number of substitutes available.	• Price of substitutes • Quality/performance of substitutes

The stronger each of the five forces is, the lower the profitability of the industry.

Porter's 5 forces and performance management

When conducting a 5 forces assessment an organisation should consider the following:

- How to measure the strength of the forces

- How reliable those measurements are

- How to manage the forces identified to optimise organisational performance. The organisation should:

    - avoid business sectors which are unattractive because of the 5 forces

    - try to mitigate the effects of the 5 forces. For example, supplier power is lessened if a long-term contract is negotiated or competition is reduced by taking over a rival.

- Suitable performance indicators and targets to monitor the forces.

It is important that an organisation considers its performance in the context of its industry. For example, rising supplier prices may initially be blamed on an inefficient purchasing function. However, on further investigation it may be found that the industry is supplied by a relatively small number of large suppliers who have the power to increase prices.

Student accountant articles: visit the ACCA website, accaglobal.com, to review the article on 'performance management models'.

7 Strategic choice

7.1 Purpose of strategic choice

During the strategic choice stage, the managers will identify different strategic options available to the organisation and choose the strategic options which are most likely to **close the gap** between the organisation's current strategic position and its long-term goals and objectives.

7.2 Gap analysis

After completing the strategic analysis stage, the managers should have a better understanding of the organisation's current position and can now identify if there is a **gap** between **the forecast position** and its **long-term targets**.

The difference between these two is known as a **planning gap**.

The gap may be measured in terms of earnings, demand, return on capital employed (ROCE) etc. The example below shows a planning gap for 'earnings':

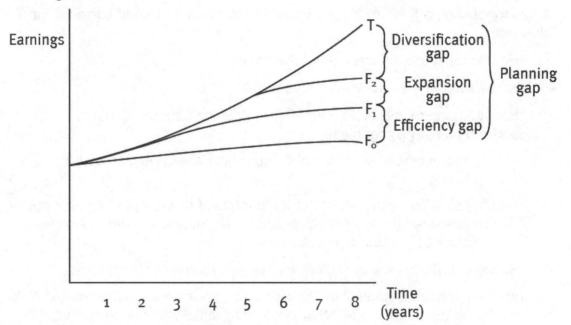

T = target

F_0 = initial forecast

F_1 = forecast after addressing efficiency gap

F_2 = forecast after also addressing expansion gap

The planning gap may be caused by a combination of the following factors:

- **Efficiency gap** – this relates to organisational inefficiencies. The efficiency gap can be addressed, for example, by better use of resources or divestment of a loss making business unit. Business Process Re-engineering (BPR) or value chain analysis (Chapter 6) could be used here.

- **Expansion gap** – this part of the planning gap may be closed by developing new products **or** diversifying into new markets.

- **Diversification gap** – this part of the planning gap may be closed by developing new products **and** diversifying into new markets.

7.3 Ansoff's matrix and its use in closing the performance planning gap

Ansoff represented the choices for closing the planning gap in his **product/market matrix**.

	Existing product	New product
Existing market	Market penetration	Product development
New market	Market development	Diversification

Managers can use their knowledge of the environment in which the organisation operates (for example, the level of competition or the availability of resources) to successfully identify the direction for strategic development and closure of the planning gap.

	Existing Product	**New Product**
Existing Market	**Market penetration** • A low risk strategy that involves increasing the market share in the existing market with the existing products. • Techniques used include improved quality and efficiency (hence addressing the **efficiency gap**), increased marketing activity or repositioning of the brand.	**Product development** • Attempts to sell new products to existing customers (hence addressing the **expansion gap**). • Builds on the organisation's knowledge and understanding of the market, allowing it to identify gaps and highlight customer needs not currently met by existing products. • New products could arise from R&D, joint ventures, buying in other organisation's products, copying innovations of rivals or licensing.

	Key risks: • Can lead to stagnation – it is unlikely to lead to high rates of growth since the emphasis is solely on 'selling more of the same products to the same customers'. • Need to consider competitor reaction.	• Could also come from product modifications or innovations (for example, Mars Ice-cream as an alternative to a Mars Bar). Key risks: • Market size and demand are unknown. • Need to consider impact on profitability of existing products.
New Market	**Market development** • The organisation keeps tried and tested existing products but attempts to sell them to new customers, i.e. new customer segments or geographical regions (for example, McDonald's and its geographical market development). • Used to close the **expansion gap**. Key risks: • The identified market may be less profitable than expected. • It puts a strain on existing strategic capabilities.	**Diversification** • Involves attempting to sell a new product to new customers. • Used to address the **diversification gap**. Key risks: • The most risky of all of the strategies since it involves both new products and markets. **Note:** There are two types of diversification: • **Related** – the organisation remains in a market or industry in which is it familiar. This can help reduce some of the risks of diversification. • **Unrelated** – the organisation has no previous experience in the market or industry. This is the riskiest diversification approach and likely involves greater market and product development research.

KAPLAN PUBLISHING

7.4 Porter's generic strategies

Another important part of strategic choice is deciding on what basis to compete. Porter identified three generic strategies through which an organisation could achieve competitive advantage and optimise performance.

	Lower cost	Higher cost
Broad target	Cost leadership	Differentiation
Narrow target	Focus	
	Cost focus	Differentiation focus

Cost leadership

 The organisation sets out to be the lowest cost producer in the industry.

Differentiation

 The organisation offers a product that can't be matched by rivals and charges a premium for this 'difference'.

Focus

 Position the business in one particular niche in the market. Competition may be on the basis of costs or differentiation.

 Porter's generic strategies

Cost leadership

The organisation sets out to be the lowest cost producer in the industry.

Performance should improve due to:

- the ability to earn the highest unit profits

- lower costs acting as a barrier to entry and reducing competition.

However:

- There is no fall back if the leadership position is lost, for example strengthening of the currency may make imports of substitute goods cheaper.

- The organisation must continually adapt to ensure unit prices are kept low and consumer needs are met.

Requirements include:

- Mass production facilitating the achievement of economies of scale.

- Investment in the latest technology reducing labour costs.

- Improving productivity, for example through the use of value chain analysis (Chapter 6) or zero based budgeting (Chapter 5).
- Use of bargaining power to lower the cost of supplies and overheads.

Differentiation

The organisation offers a product that can't be matched by rivals and charges a premium for this 'difference'.

Methods of differentiation include:

- quality differentiation, e.g. better reliability, durability or performance
- image and branding
- design
- support, for example offering 0% finance or next day delivery.

Performance should improve due to:

- higher margins
- loyalty increases with repeat custom
- reduction in the power of customers.

However:

- there is a need to continually innovate to defend the position
- smaller volumes
- associated costs, such as marketing, are higher
- performance in a recession may be poor.

Focus

Position the business in one particular niche in the market. Competition may be on the basis of costs or differentiation.

Performance should improve due to:

- little competition often exists in the identified niche
- the development of brand loyalty.

However:

- if successful it may attract other cost leaders/differentiators due to potential low barriers to entry
- low volumes may be sold.

Student accountant article: visit the ACCA website, www.accaglobal.com to review the article on 'Performance management models'.

8 Strategic implementation

8.1 Purpose of strategic implementation

The purpose of **strategic implementation** is set **detailed plans and targets** for each level, division and function of the organisation which aim to ensure that the organisation's long-term strategy is achieved.

Once these plans and targets have been set, progress should be **monitored** using **key performance indicators**, as we have seen previously in Chapter 1.

8.2 A revisit of the performance hierarchy

It is useful to consider strategic implementation in the context of the performance hierarchy that was introduced in Chapter 1:

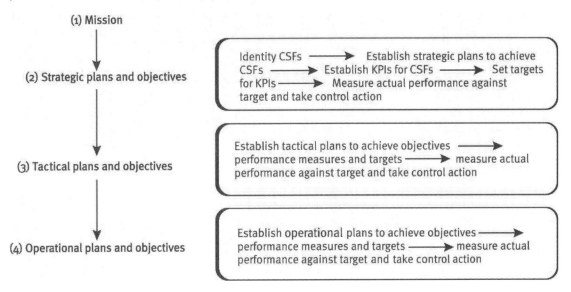

Chapter summary

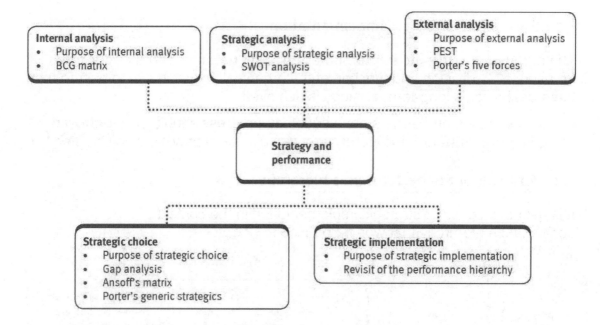

Test your understanding answers

Test your understanding 1

(a) **Strengths:**

- Successful company
- Steady increase in market share
- Experience in the market
- Founder's entrepreneurial skills
- Good designs
- Good quality control
- Keen to exploit to technology
- Strong IT

Weakness:

- Management of information is often out of date – No in-house IT expertise
- No web experience
- Not sure if the new system will generate new sales – Lack of control over store managers
- Out of date reporting from some stores
- Over reliance on IT provider

Opportunities:

- E-trading can provide a new sales channel and revenue stream
- Identification and recording of customer details to enhance customer relationships
- Extension of customer base
- Global market potential
- Cut costs in many areas
- Create a vision of a modern company
- Develop product range further
- Look at employing an IT specialist

Threats:

– Customer resistance to on-line shopping

– Loss of unique identity; may become just another website trader

– Resistance within the company

– Effects on existing personnel and working conditions

– Costs of developing the website may outweigh the benefits

– Security issues

– Loss of competitive edge

Note: marks would be awarded for other relevant points.

(b) It is important to consider how these factors link to performance measurement in Envie Co:

– **Identifying weaknesses:** SWOT analysis has identified that Envie's lack of web experience is a weakness and therefore Envie needs to try to address this weakness and turn it into a strength by developing a website to reach global markets. It will be important for Envie Co to measure revenue and revenue growth for its website in order to assess how well it is performing. The use of SWOT analysis will focus management attention on current strengths and weaknesses of the organisation which will be of assistance in formulating the business strategy. It will also enable management to monitor trends and developments in the changing business environment. Each trend or development may be classified as an opportunity or a threat that will provide a stimulus for an appropriate management response. Management can make an assessment of the feasibility of required actions in order that the company may capitalise upon opportunities whilst considering how best to negate or minimise the effect of any threats.

– **Identifying CSFs:** SWOT analysis has identified unique designs and good quality control as key to the expansion of Envie Co. This therefore suggests that it will be important to have performance measures which look at the effectiveness of the design team and the quality of the products produced.

– **Setting targets:** one of the opportunities identified is 'the extension of the customer base'. This could be linked to financial objectives, such as revenue growth targets for new customers. Envie's managers will need to monitor the targets set to assess how well performance compares to them.

– **Information needs:** Envie Co will need to collect information in relation to measuring and reporting on the KPIs set

Test your understanding 2

	Market growth (% change in annual market revenue)*	Division's market share (most recent divisional revenue/market revenue)	Relative market share (division's market share/largest competitor's market share)
Premier	14.6%	10%	0.58
Organic	1.9%	78%	3.90
Baby	10.2%	3%	0.12
Convenience	2.8%	3%	0.10

* This is the average growth over the four year period.

The management could use the BCG matrix in order to classify its subsidiaries in terms of their rate of market growth and relative market share. The model has four categories. These are:

Stars

A star product has a relatively high market share in a growth market.

The **Premier** division is experiencing strong growth in a growing market. It has a 10% market share and therefore it seems reasonable to categorise the Premier division as a star.

Problem child

They have a relatively low market share in a high growth market. The **Baby** division would appear to fall into this category. The market leader enjoys a 25% share whilst the Baby division appear to be struggling to achieve growth in turnover and hence profits.

Cash cow

A cash cow is characterised by a relatively high market share in a low growth market and should generate significant cash flows.

The **Organic** division appears to be a cash cow since it has a very high market share in what can be regarded as a low growth market.

Dog

A dog is characterised by a relatively low market share in a low growth market and might well be loss making. The **Convenience** division would appear to fall into this category since its market share is very low and it has low growth.

Food for thought has a dog and a problem child that both require immediate attention. Competitors within the sector will resist any attempts to reduce their share of a low growth or declining market. As far as the problem child is concerned, the management need to devise appropriate strategies to convert them into stars.

Remuneration package

The existing remuneration policy links the divisional manager's bonus to the achievement of the cost budget set at board level. This may be seen as appropriate for the Organic and the Convenience divisions since they are both in low growth markets and therefore adherence to cost budgets should be possible. However, the Premier and Baby divisions are in high growth markets. Therefore, linking the manager's bonus to the achievement of the cost budget may discourage the manager from making the investment that is required to take advantage of the growth opportunity.

There also seems to be an inconsistency between the way the remuneration package is determined and the method used to evaluate divisional performance. Divisional performance is measured using EVA and this is broadly consistent with the company's objective of maximisation of shareholder wealth. However, by failing to link the remuneration policy to EVA and the company's objective, dysfunctional behaviour may occur.

Professional skills may be awarded for the following:

- **Analysis and Evaluation** – appropriate use of the data to perform suitable calculations for market growth and relevant market share to support discussion and draw conclusions on FFT's competitive position.

- **Scepticism** – recognition that the current reward scheme is not consistent with divisional performance measures and is unsuitable for all divisions.

- **Commercial acumen** – effective use of the scenario information and other practical considerations to provide a comprehensive assessment of FFT's competitive position

Managing risk and uncertainty

Chapter learning objectives

Upon completion of this chapter you will be able to:

- evaluate how risk and uncertainty play an important role in long-term strategic planning and decision-making, including the impact of the different risk appetites of stakeholders.

PER

One of the PER performance objectives (PO1) is to take into account all relevant information and use professional judgement, your personal values and scepticism to evaluate data and make decisions. You should identify right from wrong and escalate anything of concern. You also need to make sure that your skills, knowledge and behaviour are up-to-date and allow you to be effective in you role. Another PER performance objectives (PO5) is to manage yourself and your resources effectively and responsibly. You contribute to the leadership and management of your organisation – delivering what's needed by stakeholders and the business. PER performance objective (PO22) is data analysis and decision support, which involves enabling relevant stakeholders to make decisions. Working through this chapter should help you understand how to demonstrate these objectives.

1 Common knowledge

Chapter 3 builds on the following knowledge from PM:

- Risk and uncertainty
- Pay off tables
- Expected values
- Maximax, maximin and minimax regret decisions.

2 Introduction

In Chapter 1, we learned that an important part of performance management is to identify the organisation's **strategy** and **objectives**.

When setting an organisation's strategy and objectives, it is important to consider the potential impact of **risk and uncertainty** which may be identified as part of analysis of the organisation's external environment.

In this chapter, we discuss the **difference between risk and uncertainty** and look at the different types of variables that needs to be considered.

Following this, we explore a number of different **decision-making techniques** that can be applied when dealing wish risk and uncertainty, including:

- **expected values**
- **maximax**, **maximin** and **minimax regret** criteria.

Finally, we discuss how **different risk appetites** of stakeholders can affect the organisation's overall approach to decision-making and managing risk.

.

3   Risk and uncertainty

3.1   Introduction

The business landscape has become increasingly unpredictable and uncertain in recent times due to rapid changes in technology and fierce competition, as well as major global events such as COVID-19.

Strategic, tactical and operational planning deal with future events but these future events cannot always be accurately predicted. Planning, decision-making and reporting must therefore take risk and uncertainty into account.

Although the terms are often used interchangeably, there is a small distinction between risk and uncertainty:

 Risk is the variability of possible returns. There are a number of possible outcomes and the probability of each outcome is **known**.

 Uncertainty also means that there are a number of possible outcomes. However, the probability of each outcome is **not known**.

Exogenous variables are variables that do not originate from within the organisation itself and are not controllable by management, e.g. government policy, weather conditions, state of the economy, competitors' actions etc. Their existence means that strategic planning will always be subject to some risk and uncertainty. **Endogenous variables**, on the other hand, are factors under the control of management.

All businesses face risk/uncertainty. Risk management is the process of understanding and managing the risks that an organisation is inevitably subject to.

 The impact of exogenous variables

A hospital has developed a new surgical technique as a more expensive alternative to existing treatments. It is considering whether to begin to provide the treatment to all its patients, which would mean building a new facility. In order to inform the decision, the hospital is considering the likely effect of a number of variables.

- The likelihood that another alternative cheaper treatment, either a surgical technique or a drug regime, will be discovered.

- The likelihood that other hospitals will begin to offer similar services which will limit demand.

- Government policy – changes in the way that treatment is funded and therefore whether the costs of the treatment will be paid for.

3.2 Measuring variability

In order to measure the risk associated with a particular project, it is helpful to find out how wide ranging the possible outcomes are. The conventional measure is the **standard deviation**.

 The **standard deviation** compares all the actual outcomes with the mean. It then calculates how far on average the outcomes deviate from the mean.

The basic idea is that the standard deviation is a measure of volatility: the more that actual outcomes vary from the average outcome, the more volatile the returns and therefore the more risk involved in the investment/decision.

In a normal distribution curve, approximately 68% of data would fall within one standard deviation of the mean.

3.3 Dealing with risk/uncertainty

A number of tools can be used to incorporate the impact of risk/uncertainty.

Tool	Explanation
Scenario planning	Looks at a number of different but plausible future situations. For example, Shell was the only major oil company to have prepared for the shock of the 1970s oil crisis through scenario planning and was able to respond faster than its competitors.
Computer simulations	A modelling technique which shows the effect of more than one variable changing at a time and gives management a view of the likely range and level of outcomes so that a more informed decision can be taken.
Sensitivity analysis	Takes each uncertain factor in turn, and calculates the change that would be necessary in that factor before the original decision is reversed.
Expected values (EVs)	Shows the weighted average of all possible outcomes.
Maximax, maximin and minimax regret	Three different tools for incorporating risk/ uncertainty. The attitude of management towards risk will determine which of the three tools is used.

EVs and maximin, maximax and minimax regret will be explored in more detail below.

Note: You will not be required to carry out any calculations using these tools. Any illustrative calculations are included only as an aid to understanding the tool in question.

4 Impact on decision making

4.1 Expected values

 The **expected value (EV)** is the average return that will be made if a decision is repeated again and again.

Each of the possible outcomes is weighted with their relative probability of occurring. It is the weighted arithmetic mean of the outcomes.

The formula for expected values is: **EV = $\sum$px**

where: x = the value of the possible outcome

p = the probability of the possible outcome.

Illustration 1 – Simple EV calculation			

Returns from a new restaurant depend on whether a company decides to open in the same area. The following estimates are made:

Competitor opens up	Probability (p)	Project NPV (x)	px
Yes	0.30	($10,000)	($3,000)
No	0.70	$20,000	$14,000
			$11,000

The EV = $\sum$px = $11,000. Since the expected value shows the long run average outcome of a decision which is repeated time and time again, it is a useful decision rule for a **risk neutral decision maker**. This is because a risk neutral decision maker neither seeks nor avoids risk; they are happy to accept the average outcome.

Since the expected value shows the long-run average outcome of a decision which is repeated again and again, it is a **useful** decision tool for a **risk neutral** decision maker. This is because a risk neutral person neither seeks risk nor avoids it; they are happy to accept an average outcome. This technique would **not be useful**:

- for **decisions which occur only once** (the EV is the average and not an actual outcome) (the techniques below are suited to either one off or repeated decisions)

- if the **probabilities** and/or the **values** of the various outcomes are **unknown or uncertain**

- for a **non-risk neutral** decision maker.

4.2 Maximax

 The **maximax rule** looks at the best possible outcome for each course of action and selects the alternative that maximises the maximum pay-off achievable.

With maximax the decision maker chooses the **outcome which is guaranteed to maximise their profit**.

It is often seen as an **optimistic** approach to decision making (assuming the best outcome will occur) and is used by decision makers who are **risk seeking**.

It may be viewed as being an **overly optimistic** approach since it **risks making a lower profit** if the maximum outcome is not achieved. It can be used for **one-off or repeated decisions**.

4.3 Maximin

 The **maximin rule** looks at the worst possible outcome for each course of action and selects the alternative that maximises the minimum pay-off achievable.

With maximin the decision maker chooses the **outcome which is guaranteed to minimise their losses**.

It is often seen as a **pessimistic** approach to decision making (assuming the worst outcome will occur) and is used by decision makers who are **risk averse**.

It may be viewed as being an **overly pessimistic** approach since **they lose out on the opportunity to make big profits**. It can be used for **one-off or repeated decisions**.

4.4 Minimax regret

 The **minimax regret** looks at the maximum regret (opportunity cost) for each course of action and aims to choose the strategy that minimises the maximum regret.

With minimax regret the decision maker **chooses the outcome which minimises the maximum regret**. It is a technique for a decision maker who **does not want to make the wrong decision and miss out** and is **neither risk seeking nor risk averse**.

However, in the process, they **risk making a lower profit**. This technique can also be used for **one-off or repeated decisions**.

Illustration of these tools

Illustration 2 – Decision making

Geoffrey Ramsbottom runs a kitchen that provides food for various canteens throughout a large organisation. A particular salad generates a profit of $2 based on a selling price of $10 and a cost of $8. Daily demand is as follows:

Demand	Probability
40 salads	0.10
50 salads	0.20
60 salads	0.40
70 salads	0.30
	———
	1.00

Required:

The kitchen must prepare the salad in batches of 10. Its staff have asked you to help them decide how many salads it should supply per day using:

- Expected values

- Maximax

- Maximin

- Minimax regret

Answer:

There are a range of possible outcomes (levels of demand) and a variety of possible responses (number of salads to supply) and therefore it is useful to construct a payoff table:

Expected values

		Daily supply profit/(loss) outcome (x)			
Daily demand	**Prob (p)**	**40 salads**	**50 salads**	**60 salads**	**70 salads**
40 salads	0.10	$80 (W1)	$0	($80)	($160)
50 salads	0.20	$80	$100	$20	($60)
60 salads	0.40	$80	$100	$120	$40
70 salads	0.30	$80	$100	$120	$140
		———	———	———	———
	EV =	$80	$90	$80	$30 (W2)
		———	———	———	———

Workings:

W1 Profit is calculated as follows = 40 salads × $2 = **$80**

W2 EV is calculated as follows = (0.10 × –$160) + (0.20 × –$60) + (0.40 × $40) + (0.30 × $140) = **$30**

Conclusion: Therefore, based on EVs, daily supply should be **50 salads** since this yields the highest expected value of $90.

Maximax

Daily demand	Prob (p)	Daily supply profit/(loss) outcome (x)			
		40 salads	50 salads	60 salads	70 salads
40 salads	0.10	$80	$0	($80)	($160)
50 salads	0.20	$80	$100	$20	($60)
60 salads	0.40	$80	$100	$120	$40
70 salads	0.30	$80	$100	$120	$140
Maximum profit =		$80	$100	$120	**$140**

The maximax rule involves selecting the alternative that maximises the maximum pay-off achievable. Looking at the table above, the maximum profit achievable is $140. This will be achieved if **70 salads** are supplied.

Maximin

Daily demand	Prob (p)	Daily supply profit/(loss) outcome (x)			
		40 salads	50 salads	60 salads	70 salads
40 salads	0.10	$80	$0	($80)	($160)
50 salads	0.20	$80	$100	$20	($60)
60 salads	0.40	$80	$100	$120	$40
70 salads	0.30	$80	$100	$120	$140
Minimum profit =		**$80**	$0	($80)	($160)

The maximin rule involves selecting the alternative that maximises the minimum pay-off achievable. Looking at the table above, the maximum of the minimum profits is $80. This will be achieved if **40 salads** are supplied.

Minimax regret

The minimax regret strategy is the one that minimises the maximum regret (opportunity cost). A regret table should be used:

Daily demand	Daily supply regret (opportunity cost)			
	40 salads	50 salads	60 salads	70 salads
40 salads	Right decision	$80 (W1)	$160 (W1)	$240 (W1)
50 salads	$20	Right decision	$80	$160
60 salads	$40	$20	Right decision	$80
70 salads	$60	$40	$20	Right decision
	——	——	——	——
Maximum regret =	**$60**	$80	$160	$240
	——	——	——	——

Therefore, to minimise the maximum regret, 40 salads should be supplied.

(W1): If daily demand is 40 salads, it would be the right decision for the business to supply 40 salads since the profit of supplying **40 salads** is the highest, i.e. $80.

- If the business decided instead to supply 50 salads, the regret (opportunity cost) would be the $80 it could have made supplying 40 salads minus the $0 it did make supplying the 50 salads = $80.

- If the business decided instead to supply 60 salads, the regret (opportunity cost) would be the $80 it could have made supplying 40 salads minus the $80 loss it did make supplying the 60 salads = $160.

- If the business decided instead to supply 70 salads, the regret (opportunity cost) would be the $80 it could have made supplying 40 salads minus the $160 loss it did make supplying the 70 salads = $240.

5 Impact of risk appetite of stakeholders

Stakeholders will be discussed in detail in Chapter 4. However, we know from earlier studies that a stakeholder is a group or individual who has an interest in what the organisation does or an expectation of the organisation.

Different stakeholders will have different risk perspectives or different risk appetites. In order to effectively manage business performance, it will be necessary for the business to align its decisions with the stakeholder's risk appetite.

Some examples of stakeholders and discussion of their risk appetite is included below:

Shareholders

May be prepared to take a risk (risk seeking) in order to maximise the possible return, especially since shareholders are able to spread their risk by holding a portfolio of investments. A maximax approach to decision making may be suitable.

However, shareholders are not always classed as risk seeking. For example, the shareholders of a company that is in financial distress may prefer the business to take a more risk neutral or risk averse approach in order to secure the future of the business. In this situation, an expected value or maximin approach would be more suitable.

Employees and managers

They should act in the best interests of the shareholders but this does not always happen since they may be:

- **risk averse:** employees and managers may be reluctant to take risks, e.g. to invest in a new project, if an unsuccessful outcome would impact their performance evaluation or the survival of the company (and hence their job). Therefore, even though risk taking may be in the best interests of the company and its shareholders they tend to exercise caution and are unwilling to take risks. A maximin approach to decision making would be most used.

- **risk seeking:** employees and managers may be encouraged to take risks by the promise of huge rewards or bonuses. In this situation, a maximax approach to decision making would be used.

Illustration 3 – Risk appetite of employees

The collapse of Lehman brothers, a sprawling global bank, almost brought down the world's financial system. The then governor of the bank of England, Mervyn King, criticised City banks who rewarded staff with huge sums for taking risks and concluded that the credit crisis was caused, in part, by bankers betting on high-risk complex financial products. A culture of risk taking had developed due to the huge potential bonuses and rewards offered to bankers.

Financiers

These include:

- **Venture capitalists** (VCs) – VCs are likely to be rational investors seeking the maximum return for minimum risk. A maximax approach may seem to be most relevant here. They will invest in a number of companies and so are prepared for some of their investments to fail, provided that some of their investments perform well. Steps will be taken to reduce risks, for example performance will be monitored on a regular basis to ensure that targets are met and/or any agreed exit strategy can be achieved. In addition, the VCs will also place employees on the management team so that they can influence decisions.

- **Banks** – traditionally, banks would have been considered to have a reasonably conservative approach to risk with a desire to secure their funds and guarantee returns. A risk neutral (EV) or risk averse (maximin) approach would be most relevant.

Illustration 4 – Banks and risk taking

As mentioned above, banks are not normally considered to be risk seeking. However, the financial crisis which commenced in 2007 was triggered by US banks giving high risk loans (sub-prime mortgages) to people with poor credit histories. A sharp rise in US interest rates resulted in a huge number of American home owners defaulting on their mortgages. The impact of these defaults were felt across the financial system as many of the mortgages had been sold to big banks who turned them into supposedly low risk securities. However, this assumption proved wrong. In fact, huge uncalculated risks had been taken with the bankers being spurred on by the potential to earn huge bonuses.

Student accountant articles: visit the ACCA website, accaglobal.com, to review the two articles on 'the risks of uncertainty'.

Chapter summary

Environmental, social and governance factors

Chapter learning objectives

Upon completion of this chapter you will be able to:

- discuss the ways in which stakeholder groups operate and how they influence an organisation and its performance measurement and performance management systems (e.g. using Mendelow's matrix)

- discuss the social and ethical issues that may impact on strategy formulation and evaluate the role of the management accountant in the collection of data, measurement and reporting of social and environmental factors, such as are used to demonstrate a wider view of performance in reporting, for example, sustainability

- discuss, evaluate and apply environmental management accounting using for example lifecycle costing, input-output analysis and activity-based costing

- explore the role of the management accountant in providing key performance information for integrated reporting to stakeholders

PER

One of the PER performance objectives (PO1) is to take into account all relevant information and use professional judgement, your personal values and scepticism to evaluate data and make decisions. You should identify right from wrong and escalate anything of concern. You also need to make sure that your skills, knowledge and behaviour are up-to-date and allow you to be effective in you role. PER performance objectives (PO12) is to apply different management accounting techniques is different business contexts to effectively manage and use resources. Working through this chapter should help you understand how to demonstrate that objective. Another PER performance objective (PO22) is data analysis and decision support, which involves enabling relevant stakeholders to make decisions. Working through this chapter should help you understand how to demonstrate these objectives.

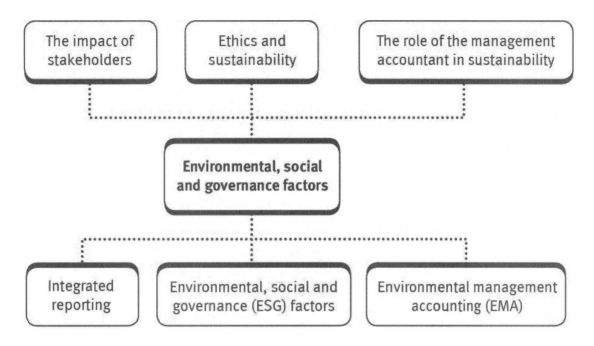

1 Common knowledge

Chapter 4 builds on your knowledge of environmental management accounting (EMA) from PM.

2 Introduction

Much of the focus of APM will be on profit seeking organisations and more specifically companies. Companies have the primary objective to maximise shareholder wealth. When considering how best to achieve this objective it can be easy to focus:

- primarily on the shareholders and not the other stakeholders and

- on managing and measuring financial performance (e.g. return on capital employed (ROCE) or gross profit margins) and/or more traditional non-financial areas of performance (e.g. employee and customer satisfaction, or product quality).

Although this focus is important (it will be discussed in depth in Chapters 10, 11 and 13), it is also necessary for organisations (and for us in the early stages of the APM course) to understand how vital it is to consider a range of other issues when managing and measuring performance (such as environmental and social factors) and for an organisation to consider its different stakeholders and not just its shareholders.

3 The impact of stakeholders

3.1 Introduction

 A **stakeholder** is a group or individual who has an interest in what the organisation does, or an expectation of the organisation.

Organisations will have a range of different stakeholders, such as:

Shareholders   **Society**

Competitors   **Managers**

Government   **Employees**

Suppliers   **Customers**

Community   **Lenders**

The primary objective of profit seeking organisations is to maximise shareholder wealth. However, an organisation (whether profit seeking or not-for-profit) must consider the needs of all of its stakeholders.

This is particularly relevant in the context of the remainder of this chapter; there is an increasing recognition amongst governments, businesses, customers, society, investors and other stakeholders of the importance of sustainability and the impact of businesses on society and the environment. Stakeholders are interested in how an organisation is performing in these areas.

Test your understanding 1

Chatman Theatre is a charitable trust with the objective of making multicultural films and stage productions available to a regional audience. The organisation is not for profit. The aim is to bring diversity of films, plays and dance that would otherwise be inaccessible to a regional audience.

The theatre needs to have strict budget focus, since a charity can become bankrupt. In order to achieve the required income, relationships must be built with a range of stakeholders.

Required:

Identify a few key stakeholders and ideas that would assist in building relationships and hence improving performance.

3.2 Stakeholder mapping

It was noted above that an organisation will have a range of different stakeholders with diverse, and sometimes conflicting, objectives. **Stakeholder mapping (Mendelow's matrix)** can be used to **effectively manage and optimise performance**.

Mendelow's matrix looks at the **level of power** and the **level of interest** of different stakeholder groups.

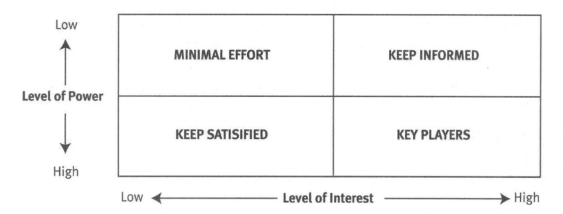

Note: In the exam, it is unlikely that you will have to produce a Mendelow matrix. Instead, you may be asked, for example:

- To evaluate how different stakeholders should be managed depending on their specific needs and their levels of interest and power

- To recommend and justify appropriate performance measures for different stakeholder groups.

 Illustration 1 – Stakeholders' influence

The airline, Ryanair, has regular labour relations problems with pilots, cabin attendants and check-in staff. For example, in recent years pilots at Ryanair threatened a mass strike (and possible desertion to a competitor airline) if there were not significant improvements in pay and conditions. Ryanair cannot operate without these staff so these employees have great power and have shown that they are happy to exercise that power.

3.3 Optimising performance

In order to optimise performance, an organisation must carry out a number of steps:

Step 1: Identify all stakeholders and their needs/objectives.

Step 2: Consider the relative levels of power and interest of the stakeholders and plot these on the matrix.

Step 3: Evaluate, using the matrix, how the different stakeholders should be managed.

There are **four possible classifications of stakeholder** and each group will be managed differently.

- **Key players:** These stakeholders are the major drivers of change and could stop management plans and hinder success if not satisfied. Their participation in the planning process is vital.

- **Keep satisfied:** These stakeholders have high power and need to be reassured of the outcome of the strategy well in advance to stop them from gaining interest and negatively impacting business performance.

- **Keep informed:** These stakeholders are interested in the strategy but lack power. Managers must justify their plans to these stakeholders. Otherwise, they will gain power by joining forces with other stakeholders.

- **Minimal effort:** These stakeholders lack interest and power and are more likely than others to accept what they are told and follow instructions.

Step 4: Establish priorities (for example, prioritise 'key players').

Step 5: Manage conflicting demands

Stakeholders' requirements and aspirations often conflict:

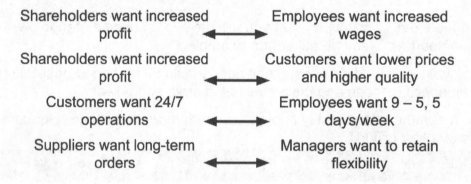

Shareholders want increased profit	⟷	Employees want increased wages
Shareholders want increased profit	⟷	Customers want lower prices and higher quality
Customers want 24/7 operations	⟷	Employees want 9 – 5, 5 days/week
Suppliers want long-term orders	⟷	Managers want to retain flexibility

Unless these conflicts are managed (for example, using prioritisation and compromise), performance will be affected.

Resolving conflicting (Cyert and March)
Management can seek to manage conflicting objectives through the following:
Prioritisation – this could follow from Mendelow's matrix above.
Negotiation and 'satisficing' – finding the minimum acceptable outcome for each group to achieve a compromise.
Sequential attention – each period a different stakeholder group is focused upon, e.g. the workers' canteen could be updated this year with the implication that employees should not expect any improvements in working conditions for the next few years.

> **Side payments** – this can often involve benefiting a group without giving them what they actually want, e.g. the local community may be concerned with cuts in jobs and increased pollution but the firm seeks to placate them by building new sports facilities and sponsoring a local fete.
>
> **Exercise of power** – when a deadlock is resolved by a senior figure forcing through a decision simply based on the power they possess.

Step 6: Once the stakeholders' needs have been prioritised and any conflicts managed, the mission and strategic objectives of the organisation should to be developed with these needs in mind.

Step 7: Once the organisation has developed the mission and strategic objectives (with the needs of its stakeholders in mind) it will establish CSFs and KPIs that are aligned to the achievement of the above mission and strategic objectives (as discussed in Chapter 1).

Step 8: The strategic objectives should be translated into tactical and operational objectives and performance measures should be established for these (again, as discussed in Chapter 1). Alignment between the stakeholders' needs, mission, objectives and measures (at all levels) underpins the performance management process.

4 Ethics and sustainability

4.1 Ethics

 Ethics is a set of moral principles that examines the concept of right and wrong. It relates to behaviour expected by society, but not codified in law.

 Business ethics is the application of ethical values to business behaviour.

Business ethics are a key component of an organisation's ESG strategy. Ethical businesses are starting to consider corporate decency, for example, climate change may not lead to collapse in this generation but it could in the next.

Illustration 2 – Examples of ethical issues

Is it ethical to:

- experiment on animals
- drill for oil
- build roads through the countryside
- allow smoking in public areas
- pay senior executives large increases in salary
- train students to pass exams?

4.2 Corporate social responsibility

 Corporate social responsibility (CSR) refers to the idea that a company should be sensitive to the needs of all stakeholders in its business operations and not just shareholders.

Over recent decades, organisation's have recognised a growing expectation that they should behave as responsible members of society.

 Illustration 3 – Examples of CSR practices

Clothing brand Patagonia has developed a strong reputation for good CSR practices by introducing a number of internal practices including Fair Trade programs, responsible purchasing, use of recycled materials and organic cotton. They also regularly campaign against big oil companies and other major polluters.

4.3 Sustainability

One area of CSR that is becoming increasingly important is **sustainability**. This is an **important term and will be a key focus of this chapter**. There are many different definitions of sustainability. Two common ways of defining or considering sustainability are as follows:

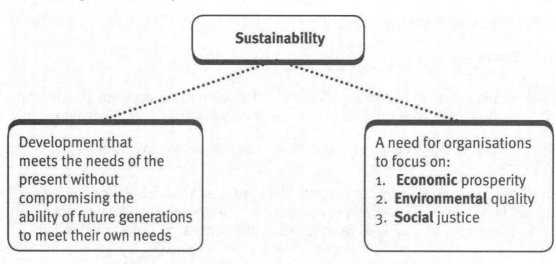

 Illustration 4 – Leon Restaurants

Leon Restaurants (a chain of more than 60 fast food eateries) pride themselves on sustainability. They focus on seasonal and local produce, limit meat on the menu and are in the process of reducing plastic usage.

Leon takeaways are served in compostable packaging and the company have replaced plastic straws and cutlery with biodegradable alternatives. What's more, over one third of the menu is vegan, and over two-thirds of dishes are vegetarian.

Let's consider the second definition of sustainability in more detail:

Environmental	The impact a business has on the natural environment; for example, through its supply chain sourcing, its use of natural resources, waste and emissions.
Social	The impact a business has on its most 'important' stakeholders: employees and their families, customers, suppliers and local communities.
Economic	Not simply financial profit but includes the wider impact a business has on the local, national and international economy, for example, through creating employment, generating innovation, paying taxes and creating wealth.
Sometimes summarised as the 3 P's of **P**lanet (environment), **P**eople (social) and **P**rofit (economic).	

The final term to be defined relates to this discussion above:

 Triple bottom line (TBL) accounting means expanding the traditional company reporting framework to take into account environmental (**planet**) and social performance (**people**) in addition to economic performance (**profit**).

5 The role of the management accountant in sustainability

5.1 Introduction

Management accountants, as trusted advisors, will be at the heart of action on sustainability. They will apply their skills and competencies to help develop sustainable strategies that are **more forward looking**, about **value creation** and **risk mitigation** and are not focused on unsustainable behaviour such as **short-termism** or **adverse resource usage.** Management accountants need to ensure that **resource is allocated** within the finance team and across the organisation to engage in ESG issues.

In the exam, you may be asked to evaluate the role of the management accountant in the collection of data, measurement and reporting of social and environmental factors.

Management accountants will have a significant role in **embedding performance measures in the area of sustainability into the core performance measurement process**:

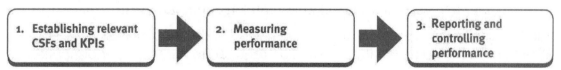

Each of these will be discussed below.

5.2   Identifying CSFs and establishing relevant KPIs

The management accountant will act as the voice of conscience and sustainability, using their skills to collaborate with those from across the business and working alongside the CEO in identifying CSFs and establishing relevant KPIs.

Sustainability issues should be **embedded** in the entire **performance management process**:

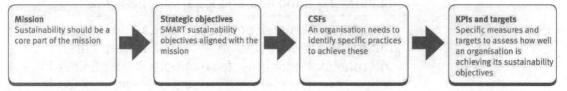

Mission	Strategic objectives	CSFs	KPIs and targets
Sustainability should be a core part of the mission	SMART sustainability objectives aligned with the mission	An organisation needs to identify specific practices to achieve these	Specific measures and targets to assess how well an organisation is achieving its sustainability objectives

Some potential KPIs are as follows:

Area of sustainability	Examples of KPIs
Energy and water	Energy and water consumption
Materials	% recycled materials used
Supply chain	% of suppliers that comply with established sustainability strategy
Waste	Waste by type and disposal method
Social	Number of health and safety incidents
Emissions	Carbon footprint

Businesses cannot measure every aspect of performance, so the management accountant must decide the **most appropriate KPIs to focus on** in relation to sustainability.

The KPIs should:

- actually measure sustainability

- align with the organisation's mission, strategic objectives and CSFs

- provide a balanced picture of the organisation's performance (good and bad)

- recognise the interconnectedness between the measures

- focus on the areas that have the greatest potential impact on sustainability

- be measured over time to aid tracking of trends

- be clear and consistent to aid benchmarking comparisons.

Additionally, the organisation may face challenges due to conflicts between KPIs or difficulty collecting the information required to measure performance.

5.3 Measuring performance

Once appropriate KPIs have been established, the management accountant will have a role in collecting KPI data and transforming it into useful information so that sustainability can be measured.

The management accountant will have an important role in analysing information to draw out patterns and insights for those who use the information.

Information technology (IT) will assist with this. IT will be discussed in Chapter 7.

Note: In the exam, you may need to do the following:

- Recommend how to measure sustainability in a given scenario; recommended KPIs will only score marks if they are relevant to the scenario in the question.

- Evaluate how effectively an organisation measures sustainability in its performance measurement system. Does it do the following?

  - Align to the mission and strategic objectives.

  - Is prioritised, balanced and contains measures both good and bad.

  - Is integrated into the core performance management and measurement process.

  - Covers all areas that the organisation is trying to achieve.

  - Information is presented in a way that maximises its usefulness.

5.4 Reporting and controlling performance

Once measured, the management accountant will have a role in reporting and controlling performance:

- Comparing actual performance against a target or appropriate benchmark

- Monitoring performance consistently over time and identifying trends

- Understanding the reasons for the differences between actual and target performance and making recommendations to get back on track (in the case of negative variances)

- Communicating insights in an objective and responsible way to influence the organisation's decision making

- Helping apply these decisions to harness value for the organisation through its ongoing strategic planning and control.

Given the increased importance of sustainability as a major global issue, there has been a focus on establishing a **globally accepted framework** within which an organisation can frame its sustainability strategy. Although there is a recognition of the need to set a sustainability equivalent of the International Financial Reporting Standards (IFRS), to put financial and non-financial information on the same footing, this has not been achieved as yet.

However, a number of possible frameworks do exists. Two of these are discussed below.

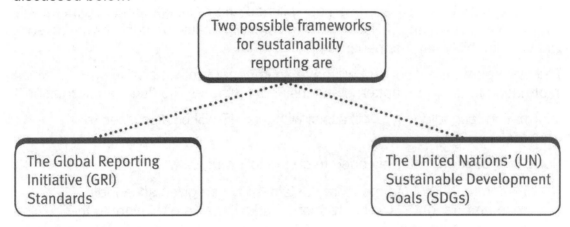

5.5 The GRI standards

- The GRI standards provide **best practice for reporting** on a range of **economic**, **environmental** and **social** impacts, creating a common language for reporting on sustainability in a credible and consistent way.

- Specific guidance is given to companies on what areas they should report on, helping organisations understand and disclose their impacts in a way that meets the needs of multiple stakeholders.

- GRI standards are not mandatory.

Illustration 5 – GRI standards

The GRI guidelines encourage disclosure of various aspects of the three categories; economic, environmental and social. For example:

Economic	Environmental	Social
<ul><li>Economic performance</li><li>Procurement practices</li><li>Anti-corruption</li></ul>	<ul><li>Materials</li><li>Energy</li><li>Emissions</li></ul>	<ul><li>Diversity and equality policies</li><li>Humans rights assessment</li><li>Customer privacy</li></ul>

5.6 UN SDGs

Introduction

The UN SDGs build on decades of work by countries and the UN. They encourage countries to embed sustainability measures into their 'core' performance reporting.

In 2015, the UN launched 17 SDGs to end poverty, fight inequality and justice and tackle climate change by 2030. Each goal has a related set of targets.

Illustration 6 – UN's urgent call to action 2020

A 15 year plan was set out by the UN in 2015 but their view is that it is not advancing at the scale or speed required. This prompted the UN's call in 2020 for a decade of ambitious action.

The call to action by the UN is on three levels:

1 Global action (e.g. more resources)

2 Local action (e.g. embedding changes in regulations)

3 People action (by society in general to generate this unstoppable move).

Businesses and organisations are responding to the challenge, sharing their commitment to contributing to the UN's SDGs because:

- It's the right thing to do

- It aligns with the mission and objectives

- It responds to the UN's call to action and is a response to Covid-19 and beyond

- It will build trust, reputation and lead the way

- Of the expectations of new generations and wider society.

Goals, targets and indicators

The 17 SDGs are broad and aspirational.

Illustration 7– UN SDGs

Sustainable development goals	(1) No poverty	(2) Zero hunger	(3) Good health and well-being	(4) Quality education	(5) Gender equality
(6) Clean water and sanitation	(7) Affordable and clean energy	(8) Decent work and economic growth	(9) Industry, innovation and infrastructure	(10) Reduced inequalities	(11) Sustainable cities and communities
(12) Responsible consumption and production	(13) Climate action	(14) Life below water	(15) Life on land	(16) Peace, justice and strong institutions	(17) Partnerships for the goals

Each goal is supported by:

- a wide range of associated **targets** (169 in total)

- and **indicators**, which provide a quantifiable framework for assessing whether the goals are being achieved.

Some examples are discussed below.

Note: These are included to enhance your knowledge and understanding of sustainability reporting. However, in APM questions you will not be expected to have any detailed knowledge of the UN SDGs, associated targets or indicators.

Goal number/title	Example of target	Example of indicator
(5) Gender equality (nine associated targets and indicators)	End all forms of discrimination against all girls and women everywhere	Whether or not legal frameworks are in place to promote, enforce and monitor equality and non-discrimination on this basis

Illustration 8 – Companies aiming to achieve gender equality

In the United Kingdom (UK), only 22% of senior leadership roles are held by women, almost 80% of companies still pay men more than women and the average gender pay gap is 17.4%.

Two examples of the best UK companies for women to work for are:

Sky

In 2018, Sky reported an average gender pay gap of 11.5% and a bonus gap of 40.2%. Through its Women in Leadership programme, Sky made a 5-year commitment to have 50% representation by women in leadership roles and every position that emerges will need an equal gender split on the short list.

Marks and Spencer

Retail giant Marks and Spencer paints a similar picture to Sky with an average gender pay gap of 12.3% and a bonus gap of 53.4%. As part of its 'Plan A 2025', the company upholds its mentoring system and 1:1 coaching for mid-senior women to allow better opportunities to progress into senior roles. Expectant and prospective parents are given time off to attend parental appointments, IVF treatments and fostering and adoptive meetings. They also committed to flexible working hours allowing parents to opt for term time only and part time schedules.

Goal number/title	Example of target	Example of indicators
(12) Responsible consumption and production (eleven associated targets and indicators)	By 2030 substantially reduce waste generation through prevention, reduction, recycling and reuse	Recycling rate, tonnes of material recycled

Illustration 9 – Responsible consumption and production

Brunel University

The responsible way in which Brunel University in London researches, sources, uses and disposes of materials has resulted in it being ranked as one of the best universities in the world for delivering against the UN SDG of responsible consumption and production. Brunel University has worked towards this goal in a number of ways. For example:

- Looking at how food and other supplies are ethically sourced, through a responsible procurement strategy; minimising the use of plastic and policies on recycling waste sent to landfill through elimination, reduction, re-use and recycling.

- Tracking the way in which hazardous and toxic materials are handled.

Nike

International sportswear company Nike's mission is to 'Move to Zero, meaning moving towards zero carbon and zero waste to help protect the future of sports'.

Goal number/title	Example of target	Example of indicators
(4) Quality education (nine associated targets and indicators)	By 2030 ensure that all girls and boys complete free, equitable and quality primary and secondary education leading to relevant and effective learning outcomes	Proportion of young people achieving at least a minimum proficiency level in reading and mathematics by gender

> **Illustration 10 – Ensuring quality education at Lego**
>
> Lego believes in play and advocates transformative power to have this adopted in education and early childhood development worldwide. To do this, they provide their famous bricks and promote play in the classroom and other education partnerships and projects worldwide, which in turn supports SDG (4) Quality education.
>
> Inspiring and engaging children in sustainability is a big part of this mission. For example, the company launched a LEGO wind turbine model containing an instruction booklet with interesting facts about climate change and wind energy.

17 SDGs and 169 related targets is a lot. Organisations need to:

- Prioritise the choice of SDGs and related targets to those where they can make a meaningful contribution and should be ambitious.

- Should focus on and pick out the SDGs and targets that are aligned to the mission and objectives (in which sustainability issues should be embedded).

For example, a common commitment by organisations is to be net zero in terms of carbon emissions by 2030.

Monitoring performance

Organisations need to take steps to measure and monitor performance in order to keep on track of their commitments, reviewing these commitments and accelerating action where necessary so that the 2030 target can be achieved.

The management accountant will have an important role in this:

- Capturing reliable data

- Assessing performance against relevant targets and benchmarks

- Ensuring information required is part of the management information flows

- Presenting information in a way which maximises its usefulness to the audience.

> **Illustration 11 – SDG Action Manager**
>
> The SDG Action Manager is a tool created by the B Corp movement; a worldwide movement that is promoting business as a force for good.
>
> The SDG Action Manager enables businesses to:
>
> - Set goals for improvement and consider how these goals can be achieved; actionable, impactful and relevant advice is given
>
> - Learn about the company's current performance with a useful and visual snapshot of performance
>
> - Track progress using a company-wide dashboard that is effective and user friendly and allows collaboration across the company
>
> - Accelerate action by encouraging the company to join a global movement of companies working to build a better world by 2030.

Illustration 12 – Skills required by management accountants

The involvement of management accountants in sustainability is essential but should be viewed by them as an opportunity.

The modern management accountant will need to successfully combine traditional technical accounting skills with business, people, leadership and digital skills (all underpinned by ethics and professionalism) but is well positioned to meet the changing mandate since:

- it has a unique end-to-end view of the organisation, understanding that every activity has a financial consequence

- its accounting information is trusted and credible

- it already provides a framework for performance management through management accounting

- it brings professional, evidence-based objectivity to decision making.

Accountants need to commit to professional development, equipping themselves with the skills required to apply the tools that exist for tackling sustainability issues throughout the business and ensuring that they can collaborate with those across the business to ensure that the relevant regulations and standards (and related disclosure requirements) are followed.

The role of the management accountant will become much more varied and potentially interesting and will require the accountant to build competencies in a range of areas, such as:

- Understanding scientific literacy

- Understanding societal impact

- Collaborating internally and externally

- Recognising the interconnectedness of social and environmental issues.

Student accountant article: visit the ACCA website, www.accaglobal.com, to review the article on 'Sustainability and performance management'.

6 Integrated reporting

6.1 Introduction

The Integrated Reporting Council (IIRC) was formed in 2010 to create a globally accepted framework for a process that results in communication by an organisation about value creation over time.

The Integrated Reporting (IR) framework recognises the **importance of looking at financial and sustainability performance in an integrated way**:

- identifying the relationship between 'six capitals' (see discussion below)

- encouraging a focus on business sustainability and an organisation's long-term success.

With IR, instead of having environmental and social issues reported in a separate section of the annual report, or a standalone 'sustainability' report, the idea is that one report should capture the strategic and operational actions of management in its holistic approach to business and stakeholder 'wellbeing'.

6.2 Triple bottom line (TBL) and different types of capital

There is an increasing recognition that the long-term pursuit of shareholder value is linked to the preservation and enhancement of six different types of capital. These can be broadly related to the three aspects of the TBL (defined in section 4.2).

Aspect of TBL	Type of capital affected
Environmental	**Natural capital** – Natural renewable and non-renewable resources (for example, air, water, land and energy) and processes used by a business in delivering its products/services. Considers, for example, waste, recycling and emissions.
Social	**Human capital** – Health, skills, motivation of employees. **Social capital** – Relationships, partnerships and co-operation, for example with suppliers. **Intellectual capital** – Patents, brand value and tacit knowledge (i.e. knowledge that is held by people in the organisation but is not formally documented).
Economic	**Manufactured capital** – Buildings, equipment and infrastructure used by the business. **Financial capital** – Funds available to enable the business to operate. Reflects the value generated from the other types of capital.

6.3 The role of the management accountant

The **role of the management accountant in providing key performance information for IR to stakeholders** is the emphasis of how IR may be examined in APM.

Note: Many of the points covered in Section 5 on 'The role of the management accountant in sustainability' are relevant to the role of the management accountant in IR and can be used as part of this discussion.

The management accountant must now be able to collaborate with top management in the integration of financial wellbeing with community and stakeholder wellbeing. This is a more strategic view considering factors that drive long-term performance.

IR will bring statutory reporting closer to the management accountant and will make management accountants even more important in bridging the gap between stakeholders and the company's reports.

The management accountant will be expected to produce information that:

- is a balance between quantitative and qualitative information. The information system must be able to capture both financial and non-financial measures

- links past, present and future performance. The forward looking nature will require more forecasted information

- considers the potential impact of relevant laws and regulations on performance and any necessary action that should be taken

- provides an analysis of opportunities and risks that could impact in the future

- considers how resources should be best allocated

- is tailored to the specific business situation but remains concise.

An **emphasis on the six types of capital could result in more focussed performance management** in the following ways:

- KPIs can be set up for each of the six capitals, ensuring that each of the drivers of sustainable value creation are monitored, controlled and developed.

- These can be developed further to show how the KPIs connect with different capitals, interact with, and impact each other.

- The interaction and inter-connectedness of these indicators should then be reflected in greater integration and cooperation between different functions and operations within the firm.

- This should result in greater transparency of internal communications allowing departments to appreciate better the wider implications of their activities.

- Together this should result in better decision making and value creation over the longer term.

Test your understanding 2

For each of the six capitals outlined in the IR Framework, suggest appropriate KPIs.

There is clearly a need for the profession to accept the challenge for being the mechanism for a new type of transparency and accountability; one that incorporates social and environmental impacts as well as economic ones.

The role of the management accountant in sustainability is as yet not well established. However, it is anticipated that over time, IR will become the corporate reporting norm. This will offer a productive and rewarding future, not only for the management accountant but for society as a whole.

Student accountant article: visit the ACCA website, www.accaglobal.com, to review the article on 'Integrated Reporting'.

7 . Environmental, social and governance (ESG) factors

7.1 Introduction

In recent years, there has been a growing number of large (and many small) organisations that have introduced ESG reporting as a method of demonstrating to stakeholders the organisation's commitment to sustainable practices.

Organisations have started to recognise that focusing solely on profit maximisation, without considering the interaction of the business with its operating environment will not be a sustainable approach.

At the same time, there has been increasing demand for environmentally friendly products and processes.

Adopting a sustainable business model could be:

*   not only a **challenge**

*   but also an **opportunity**; it is not simply about complying with the minimum legal/regulatory standards but is about value creation and risk mitigation.

Senior leaders are starting to accept the challenge and the responsibility and this has been accelerated by the events of 2020, including Covid-19 and the Black Lives Matter movement. However, it is recognised that a more significant and systematic approach is needed. Businesses are starting to ask 'What are the issues that matter most to us and society and that have a financial impact?'

Illustration 13– Jamie Oliver Group – B Corp

The Jamie Oliver Group reached a significant milestone in July 2020, achieving certification as a B Corporation (B Corp).

To become a B Corp, the business was assessed and audited against rigorous standards of social and environmental performance, accountability and transparency. The Jamie Oliver Group has always held social impact at its heart – from campaigning for a better food system, advocating high food and animal welfare standards, to creating a happy, healthy and inclusive workplace.

The certification is recognition of the high standards the group upholds, plus it gives the group the ideal framework to pursue their campaign of halving UK childhood obesity by 2030.

7.2 Environmental, social and governance factors

Environmental, social and (corporate) **governance (ESG)** refers to the three central factors in measuring the sustainability and societal impact of an organisation and that help to determine the long-term performance of an organisation.

Illustration 14 – Examples of ESG factors

Environmental	Social	Governance
<ul><li>Climate change risks</li><li>Raw material and water scarcity</li><li>Pollution and waste innovation</li><li>Clean technology</li><li>Renewable energy</li></ul>	<ul><li>Employment policies and industrial relations. For example, working conditions (including child labour) and diversity</li><li>Health and safety</li><li>Treatment of customers</li><li>Impact on communities (for example, indigenous communities)</li></ul>	<ul><li>Board diversity and structure</li><li>Executive pay</li><li>Audits</li><li>Internal controls</li><li>Fair tax strategy</li><li>Shareholder' rights</li><li>Bribery and corruption</li></ul>

7.3 Corporate governance

Corporate governance (or the 'G' in 'ESG') is concerned with the overall control and direction of a business so that the business's objectives are achieved in an acceptable manner by **all stakeholders**.

 Corporate governance is the set of processes and policies by which a company is directed, administered and controlled. It includes the appropriate role of the board of directors and the auditors of the company.

Illustration 15 – UK Corporate Governance Code

The revised 2018 UK Corporate Governance Code includes a number of reforms focusing on ESG issues. For example:

- The company should state how it has engaged with suppliers, customers, employees and others in a business relationship with the company. For example, what concerns have been raised by employees and have their views been taken into account?

- Quoted companies must report, as part of their directors' report, information on energy usage and any energy efficient action taken in the financial year.

Arguments for ESG	Arguments against ESG
• Can help **attract and retain customers** – It enhances reputation and hence strengthens the brand and acts as a method of differentiation in a competitive market. • Can help **attract and retain high calibre staff** and **access to a wider human resource base** – Good ESG involves, for example, good working conditions, avoids discrimination and focuses on good labour relations. • Avoiding pollution and reducing wastage, water and energy use will help to **reduce costs, fines and lawsuits** and potentially offer **access to subsidies and government support**. • **Fulfils the needs of stakeholders such as environmental groups, who may otherwise join forces with other stakeholders** (such as consumers and the government) to **increase power** (and this may in turn result in a damage to reputation and/or increased time managing stakeholders). • Can reduce risk and hence **lower the cost of raising finance** and also serves as a tool for **attracting investors**. All of the above should contribute to **long-term performance improvements and sustainable competitive advantage**. • In addition to performance improvements, consideration of ESG factors is the **ethically correct** thing to do.	• The **primary purpose of a company is to earn a profit** and it is the manager's duty to act in a way to maximise shareholder wealth. For example, it could be argued that it is not right for them to donate company funds to charity. • Focusing on **maximising shareholder wealth could be said to be aligned with ESG issues**. For example, increased returns will result in increased tax payments. • Potential **increased cost** of sourcing from ethical suppliers, for example Fairtrade products. • **Lack of knowledge** on the benefits plus what actions to take, how these should be reported and how their impact should be measured. • Reluctance to commit to ESG due to a **lack of skills and resources**, for example due to management time taken up by ESG planning and implementation or a requirement for information systems to be adapted to capture the information required. • Having to **turn away business from customers considered to be unethical**. For example, an 'ethical' bank may choose not to invest in a company that manufactures weapons. • An organisation may argue that it is **enough for them to comply with relevant laws and regulations** and that they do not need to go above and beyond this.

Illustration 16 – ESG success stories

Microsoft

Microsoft has taken the lead in its commitment towards carbon mitigation to become the first company among its peers to target 'carbon negative' status by 2030. It has created a US$1 billion fund to reduce emissions and start clearing carbon. The ambitious commitment is unprecedented and sets Microsoft apart from its entire sector.

GlaxoSmithKline (GSK)

The UK-based pharmaceutical giant has some giant ESG initiatives. It has made a total of 13 commitments that contribute to various UN Sustainable Development Goals. The company aims to reduce its environmental impact by 25% by 2030.

On the social front, the company aims to reach 800 million underserved people by 2025. On the governance front, GSK is working towards greater female representation in senior roles and LGBTQ+ advancement. All the company's goals and the progress towards those goals are published in an annual summary report.

Starbucks

In 2022, Starbuck's tried to ensure that its executive board remained focused on environmental and social practices by including this as part of the criteria to award bonuses to its executives. 10% of the overall bonus payment was linked 'planet-positive' results and another 10% was linked to 'fostering an inclusive environment where all employees feel valued and included'.

Salesforce (customer relationship management software)

Salesforce has some important goal-based ESG initiatives and has committed 1 million employee hours to the UN's Sustainable Development Goals.

Salesforce have also joined the UN Global Compact, a platform for companies to align with responsible business practices. In addition, the company recently launched Salesforce Sustainability Cloud, a system that helps business track, analyse and report vital environmental information.

These actions can ultimately help in the overall reduction of carbon emissions. In early 2020, the company launched It.org, an initiative to connect, empower and mobilise global restoration of 100 million trees.

Student accountant article: visit the ACCA website, www.accaglobal.com, to review the article on 'Sustainability reporting'.

8 Environmental management accounting (EMA)

8.1 Introduction

As discussed already in this chapter, organisations are becoming increasingly aware of the environmental implications of their actions (their operations/ products/services).

Illustration 17 – Environmental management at BP
BP, one of the world's leading oil and gas companies, describe a number of activities aimed at reducing the environmental impact of the company's operations in its annual review. These include: • Improving the integrity of its equipment and pipelines to reduce the spillage of oil • Reducing the emissions of greenhouse gases, which is measured and reported within the Annual Review • Introducing environmental requirements for new projects • Supporting the use of market mechanisms to bring about emission reductions across the industry • Launching a new business providing energy from alternative sources • Investing in research into biofuels • Developing and marketing fuel which produces lower emissions compared with standard fuels.

8.2 Traditional management accounting and environmental costs

In section 6 we discussed reporting on environmental matters using sustainability reports or integrated reporting.

Before reporting on these matters the organisation needs to identify its environmental costs (section 7.3), measure its existing performance and monitor the effectiveness of any environmental-related activities undertaken.

However, traditional management accounting systems were unable to identify or to deal adequately with environmental costs.

As a result, managers were unaware of these costs and had no information with which to manage or reduce them.

8.3 Categories of environmental costs

There are four categories of environmental cost that should be identified, measured, monitored and controlled by the organisation.

Environmental cost category	Description	Problem with traditional management accounting system
Conventional costs	Costs having an environmental impact such as raw material and energy costs	Traditional management accounting systems would have 'hidden' these within overheads making it difficult for managers to identify and control them
Contingent costs	Include future compliance costs (such as clear up costs) or remediation costs when a site is decommissioned	Traditional management accounting systems would have focused on annual periods rather than the entire life of a project and therefore managers will have overlooked these costs due to a focus on the short-term
Relationship costs	Image costs such as the cost of producing environmental information for public reporting (including integrated reporting or sustainability reports)	Traditionally management accounting systems would not have adequately captured this cost information meaning that managers were unaware of the existence of these costs or did not realise the extent of these costs
Reputational costs	Costs associated with failing to address environmental issues, for example, lost sales due to brand damage	Ignored by managers who were unaware of the risk of incurring them and hence did not take adequate steps to manage them

Illustration 18 – Reputational costs

In 2010 a blast at the Deepwater Horizon rig in the Gulf of Mexico killed eleven people and caused one of the worst oil spills in history. The environmental impact of the oil spill is ongoing. For example, in more recent years traces of oil from the spill were found in the feathers of birds eaten by land animals. The US presidential commission concluded that the oil spill was an avoidable disaster caused by a series of failures and blunders made by BP, its partners and the government departments assigned to regulate them. It also warned that such a disaster was likely to recur because of complacency in the industry.

> For BP, the company at the heart of the disaster, the effects have had a deep and widespread impact. The company has become synonymous with everything that is dangerous about oil exploration causing massive reputational damage.
>
> BP is working to restore their reputation. For example, in recent years they joined forces with two other oil and gas companies to create a $1 billion climate change fund focused on researching renewable energy, sharing techniques and reducing the leakage of methane (a big contributor towards global warming).

8.4 What is EMA?

EMA was developed in recognition that environmental costs were often left out of or not identified in traditional management accounting techniques leading to ill-informed or poor decision making, with both adverse environmental and economic consequences.

 EMA is concerned with the accounting information needs of managers in relation to the organisation's activities that affect the environment as well as environment-related impacts of the organisation. It involves the identification and estimation of the financial and non-financial costs of environmental-related activities with a view to control and reduce these costs.

As mentioned in the definition above, EMA **identifies and estimates the costs of environment-related activities** (covered in section 7.3) and **seeks to control** these costs. For example it:

- Identifies and separately monitors the usage and cost of resources such as water, electricity and fuel (**conventional costs**) and enables these costs to be reduced, for example through redesigning the product or the production process. ABC and lifecycle costing are effective techniques here (see section 7.5).

- Estimates future **contingent costs** ensuring they form part of any investment decision and giving scope upfront to reduce these costs through product or process redesign. Lifecycle costing is an effective technique here (see section 7.5).

- Makes managers aware of **relationship costs** in order to focus their attention on building these costs into project appraisal and taking steps to potentially reduce these costs. Lifecycle costing is an effective technique here (see section 7.5).

- Makes managers aware of **reputational costs** in order to focus their attention on managing the risk of them occurring.

Importantly, the focus of EMA is not entirely on **financial costs** but it also considers the **non-financial** environmental cost or benefit of any decisions made.

A clearer understanding of costs should mean that **budgets are more realistic** and therefore more useful for planning purposes, such as **pricing decisions**.

EMA includes **environment-related KPIs and targets** as part of routine performance monitoring and management appraisal. These will be both **financial and non-financial**, **internal and external** and relating to **short-term and long-term performance**.

EMA will also often **benchmark** activities against environmental best practice.

8.5 EMA techniques

EMA techniques deliver a means of connecting an organisation's environmental and economic performance and provide a financial incentive for organisations to more consciously consider sustainable aspects of their operations. Four key techniques will be covered below.

Note: The full **cost of EMA** (for example, adapting the information system so that it is capable of capturing the information required) must be **compared with the benefit of EMA**.

Activity- based costing (ABC)

ABC was covered in PM and will be discussed in Chapter 5. It can be applied to environment-related costs.

Environment-related costs can be analysed into:

- Costs which can be attributed directly to a cost centre, for example a waste filtration plant. It should be relatively straightforward to identify and, to some extent, control these costs.

- Environment-driven costs which are generally hidden in overheads (for example, conventional costs). ABC will aim to separately identify and control these costs:
    - The costs are removed from general overheads and traced to individual environmental-related cost pools for the products or services.
    - This means that cost drivers are determined for these costs and products are charged for the use of these environmental costs based on the amount of cost drivers that they contribute to the activity.
    - This should result in a more realistic product cost.
    - It should also result in better control of environment-related costs by reducing the incidental cost drivers or eliminating certain activities.

Note: Much of the detail covered in Chapter 5, for example on the steps involved in ABC and the evaluation of ABC is relevant when discussing its use in EMA.

Advantages and disadvantages of ABC

Advantages	Disadvantages
• Better/fairer product costs.	• Time consuming.
• Improved pricing – so that the products which have the biggest environmental impact reflect this by having higher selling prices.	• Expensive to implement.
	• Determining accurate costs and appropriate cost drivers is difficult.
• Better environmental control.	• External costs, i.e. not experienced by the company (e.g. carbon footprint) may still be ignored/unmeasured.
• Facilitates the quantification of cost savings from 'environmentally-friendly' measures.	• A company that integrates external costs voluntarily may be at a competitive disadvantage to rivals who do not do this.
• Should integrate environmental costing into the strategic management process.	• Some internal environmental costs are intangible (e.g. impact on employee health) and these are still ignored.

Lifecycle costing

Traditional costing techniques based around annual periods may give a misleading impression of the costs and profitability of a product. Lifecycle costing considers the costs and revenues of a product over its whole life rather than one accounting period. Therefore, the full cost of producing a product over its whole life will be taken into account. These costs include costs incurred **prior to, during** and **after** production and will therefore include the **full environmental cost** of producing a product over its whole life.

It is important that all of the environmental costs are identified and included in the initial project appraisal. For example:

- Managers should identify conventional costs such as energy and raw material costs and design products carefully to reduce waste over the manufacturing life of the product

- Managers must pay attention to relationship costs and build these into project appraisal

- Managers must pay attention to decommissioning costs that will be incurred after the end of the project and should plan for these costs.

For an organisation to be able to claim to be financially and environmentally responsible, it must have plans in place to cover these costs.

Test your understanding 3

The following details relate to a new product that has finished development and is about to be launched.

	Development	Launch	Growth	Maturity	Decline
Time period	Finished	1 year	1 year	1 year	1 year
R & D costs ($m)	20				
Marketing costs ($m)		5	4	3	0.9
Production cost per unit ($) (see note)		1.00	0.90	0.80	0.90
Production volume		1m	5m	10m	4m
Other costs ($m) (see note)					1m

Note: The production cost per unit includes environmental-related production costs. The 'other costs' relate to decommissioning costs that will be incurred at the end of the decline stage.

The launch price is proving a contentious issue between managers. The marketing manager is keen to start with a low price of around $8 to gain new buyers and achieve target market share. The accountant is concerned that this does not cover costs during the launch phase and has produced the following schedule to support this:

Launch phase:		$ million
Amortised R&D costs	(20 ÷ 4)	5
Marketing costs		5
Production costs	(1 million × $1 per unit)	1
		———
Total		11
		———
Total production (units)		1 million
Cost per unit		$11

Required:

Prepare a revised cost per unit schedule looking at the whole lifecycle and comment on the implications of this cost with regards to the pricing of the product during the launch phase.

Input-output analysis

This technique focuses on waste in processes. It records material inflows and balances this with outflows on the basis that what comes in, must go out.

For example, if 100 kg of materials have been bought and only 90 kg of materials have been produced, then the 10 kg difference must be accounted for in some way. It may be, for example, that 20% of this difference (i.e. 2 kg) has been sold as scrap and 80% (i.e. 8 kg) of it is waste.

By accounting for outputs in this way, both in terms of physical quantities, and, at the end of the process, in monetary terms too, businesses are forced to focus on environmental costs.

Flow cost accounting

There are similarities between input-output analysis and another EMA technique called flow cost accounting (FCA).

This technique uses not only material flows, but also the organisational structure; looking at material flows and material losses incurred at various stages of the production process.

It makes material flows transparent by looking at the physical quantities involved, their costs and their value. The costs can be divided into different types (an example is given in Illustration 4 below) and the values and costs of each of these types can then be calculated.

The aim of flow cost accounting is to reduce the quantity of materials which, as well as having a positive effect on the environment, should have a positive effect on the organisation's total costs in the long run.

Illustration 19 – Cost reduction at McCain Foods

One example of energy saving is McCain Foods, which buys an eighth of the UK's potatoes to make chips. It has cut its Peterborough plant's CO_2 footprint by two-thirds, says corporate affairs director Bill Bartlett. It invested £10m (approximately $15m) in three 3MW turbines to meet 60 per cent of its annual electricity demand. McCain spent another £4.5m (approximately $6.75m) on a lagoon to catch the methane from fermenting waste water and particulates, which generates another 10 per cent of the site's electricity usage. It also wants to refine its used cooking oil, either for its own vehicles fleet or for selling on.

McCain want to become more competitive and more efficient.

Illustration 20 – FCA

FCA is used to increase the transparency with which a company can trace the flows, transformations, inventory and losses of physical inputs through its **processes**.

Since 'what gets measured gets done' it provides a tool for better understanding the processes and resource usage, in the hope that steps can be taken to better manage waste and reduce material losses.

FCA can cover as much or as little as on organisation desires including:

- a single isolated process

- a whole factory production line

- a product's full supply chain.

For example, if we look at a single process in a t-shirt production line, a known amount of cotton is **input** into the production process and we get a certain amount of **product output** (t-shirts). The difference between the input and product output is **material loss**. A significant benefit of FCA is that it quantifies the effect of material losses in monetary units, thus providing the necessary incentive for the organisation to take action.

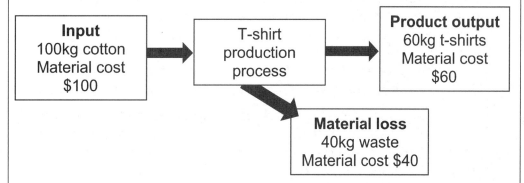

The above example could be extended to include **three types of costs**:

- The **material cost**, i.e. the $100 cotton.

- The **system and delivery cost**, e.g. energy cost of the production process and other running costs.

- The **disposal cost**, e.g. waste management cost.

Question practice

The question below is an excellent question on EMA. Make sure that you take the time to attempt the question and review/learn from the answer.

Test your understanding 4

FGH Telecom (FGH) is one of the largest providers of mobile and fixed line telecommunications in Ostland. The company has recently been reviewing its corporate objectives in the light of its changed business environment. The major new addition to the strategic objectives is under the heading: 'Building a more environmentally friendly business for the future'. It has been recognised that the company needs to make a contribution to ensuring sustainable development in Ostland and reducing its environmental footprint. Consequently, it adopted a goal that, by year 17, it would have reduced its environmental impact by 60% compared to year 1. It is currently year 11.

The reasons for the board's concern are that the telecommunications sector is competitive and the economic environment is increasingly harsh with the markets for debt and equities being particularly poor. On environmental issues, the government and public are calling for change from the business community. It appears that increased regulation and legislation will appear to encourage business towards better performance. The board have recognised that there are threats and opportunities from these trends. It wants to ensure that it is monitoring these factors and so it has asked for an analysis of the business environment with suggestions for performance measurement.

Additionally, the company has a large number of employees working across its network. Therefore, there are large demands for business travel. FGH runs a large fleet of commercial vehicles in order to service its network along with a company car scheme for its managers. The manager in charge of the company's travel budget is reviewing data on carbon dioxide emissions to assess FGH's recent performance.

Recent initiatives within the company to reduce emissions have included:

(a) the introduction in year 10 of a homeworking scheme for employees in order to reduce the amount of commuting to and from their offices and

(b) a drive to increase the use of teleconferencing facilities by employees.

Data on FGH Telecom's Carbon Dioxide Emissions			
Measured in millions of kgs	Year 1 Base year	Year 9	Year 10
Commercial Fleet Diesel	105.4	77.7	70.1
Commercial Fleet Petrol	11.6	0.4	0.0
Company Car Diesel	15.1	14.5	12.0
Company Car Petrol	10.3	3.8	2.2
Other Road Travel (Diesel)	0.5	1.6	1.1
Other Road Travel (Petrol)	3.1	0.5	0.3
Rail Travel	9.2	9.6	3.4
Air Travel (short haul)	5.0	4.4	3.1
Air Travel (long haul)	5.1	7.1	5.4
Hire Cars (Diesel)	0.6	1.8	2.9
Hire Cars (Petrol)	6.7	6.1	6.1
Total	172.6	127.5	106.6

Required:

(a) Perform an analysis of FGH's business environment to identify factors which will affect its environmental strategy. For each of these factors, suggest performance indicators which will allow FGH to monitor its progress. **(8 marks)**

(b) Evaluate the data given on carbon dioxide emissions using suitable indicators. Identify trends from within the data and comment on whether the company's behaviour is consistent with meeting its targets. **(9 marks)**

(c) Suggest further data that the company could collect in order to improve its analysis and explain how this data could be used to measure the effectiveness of the reduction initiatives mentioned. **(3 marks)**

Professional marks will be awarded for the demonstration of skill in analysis and evaluation, scepticism and commercial acumen in your answer. **(5 marks)**

(Total: 25 marks)

8.6 EMA and quality-related costs

As mentioned earlier in this chapter, EMA **identifies and estimates the costs of environment-related activities** and **seeks to control** these costs.

In the context of quality, we could consider **environment-related costs as being the costs of ensuring the quality of an organisation's processes or activities in relation to the environment**.

Quality-related costs will be covered in more detail in Chapter 14 but in terms of environment-related costs can be categorised as follows.

Environment-related cost	Description and example
Environmental prevention costs	Costs of implementing a quality improvement programme to prevent the negative impact of an organisation's processes or activities in relation to the environment. Should lead to continuous improvement. For example, the cost of designing products or services with built in quality to minimise waste.
Environmental appraisal costs	Costs of quality inspection and testing. For example, the costs incurred to ensure the organisation complies with regulations and voluntary standards.
Environmental internal failure costs	Costs arising from a failure to meet quality standards before the product or service reaches the customer. For example, an organisation's processes may produce carbon dioxide and other potentially damaging gases and it therefore invests in filters to adsorb the carbon dioxide before emission to the atmosphere.
Environmental external failure costs	Costs arising from a failure to meet quality standards after the product or service reaches the customer. For example, the cost of cleaning up an oil spill.

Importantly, the focus of is not entirely on **financial quality-related costs** but also considers **non-financial quality-related costs** of the organisation's activities and processes, with the **overall aim of minimising the quality-related costs**. For example, an organisation may choose to invest more in environmental prevention costs (such as the financial cost of quality product design) with the objective of reducing or minimising the financial (for example, fines for not meeting quality standards) and non-financial (for example, harmful emissions) environmental external failure costs.

8.7 EMA and TQM

In order to reduce lifecycle costs an organisation may adopt a total quality management (TQM) approach (TQM will be discussed in Chapter 14) with the focus being on 'continuous improvement' and the pursuit of excellence.

It is arguable that TQM and environmental management are inextricably linked insofar as good environmental management is increasingly recognised as an essential component of TQM. Such organisations pursue objectives that may include zero complaints, zero spills, zero pollution, zero waste and zero accidents.

Information systems need to be able to support such environmental objectives via measurement of environment-related KPIs and the provision of feedback – on the success or otherwise – of the organisational efforts in achieving the targets and the objectives set.

Student accountant article: visit the ACCA website, www.accaglobal.com, to review the article on 'Environmental management accounting'.

Chapter summary

The role of the management accountant in sustainability
- Introduction
- Identifying CSFs and establishing relevant KPIs
- Measuring performance
- Reporting and controlling performance
- The GRI standards
- UN SDGs

Ethics and substainability
- Ethics
- CSR
- Substainability

The impact of stakeholders
- Introduction
- Stakeholder mapping

Environmental, social and governance factors

Integrated reporting
- Introduction
- Triple bottom line and types of capital
- The role of the management accountant

Environmental, social and governance (ESG) factors
- Introduction
- Definitions
- ESG and performance management

Environmental management accounting (EMA)
- Introduction
- Traditional management accounting and environmental costs
- Categories of environmental cost
- What is EMA?
- EMA techniques
- EMA and quality-related costs
- EMA and TQM

Test your understanding answers

Test your understanding 1

Loyal customers

Chatman Theatre, which is a charity, can make use of a database to profile their interests and wants. A tailored communication can then be sent.

Given the need to contain costs, this might be by getting customers to sign up to an e-list to get up-to-date news and information on future performances.

They could set up a website with booking facilities and send confirmation by email rather than post.

Develop a friend of the theatre group, giving discounts to regular loyal customers.

First time customers

The website could be linked to other relevant websites, such as local attractions and tourist boards, to attract new customers.

The theatre could produce an information pack to attract new mailing list subscribers. These could be made available in local churches and shops.

Local arts groups

A partnership agreement could be established with arts groups, to co-sponsor events of special interest to given groups of customers.

Local organisations

Try to obtain commercial sponsorship from local companies. Acknowledgement could be given in the monthly programme mailings and preferential facilities offered for corporate hospitality.

Media

Personal invitations could be issued to opening nights, to interview the performers and give an overview of the show.

Note: The above is just a selection of potential relationships with stakeholders.

Test your understanding 2

KPIs need to be matched to CSFs, which will depend on the precise circumstances of an organisation and the environment within which it operates.

However, some generic KPIs could include the following:

Financial capital

- Conventional performance measures may be relevant here including revenue growth, margins, ROCE, interest cover, key costs as a % of revenue, etc (Chapter 10).

- EVA™ (Chapter 11).

Manufactured capital

- Inventory days, inventory turnover, size of forward order book compared to annual production, etc.

- Investment in different classes of non-current assets. These could also include intangible assets, such as measuring annual investment in research and development as a % of revenue.

Intellectual capital

- Staff turnover of skilled staff

- Utilisation of skilled staff

- Percentage of patented products

- A measurement of brand strength such as elasticity of demand (i.e. the change in demand as a result of a change in price)

- Research and development expenditure.

Human capital

- Number of staff, staff turnover

- Productivity/efficiency measures such as sales per employee for a sales team

- Sickness rates.

Social capital

- Staff satisfaction surveys, looking in particular at staff confidence in leadership, opinions about growth and wellbeing.

Natural capital

- Any environmental KPIs could be used here such as energy consumption and efficiency, output of greenhouse gasses and carbon footprint, water usage, % of waste recycled verses landfill, % of products produced that can be recycled, etc.

Test your understanding 3

Lifecycle costs		$ million
Total R&D costs		20.0
Total Marketing costs	(5 + 4 + 3 + 0.9)	12.9
Total Production costs	((1 × 1) + (5 × 0.9) + (10 × 0.8) + (4 × 0.9))	17.1
Decommissioning cost		1.0
		51.0
Total production (units)	(1 + 5 + 10 + 4)	20 million
Cost per unit	(51 ÷ 20)	$2.55

Comment

- The cost was calculated at $11 per unit during the launch phase. Based on this cost, the accountant was right to be concerned about the launch price being set at $8 per unit.

- However, looking at the whole life-cycle the marketing manager's proposal seems more reasonable.

- The average cost per unit over the entire life of the product is only $2.55 per unit. Therefore, a starting price of $8 per unit would seem reasonable and would result in a profit of $5.45 per unit.

Test your understanding 4

(a) Government regulations relevant to FGH's environmental strategy include requirements to recycle materials, limits on pollution and waste levels along with new taxes such as carbon levies to add additional costs. Performance indicators would be additional costs resulting from failure to recycle waste, fines paid for breaches and the level of environmental tax burdens.

The general economic climate is relevant to the strategy including factors such as interest, inflation and exchange rates. For FGH, the general economic environment is not good and cost savings from reductions in energy use would help to offset falling profits. Also, the difficulties indicated in raising capital could be monitored through the firm's cost of capital. This would be especially relevant if the environmental initiatives lead to significant capital expenditure for FGH.

Trends and fashions among the general public appear to be relevant for FGH as the public will be end-users of its services and environmental action could improve the brand image of FGH. Suitable performance indicator would be based around a score in a customer attitude survey.

Technological changes in the capabilities available to FGH and its competitors will affect its environmental strategy. New environmentally efficient technologies such as hybrid cars and solar recharging cells would be relevant to the cost and product sides of FGH. Performance indicators would involve measuring the impact of the use of new technology on existing emission data.

(b) The company has a target of cutting emissions by 60% of their year 1 values by the year 17. Overall, it has cut emissions by 38% in the first nine years of the 16-year programme. There was a reduction of 16% in the last year of measurement. If this rate of improvement is maintained then the company will reduce its emissions by 82% (62% × (84% ^ 7)) by year 17. However, it should be noted that it is unlikely that there will be a constant rate of reduction as it normally becomes more difficult to improve as the easy actions are taken in the early years of the programme.

The initial data are rather complex and so to summarise, three categories for the three types of transport were considered (Road, Rail and Air). The largest cut has been in rail related emissions (63%) while the contribution from road transport has only fallen by 38%. The road emissions are the dominant category overall and they are still falling within the programmed timetable to reach the target. However, it is clear that air travel is not falling at the same pace but this may be driven by factors such as increasing globalisation of the telecommunication industry which necessitates travel by managers abroad to visit multinational clients and suppliers.

One unusual feature noted is that the mix of transport methods appears to be changing. Rail travel appears to be declining. This is surprising as rail is widely believed to be the lowest emitting method from these forms of travel. However, caution must be exercised on this conclusion which may be due to a change in the emissions technology relating to each category of travel rather than the distance travelled using each method.

The major change that is apparent from the basic data is the move from petrol to diesel-powered motor vehicles which in the commercial fleet appears nearly complete. It will be more difficult to move company and private cars to diesel-power as there will be an element of choice on the part of the car user in the type of car driven.

Working

Measured in millions of kgs	Year 1	Year 9	Year 10	Change on base year
Commercial Fleet Diesel	105.4	77.7	70.1	−33%
Commercial Fleet Petrol	11.6	0.4	0.0	−100%
Company Car Diesel	15.1	14.5	12.0	−21%
Company Car Petrol	10.3	3.8	2.2	−79%
Other Road Travel (Diesel)	0.5	1.6	1.1	120%
Other Road Travel (Petrol)	3.1	0.5	0.3	−90%
Rail Travel	9.2	9.6	3.4	−63%
Air Travel (short haul)	5.0	4.4	3.1	−38%
Air Travel (long haul)	5.1	7.1	5.4	6%
Hire Cars (Diesel)	0.6	1.8	2.9	383%
Hire Cars (Petrol)	6.7	6.1	6.1	−9%
Total	172.6	127.5	106.6	
Index	100%	74%	62%	
YoY change		−16%		

Simplifying categories

	Year 1	Year 9	Year 10	Change on base year
Road travel	153.3	106.4	94.7	−38%
Air travel	10.1	11.5	8.5	−16%
Rail travel	9.2	9.6	3.4	−63%
Total	172.6	127.5	106.6	−38%

Mix of travel method in each year

	Year 1	Year 9	Year 10	
Road travel	89%	83%	89%	
Air travel	6%	9%	8%	
Rail travel	5%	8%	3%	

(c) The analysis could be improved by collecting data on the total distances travelled so that employee behaviour can be tracked. This would allow measurement of the effect of switching away from physical meetings and using teleconferencing facilities. This may be particularly effective in cutting air travel which has been noted as a problem area.

It would also allow assessment of the homeworking scheme which should reduce total distance travelled. Although, the full environmental benefit will not be apparent as much of the travel would have been a regular commute to work which an employee will not be able to claim and so is unlikely to record.

Finally, the collection of distance travelled data will allow a measure of the effect of changing modes of transport by calculating an average emission per km travelled.

Professional skills marks (maximum 5 marks)

Analysis and Evaluation:

- Appropriate use of data to perform suitable calculations and support discussion on whether the company's behaviour is consistent with meeting its targets

- Comprehensive analysis of the business environment, clearly supported with relevant suggested PIs.

Scepticism:

Recognition of additional data required to improve analysis performed.

Commercial Acumen:

- Effective use of example drawn from across the scenario information and other practical considerations related to the context to illustrate the points being made.

Budgeting and control

Chapter learning objectives

Upon completion of this chapter you will be able to:

- evaluate the strengths and weaknesses of alternative budgeting models and compare such techniques as fixed and flexible, rolling, activity based, zero based and incremental

- evaluate different types of budget variances and how these relate to issues in planning and controlling organisations

- evaluate the increased use of non-traditional profit-based performance measures in controlling organisations (e.g. beyond budgeting)

- discuss and evaluate the application of activity-based management.

PER

One of the PER performance objectives (PO13) is to plan business activities and control performance, making recommendations for improvement. Another PER performance objective (PO22) is data analysis and decision support. Working through this chapter should help you understand how to demonstrate these objectives.

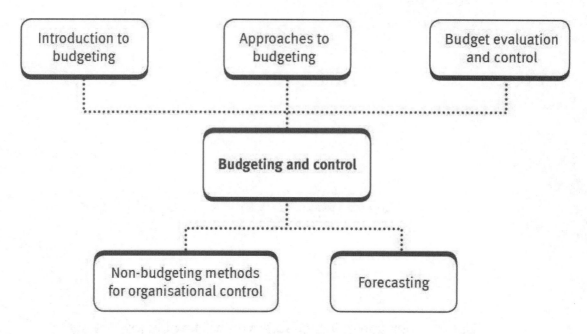

1 Common knowledge

Chapter 5 builds on the following knowledge from PM:

- Alternative budgeting models
- Absorption costing and activity-based costing
- Beyond budgeting
- Standard costing and variances
- Forecasting.

2 Introduction

In Chapter 1, we said that 'performance management is any activity that is designed to improve an organisation's performance and ensure that its goals are being met'. Budgeting will assist with performance management since it is an important tool for **planning** and **control** within an organisation and contributes to performance management by providing targets (or benchmarks) against which to compare actual results (through **variance analysis**) and develop corrective measures.

It is important that the organisation understands the relative merits of the different budgeting approaches and chooses the approach that is most suitable for them.

In addition, it is important to acknowledge that the business environment has become more complex, dynamic, turbulent and uncertain. Organisations need to be more adaptive to change, rather than be stifled by a need to comply with a fixed plan (budget). As a result, there has been an increased use of non-traditional profit-based performance measures in controlling organisations (e.g. beyond budgeting).

3 Introduction to budgeting

3.1 What is a budget?

 A budget is a quantitative plan prepared for a specific time period. It is normally expressed in financial terms and prepared for one year.

3.2 What is the purpose of budgeting?

Budgeting serves a number of purposes:

Planning

A budgeting process forces the business to look into the future. This is essential for survival since it stops management from relying on ad hoc or poorly co-ordinated planning.

Control

Actual results are compared against the budget and action is taken as appropriate.

Communication

The budget is a formal communication channel that allows junior and senior staff to converse.

Co-ordination

The budget allows co-ordination of all parts of the business towards a common corporate goal.

Evaluation

Responsibility accounting divides the organisation into budget centres, each of which has a manager who is responsible for its performance. The budget may be used to evaluate the actions of a manager within the business in terms of costs and revenues over which they have control.

Motivation

The budget may be used as a target for managers to aim for. Rewards should be given for operating within or under budgeted levels of expenditure. This acts as a motivator for managers.

Authorisation

The budget acts as a formal method of authorisation for a manager for expenditure, hiring staff and the pursuit of plans contained within the budget.

Delegation

Managers may be involved in setting the budget. Extra responsibility may motivate managers. Management involvement may also result in more realistic targets.

3.3   Setting targets

For performance management purposes, one of the main purposes of a budget is to get targets. These targets can then be compared to the actual level of performance to evaluate whether the organisation's objectives have been achieved and to identify whether corrective action is required.

Using budgets should motivate divisions and individual employees to work towards targets and help the organisation to meet its objectives. This becomes even more effective if rewards are used, such as bonuses, which provide an incentive for staff to aim to achieve their targets.

However, for the budgets to increase motivation they must be set at a level which is not too easy to achieve because this can result in staff 'slowing down' or relaxing once they have achieved their targets. If bonuses are being offered, then targets which are too easy will result in the organisation rewarding staff unnecessary. This may even cost the organisation more than it has gained.

Ideally, targets should be challenging so that staff are motivated to work harder or more effectively than they would have done without these targets. However, if the targets become too challenging then staff may believe that they are unachievable. At this stage, staff can become demotivated. Not only will they no longer believe that they can achieve their target, they may also feel frustrated that their managers have unrealistic expectations and do not understand what is achievable and realistic.

One of the most difficult aspects of setting targets is ensuring the that they are set at the current level of difficulty.

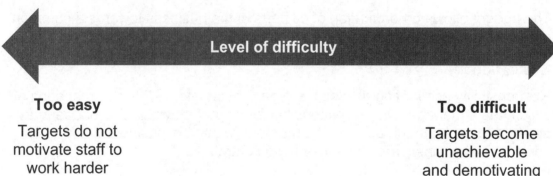

Level of difficulty

Too easy

Targets do not motivate staff to work harder

Too difficult

Targets become unachievable and demotivating

4 Approaches to budgeting

Different approaches to budgeting were studied in PM. In this exam it is important that you:

- not only understand each of the techniques but

- that you can compare the techniques and

- evaluate their relative strengths and weaknesses.

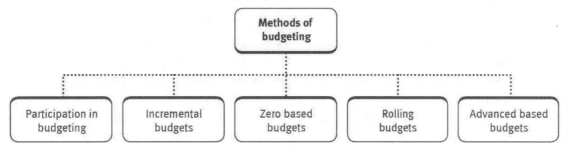

Note: Some calculations may be required but this will not be the emphasis of a question on budgeting, rather it will serve as the basis for more detailed discussion.

4.1 Participation in budgeting

 A **top-down** (or non-participative) budget is one that is imposed on the budget holder (e.g. the divisional manager responsible for achieving the budget targets) by senior management. The budget holder does not participate in the budget setting process.

Advantages	Disadvantages
• **Senior managers retain control**.	• Lack of **acceptance** from divisional managers who feel excluded from the process.
• Budget setting process can be **quicker**.	• Takes up **more time for senior management**.
• **Avoids the problem of bad decisions from inexperienced managers**.	• Senior managers may have a **lack of local knowledge** and not fully appreciate what is actually achievable in each division.
• **Avoids budgetary slack** (i.e. divisional managers may be tempted to set targets that are too easy to achieve).	
• **Avoids dysfunctional behaviour** (i.e. divisional managers lack a strategic perspective, focusing on the needs of the division and, as a result, budgets may not be in line with corporate objectives).	

A **bottom-up** (or participative) budget involves the budget holders (e.g. divisional managers) of an organisation having the opportunity to participate in the setting of the budgets.

Advantages	Disadvantages
• Improved **motivation** due to a sense of ownership and empowerment. • It **increases divisional managers' understanding** (which has an additional benefit if personal targets are set from the budget). • **Frees up senior management resource**. • **Improves the quality of decision making** since divisional managers are close to their product markets.	• **Can lead to budgetary slack** (i.e. divisional managers may be tempted to set targets that are too easy to achieve). • **Can lead to dysfunctional behaviour** (i.e. divisional managers lack a strategic perspective, focusing on the needs of the division and, as a result, budgets may not be in line with corporate objectives). • **Senior managers lose control**. • Budget setting process can be **more time-consuming**. • **Can lead to bad decisions from inexperienced managers**.an increment from the highest possible base figure in the following year.

An organisation may use a mix of the two approaches and each approach may be used to a greater or lesser extent in different divisions. It will be up to senior management to decide on the level of central control to exercise, based on the skills and needs of the divisional managers.

4.2 Incremental budgets

 An incremental budget starts with the previous period's budget or actual results, and adds (or subtracts) an incremental amount to cover inflation and other known changes (e.g. an extra worker or additional machine).

It may be viewed as a **traditional approach** to budgeting.

Suitability

- It is suitable for **stable** businesses, in which costs are not expected to change significantly.

- There should be **good cost control** (i.e. managers are efficient in controlling costs, work hard to be as efficient as possible and to eliminate waste.

- There should be **limited discretionary costs** (i.e. avoidable costs such as advertising, training or research and development). The non-essential nature means that inclusion in the budget should be justified rather than automatic.

Advantages	Disadvantages
• Quickest and easiest method (and therefore low cost). • Assuming that the historic figures are acceptable, only the increment needs to be justified. • Avoids 'reinventing the wheel' if the environment is stable and therefore costs are not expected to change significantly. • Works well in an environment where there is good cost control and/or limited discretionary costs (see discussion above).	• Backward looking – the modern business environment is more dynamic (i.e. less stable), making this approach to budgeting less suitable. • Builds in previous problems, inefficiencies and wastage. • Simply increasing the budget by an increment does not encourage managers to be more efficient in controlling costs, reducing waste or to find new, innovative ways of doing things. • Activities do not have to be justified and so uneconomic activities may be continued. • Managers may build in slack (i.e. make the budget easy to achieve), for example, to help secure the receipt of a reward that is aligned to the achievement of the budget. • Managers may spend up to their budget (i.e. spend more than is required) to ensure that they get an increment from the highest possible base figure in the following year.

Test your understanding 1

AW produces two products, A and C. In the last year (20X4) it produced 640 units of A and 350 units of C incurring costs of $672,000. Analysis of the costs has shown that 75% of the total costs are variable. 60% of these variable costs vary in line with the number of A produced and the remainder with the number of C.

The budget for the year 20X5 is now being prepared using an incremental budgeting approach. The following additional information is available for 20X5:

- All costs will be 4% higher than the average paid in 20X4.

- Efficiency levels will remain unchanged.

- Expected output of A is 750 units and of C is 340 units.

Required:

What is the budgeted total variable cost of product C (to the nearest $100) for the full year 20X5?

Question practice

The NW Entertainments Company (NWEC) is a privately owned organisation which operates an amusement park in a rural area within the North West region of a country which has a good climate all year round. The amusement park comprises a large fairground with high-quality rides and numerous attractions designed to appeal to people of all ages.

The park is open for 365 days in the year.

Each day spent by a guest at the park is classed as a 'Visitor Day'. During the year ended 30 November 20X3 a total of 2,090,400 visitor days were paid for and were made up as follows:

Visitor category	% of total visitor days
Adults	40
14–18 years of age and Senior Citizens	20
Under 14 years of age	40

Two types of admission pass are available for purchase, these are:

The 'One-day Visitor's pass' and the 'Two-day Visitor's pass', which entitles the holder of the pass to admission to the amusement park on any two days within the year commencing 1 December.

The pricing structure was as follows:

(i) The cost of a One-day pass for an adult was $40. Visitors aged 14–18 years and Senior Citizens receive a 25% discount against the cost of adult passes. Visitors aged below 14 years receive a 50% discount against the cost of adult passes.

(ii) The purchase of a Two-day Visitor's pass gave the purchaser a 25% saving against the cost of two One-day Visitor's passes.

(iii) 25% of the total visitor days were paid for by the purchase of One-day passes. The remainder were paid for by the purchase of Two-day passes.

Total operating costs of the park during the year amounted to $37,600,000.

NWEC receives income from traders who provide catering and other facilities to visitors to the amusement park. There are 30 such traders from whom payments are received. The amount of the payment made by each trader is dependent upon the size of the premises that they occupy in the amusement park as shown in the following summary:

Size of premises	No. of Annual Traders	Payment per Trader
		$
Large	8	54,000
Medium	12	36,000
Small	10	18,000

The income from each trader is received under 3 year contracts which became effective on 1 December 20X3. The income is fixed for the duration of each contract.

All operating costs of the park incurred during the year ending 30 November 20X4 are expected to increase by 4%. This has led to a decision by management to increase the selling price of all categories of admission passes by 4% with effect from 1 December 20X3. Management expect the number of visitor days, visitor mix and the mix of admission passes purchased to be the same as in the previous year.

NWEC also own a 400 bedroom hotel with leisure facilities, which is located 20 kilometres from the amusement park.

During the year ended 30 November 20X3, the charge per room on an all-inclusive basis was $100 per room, per night. The total operating costs of the hotel amounted to $7,950,000. Average occupancy during the year was 240 rooms per night. The hotel is open for 365 days in the year.

It is anticipated that the operating costs of the hotel will increase by 4% in the year ending 30 November 20X4. Management have decided to increase the charge per room, per night by 4% with effect from 1 December 20X3 and expect average occupancy will remain at the same level during the year ending 30 November 20X4.

The revenue of the hotel is independent of the number of visitors to the amusement park.

Required:

Prepare a statement showing the budgeted net profit or loss for the year to 30 November 20X4.

Answer

NWEC Budgeted Profit and Loss Statement for year to 30 November 20X4

Amusement Park – admission receipts:	$	$
One-day pass:		
Adults:	8,696,064	
14–18 years, senior citizens	3,261,024	
Under 14 years	4,348,032	
Two-day pass:		
Adults:	19,566,144	
14–18 years, senior citizens	7,337,304	
Under 14 years	9,783,072	
	———	
		52,991,640
Other revenue Income from traders		1,044,000
		———
Total revenue – park		54,035,640
Operating costs		39,104,000
		———
Budgeted profit of park		14,931,640
Hotel income	9,110,400	
Hotel operating costs	8,268,000	
	———	
Budgeted profit of hotel		842,400
		———
		15,774,040
		———

Workings:

No. of Visitor days for year to 30 November 20X4   = 2,090,400

One-day passes = 2,090,400 × 25%   = 522,600

Two-day passes (2,090,400 × 75%)/2   = 783,900

Admission fees applicable from 1 December 20X3. (increased by 4% per annum).

	One-day pass ($)	Two-day pass ($)
Adults	41.60 (40*1.04)	62.40 (41.60*2 less 25%)
14–18 years; senior citizens	31.20 (30*1.04)	46.80 (31.20*2 less 25%)
Under 14's	20.80 (20*1.04)	31.20 (20.80*2 less 25%)

Split	One-day pass revenue			Two-day pass revenue		
40%	209,040	$41.60	$8,696,064	313,560	$62.40	$19,566,144
20%	104,520	$31.20	$3,261,024	156,780	$46.80	$ 7,337,304
40%	209,040	$20.80	$4,348,032	313,560	$31.20	$ 9,783,072
	522,600			783,900		

4.3 Zero based budgets

 Zero based budgeting (ZBB) is a method of budgeting that requires each cost element to be specifically justified, as though the activities to which the budget relates were being undertaken for the first time. Without approval, the budget allowance is zero.

It is an alternative to incremental budgeting.

Suitability

- **Fast moving** (dynamic) businesses/industries.

- For allocating resources in areas of **discretionary spending**.

- **Public sector organisations** such as local authorities. These organisations have strict constraints on the amount of funding they receive and this funding should be put to the best use (this will be discussed further in Chapter 12).

ZBB process

There are **four distinct stages to the implementation of ZBB**:

1   **Determine the activities that are to be used as the objects of a decision package.** Managers should specify for their responsibility centres those activities that can be individually evaluated.

    For example, if ZBB was used in a school, one of the activities identified by the head teacher (i.e. 'manager') could be the provision of school lunches.

2   **Each of the individual activities is then described in a decision package.** The decision package should:

    •   state the purpose of the activity

    •   state the costs and benefits expected from the given activity

    •   be drawn up in such a way that the package can be evaluated and ranked against other packages.

    Carrying on from our example above, the purpose of the activity would be to provide school lunches to pupils. The cost would be the cost of the food, drinks, facilities and staff, and the benefit would be that pupils would have access to lunch in the school day.

    (**Note**: The example here will focus on the simple activity of provision of school lunches to pupils. In reality, there would be multiple ways to carry out this activity and each would be considered. For example, option 1 may be to provide an area where pupils can eat their own packed lunches or buy and eat a pre-prepared selection of prepared cold snacks and sandwiches, option 2 may be to provide a self-service canteen with hot and cold food and drinks available and option 3 may be to provide a full hot food catered service for pupils.).

3   **Each decision package is evaluated and ranked using cost/benefit analysis.** In this example, the cost/benefit of the activity of providing school lunches would be compared with the cost/benefit of other activities, for example the provision of IT equipment, sporting facilities, additional staff etc.

4   **The resources are then allocated to the various packages** based on the order of priority (ranking above) and up to the spending level.

Advantages	Disadvantages
• Resources should be allocated efficiently and economically. • Inefficient or obsolete operations will be identified and either discontinued or budgetary allocation altered. • ZBB leads to increased staff involvement at all levels. This should lead to better communication and motivation. • It responds to changes in the business environment and so is more suited in fast moving organisations/industries. • Knowledge and understanding of the cost-behaviour patterns of the organisation will be enhanced.	• The time involved and the cost of preparing the budget are much greater than for incremental budgeting. For this reason, organisations (and more specifically profit-seeking organisations) are unlikely to use ZBB across the whole business. Instead, it may be used in a particular area or areas of the organisation where the benefit will be greatest. • It may emphasise short-term benefits to the detriment of long-term benefits. • The budgeting process may become too rigid and the company may not be able to react to unforeseen opportunities or threats. • There is a need for management skills that may not be present in the organisation. • Managers may feel demotivated due to the large amount of time spent on the budgeting process. • It is difficult to compare and rank different types of activity. • The rankings of packages may be subjective where the benefits are of a qualitative nature.

4.4 Rolling budgets

A criticism of some of the other methods of budgeting discussed in this section (i.e. incremental and ZBB) is that they prevent managers from responding quickly to changes in today's business environment but instead place undue focus on creating a budget for a fixed, rigid period (for example, an annual incremental budget or ZBB process).

 A rolling budget is one that is kept continuously up to date by adding another accounting period (e.g. month or quarter) when the earliest accounting period has expired.

Suitability

- Accurate forecasts cannot be made, e.g. in a dynamic business environment or in a new business.

- For any area of business that needs tight control since the budget should be more realistic and accurate.

Advantages	Disadvantages
• Planning and control based on a more accurate budget. • Much better information upon which to appraise the performance of management; rolling budgets reduce the element of uncertainty since they concentrate on the short-term. • There is always a budget that extends for a fixed period into the future (normally 12 months). • It forces management to take the budgeting process more seriously; the budget is reassessed and updated regularly.	• More costly and time consuming than, for example, incremental budgeting. • An increase in budgeting work may lead to less control of the actual results. • There is a danger that the budget may become the last budget 'plus or minus a bit'. • The budget may be demotivating because the targets are changing regularly and/or employees feel that they spend a large proportion of their time budgeting.

Test your understanding 2

A company uses rolling budgeting and has a sales budget as follows:

	Quarter 1 $	Quarter 2 $	Quarter 3 $	Quarter 4 $	Total
Sales	125,750	132,038	138,640	145,572	542,000

Actual sales for Quarter 1 were $123,450. The adverse variance is fully explained by competition being more intense than expected and growth being lower than anticipated. The budget committee has proposed that the revised assumption for sales growth should be 3% per quarter for Quarters 2, 3 and 4.

Required:

Update the budget figures for Quarters 2–4 as appropriate.

Question practice

The question below is an example of how you may be expected to compare the different budgeting techniques. Make sure that you attempt this question and review the answer.

Test your understanding 3

The Drinks Group (DG) has been created over the last three years by merging three medium-sized family businesses. These businesses are all involved in making fruit drinks. Fizzy (F) makes and bottles healthy, fruit-based sparkling drinks. Still (S) makes and bottles fruit-flavoured non-sparkling drinks and Healthy (H) buys fruit and squeezes it to make basic fruit juices. The three companies have been divisionalised within the group structure. A fourth division called Marketing (M) exists to market the products of the other divisions to various large retail chains. Marketing has only recently been set up in order to help the business expand. All of the operations and sales of DG occur in Nordland, which is an economically well-developed country with a strong market for healthy non-alcoholic drinks.

The group has recruited a new finance director (FD), who was asked by the board to perform a review of the efficiency and effectiveness of the finance department as her first task on taking office. The finance director has just presented her report to the board regarding some problems at DG.

Extract from the finance director's Report to the Board

'The main area for improvement, which was discussed at the last board meeting, is the need to improve profit margins throughout the business. There is no strong evidence that new products or markets are required but that the most promising area for improvement lies in better internal control practices.

Control

As DG was formed from an integration of the original businesses (F, S, H), there was little immediate effort put into optimising the control systems of these businesses. They have each evolved over time in their own way. Currently, the main method of central control that can be used to drive profit margin improvement is the budget system in each business. The budgeting method used is to take the previous year's figures and simply increment them by estimates of growth in the market that will occur over the next year. These growth estimates are obtained through a discussion between the financial managers at group level and the relevant divisional managers. The management at each division are then given these budgets by head office and their personal targets are set around achieving the relevant budget numbers.

Divisions

H and S divisions are in stable markets where the levels of demand and competition mean that sales growth is unlikely, unless by acquisition of another brand. The main engine for prospective profit growth in these divisions is through margin improvements. The managers at these divisions have been successful in previous years and generally keep to the agreed budgets. As a result, they are usually not comfortable with changing existing practices.

F is faster growing and seen as the star of the Group. However, the Group has been receiving complaints from customers about late deliveries and poor quality control of the F products. The F managers have explained that they are working hard within the budget and capital constraints imposed by the board and have expressed a desire to be less controlled.

The marketing division has only recently been set up and the intention is to run each marketing campaign as an individual project which would be charged to the division whose products are benefiting from the campaign. The managers of the manufacturing divisions are very doubtful of the value of M, as each believes that they have an existing strong reputation with their customers that does not require much additional spending on marketing. However, the board decided at the last meeting that there was scope to create and use a marketing budget effectively at DG, if its costs were carefully controlled. Similar to the other divisions, the marketing division budgets are set by taking the previous year's actual spend and adding a percentage increase. For M, the increase corresponds to the previous year's growth in group turnover.'

End of extract

At present, the finance director is harassed by the introduction of a new information system within the finance department which is straining the resources of the department. However, she needs to respond to the issues raised above at the board meeting and so is considering using different budgeting methods at DG. She has asked you, the management accountant at the Group, to do some preliminary work to help her decide whether and how to change the budget methods. The first task that she believes would be useful is to consider the use of rolling budgets. She thinks that fast-growing F may prove the easiest division in which to introduce new ideas.

F's incremental budget for the current year is given below. You can assume that cost of sales and distribution costs are variable and administrative costs are fixed.

	Q1	Q2	Q3	Q4	Total
	$000	$000	$000	$000	$000
Revenue	17,520	17,958	18,407	18,867	72,752
Cost of sales	9,636	9,877	10,124	10,377	40,014
Gross profit	7,884	8,081	8,283	8,490	32,738
Distribution costs	1,577	1,616	1,657	1,698	6,548
Administration costs	4,214	4,214	4,214	4,214	16,856
Operating profit	2,093	2,251	2,412	2,578	9,334

The actual figures for quarter 1 (which has just completed) are:

	$000
Revenue	17,932
Cost of sales	9,863
Gross profit	8,069
Distribution costs	1,614
Administration costs	4,214
Operating profit	2,241

On the basis of the Q1 results, sales volume growth of 3% per quarter is now expected.

The finance director has also heard you talking about bottom-up budgeting and wants you to evaluate its use at DG.

Required:

(a) Evaluate the suitability of incremental budgeting at each division

(6 marks)

(b) Recalculate the budget for Fizzy division (F) using rolling budgeting and briefly assess the use of rolling budgeting at F. **(6 marks)**

(c) Recommend any appropriate changes to the budgeting method at the Marketing division (M), providing justifications for your choice.

(3 marks)

(d) Analyse and recommend the appropriate level of participation in budgeting at Drinks Group (DG). **(5 marks)**

Professional marks will be awarded for the demonstration of skill in analysis and evaluation and commercial acumen in your answer.

(5 marks)

(Total: 25 marks)

4.5 Activity-based budgeting

 Activity-based budgeting (ABB) prepares budgets using overhead costs derived from activity-based costing. It aims to bring greater discipline to the process of budgeting for overhead costs (compared to, say, a traditional incremental approach).

Before we look at ABB in more detail, it is useful to review the activity-based models in general, i.e. activity-based costing and activity-based management.

4.5.1 Activity-based costing (ABC)

Aim: the aim of ABC is to calculate the full production cost per unit. It is an alternative to absorption costing in a modern business environment.

Reasons for the development of ABC
• Absorption costing is based on the principle that production overheads are driven by the level of production. This was true in the past when businesses tended to produce only one product or a few simple and similar products. However, a higher level of competition has resulted in the diversity and complexity of the products increasing. As a result, there are a number of different factors that drive overheads, not simply the level of production.
• Production overheads are a larger proportion of total costs in modern manufacturing since manufacturing has become more machine intensive and less labour intensive. Therefore, it is important that an accurate estimate is made of the production overhead per unit.

Steps in ABC

- **Step 1:** Group production overheads into activities (cost pools), according to how they are driven.

- **Step 2:** Identify cost drivers for each activity, i.e. what causes the activity costs to be incurred.

- **Step 3:** Calculate an overhead absorption rate (OAR) for each activity.

- **Step 4:** Absorb the activity costs into the product.

- **Step 5:** Calculate the full production cost and/or the profit or loss.

The question below recaps the calculation of the full production cost per unit using traditional absorption costing and using ABC. Make sure that you understand the calculation and that you can comment on the reasons for the differences between the full production cost per unit under the two costing methods.

Test your understanding 4

Trimake makes three main products, using broadly the same production methods and equipment for each. A conventional absorption costing system is used at present, although an activity based costing (ABC) system is being considered. Details of the three products for a typical period are:

Product	Hours per unit Labour	Hours per unit Machinery	Materials per unit $	Volumes Units
X	½	1½	20	750
Y	1½	1	12	1,250
Z	1	3	25	7,000

Direct labour costs $6 per hour and production overheads are absorbed on a machine hour basis. The rate for the period is $28 per machine hour (i.e. the OAR) and a total of 23,375 machine hours were worked.

Traditional absorption costing would give a full production cost per unit as follows:

	X $	Y $	Z $
Materials	20	12	25
Labour	3	9	6
	—	—	—
Total direct cost	23	21	31
Production overhead @ $28 per hour	42	28	84
	—	—	—
Total	65	49	115

Further analysis shows the total production overhead of $654,500 is not entirely driven by machine hours and can be divided as follows:

	%
Costs relating to set-ups	35
Costs relating to machinery	20
Costs relating to materials handling	15
Costs relating to inspection	30
	—
Total production overhead	100

The following total activity volumes are associated with the product line for the period as a whole:

	Number of set-ups	Number of movements of materials	Number of inspections
Product X	75	12	150
Product Y	115	21	180
Product Z	480	87	670
Total	670	120	1,000

Required:

Calculate the cost per unit for each product using ABC principles.

Advantages and disadvantages of ABC

Advantages	Disadvantages
• Provides a more accurate cost per unit since it recognises that overhead costs are not all related to production and sales volumes, leading to better: – pricing – decision making (e.g. products or services that could only be sold at an unsustainable loss will be discontinued) and – performance management and control (actual results compared to a more accurate budget). • It provides a better insight into what drives overhead costs resulting in better control of costs. • It can be applied to all overhead costs, not just production overheads. • It can be used just as easily in service costing as product costing.	• The benefits might not justify the costs (initial set up costs, staff training costs, cost of potential staff resistance, cost of changing systems to capture information required and the ongoing cost of using ABC), particularly if overheads are primarily volume related or a small proportion of total costs. • It is impossible to allocate all overheads to specific activities (step 1). • The choice of cost drivers (step 2) might be inappropriate. • It may be difficult to assign responsibility for individual costs pools. • Limited benefit if activity costs are already well controlled and the process is already efficient. • Customers may not tolerate the changes made as a result of the exercise. For example, a price increase may result in lost sales in a competitive market, or eliminating an unprofitable product may drive customers away if they expect the organisation to supply a range of products.

4.5.2 Activity based management

 Activity-based management (ABM) is the use of ABC information for management purposes to improve **operational** and **strategic** decisions. **ABM** applies ABC principles in order to satisfy customer needs using the least amount of resources.

Operational ABM

ABM can help operational managers make decisions that can **improve operational efficiency** and hence performance:

- It may identify and then **reduce or eliminate activities that do not add value** to the customer and **refocus on only value adding activities** (e.g. using appropriate machines or materials to produce goods demanded by the customer). This should cut costs without reducing product value.

- Finding ways to **continually improve the value-adding activities**. ABM may establish ways to produce the product more efficiently by understanding what drives the cost of activities and finding ways to **reduce the incidence of these cost drivers** without negatively impacting quality (e.g. using a standardised rather than a bespoke product design or perhaps by assembling products in batches rather than switching between different products).

- It may **identify design improvements**, for example a change to the design to prevent quality problems and associated costs such as wastage.

However, there are **risks** associated with the use of operational ABM. Some activities will have an implicit value that is not necessarily reflected in the financial value. For example, a pleasant workplace can help attract/retain the best staff but a risk of operational ABM is that this activity is eliminated.
In addition, many of the disadvantages of ABC (discussed in section 5.5.1) are relevant when discussing the risks of ABM.

Illustration 1 – Operational ABM

One of the biggest advantages of ABM is that costs are categorised by activities rather than traditional cost categories. For example:

Traditional costing system		ABM system	
Cost of sales	X	Direct material cost	X
Staff costs	X	Direct labour cost	X
Factory rent	X	**Indirect costs**	
Maintenance	X	Schedule production jobs	X
Depreciation	X	Machine set-up	X
	——	Receiving materials	X
Total costs	X	Supporting existing products	X
	——	Introducing new products	X
			——
		Total costs	X
			——

Having costs categorised by activity provides more relevant information to managers:

- There may be activities that don't add value and these could be stopped.

- There may be activities that cost more than expected and the manager can use their knowledge of the activity's cost driver to reduce the cost. For example, the cost of setting up the machines could be reduced by having longer production runs.

Strategic ABM

- Strategic ABM uses ABC information to decide which products to develop and sell based on profitability:

  - By identifying the underlying drivers of activities (cost pools), ABM provides an understanding of the resource implication of various courses of action and therefore ensures unfeasible courses of action are not taken and that **unprofitable products are eliminated**.

  - It can assist in **re-pricing**. For example, customers may be willing to pay a premium for a product due to a special finish or a particular material used.

  - It helps **determine the profitability of new products**.

- As well as focusing on product profitability, it **can assist with customer profitability analysis** (CPA). This involves apportioning overheads to different types of customer using ABM principles. In doing so, it enables a better understanding of the profitability of selling to different customers so that decisions can be made as to which customers should be focused on and where cost efficiencies can be made.

- It can assist in **improving relationships with customers and suppliers** through working closely with customers to understand their needs and with suppliers to improve quality and costs.

However, in addition to the relevant disadvantages of ABC (discussed in section 5.5.1), there are **risks** associated specifically to strategic ABM. For example, some strategic decisions may have an implicit value that is not reflected in the financial value; such as low value customers opening up leads in the market (a risk of strategic ABM is that this customer is eliminated).

Summary of ABM

A full **cost-benefit analysis** should be carried out to establish if the risks discussed above and the cost of the extra work required to obtain the more accurate information are less than the potential savings from the benefits discussed above to be enjoyed as a result of the more accurate assessment.

Question practice

The question below is a scenario-based question including both numerical and discursive requirements. Calculations may be tested but they will be used to form the basis of your decisions and will generally only be worth a small number of marks. Make sure that you attempt this question and learn from the answer. You may find it difficult to attempt a long question in full at this stage of your studies but it is important that you understand the level that you are expected to reach by the time you come to sit the exam.

Test your understanding 5

Navier Aerials Co (Navier) manufactures satellite dishes for receiving satellite television signals. Navier supplies the major satellite TV companies who install standard satellite dishes for their customers. The company also manufactures and installs a small number of specialised satellite dishes to individuals or businesses with specific needs resulting from poor reception in their locations.

The chief executive officer (CEO) wants to initiate a programme of cost reduction at Navier. His plan is to use activity-based management (ABM) to allocate costs more accurately and to identify non-value adding activities. The first department to be analysed is the customer care department, as it has been believed for some time that the current method of cost allocation is giving unrealistic results for the two product types.

At present, the finance director (FD) absorbs the cost of customer care into the product cost on a per unit basis using the data in table 1. He then tries to correct the problem of unrealistic costing, by making rough estimates of the costs to be allocated to each product based on the operations director's impression of the amount of work of the department. In fact, he simply adds $100 above the standard absorbed cost to the cost of a specialised dish to cover the assumed extra work involved at customer care.

The cost accountant has gathered information for the customer care department in table 2 from interviews with the finance and customer care staff. She has used this information to correctly calculate the total costs of each activity using activity-based costing in table 3. The CEO wants you, as a senior management accountant, to complete the work required for a comparison of the results of the current standard absorption costing to activity-based costing for the standard and specialised dishes.

Once this is done, the CEO wants you to consider the implications for management of the customer care process of the costs of each activity in that department. The CEO is especially interested in how this information may impact on the identification of non-valued added activities and quality management at Navier.

Navier Dishes (information for the year ending 31 March 20X3)
Customer care (CC) department

Table 1: Existing costing data

	$000
Salaries	400
Computer time	165
Telephone	79
Stationery and sundries	27
Depreciation of equipment	36
	707

Note:

1 CC cost is currently allocated to each dish based on 16,000 orders a year, where each order contains an average of 5.5 dishes.

Table 2: Activity-costing data

Activities of CC dept		Staff Comments time
Handling enquiries and preparing quotes for potential orders	40%	relates to 35,000 enquiries/ quotes per year
Receiving actual orders	10%	relates to 16,000 orders in the year
Customer credit checks	10%	done once an order is received
Supervision of orders through manufacture to delivery	15%	
Complaints handling	25%	relates to 3,200 complaints per year

Notes:

1   Total department cost is allocated using staff time as this drives all of the other costs in the department.

2   90% of both enquiries and orders are for standard dishes. The remainder are for specialised dishes.

3   Handling enquiries and preparing quotes for specialised dishes takes 20% of staff time allocated to this activity.

4   The process for receiving an order, checking customer credit and supervision of the order is the same for both a specialised dish order and a standard dish order.

5   50% of the complaints received are for specialised dish orders.

6   Each standard dish order contains an average of six dishes.

7   Each specialised dish order contains an average of one dish.

Table 2: Activity-based costs

	Total	Standard	Specialised
Handling enquiries and preparing quotes	282,800	226,240	56,560
Receiving actual orders	70,700	63,630	7,070
Customer credit checks	70,700	63,630	7,070
Supervision of order through manufacture to delivery	106,050	95,445	10,605
Complaints handling	176,750	88,375	88,375
Total	707,000	537,320	169,680

Required:

(a)   Evaluate the impact of using activity-based costing, compared to the existing costing system for customer care, on the cost of both types of product.   **(10 marks)**

(b)   Assess how the information on each activity can be used and improved upon at Navier in assisting cost reduction and quality management in the customer care department.

       Note: There is no need to make comments on the different product types here.   **(10 marks)**

Professional marks will be awarded for the demonstration of skill in analysis and evaluation and commercial acumen in your answer.

       (5 marks)

       (Total: 25 marks)

Student accountant article: visit the ACCA website, www.accaglobal.com, to review the article on 'Activity-based management'.

4.5.3 Activity-based budgeting

Now that we understand the concepts of ABC and ABM, we can review the final approach to budgeting, activity-based budgeting.

 Activity-based budgeting (ABB) uses the costs determined in ABC to prepare budgets for each activity.

- The cost driver for each activity is identified. A forecast is made of the number of units of the cost driver that will occur in the budget period.

- Given the estimate of the number of units of the cost driver, the activity cost is estimated.

Illustration 2 – ABB

Tiddleypeeps is a private childcare provider and operates from two different sites. Site 1 currently employs 15 staff and has 120 children registered for childcare provision. Site 2 employs 24 staff and has 160 children registered. The total overhead for salaries at Tiddleypeeps this year was $624,000.

Tiddleypeeps is looking to expand both of its premises next year such that it can provide childcare for an additional 15 more children at Site 1 and 24 additional children at Site 2.

Management use staff numbers to allocate costs between the sites and believe that the number of registered children is the most appropriate cost driver for salaried costs.

Required:

Using an activity-based budgeting approach, calculate the budgeted cost for salaries for both sites at Tiddleypeeps for next year.

Answer

Step 1: Group production overheads into activities according to how they are driven.

In this example, we are focusing on one activity cost (cost pool); salaries. This is allocated between the two sites based on staff numbers:

	Site 1	Site 2
Salary cost (W1)	$240,000	$384,000

(W1)

Total staff: 15 site 1 + 24 site 2 = 39

Salary cost site 1 = 15/39 × $624,000

Salary cost site 2 = 24/39 × $624,000

Step 2: Identify the cost driver for the activity.

This is the number of registered children (given in the question).

Step 3: Calculate and OAR for each activity

	Site 1	Site 2
Salary cost (W1)	$240,000	$384,000
Number of children	120	160
Cost driver rate per child	$2,000	$2,400

Step 4: Absorb the activity costs into each site to produce an ABB for the next year.

Budgeted salary cost site 1 = $2,000 per child × 135 children = $270,000

Budgeted salary cost site 2 = $2,400 per child × 184 children = $441,600

Advantages	Disadvantages
• ABB draws attention to the costs of overhead activities, which can be a large proportion of total operating costs. • It recognises that it is activities that drive costs. If we can control the causes (drivers) of costs, then costs should be better managed and understood. • It can be used to identify CSFs, for example a specific activity that must be done quickly, accurately or efficiently. • ABB can provide useful information for a total quality management (TQM) environment, by relating the cost of an activity to the level of service provided. It focuses on controlling costs but without a negative impact on quality. (**Note**: TQM will be discussed in Chapter 14)	• A considerable amount of time and effort may be required to establish an ABB system (e.g. identifying the key activities and their cost drivers). • Staffing issues, for example resistance to change or the cost of training staff. • The cost of adapting information systems so that they can collect and process a large amount of activity and cost driver information. • ABB might not be appropriate for the organisation and its activities and cost structures, i.e. it is only suited to ABC users. • It may be difficult to identify clear individual responsibilities for activities and hence accountability for the achievement of the activity budget.

	•	It could be argued that in the short-term many overhead costs are not controllable and do not vary directly with changes in the volume of activity of the cost driver. For example, this could be due to fixed price agreements with suppliers or fixed employee wages. The only cost variances to report would be fixed overhead expenditure variances for each activity.

5 Budget evaluation and control

5.1 Fixed and flexible budgeting

 A **fixed budget** is a budget prepared at a single level of activity.

 A **flexible budget** is prepared at a number of activity levels and can be 'flexed' or changed to the actual level of activity for budgetary control purposes. The cost behaviour of all cost elements known and classified as either fixed or variable.

Before we can investigate any variances between the budget and actual results, a flexed budget is required to adjust for any changes to revenue and variable costs that have occurred as a result of changes in activity levels.

Note: The test your understanding below serves as a quick reminder of fixed and variable costs.

Test your understanding 6

A company has the following budgeted and actual information for a department.

	Budget	Actual
Level of activity (units of output)	1,000	1,200
Cost ($)	20,000	23,000

Required:

(a) Assuming all costs are variable, has the company done better or worse than expected?

(b) If $10,000 of the budgeted costs are fixed costs, the remainder being variable, has the company performed better or worse than expected?

Test your understanding 7

Redfern hospital is a government-funded hospital in the country of Newland. Relevant cost data for the year ended 31 December 20X0 is as follows:

1 Salary costs per staff member were payable as follows:

	Budget ($)	Actual ($)
Doctors	100,000	105,000
Nurses	37,000	34,500

Budgeted and actual staff were 60 doctors and 150 nurses.

2 Budgeted costs for the year based on 20,000 patients per annum were as follows:

	$	Variable cost (%)	Fixed cost (%)
Other staff costs	1,440,000	100	–
Catering	200,000	70	30
Cleaning	80,000	35	65
Other operating costs	1,200,000	30	70
Depreciation	80,000	–	100

Variable costs vary according to the number of patients.

3 The actual number of patients for the year was 23,750. Actual costs (excluding the cost of doctors and nurses) incurred during the year were as follows:

	$
Other staff costs	1,500,000
Catering	187,500
Cleaning	142,000
Other operating costs	1,050,000
Depreciation	80,000

Required:

Prepare a statement which shows the actual and budgeted costs for Redfern hospital in respect of the year ended 31 December 20X0 on a comparable basis.

Advantages and disadvantages of flexible budgeting

Advantages	Disadvantages
Should enable better performance evaluation as comparing like with like.	• May be perceived by some as 'moving the goal posts' resulting in demotivation – especially if bonuses are lost despite beating the original budget. • Difficulties splitting costs into fixed and variable elements. • In the long -run it could be argued that all costs are variable.

5.2 Recap of the basics of variance analysis

In section 3.2, we discussed the purposes of budgeting. Two key reasons for budgeting are to facilitate planning and control. Variance analysis is used as part of this 'control'.

In PM you learnt that variance analysis is a key element of management control:

1   Targets and standards are set reflecting what should happen

2   Actual performance is then measured

3   Actual results are then compared with the (flexed) standards, using variance analysis

4   'Significant' variances can then be investigated and appropriate action taken.

This process thus facilitates 'management by exception'.

Note: In APM, you may be asked to calculate a variance, although it is likely that calculation marks will account for only the minority of marks available for a question on variances. However, do spend a little bit of time reviewing the variances covered in PM to ensure you are comfortable with the calculations and the meaning of each variance. Without being able to do this first, it will be difficult to address the requirements of the APM syllabus area on variances.

KAPLAN PUBLISHING

5.3 A quick reminder of some of the different types of budget variance

Basic variances	Advanced variances
• Sales price and sales volume variances • Material price and material usage variances • Labour rate, labour efficiency and labour idle time variances • Variable overhead efficiency and variable overhead expenditure variances • Fixed overhead expenditure and fixed overhead volume variances.	• Material mix and yield variances • Sales mix and quantity variances • Planning and operational variances (discussed in section 5.4).

Any of the basic or advanced variances may be examined in APM and, as mentioned, a little bit of time should be spent reviewing these.

5.4 Planning and operating variances

The APM syllabus requires you to evaluate different types of budgetary variance and how these relate to issues in planning and controlling organisations. One type of advanced variance, planning and operational variances, will be particularly relevant here.

Any variance calculated can be further divided into planning and operational elements if at the end of the period, with the benefit of hindsight, it is known that the original budget was unrealistic and therefore a decision is taken to amend the budget.

Planning variances

• The planning variance is the difference between the original standard and the revised one.

• Planning variances are thus those which arise due to inaccurate forecasts or standards in the original budget setting.

Operational variances

• Operational variances are then the remainder due to the decisions of operational managers.

• An operational variance is the difference between this revised standard and actual performance.

Advantages of splitting variances into planning and operational elements

From a performance management perspective the advantage of this approach is that line managers can concentrate on improving operational matters for which they are genuinely responsible and accountable.

For example, a sales price variance could be split to indicate how far sales prices were incorrectly estimated in the budget (planning) and how well the sales managers have done in negotiating high prices with customers (operational).

Disadvantages of splitting variances into planning and operational elements

On the other hand, the disadvantage of planning and operational variances is that too often all adverse variances are explained away as being planning errors.

Another problem is if the revised standard is harder to achieve than the original one. The manager could become unmotivated by this moving target, especially if, for example, they miss out on a bonus that they would have achieved under the original standard.

The **calculations were covered in PM**. However, some examples have been included below for revision purposes.

Planning and operational variances for sales volume

Test your understanding 8 – Market size and share

Hudson has a sales budget of 400,000 units for the coming year based on 20% of the total market. On each unit, Hudson makes a profit of $3. Actual sales for the year were 450,000, but industry reports showed that the total market volume had been 2.2 million.

(a)   Find the traditional sales volume variance.

(b)   Split this into planning and operational variances (market size and market share). Comment on your results.

Planning and operational variances for labour efficiency

Test your understanding 9

The standard hours per unit of production for a product is 5 hours. Actual production for the period was 250 units and actual hours worked were 1,450 hours. The standard rate per hour was $10. Because of a shortage of skilled labour it has been necessary to use unskilled labour and it is estimated that this will increase the time taken by 20%.

Required:

Calculate the planning and operational labour efficiency variances.

Planning and operational variances for material price and usage

> **Test your understanding 10**
>
> Holmes uses one raw material for one of their products. The standard cost per unit at the beginning of the year was $28, made up as follows:
>
> Standard material cost per unit = 7 kg per unit at $4 per kg = $28.
>
> In the middle of the year the supplier had changed the specification of the material slightly due to problems experienced in the country of origin, so that the standard had to be revised as follows:
>
> Standard material cost per unit = 8 kg per unit at $3.80 per kg = $30.40.
>
> The actual output for November was 1,400 units. 11,000 kg of material was purchased and used at a cost of $41,500.
>
> **Calculate**
>
> (a) material price and usage variances using the traditional method
>
> (b) all planning and operational material variances.

6 Non-budgetary methods for organisational control

6.1 Introduction

So far in this chapter, we have explained that budgeting is an important tool for planning and control in an organisation and contributes to performance management by providing benchmarks against which to compare actual results (through variance analysis) and develop corrective measures.

The use of traditional budgeting (including methods such as incremental budgeting) is comfortable and predictable and it may still have its place in organisations.

However, there are also many **weaknesses and limitations of traditional approaches to budgeting**. These can be summarised as follows:

- **Costly and time consuming** – The process of setting budgets and targets, implementing tools, inspecting and controlling performance, managing people and budgets (often from remote locations) is costly and time consuming. Finance teams, with their wealth of competencies and experience, spend far too much time on this arguably non-value adding activity.

- **Focus is on short-term results** – There is a trade-off between the achievement of (short-term) budgetary targets and long-term value creation. Traditional budgeting creates a fixed mind-set; it is constraining, allowing limited flexibility to respond to events in an ever-changing world and with undue focus on the past rather than current and future events and on continuous improvement.

- **Insufficient external focus** – Organisational success will require consideration of internal and external factors.

- **Top-down approach to strategy and decision-making** – Traditional budgeting commonly uses a hierarchy of control and accountability. Strategies, decision-making and budgets may be imposed by senior management with limited involvement of those who are responsible for executing and achieving the plan set.

- **Less suited to modern organisations** – Traditional budgeting is comfortable and predictable but is less suited to modern organisations (in both the private and public sector) where:

  - **Change is the new norm** due to seismic shifts in the level of competition, customers' expectations and the global political outlook, combined with a fast pace of technological change. These changes present both risks and opportunities and organisations will have to plan for a different way of doing things.

  - **The importance of an empowered and adaptive organisation** is much greater than the need for a traditional command and control budgeting model.

Illustration 3 – Reasons to replace traditional budgeting

Ten reasons why budgeting causes significant problems today and needs to be replaced:

1 **Budgeting prevents rapid response**: Organisations need to respond rapidly to unpredictable events but the annual budgeting process was never designed for this purpose.

2 **Budgeting is too detailed and expensive**: Budgeting is highly bureaucratic and very expensive.

3 **Budgeting is out-of-date within a few months**: Many of the key assumptions change frequently (such as commodity prices, exchange and interest rates and of course customer demand) causing confusion and much rework.

4 **Budgeting is not aligned with the competitive environment**: Today's drivers of success are concerned more with fast response and continuous innovation than managing people and budgets.

5 **Budgeting is divorced from strategy**: Budgets are based on functions and departments rather than strategic themes. The chances of the goals and plans of many disparate functions and departments being aligned with a coherent corporate strategy are often negligible.

6 **Budgeting stifles initiative and innovation**: Budgeting tends to support an authoritarian management regime that stifles innovation.

7 **Budgeting protects non-value adding costs**: Cost budgets are commonly compiled and agreed based on prior year outcomes. There is little time and incentive to understand and challenge the root causes of costs allowing huge amounts of waste to fester and grow.

8   **Budgeting reinforces command and control**: Budgets were designed to enable functional leaders to manage organisations from the centre, thus local decision-making is usually delegated within strict budgetary controls.

9   **Budgeting demotivates people**: When starting a new job most people are usually highly motivated to maximise their performance but soon they learn not to fight the system and to 'go with the flow'. This means doing little more than their job description specifies and the minimum to achieve targets.

10   **Budgeting encourages unethical behaviour and increases reputational risk**: Aggressive targets and incentives drive people to meet the numbers at almost any cost. This can lead to unethical selling and 'creative' accounting placing the organisation's reputation in jeopardy.

6.2   The use of non-budgetary methods in organisations

The weaknesses and limitations of traditional budgeting discussed above have resulted in some organisations re-thinking their approach to performance management and control, instead increasing their use of non-traditional performance measures in controlling organisations.

Non-budgetary methods will focus less on layers of control and more on **team empowerment, learning and responsibility**; teams will have a growth mind-set and be change adept. They will also **focus on innovation**, enabling a rapid response to threats and opportunities; products will have a short lifecycle and design and production will be flexible to meet the changing needs of the environment.

One example of this approach is **beyond budgeting**. This is discussed below.

6.3   What is beyond budgeting?

Beyond budgeting is an approach to performance management and control that tries to resolve the weaknesses and limitations of traditional approaches to budgeting.

There is no one set definition of beyond budgeting but is can be thought of as follows:

 Beyond budgeting (BB) is the generic term given to the body of practices intended to replace traditional budgeting as a management model. The core concept is the need to move from a business model based on centralised organisational hierarchies and control to organisations based on empowerment and adaption. A range of techniques, such as rolling forecasts and market related targets, can take the place of traditional budgeting.

BB approaches are commonly used in organisations that face regular environmental changes and/or where continuous improvement is critical to the organisation's success.

There are many examples of organisations that have adopted a BB approach including Google, American Express, Toyota, Southwest Airlines, Leyland Trucks and Whole Foods Markets.

6.4 The principles of BB

There is no defined list of BB principles that should be adopted by an organisation in order to succeed at this approach. However, the following is a list of **common best practices** adopted by organisations using a BB approach:

Area of best practice	Explanation
Governance and transparency	• Employees are bound, by a clear organisational **mission and set of values**, to a common cause, rather than being controlled by a central plan. • **Governance** is through shared values and sound judgement, not detailed rules and regulations. • **Information is open and transparent**, not restricted and controlled. For example, information systems may be activity-based, reporting on activities for which managers and teams are responsible.
Accountable teams	• The organisation consists of a **network of accountable teams** who are empowered and trusted to regulate their performance with limited centralised and hierarchical control and no micro management. • Team managers and employees are given a **high degree of freedom** to make decisions that generate value. This is consistent with concepts such as Business Process Re-engineering (Chapter 6) and total quality management (Chapter 14). • Teams are **responsible for relationships** with customers, suppliers and other stakeholders. • **Budgets** may still be used but these will be set at **local level** (bottom-up) using local knowledge.
Goals, targets and rewards	• Managers will be given a **range of challenging, but controllable, goals and targets linked to shareholder value**, e.g. recognising the importance of both financial measures (such as gross profit margin or ROCE) and non-financial measures (such as customer satisfaction, innovation or sustainability). A performance management model such as the balanced scorecard (Chapter 13) may be used. • Targets will often be based on **external benchmarks**. • **Innovation and continuous improvement is encouraged and rewarded.**

Planning and control	• **Planning is a continuous and inclusive process**, not a top-down annual event.
	• **Rolling budgets** may be used. These are flexible and can be quickly adjusted to changes in the organisation's environment and should result in more timely allocation of resources.
	• The **focus is on future events, not the past**. Controls that do exist are based on fast, frequent feedback and **not budget variances**.

Illustration 4 – Toyota, a world class management model

Toyota is an example of an organisation that has moved away from traditional budgetary methods for organisational control.

Toyota is one of the best-managed manufacturing companies in the world. Its Toyota Production System is legendary. Management focuses on continuous improvement and meeting customers' needs. Everyone has a voice and is expected to contribute to the continuous improvement of their work. Medium-term goals aimed at best practice are set at every level. Planning takes place at team level and happens monthly within a clear strategic framework (12 month rolling forecasts support capacity planning. Resources are made available just-in-time to meet each customer order. There are no fixed targets, no annual budget constraints and people are trusted with information to make the right decisions).

6.5 Advantages and disadvantages of BB

Advantages

- Planning is continuous and the organisation is more likely to be proactive rather than reactive to changes in its environment. Lower costs should result from a move away from the concept of a budget entitlement towards a focus on the purpose for which costs are being incurred.

- Targets become more challenging and have a more external focus. They stretch staff and encourage staff to find better ways to do things. They also make the organisation more customer and supplier focused, improving relationships with key stakeholders.

Disadvantages

- Planning, coordination and performance evaluation become more complicated. This has the added impact that reward systems also become more complex.

- If benchmarks and targets are viewed as being unachievable then effort to achieve them is reduced rather than improved. (Targets should be viewed as challenging 'stretch' targets rather than unachievable, uncontrollable or out of reach).

- The organisation becomes more innovative and continuously improves.

- Managers are more involved in the decision making process, which provides better information for decisions as well as providing better motivation for managers.

- Managers can take decisions much more quickly. They are empowered to make decisions and are not constrained by traditional budgets and fixed resources.

- It creates information systems which provide fast and open information throughout the organisation.

- Although employees should be bound by a clear mission and set of values, sometimes organisational goals are less clear and are not communicated throughout the organisation. This means, for example, that many key stakeholders such as providers of finance and shareholders may lose out as the organisation focuses more on customers and innovation.

- Organisations that move to a BB structure can often face a lot of resistance from staff and managers where traditional budgets may be very deeply ingrained in the organisation's culture. If staff fail to fully embrace the new system and targets then the system is set to fail. For example, this may be the case in public sector organisations (discussed in Chapter 12) where managers are under pressure to adhere to traditional budgets in a resource constrained environment.

- It may be very difficult or impractical for organisations to adopt the culture of decentralisation on which successful BB depends.

- The need for more up-to-date and accurate information requires costly investment. (Information systems will be discussed in Chapter 7).

7 Forecasting

7.1 Introduction

Forecasting is closely related to budgeting and may be touched upon in an APM question.

A number of forecasting methods were reviewed in PM including:

Method	Explanation
The hi-low method	Analyses, for example, a semi-variable cost into its fixed and variable elements. These elements are then used to forecast the total cost at any level of activity.
Regression analysis	A more accurate technique than hi-low. Used to estimate the line of best fit and can be used for forecasting whenever a linear relationship is assumed between two variables, e.g. total cost and level of activity, or total sales and marketing spend.
Time series analysis	Makes assumptions about past patterns in data, such as the general trend, seasonality and cyclical variations, to forecast figures. (**Note**: A brief understanding of this will be adequate in APM; the emphasis is more likely to be on interpreting results of a set of forecasting calculations provided.)
The learning curve model	Takes account of the learning curve effect to forecast the average labour time/unit or labour cost/unit.

7.2 Hi-low method

Test your understanding 11 – Hi-low method

Cost data for the six months to 31 December 20X8 is as follows:

Month	Units	Inspection costs $
July	340	2,240
August	300	2,160
September	380	2,320
October	420	2,400
November	400	2,360
December	360	2,280

Required:

Use high/low analysis to find the variable cost per unit, and the total fixed cost. Forecast the total cost when 500 units are produced.

7.3 Regression analysis

Regression analysis – linear regression equation and example

Linear regression equation

The equation of a straight line is:

$$y = a + bx$$

where y = dependent variable
    a = intercept (on y-axis)
    b = gradient
    x = independent variable

and b = $\dfrac{n\Sigma xy - \Sigma x\Sigma y}{n\Sigma x^2 - (\Sigma x)^2}$

where n = number of pairs of data

and a = $\bar{y} - b\bar{x}$

Example

Aurelius is a small supermarket chain that has 6 shops. Each shop advertises in their local newspapers and the marketing director is interested in the relationship between the amount that they spend on advertising and the sales revenue that they achieve. She has collated the following information for the 6 shops for a previous week:

Shop	Advertising expenditure	Sales revenue
1	80	730
2	60	610
3	120	880
4	90	750
5	70	650
6	30	430

She has further performed some calculations for a linear regression calculation as follows:

- the sum of the advertising expenditure (x) column is 450

- the sum of the sales revenue (y) column is 4,050

- when the two columns are multiplied together and summed (xy) the total is 326,500

- when the advertising expenditure is squared (x^2) and summed, the total is 38,300

Required

Calculate the line of best fit using regression analysis.

Solution

$$b = \frac{n\sum xy - \sum x \sum y}{n\sum x^2 - (\sum x)^2}$$

$$= \frac{6 \times 326{,}500 - 450 \times 4{,}050}{6 \times 38{,}300 - 450^2}$$

$$= \frac{136{,}500}{27{,}300} = 5$$

$$a = \bar{y} - b\bar{x}$$

$$= \frac{4{,}050}{6} - 5 \times \frac{450}{6} = 300$$

The regression equation is y = 300 + 5x

7.4 The learning curve effect

The learning curve effect

As workers become more familiar with the production of a new product, the average labour time (and average labour cost) per unit will decline.

Wright's Law states that as output doubles, the average time per unit falls to a fixed percentage (referred to as the learning rate) of the previous average time.

The learning curve effect can be calculated using the following formula:

$$y = ax^b$$

where:

y = the average time (or average cost) per unit/batch

a = time (or cost) for the first unit/batch

x = output in units/batches

b = log r/log 2 (r = rate of learning, expressed as a decimal).

The formula can be used to forecast the cost of labour but would normally be examined as part of a bigger forecasting question such as the one below.

The learning curve and the steady state

The learning effect will only apply for a certain range of production. Once the steady state is reached the direct labour hours will not reduce any further.

The learning curve effect – example

BFG is investigating the financial viability of a new product, the S-pro. The S-pro is a short-life product for which a market has been identified at an agreed design specification. The product will only have a life of 12 months.

The following estimated information is available in respect of the S-pro.:

1. Sales should be 120,000 in the year in batches of 100 units. An average selling price of $1,050 per batch of 100 units is expected.

2. An 80% learning curve will apply for the first 700 batches after which a steady state production time will apply, with the labour time per batch after the first 700 batches being equal to the time of the 700th batch. The labour cost of the first batch was measured at $2,500. This was for 500 hours at $5 per hour.

3. Variable overhead is estimated at $2 per labour hour.

4. Direct material will be $500 per batch for the S-pro for the first 200 batches produced. The second 200 batches will cost 90% of the cost per batch of the first 200 batches. All batches from then on will cost 90% of the batch cost for each of the second 200 batches.

5. S-pro will require additional space to be rented. These directly attributable fixed costs will be $15,000 per month.

A target net cash flow of $130,000 is required in order for the project to be acceptable.

Note: At the learning curve rate of 80% the learning factor (b) is equal to – 0.3219.

Required:

Prepare detailed calculations to show whether S-pro will provide the target net cash flow.

Answer:

BFG net cash flow calculation

Sales units	120,000
	$
Sales revenue	1,260,000
Costs:	
Direct material (W1)	514,000
Direct labour (W2)	315,423
Variable overhead (W3)	126,169
Rent	180,000
Net cash flow	124,408
Target cash flow	130,000

Conclusion: The target cash flow will not be achieved.

Workings:

(W1) **Direct material**

Batches	$
First 200 @ $500	100,000
Second 200 @ $450	90,000
Remaining 800 @ $405	324,000
Total	514,000

(W2) **Direct labour**

$y = ax^b$

where; a = 2,500 and b = −0.3219

Total cost for first 700 batches (x = 700);

$700 \times 2,500 \times 700^{-0.3219}$	$212,423

Total cost for first 699 batches (x = 699);

$699 \times 2,500 \times 699^{-0.3219}$	$212,217
Cost of 700th batch ($212,423 − $212,217)	$206

Total cost of final 500 batches;

$206 × 500	$103,000
Total labour cost ($212,423 + $103,000)	$315,423

(W3) **Variable overhead**

Variable overhead is $2 per labour hour, or 40% of the direct labour cost.

Chapter summary

Methods of budgeting
- Participation in budgeting
- Incremental budgets
- Zero based budgets
- Rolling budgets
- Activity-based budgeting

Introduction to budgeting
- What is a budget?
- What is the purpose of budgeting?

Budgeting and control

Budget evualation and control
- Fixed and flexible budgets
- Different types of variances
- Planning and operational variances

Non-budgeting methods for organisational control
- Introduction
- The use of non-budgeting methods in organisations
- What is beyond budgeting (BB)?
- The principles of BB
- Advantages and disadvantages of BB

Forecasting
- Introduction
- Hi-low method
- Regression analysis
- The learning curve model

Test your understanding answers

Test your understanding 1

Solution:

20X4 costs:

Total variable costs	=	75% × $672,000	=	$504,000
Proportion relating to product C	=	40% × $504,000	=	$201,600
Cost per unit of product C	=	$201,600/350	=	$576

20X5 budget costs:

Inflated cost per unit of C	=	1.04 × $576	=	$599.04
Total variable cost for product C	=	340 × $599.04	=	$203,674

i.e. $203,700 to nearest $100.

Test your understanding 2

The revised budget should incorporate 3% growth starting from the actual sales figure of Q1.

	Quarter 2 $	Quarter 3 $	Quarter 4 $
Sales	127,154	130,969	134,898

Workings

- Budget = $123,450 × 103%
- Budget = $127,154 × 103%
- Budget = $130,969 × 103%

Test your understanding 3

(a) The current method of budgeting at all divisions is incremental budgeting. The advantages of incremental budgeting are that it is simple and easy; therefore, it does not take up much time and resources in the finance department, which is constrained by the new information system implementation. It is suitable in organisations where the business is stable and so historic figures represent a solid base from which to consider small changes. The problems associated with incremental budgeting are that it consolidates existing practices into the targets and so tends to stifle innovation. As a result, inefficient and uneconomic activities will not be challenged and opportunity for cost savings may be missed. Also, managers may deliberately spend up to their budget limits in order to ensure that they get an increment from the highest possible base figure in the next budget.

At the different divisions

As S and H are stable businesses, it makes sense to continue to use incremental budgeting at these divisions. Change at these divisions may not seem necessary as it would create resistance from the divisional managers. However, incremental budgeting is not consistent with continuous improvement which may be required to reduce costs and improve profit margins in these divisions.

At F, the incremental budgets will be rapidly out of date in such a growing business. The current problems of management dissatisfaction and poor quality control may be resulting from divisional management trying to meet their targets with a budget that is not suitable for the growth occurring. They may be cutting corners to meet budget and so buying poorer materials or failing to increase capacity and so not making deliveries.

At M, incremental budgeting is intensifying complaints from the other divisions, who already see M as an unnecessary expense. Incremental budgeting is insufficiently critical of the existing spending and it can lead to unjustified increases.

(b) A rolling budget is one where the budget is kept up to date by adding another accounting period when the most recent one expires. The budget is then rerun using the new actual data as a basis. At Drinks Group, with its quarterly forecasting, this would work by adding another quarter to the budget and then re-budgeting for the next four quarters.

Rolling budgets are suitable when the business environment is changing rapidly or when the business unit needs to be tightly controlled.

The new budget at F would be:

	Current year Q1	Current year Q2	Current year Q3	Current year Q4	Current year Total	Next year Q1
	$000	$000	$000	$000	$000	$000
Revenue	17,932	18,470	19,024	19,595	75,021	20,183
Cost of sales	9,863	10,159	10,464	10,778	41,264	11,101
Gross profit	8,069	8,311	8,560	8,817	33,757	9,082
Distribution costs	1,614	1,662	1,712	1,764	6,752	1,817
Administration costs	4,214	4,214	4,214	4,214	16,856	4,214
Operating profit	2,241	2,435	2,634	2,839	10,149	3,051

Based on the assumptions that cost of sales and distribution costs increase in line with sales and that administration costs are fixed as in the original budget.

The budget now reflects the rapid growth of the division. Using rolling budgets like this will avoid the problem of managers trying to control costs using too small a budget and as a result, choking off the growth of the business. The rolling budgets will require additional resources as they now have to be done each quarter rather than annually but the benefits of giving management a clearer picture and more realistic targets more than outweigh this.

However, it may also be worth considering going beyond budgeting altogether in order to avoid this constraint problem.

(c) At M, as noted in part (a), incremental budgeting may not be a suitable choice of budget method. A more appropriate budgeting system for such a project-based function is zero-based budgeting (ZBB). Marketing operates around campaigns that often run for fixed periods of time and do not fit neatly into accounting periods which further undermines the use of incremental budgeting. It can be seen as a series of projects. This type of operation is best controlled by having individual budgets for each campaign that the divisional managers must justify to senior management at the start

ZBB requires each cost element to be justified, otherwise no resources are allocated. This approach would please the manufacturing divisional managers, as they will see tight control. It will not hobble M as there are few fixed overheads in marketing as it mainly involves human capital. ZBB is often used where spending is discretionary in areas such as marketing and research and development.

(d) The management style currently used at DG is top-down, budget-based with some degree of participation by divisional managers. Given the irritation being expressed by the divisional managers, the senior management could consider making the control process more participatory. This would involve shifting to more bottom-up setting of control targets. This could involve the divisions preparing budgets or else dropping budgeting altogether. Bottom-up control involves the divisional managers at DG having an opportunity to participate in the setting of their budgets/targets. It is also known as participative control for that reason. It has the advantages of improving motivation of the divisional managers by creating a greater sense of ownership in the budget/targets. It increases the manager's understanding, which has additional benefits if personal targets are then set from the budget. Bottom-up processing frees up senior management resource as the divisional managers do more of the work. It can also improve the quality of decision making and budgeting as divisional managers are closer to their product markets.

Bottom-up control can be contrasted with top-down budgeting. A top-down budget is one that is imposed on the budget holder by the senior management. It is controlled by senior management and avoids budgets that are not in line with overall corporate objectives or that are too easily achieved.

At DG, the current approach does have involvement from the budget holders and so is participatory. This is important as the managers are set targets based on budgets, although the finance department involvement should help to avoid the issues of lack of strategic focus and slack that are noted above. The introduction of rolling budgets could be delegated to the F managers as they will be happy to take on the solution to their constraint problems. It would be wise to keep some involvement by senior finance staff in reviewing the budget – particularly, the key growth assumptions. The introduction of ZBB at M will require the involvement of budget holders as they will prepare the original proposal. These suggestions will have the advantage of encouraging innovation although it will loosen central control. Senior management will need to assess whether the managers of the stable divisions (H and S) can be relied on to drive down costs without the close oversight of the head office that is provided by a top-down approach.

Thus, some level of bottom-up budgeting fits well with both the current and future plans for financial control at Drinks Group. Although, the senior management will have to decide on the different level of central control to exercise, based on the skills of the divisional management and the degree of latitude that they require in order to improve their operations.

Professional skills marks (maximum 5 marks)

Analysis and Evaluation:

- Appropriate use of the data to recalculate the budget for F and to support the assessment of the use of rolling budgeting at F

- Comprehensive evaluation of the use of incremental budgeting, with specific focus on each division as well as the organisation overall

- Problems of current budgeting system and top-down approach clearly supported with examples and reasoned recommendations.

Commercial Acumen:

- Recommendations on changes to budgeting method at M and the appropriate level of participation in DG are practical and plausible in the context of the division's and organisation's situation.

Test your understanding 4

(W1) Overheads

Type of overhead	%	Total overhead $
Set-ups	35	229,075
Machining	30	130,900
Material's handling	15	98,175
Inspection	30	196,350
	100	654,500

Step 1: Group production overhead into activities	Step 2: Identify cost drivers for each activity
Set-ups	Number of set-ups
Machining	Number of machine hours
Material's handling	Number of movements of materials
Inspection	Number of inspections

Step 3: Calculate an OAR for each activity

Activity cost (W1)	Cost driver	OAR = activity cost ÷ cost driver
Set-ups = $229,075	670 set ups	$341.90 per set up
Machining = $130,900	23,375 machine hours	$5.60 per machine hour
Materials handling = $98,175	120 material movements	$818.13 per movement of material
Inspection = $196,350	1,000 inspections	$196.35 per inspection

Step 4: Absorb activity costs into products

	Product X $	Product Y $	Product Z $	Total $
Set-ups	25,642.50	39,318.50	164,112	229,073
Machining	6,300	7,000	117,600	130,900
Materials handling	9,817.56	17,180.73	71,177.31	98,175.60
Inspection	29,452.50	35,343	131,554.50	196,350
Total production overhead	71,212.56	98,842.23	484,443.81	654,498.60
Production overhead per unit	**94.95**	**79.07**	**69.21**	

Step 5: Calculate the full production cost per unit

	Product X $	Product Y $	Product Z $
Direct costs (from question)	23.00	21.00	31.00
Production overhead (step 4)	94.95	79.07	69.21
Full production cost under ABC	**117.95**	**100.07**	**100.21**
Full production cost under absorption costing	**65**	**49**	**115**

ABC has resulted in a significant change in the full production cost per unit. The cost of products X and Y have approximately doubled whereas the cost of product Z has decreased by approximately 13%.

Test your understanding 5

(a) **Current absorption costing**

(Workings to support quantitative results are given below.)

The CC department represents an overhead to the operations at Navier. Its costs are currently allocated in a simple fashion by dividing the total departmental cost by the number of dishes to obtain a cost of customer care for each dish as $8.03. This cost will then be added to other costs (such as materials and labour used in production) to obtain a total cost per dish. This cost can then be compared to the selling price per dish in order to obtain a figure for the profit per dish.

In addition, the FD adds a further $100 per specialised dish in order to compensate for the extra work involved. However, this leads to an over-absorption of total cost since the $8.03 will absorb fully the CC costs and an additional $160,000 (1,600 specialised dishes at $100) of costs may be incorrectly absorbed.

ABC costing

The problem at Navier is that it sells two different types of dish and these products use different amounts of the company's resources. The activity-based analysis shows that the cost of customer care per standard dish is in fact lower than the current cost allocated at $6.22 per dish. This means that these dishes are making a higher profit per unit than would be given using the existing costing system. The specialised dishes are costing $106.05 each in customer care so it is vital that their price reflects this much higher cost base. The major activities that contribute to this higher cost are dealing with initial sales enquiries and handling complaints. This is not surprising, as the specialised dishes represent a bespoke service which will not be easily reduced to a standard set of steps.

Given the size of the difference between the ABC cost ($106.05) and the current initial estimate of absorbed cost ($8.03), it is not surprising that there have been efforts to correct for this difference. The finance director's estimate of $108.03 to cover the costs of customer care for the specialised dishes is fairly accurate but, of course, the addition of this extra amount should have required the cost for the standard dishes to be reduced from $8.03 in order to compensate for the allocation of more cost to the specialised dishes. It is not clear if this is being done.

The advantage of the ABC analysis is that it shows the activities that are driving the higher costs and, therefore, this analysis opens the opportunity to consider if the customers of the specialised dishes value the additional work. If not, then ABM would require the non-value adding processes be removed/reduced. A survey of customer attitudes and a comparison with competitors' service standards would shed light on the perceived value of these activities.

A question that should arise in relation to the ABC exercise undertaken here is whether it has been worth the effort, given that the finance director does appear capable of reasonably accurately estimating the costs without undertaking the time-consuming ABC analysis. Of course, the problem of over-allocation of total costs would have to be corrected in any case.

(b) The information in the workings below shows that the main cost activities of the CC department are pre-sale preparation (handling enquiries and quotes) and post-sale complaints handling. Together, these activities consume 65% of the resources of the customer care department. The pre-sale work is essential for the organisation and the department converts 46% (16,000/35,000) of enquiries to orders. It would be beneficial to try to benchmark this ratio to competitor performance although obtaining comparable data will be difficult, due to its commercially sensitive nature.

However, the complaints handling aspect is one which would be identified as non-value adding in an activity-based management analysis. Non-value adding activities are those that do not increase the worth of the product to the customer, common examples are inspection time and idle time in manufacturing. It is usually not possible to eliminate these activities but it is often possible to minimise them. Complaints handling is not value adding as it results from failure to meet the service standards expected (and so is already included in the price paid).

Complaints handling links directly to issues of quality management at Navier as improved quality of products should reduce these costs. These costs are significant at Navier as complaint numbers are 20% (3,200/16,000) of orders. Complaints may arise in many ways and these causes need to be identified. As far as the operation of the CC department is concerned, it may cause complaints through poor work at the quotation stage where the job is improperly understood or incorrectly specified to the manufacturing or installation teams. This leads to non-conformance costs as products do not meet expected standards and, in this case, complaints imply that these are external failure costs as they have been identified by customers.

Quality of the end product could also be affected by the supervision activity and in order to ensure that this is functioning well, the CC department will need to have the authority to intervene with the work of other departments in order to correct errors – this could be a key area for prevention of faults and so might become a core quality activity (an inspection and prevention cost).

The other activities in the department are administrative and the measures of their quality will be in the financial information systems. Order processing quality would be checked by invoice disputes and credit note issuance. Credit check effectiveness would be measured by bad debt levels.

Workings:

Customer care (CC) department

Standard absorption cost per dish

	$000
Salaries	400
Computer time	165
Telephone	79
Stationery and sundries	27
Depreciation of equipment	36
	707

Total CC cost	$707,000
Number of dishes (5.5 × 16,000)	88,000
Standard absorption cost per dish	$8.03
Finance director's adjusted cost per specialised dish	$108.03

Activity-based costs

	Total $	Standard $	Specialised $
Handling enquiries and preparing quotes	282,800	226,240	56,560
Receiving actual orders	70,700	63,630	7,070
Customer credit checks	70,700	63,630	7,070
Supervision of order through manufacture to delivery	106,050	95,445	10,605
Complaints handling	176,750	88,375	88,375
Total	707,000	537,320	169,680
Average dishes per order		6	1
No of orders		14,400	1,600
Total number of dishes		86,400	1,600
ABC absorption cost per dish		$6.22	$106.06

Professional skills marks (maximum 5 marks)

Analysis and Evaluation:

- Appropriate use of the data to perform suitable calculations to support discussion of the use of ABC and how the information could be used

- Problems of current absorption costing method clearly supported with examples.

Commercial Acumen:

- Recognition of the failings of absorption costing but also a recognition that the ABC exercise must be cost beneficial

- Effective use of examples drawn from across scenario information and from calculations performed to illustrate the points being made

- Comprehensive assessment of how information on each activity can be used to improve Navier's performance in the areas indicated.

Test your understanding 6

(a) At first sight, the costs are higher meaning the company has done worse, from a cost control angle, but then the activity level is 20% higher than planned. If all costs are variable, we would expect costs to rise in line with activity, making expected costs 20,000 × 1.2 = $24,000. In this case, the company has done better than expected.

(b) The fixed costs of $10,000 will NOT rise in line with activity levels where as the variable costs of $10,000 will increase in line with activity levels. Therefore, the expected cost of the actual level of activity will be ($10,000 × 1.2) + $10,000 = $22,000. The actual cost is $23,000 so the company has spent more than expected.

Test your understanding 7

(W1) Actual patient numbers were 18.75% above budget, i.e. ((23,750 – 20,000) ÷ 20,000) × 100 = 18.75%. Therefore, budgeted variable costs should be increased by 18.75%.

Cost statements for the year ended 31 December 20X0

	Budget $	Actual $
Doctors	60 × $100,000 = 6,000,000	60 × $105,000 = 6,300,000
Nurses	150 × $37,000 = 5,550,000	150 × $34,500 = 5,175,000
Other staff costs	1.1875 (W1) × 1,440,000 = 1,710,000	1,500,000
Catering	(1.1875 (W1) × $200,000 × 70%) + ($200,000 × 30%) = 226,250	187,500
Cleaning	(1.1875 (W1) × $80,000 × 35%) + ($80,000 × 65%) = 85,250	142,000
Other operating costs	(1.1875 (W1) × $1,200,000 × 30%) + ($1,200,000 ×70%) = 1,267,500	1,050,000
Depreciation	80,000	80,000
Total costs	**14,919,000**	**14,434,500**

Test your understanding 8 – Market size and share

(a) **Traditional sales volume variance**

= (Actual units sold – Budgeted sales) × Standard profit per unit

= (450,000 – 400,000) × $3 = $150,000 F.

(b) **Planning and operational variances**

The revised (ex-post) budget would show that Hudson should expect to sell 20% of 2.2 million units = 440,000 units.

Original sales × standard margin = 400,000 × $3 = $1,200,000

   Market size variance = $120,000 F

Revised sales × standard margin = 440,000 × $3 = $1,320,000

   Market share variance = $30,000 F

Actual sales × standard margin = 450,000 × $3 = $1,350,000

Total sales volume variance = $120,000 F + $30,000 F = $150,000 F

Comment:

Most of the favourable variance can be attributed to the increase in overall market size. However, some can be put down to effort by the sales force which has increased its share from 20% to 20.5% (450,000/2,200,000).

Managers should only be appraised on the operational variance, i.e. the market share variance.

Test your understanding 9

AH × SR	1,450 × $10	= $14,500		
			Operational variance	$500 F
RSH × SR	1,500 × $10	= $15,000		
			Planning variance	$2,500 A
SH × SR	1,250 × $10	= $12,500		
				$2,000 A

Test your understanding 10

(a) **Traditional variances**

AQAP =		$41,500
	Price variance	**$2,500 F**
AQSP =	11,000 × $4 =	$44,000
	Usage variance	**$4,800 A**
SQSP =	1,400 × 7 × $4 =	$39,200

(b) **Planning and operational variances**

Price

AQ × AP		= $41,500	
		Operational variance	**$300 F**
AQ × RSP	11,000 × $3.80	= $41,800	
		Planning variance	**$2,200 F**
AQ × SP	11,000 × $4	= $44,000	
		Total	**$2,500 F**

Usage

AQ × SP	11,000 × $4	= $44,000	
		Operational variance	**$800 F**
RSQ × SP	11,200 × $4	= $44,800	
		Planning variance	**$5,600 A**
SQ × SP	9,800 × $4	= $39,200	
		Total	**$4,800 A**

Test your understanding 11 – Hi-low method

Step 1: Select the highest and lowest activity levels and their costs

Six months to 31/12/X8	Units produced	Inspection costs $
Highest month	420	2,400
Lowest month	300	2,160
Range	120	240

Step 2: Find the variable cost per unit

Variable cost per unit = $240/120 = $2 per unit

Step 3: Find the fixed cost

Fixed inspection costs are, therefore:

$2,400 – (420 units × $2) = $1,560 per month

or $2,160 – (300 units × $2) = $1,560 per month

i.e. the relationship is of the form y = $1,560 + $2x.

Step 4: Use these costs to forecast the total costs for 500 units

Total cost = fixed cost + variable cost

Total cost = $1,560 + ($2 × 500)

Total cost = $2,560

Business structure and performance management

Chapter learning objectives

Upon completion of this chapter you will be able to:

- identify and discuss the particular information needs of organisations adopting a functional, divisional or network form and the implications for performance management

- assess the changes to management accounting systems to reflect the needs of modern service orientated businesses compared with the needs of a traditional manufacturing industry

- assess the influence of Business Process Re-engineering (BPR) on systems development and improvements in organisational performance

- analyse the role that performance management systems play in business integration using models such as the value chain and McKinsey's 7S's

- discuss how changing an organisation's structure, culture and strategy will influence the adoption of new performance measurement methods and techniques

- discuss, with reference to performance management, ways in which the information requirements of a management structure are affected by the features of the structure

- discuss the problems encountered in planning, controlling and measuring performance levels, e.g. productivity, profitability, quality and service levels, in complex business structures

- discuss the impact on performance management of the use of business models involving strategic alliances, joint ventures and complex supply chain structures.

PER

One of the PER performance objectives (PO3) is to contribute to the wider business strategy of your organisation through your personal and team objectives. You should identify innovative ways to improve organisational performance – which may include making or recommending business process changes and improvements.

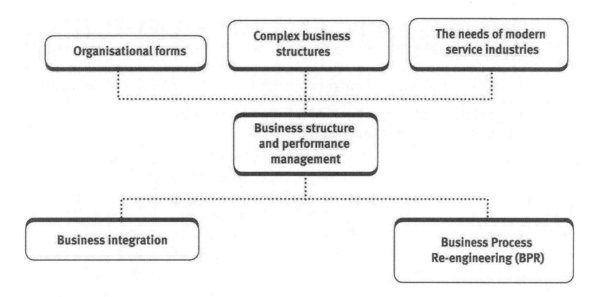

1 Introduction

In this chapter we will look at the information and information system requirements of **different business structures**. We will also discuss the implications of a particular structure for performance management.

An important element of structure is **business integration**. Performance management can improve as a result of linkages between people, operations, strategy and technology. This chapter reviews two important frameworks for understanding business integration; Porter's value chain and McKinsey's 7s model.

The chapter also introduces the topic of **business process re-engineering**. This is the fundamental redesign of business processes and, amongst other things, it can result in a change of structure.

2 Organisational forms

2.1 Functional, divisional and network (virtual) structures

In the exam, you may be asked to discuss the particular information needs of an organisation adopting a functional, divisional or network structure and the implications of these structures for performance management.

In addition, it is important to be able to discuss how changing an organisation's structure, culture (e.g. a move towards an autonomous, innovative culture) and strategy (e.g. a focus on quality rather than low cost) will influence the adoption of new performance measurement methods and techniques.

The impact of a change in structure, culture and strategy on performance management

A change in organisational structure, culture or strategy may result in a requirement for new performance measurement techniques and methods:

Organisational change	Examples of impact on performance measurement
Structure	• Highly centralised and/or functional structures will require a performance measurement system that enables data to be collected at functional level, analysed at the upper level and then fed back to the functional levels. These structures tend to inhibit a manager's discretion to try out new performance measurement techniques.
	• A task centred and/or decentralised structure will require a performance measurement system that allows data to be collected and analysed lower down the hierarchy. Managers will have more discretion to try out new performance measurement techniques.
Culture	• An innovative or creative culture will be willing to embrace new performance measurement techniques. Measurement techniques will need to focus on the performance of the innovations.
	• A restrictive, bureaucratic culture will be less open to the adoption of new performance measurement techniques.
Strategy	• The performance measurement techniques adopted should be aligned to the strategy the organisation is pursuing.
	• For example, an organisation that focuses on quality and has adopted a total quality management (TQM) approach will need performance measures that focus on factors such as the quality of the product or service, the cost of prevention and speed of response (quality is discussed in Chapter 14).

2.2 Functional structure

Functional organisations group together employees that undertake similar tasks into departments.

- A manager is placed in charge of each function.

- A narrow band of senior management co-ordinates the functions and retains the authority to make most of the decisions, i.e. decision making tends to be **centralised**.

What is a functional structure?

An example of a functional structure is:

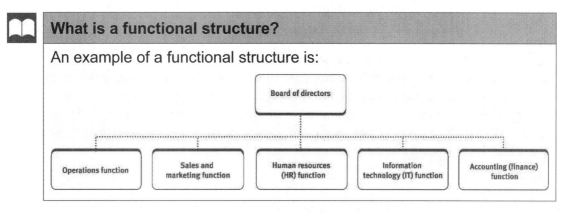

Information needs

The centralised structure results in:

- Data being passed from managers at the functional level to senior managers at the upper level.

- Data is then aggregated and analysed by senior managers at the upper level for planning and control purposes.

- Feedback is then given by the senior managers to the managers at the functional level.

Implications for performance management

There are a number of advantages and disadvantages of a functional structure for performance management:

Advantages	Disadvantages
• **Economies of scale** – Roles and activities are grouped together and not duplicated leading to lower costs • **Standardisation of outputs and systems** – Similar activities are grouped together resulting in standardisation and a focus on optimum quality • **Specialists more comfortable** – People with similar skills are grouped together and do not feel isolated • **Career opportunities** – Employees can work their way up through the function.	• **Empire building and conflicts between functions** – Functional managers may make decisions to increase their own power or that are in the best interests of their function, rather than working in the best interests of the company overall • **Slow to adapt to market changes** – Decision making is slow due to the long chain of command • **Cannot cope with rapid growth or diversification** – For example, specialists in the production function may not be able to cope with making a new product • **Integration of functions** can be difficult.

2.3 Divisional structure

In a divisional structure the organisation is split into several divisions (sometimes referred to as strategic business units or subsidiaries), each one autonomously overseeing a product or geographic region. The divisions are headed by general managers who are responsible for their own resources and have autonomy for making decisions (**decentralised** decision-making).

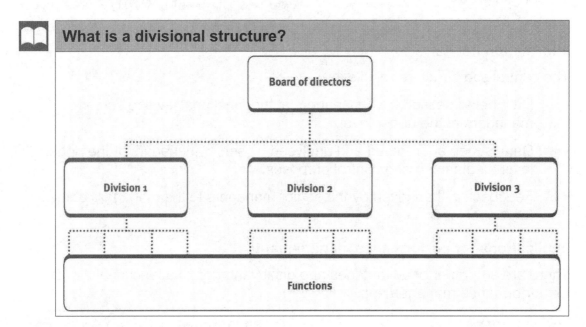

Information needs

The decentralised structure results in:

- Information being required lower down the hierarchy due to the high level of autonomy that exists. For example, information will be required by the divisional manager for budgeting purposes.

- In addition, senior management will need information so it can measure and control the performance of its divisions using similar performance measures to those used to assess the overall performance of the organisation.

Implications for performance management

Advantages	Disadvantages
• **Enables product or geographical growth** – The structure can be easily adapted for further growth and diversification • **Clear responsibility** – Divisional managers should be able to see clearly where their area of responsibility lies • **Training of general managers** – Less focus on specialisation should result in managers having a wider view of the organisation's operations • **Decision making** – Placing responsibility for divisional profitability at the divisional level should improve the speed and (hopefully) the quality of decisions (due to local knowledge) • **Top management free to concentrate on strategic matters.**	• **Co-ordination** – How to co-ordinate different divisions to achieve overall corporate objectives • **Goal congruence** – There is a potential loss of control; managers will be motivated to improve the performance of their division, possibly at the expense of the larger organisation • **Controllability** – Divisional managers should only be held accountable for those factors that they can control. The performance of a divisional manager must be appraised separately to the performance of the division. It may be difficult to determine exactly what is and what is not controllable • **Inter-dependence of divisions** – The performance of one division may depend to some extent on others, making it difficult to measure performance levels • **Head office costs** – Whether/how head office costs should be reapportioned • **Transfer prices** – How transfer prices should be set as these effectively move profit from one division to another • **Duplication of business functions** – Each division will have its own functions. This will result in more managers.

Test your understanding 1

Company A is a diversified business with strategic business units (SBUs) in very different business areas. It is organised with each SBU being a separate division.

Company B is a multinational with different parts of the supply chain in different countries. It is also divisionalised.

Required:

Comment on the differences in performance management issues for each company.

Responsibility accounting

Responsibility accounting is a system of accounting based on the identification of individual parts of a business (**responsibility centres**) which are the responsibility of a single manager. The areas of responsibility may be a cost centre, profit centre or investment centre (more on this in Chapter 11).

This is relevant to our discussion of divisional structures since the responsibility may lie with the divisional manager. Each division will be a responsibility centre.

It is important that divisional managers are only held accountable for those areas of responsibility they can control.

The information systems (management accounting systems) should be designed to reflect the responsibility structure in place and ensure that costs and revenues can be traced to those responsible. Managers of responsibility centres will require:

- the correct information
- in the correct form
- at the correct intervals.

The management accounting system must also allow senior management to measure and control the performance of its divisions using similar performance measures as those used to assess the overall performance of the organisation.

2.4 Network (virtual) structures

Much of the discussion above, on functional and divisional structures, is still relevant in today's business environment. However, the changing expectations of customers, competitive pressure, the changing political outlook and economic landscape and huge technological innovations have changed many of the traditional organisational forms and boundaries.

Organisations have adopted new structures. One example is a network (or virtual) organisation.

A network (or virtual) organisation occurs when an organisation outsources many of its functions to other organisations and simply exists as a network of contracts, with very few, if any, functions being kept in-house.

Illustration 1 – Network structure at Amazon
Many internet companies are examples of networks – Amazon being perhaps one of the best known on-line retailers.

- Amazon operates its website but relies on external suppliers, warehouses, couriers and credit card companies to deliver the rest of the customer experience. Most orders placed on Amazon's website are forwarded to suppliers, who then send the goods directly to the customer.

- These partners are also expected to provide Amazon with information on, for example, stock availability, delivery times and promotional material.

- The customer feels that they are dealing with one organisation, not many.

Characteristics

- The organisation has little or no physical premises.

- Employees and managers work remotely (often from home) in virtual teams and are connected using IT such as emails, video conferencing, intranets and extranets, enabling collaboration and co-ordination across, e.g. time zones and cultures.

- Suppliers and customers are linked using IT systems which can add to the impression that some of them form part of the same organisation.

- The organisation appears to the outside world to be just like any traditional organisation.

Information needs

- Information will be required to facilitate co-ordination and communication, decision-making and the sharing of knowledge, skills and resources.

- Control will be exercised via shared goals and targets. These will be aligned to the overall mission and objectives and, in the case of inter-organisational collaboration, communicated and enforced using contractual agreements (see discussion on service level agreements later on in this sub-section).

The IS in place should be capable of achieving the above; measuring and reporting performance. For example:

– Each party will require feedback on how they are performing in relation to targets and expectations.

– Managers responsible for controlling performance and making decisions will require this information in a user-friendly and summarised form (perhaps with the ability to drill down to the detail beneath).

– The IS can reduce the number of levels in the organisation by providing managers with information to manage and control a large number of geographically dispersed teams and individuals and by giving lower level employees more decision-making authority.

Implications for performance management

Advantages:

- The organisation has the flexibility to meet the specific needs of a project.

- In a similar way, it can assemble the components needed to exploit market opportunities.

- It can compete with large, successful organisations – they look and feel bigger than they are.

- Lower costs, for example due to low investment in assets.

Disadvantages:

- It may be difficult to establish a cohesive and trusting team and to reach agreement over common goals and measures.

- This loss of control may result in a number of problems, e.g. a fall in quality or a greater/lesser degree of risk taking than would be desired.

- Knowledge sharing, leadership and monitoring of the workforce may be difficult due to the absence of face-to-face contact and differences in time, culture, geography and language. The core organisation may not employ many of the virtual organisation's workforce and those that it does employ will often work remotely. In addition, some team members may find this way of working isolating.

- Planning and control may be difficult – a traditional system of standard costing and variance analysis is less relevant since the core organisation does not need detailed information regarding the costs incurred by its business partners. Instead, they will require financial information (such as the prices that partners will charge) and non-financial information from partners (such as the quality of the goods/services, delivery times and ethical behaviour).

- Confidentiality of information is a risk since the core organisation will share information with its partners (some of these partners may also work with competitor' organisations).

- It may be difficult to capture and share information if the systems are not integrated or are not compatible.

- Partners may work for competitors thus reducing competitive advantage. (The retention of the organisation's core competencies in-house should help to minimise this issue).

Service level agreements

Many of the problems identified above can be addressed through the use of a robust service level agreement (SLA). This is a negotiated, legal agreement between the core organisation and its partners regarding the level of service to be provided. It should include the following:

- An agreement of common goals and measures.

- Areas of responsibility should be identified. Action to be taken if KPIs are not met should be stated (for example, the use of fines).

- The activities expected of each partner together with the minimum standards expected, for example with regards to quality.

- A confidentiality agreement.

- An agreement of the standards and procedures to be adhered to by the workforce. It is worth noting that other actions outside those stated in the SLA may be used to effectively manage the workforce, for example the use of payment by results or the creation of cultural controls and a climate of trust.

- The information and reporting procedures to be followed. It is worth noting that the core organisation may put a common interface system in place to assist with information gathering.

Student accountant article: visit the ACCA website, www.accaglobal.com, to review the article on 'Complex business structures'.

3 Complex business structures

3.1 Introduction

In addition to the business structures already discussed in this chapter, there are a number of **complex** business structures. Examples include **joint ventures**, **strategic alliances**, **franchising**, **licensing**, **multinationals** and **complex supply chains**.

The complexity of these structures can result in **problems** in **planning**, **controlling** and **measuring performance** levels, e.g. how to plan for, measure and control levels of quality in a complex supply chain structure.

The **impact on performance management** of the use of three of these types of structure will be discussed below.

3.2 Joint ventures

What is a joint venture?

 A joint venture (JV) is a separate business entity whose shares are owned by two or more business entities.

Why form a JV?

There are many reasons why a business may seek a JV partner. For example:

- **To facilitate development of new products or expansion into new markets**. The JV partner may have the knowledge, skills, experience, reputation or established infrastructure in the relevant market/relating to the new product.

- **'Sharing'** is a key reason for the formation of a JV. The partners may share:

    - **resources**, e.g. pooling of machinery or technology thus reducing capital outlay

    - **costs**, e.g. making an investment feasible

    - **risks**, e.g. making the level of risk more acceptable

    - **skills, experience and intellectual property**, e.g. managers' and employees' knowledge and expertise.

- **Flexibility** since each business retains its unique identity and autonomy and may carry on business activities not related to the JV. In addition, the partners are only bound to the JV for the pre-agreed period; in which time they would hope to improve performance through business innovation and risk minimisation through the separate legal entity formed.

Each partner will bring something different to the JV arrangement (e.g. different skills, resources and experience) and when combined the object of the JV would be to improve performance.

Illustration 2 – Examples of successful JVs

Ford and Toyota

Ford and Toyota began working together to develop hybrid trucks. Toyota brings the hybrid technology knowledge, while Ford brings its leadership in the truck market. This is a great example of a JV created for access to expertise and intellectual property.

Samsung and Spotify

Samsung and Spotify struck a deal to make it easier to use Spotify on Samsung devices. Spotify is now included as a pre-installed app on many Samsung phones – even giving customers 6 months free.

JV challenges for performance management

The JV structure can make **planning**, **performance measurement** and **control difficult**. Each of these will be discussed in turn below.

Planning difficulties

- Difficult to agree on common JV goals, performance measures and targets due to different:
  - objectives from the JV, resulting in different and potentially conflicting objectives
  - time scales
  - risk appetites.

- It may be difficult to formulate a plan in which there is agreement of how best to share, e.g. resources, costs, profits, decision-making, accountability etc.

- Practically, planning may be difficult if JV partners are located in different countries, speak different languages, have different cultures or currencies or management styles or have unaligned information systems.

- A JV board should be established with agreed (a challenge in itself) representation from both parties. The effectiveness of the board will be dependent on overcoming the challenges above and working together.

Performance measurement difficulties

As mentioned above, there may be difficulties in agreeing on common performance measures to be used. Assuming this agreement is reached, the JV arrangement will still result in other potential challenges for performance measurement. For example:

- Performance measurement may be difficult if the JV does not have an integrated or common information system (IS).

- Performance measurement (such as measurement and reporting of joint profits or losses) may be difficult if partners are unwilling to share information (a climate of trust will be required).

- There may be different opinions on how the agreed performance measures should be calculated or determined.

Control difficulties

- The difficulties touched upon above will make control difficult since this control will focus on the comparison of actual performance (performance measurement may be difficult as discussed) to target performance (establishing this will be difficult, as discussed).

- Assuming effective comparison of actual results to target results can be made, attributing accountability for performance (good or bad) is difficult since each JV partner will bring different skills and knowledge to the venture. Accountability should be established at the outset.

3.3 Strategic alliances

What is a strategic alliance?

A strategic alliance is similar to a JV but a **separate business entity is not formed**.

Comparison to JVs

The reasons for forming a strategic alliance and the challenges for performance management and measurement are very similar to those discussed for a JV (and therefore the points covered in section 4.2 can, largely, be used to answer a question on strategic alliances).

However, some distinction should be made. A **relative benefit** of a strategic alliance over a JV is greater flexibility since the strategic alliance is not constrained by the reporting and compliance requirements of a separate legal entity. However, **some additional problems** more specific to a strategic alliance are:

- Independence is retained, making, for example, the establishment of common goals and the collection of information more difficult.

- Security of information may be more of a concern due the lack of a separate legal entity.

- Does not have the other benefits that a separate legal entity may have.

3.4 Complex supply chains

What is a complex supply chain?

 A **supply chain** consists of a network of organisations. Together they provide and process the necessary raw materials firstly into work-in-progress and then into finished goods for distribution and sale to the customer.

As organisations have grown in size and complexity, **complexity** in the supply chain is becoming **more commonplace**.

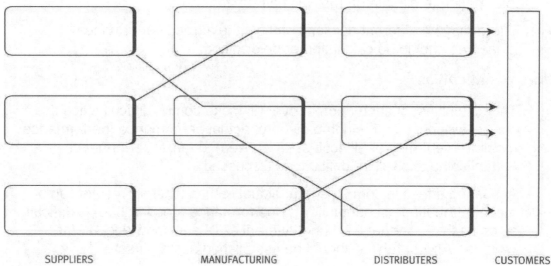

SUPPLIERS   MANUFACTURING   DISTRIBUTERS   CUSTOMERS

KAPLAN PUBLISHING

Most businesses have several suppliers and several customers. Some businesses may compete for customers and have common suppliers. There may be several supply chains serving one group of customers and they may form complex webs.

Impact of complex supply chains on performance management

A complex supply chain will require close collaboration between supply chain partners. There will be potential benefits and challenges for performance management:

Benefits for performance management	Challenges for performance management
• Harnessing the knowledge and skills of the various partners; generating new ideas, solutions and innovative products. • Aims to build positive relationships based on a joint quest to reduce costs, share technology and innovations and improve quality. • Partners will work together to fulfil customer needs in an optimum way, driving competitive advantage. • Reduces reliance on one or a small number of suppliers, manufacturers, distributors or customers.	• Can be difficult to understand and manage if the supply chain is more 'complicated' than 'complex'. • Each partner will have their own goals and motivations and these will have to be aligned to a common purpose (need a robust contract in place). • Skills required to manage the relationships. • Measuring performance may be difficult, e.g. what to measure, how to collect performance measurement information, how then to take control action.

Question practice with additional assistance

The question below is an excellent test of your ability to add depth to your answer and to use the scenario. Ensure that you attempt it and take time to review the answer before sitting the exam. Additional guidance has been included within both the question and the answer. Take the time to read this guidance and use the advice given when attempting future questions.

 Test your understanding 2

Callisto Retail (Callisto) is an on-line reseller of local craft products related to the historic culture of the country of Callistan. The business started ten years ago as a hobby of two brothers, Hassan and Ahmad. The brothers produced humorous, short video clips about Callistan which were posted on their website and became highly popular. They decided to use the website to try to sell Callistan merchandise and good initial sales made them believe that they had a viable business idea.

Callisto has gone from strength to strength and now boasts sales of $120m per annum, selling anything related to Callistan. Callisto is still very much the brothers' family business. They have gathered around themselves a number of strategic partners into what Hassan describes as a virtual company. Callisto has the core functions of video clip production, finance and supplier relationship management. The rest of the functions of the organisation (warehousing, delivery and website development) are outsourced to strategic partners.

The brothers work from their family home in the rural North of Callistan while other Callisto employees work from their homes in the surrounding villages and towns. These employees are involved in video editing, system maintenance, handling customer complaints and communication with suppliers and outsourcers regarding inventory. The employees log in to Callisto's systems via the national internet infrastructure. The outsourced functions are handled by multinational companies of good reputation who are based around the world. The brothers have always been fascinated by information technology and so they depend on email and electronic data interchange to communicate with their product suppliers and outsourcing partners.

Recently, there have been emails from regular customers of the Callisto website complaining about slow or non-delivery of orders that they have placed. Ahmad has commented that this represents a major threat to Callisto as the company operates on small profit margins, relying on volume to drive the business. He believes that sales growth will drive the profitability of the business due to its cost structure.

Hassan handles the management of outsourcing and has been reviewing the contracts that exist between Callisto and its strategic partner for warehousing and delivery, RLR Logistics. The current contract for warehousing and delivery is due for renewal in two months and currently, has the following service level agreements (SLAs):

1   RLR agree to receive and hold inventory from Callisto's product suppliers.

2   RLR agree to hold 14 days inventory of Callisto's products.

3   RLR agree to despatch from their warehouse any order passed from Callisto within three working days, inventory allowing.

4   RLR agree to deliver to customers anywhere in Callistan within two days of despatch.

Breaches in these SLAs incur financial penalties on a sliding scale depending on the number and severity of the problems. Each party to the contract collects their own data on performance and this has led to disagreements in the past over whether service levels have been achieved although no penalties have been triggered to date. The most common disagreement arises over inventory levels held by RLR with RLR claiming that it cannot be expected to deliver products that are late in arriving to inventory due to the product suppliers' production and delivery issues.

Required:

Assess the difficulties of performance measurement and performance management in complex business structures such as Callisto, especially in respect of the performance of their employees and strategic partners.

(17 marks)

Professional marks will be awarded for the demonstration of skill in analysis and evaluation and commercial acumen in your answer.

(3 marks)

(Total: 20 marks)

Question assistance

Step 1 – Review the requirements

Assessment = is an alternative to 'evaluate' where both pros and cons are needed and final judgement on their balance is required.

Performance measurement AND performance management – so need to go further than just the measures and think about how to improve performance.

'Complex business structures such as Callisto' – what constitutes a complex business structure and how does Callisto meet this definition?

Ensure employees and strategic partners are specifically addressed.

Step 2 – Review scenario for relevant information relating to requirements

Examples here include:

- 'on-line reseller'
- 'They have gathered around themselves a number of strategic partners into what Hassan describes as a virtual company'
- 'The rest of the functions of the organisation (warehousing, delivery and website development) are outsourced to strategic partners'
- 'The employees log in to Callisto's systems via the national internet infrastructure'
- 'outsourced functions are handled by multinational companies of good reputation'
- 'depend on email and electronic data interchange to communicate with their product suppliers and outsourcing partners'
- 'complaining about slow or non-delivery of orders'
- 'the company operates on small profit margins'
- The current contract for warehousing and delivery is due for renewal in two months'
- 'Each party to the contract collects their own data on performance and this has led to disagreements in the past'.

Step 3 – Plan the answer

You need to plan your answer identifying sufficient points for each part of the requirement. Use headings to structure your plan – this will help you keep focused when you write your answer.

Difficulties for Performance Measurement

- Employees
- Strategic partners.

For each heading you need to be identifying the difficulties for a virtual organisation (the 'textbook' answer) and combine this with relevant examples and information regarding Callisto. Both of these elements are essential for your answer otherwise you are either just describing the scenario or merely repeating textbook content.

Professional skills marks

Taking the time to plan your answer should help you to ensure that you include a reasoned assessment of the difficulties of both performance measurement and management and that balanced coverage of both employees and strategic partners in included. This should help you score a good mark for 'Analysis and Evaluation'. As mentioned above, part of planning the answer will be ensuring the effective use of examples drawn from across the scenario and this should help you gain a good mark for 'Commercial acumen'.

Step 4 – Check requirements

Quick recap of requirements – have you covered everything?

Step 5 – Write your answer

Use space, headings and short paragraphs to clearly signpost to the marker that you have covered all the necessary parts. If you have planned properly this will be the easiest part of the whole question.

---

4 The needs of modern service industries

4.1 Introduction

Although not strictly a type of structure, it makes sense to look at service industries as part of this chapter.

Increasingly, traditional manufacturing companies have been replaced by modern service industries, e.g. insurance, management consultancy and professional services.

The differences between the products of manufacturing companies and those of service businesses:

- can create **problems in measuring and controlling performance**
- this, in turn, **affects the information needs of service organisations**.

4.2 Characteristics of services

Services have a unique set of characteristics. These can create challenges for performance management.

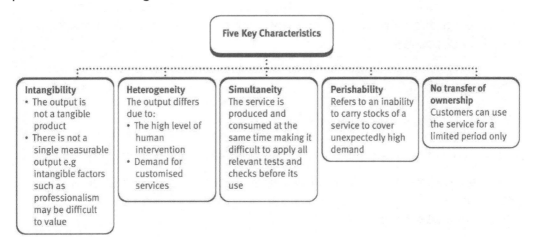

A large proportion of the cost of services is in the nature of its overheads. This together with the fact that services are often consumed at the time of purchase, will influence the type of costing system used and the extent to which costs can be traced to services.

4.3 Measuring service quality

Service providers do not have a physical product so base competitive advantage on less tangible customer benefits such as:

- soundness of advice given
- attitude of staff
- ambience of premises
- speed of service
- flexibility/responsiveness
- consistent quality.

The **service provider will establish its CSFs** and the **management accountant will have an important role in**:

- **identifying** appropriate **KPIs**
- **assembling** KPI information
- **analysing** this information for insights
- giving **guidance** to the organisation based on this insight
- **applying** what has been learned to help the organisation achieve its strategic objectives.

Technology will act as a key enabler in this; the management accounting system should be capable of assembling (and, to some extent, analysing) the relevant information and presenting it in an appropriate format so that timely and effective decisions can be made.

Test your understanding 3

Required:

State the performance measures that may be used in order to assess the surgical quality provided by a hospital indicating how each measure may be addressed.

5 Business integration

5.1 What is business integration?

An important aspect of business structure is business integration.

Business integration means that all aspects of the business must be aligned to secure the most efficient use of the organisation's resources so that it can achieve its objectives effectively.

Rather than focusing on individual parts of the business in isolation, the whole process from the initial order to final delivery of the product and after sales service needs to be considered.

Hammer and Davenport

Writers such as **Hammer** and **Davenport** argue that many organisations have departments and functions that try to maximise their own performance and efficiency at the expense of the whole. Their proposed solution is twofold and links operations, people, strategy and technology:

1   Processes need to be viewed as complete entities that stretch from initial order to final delivery of a product.

2   IT needs to be used to integrate these activities.

Test your understanding 4

XYZ has a conventional functional structure. Assess how a number of different people in the organisation may have to deal with customers, and the problems this creates.

There are two frameworks for understanding integrated processes and the linkages within them:

- Porter's value chain model.

- McKinsey's 7S model.

5.2 Porter's value chain

The value chain model is based around **activities** rather than traditional functional departments (such as finance). It considers the organisation's activities that create value and drive costs and therefore the organisation should focus on improving those activities. The activities are split into **primary** ones (the customer interacts with these and can 'see' the value being created) and **secondary** (or support) activities which are necessary to support the primary activities.

Margin, i.e. profit will be achieved if the customer is willing to pay more for the product/service than the sum of the costs of all the activities in the value chain.

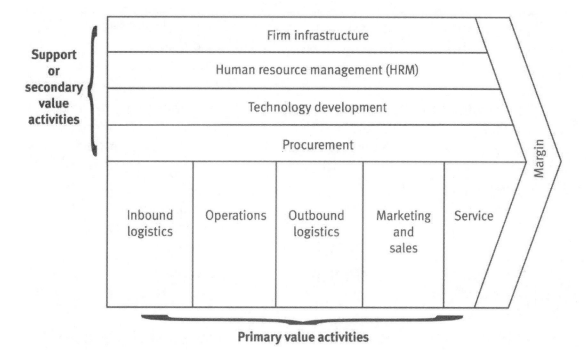

Illustration 3 – Value chain activities

Primary activity	Description	Example
Inbound logistics	Receiving, storing and handling raw material inputs	A just-in-time stock system could give a cost advantage (see Chapter 14)
Operations	Transformation of raw materials into finished goods and services	Using skilled craftsmen could give a quality advantage
Outbound logistics	Storing, distributing and delivering finished goods to customers	Outsourcing activities could give a cost advantage
Marketing and sales	Market research and the marketing mix (product, price, place, promotion)	Sponsorship of a sports celebrity could enhance the image of a product
After sales service	All activities that occur after the point of sale, such as installation, training and repair	A flexible approach to customer returns could enhance a quality image

Secondary (support) activity	Description	Example
Firm infrastructure	How the firm is organised	Centralised buying could result in cost savings due to bulk discounts
Technology development	How the firm uses technology	Modern computer-controlled machinery gives greater flexibility to tailor products to meet customer specifications
Human resource management	How people contribute to competitive advantage	Employing expert buyers could enable a supermarket to purchase better wine than their competitors
Procurement	Purchasing, but not just limited to materials	Buying a building out of town could give a cost advantage over High Street competitors

Illustration 4 – Value chain

Value chain analysis helps managers to decide how individual activities might be changed to reduce costs of operation or to improve the value of the organisation's offerings. Such changes will increase margin.

For example, **a clothes manufacturer** may spend large amounts on:

- buying good quality raw materials (inbound logistics)

- hand-finishing garments (operations)

- building a successful brand image (marketing)

- running its own fleet of delivery trucks in order to deliver finished clothes quickly to customers (outbound logistics).

All of these should add value to the product, allowing the company to charge a premium for its clothes. This is a strategy of differentiation (as per Porter's generic strategies, discussed in Section 7 of Chapter 2).

Another clothes manufacturer may:

- reduce the cost of its raw materials by buying in cheaper supplies from abroad (inbound logistics)

- making all its clothes using machinery that runs 24 hours a day (operations)

- delaying distribution until delivery trucks can be filled with garments for a particular location (outbound logistics).

All of these should enable the company to gain economies of scale and to sell clothes at a cheaper price than its rivals. This is a strategy of cost leadership (as per Porter's generic strategies, discussed in Section 7 of Chapter 2).

Test your understanding 5

Many European clothing manufacturers, even those aiming at the top end of the market, outsource production to countries with lower wage costs such as Sri Lanka and China.

Required:

Comment on whether you feel this is an example of poor integration (or poor linkage in Porter's terminology).

Value system

More recently, organisations have started to consider supply chain partnerships. The value system looks at linking the value chains of suppliers and customers to that of the organisation. A firm's performance depends not only on its own value chain, but on its ability to manage the value system of which it is part.

Illustration 5

In Chapter 4 we looked at an illustration on the UK supermarket giant, Tesco and its high wastage levels of products such as bagged salads. Tesco's 'farm to fork' methodology has engaged with producers, suppliers and customers to collect data on the levels and causes of food waste and to give an overall waste 'footprint' for a selection of products. This has shown where waste 'hotspots' have occurred and has enabled Tesco to develop a waste reduction action plan and targets for each product. For example, 'display until' dates have been removed from fruit and vegetables.

This emphasis on reduced wastage should help Tesco to cut costs and should contribute to meeting its objective of being a socially responsible retailer.

Uses of the value chain in performance management

- Used as part of **strategic analysis** to identify strengths or weaknesses and to focus on how each activity does or could add to the organisation's competitive advantage.

- Used for **ongoing performance management**. It emphasises the CSFs within each activity and targets can then be set and monitored in relation to these.

- In addition to examining primary activities (for example, production) it **looks at support activities** (for example, HRM), which may otherwise have been dismissed as overheads.

- It highlights the linkages between activities. The idea of a **chain** is important. Value will be created by linking activities and hence:

  - information systems should allow the free flow of information between activities and across departmental boundaries.

  - job descriptions and reporting hierarchies should reflect activities.

- It can be **extended to include the value chains of other key stakeholders**, for example customers and suppliers (value system). This will ensure that the needs of stakeholders are considered and that there is consistency across the value chains.

Illustration 6 – Use of the value chain in sustainability

Sustainability was covered in Chapter 4. A potential approach when selecting areas to measure in relation to sustainability could be to analyse an organisation's value chain to identify areas that have the greatest impact on sustainability and that do or could add to the organisation's competitive advantage. These can then be the priority areas to measure and the business can select and monitor KPIs to show how well it is performing in these priority areas.

Test your understanding 6

Kudos Guitar Amplifiers (KGA)

Kudos Guitar Amplifiers (KGA) was set up by Camila Garcia two years ago in the UK. Camila, an electrical engineer and musician, started repairing and then building guitar amplifiers for herself and friends. Initially Camila based her amplifiers around existing classic circuits but soon discovered a potential to tweak these to produce modern variations and improved tones. Partly as a result of the excellent sound but also the low prices compared to established brands, Camila soon found herself inundated with requests and so started the business and employed more staff.

The big break came when a number of high profile professional musicians started using KGA amplifiers. Despite operating in a highly competitive market sector, Camila has struggled to meet demand since and has waiting lists for the hand-built, top of the range models, even having increased prices considerably.

Camila is looking to expand the business further, extend the range of products offered to include cheaper models and look to sell into additional markets. She has recruited more staff, built a state of the art, dedicated factory and appointed managers. To ensure the longevity of his business Camila commissioned a strategic consultant who advised her to adopt a competitive strategy of differentiation. Below are extracts from the consultant's value chain analysis:

- **Inbound logistics** – As well as Camila's proprietary circuit designs, part of the sound of KGA amplifiers comes from the use of rare "new old stock" (NOS) components, some originally manufactured in the 1960s. Locating sufficient numbers of such components to the required quality is a major challenge and it is felt that KGA's relationship with two key suppliers is vital.

- **Operations** – The top of the range models are hand built by master craftsmen with point to point wiring and specialist components. Given normal variations in some of these, different elements are tested and matched by ear to optimise tonal characteristics. Extensive quality control tests are done before an amplifier is ready for sale. Newer, cheaper models use pre-assembled circuit boards bought from a SE Asian supplier. The factory also uses "clean room" technologies and fume extraction safety processes that far exceed current industry requirements and add to the factory running costs.

- **Outbound logistics** – Originally selling direct to customers, Camila has now agreed distribution contracts with two national UK retailers and is hoping to secure similar deals in Germany and the USA.

- **Marketing and sales** – Marketing currently consists of word of mouth, advertising in guitar magazines and sponsorship of high profile musicians. The company will also be setting up a website and Facebook page. It is felt that continued publicity from famous guitarists and online exposure are vital to achieving growth targets. The new ranges have the same brand name as the original hand-built products.

- **Service** – Camila offers a lifetime warranty on his top of the range amplifiers with a guaranteed turnaround of 5 days, although she did have a problem repairing an amplifier in time for a rock band headlining at a major festival. Cheaper ranges have an industry standard 12 months' warranty.

Required:

Discuss the performance management issues arising from the above analysis. Based on this discussion recommend and justify four possible CSFs and identify two KPIs for each of these.

5.3 McKinsey's 7s model

The **McKinsey 7S model** describes an organisation as consisting of **seven interrelated internal elements**.

A change in one element will have repercussions on the others.

All seven elements must be aligned to ensure organisational success.

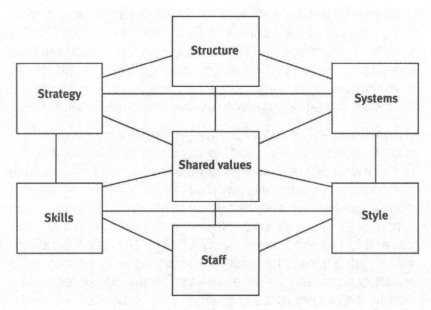

There are **three hard elements** of business behaviour. Hard elements provide the framework of how the organisation operates and include:

Strategy

What is the organisation's overall strategy? What will the organisation do? How will it set itself apart from its competitors and what position do they want to hold in the industry?

Structure

How is the organisation structured? When deciding on an appropriate structure, an organisation will consider what teams they need in place, what tasks they should be responsible for and how the teams will cross over and interact.

Systems

These are the processes, procedures and information systems that support the organisation. Systems must be properly managed and maintained and authority in systems must be clear.

The model also consists of **four soft elements**. The hard elements are easier to define or identify and management can directly influence them where as the soft elements are more difficult to describe, less tangible and are more influenced by the culture of the organisation and are demonstrated through its work. Soft elements include:

Skills

What skills will our staff/organisation need? The skill set of the staff should be aligned to what the organisation is trying to achieve. For example, a strategy focused on maximising sales may mean that staff are trained in terms of sales techniques where as a strategy focused on customer needs may emphasise the need for training with regard to product/service knowledge.

Staff

Considers types of employees, remuneration packages, how employees are attracted and retained. Staff should be recruited with appropriate skills (as discussed above) or an ability/desire to develop these skills. They should be motivated by the style and shared values (discussed below).

Style

Style usually represents the corporate culture of the organisation and includes elements such as management style and how the organisation interacts with staff and other stakeholders.

Shared values

Summarised in the organisation's mission. The attitudes, beliefs and behaviours of people in the organisation should be aligned to achieve the organisation's mission and objectives.

McKinsey's 7S model hard and soft elements

Think of it like this – **hard** elements answer many '**what**' questions about an organisation:

- Strategy – what is the organisation's driving strategy?

- Structure – what teams are in place?

- Systems – what formal systems ensure work progresses?

Whereas **soft** element answer many '**who**' and '**how**' questions about an organisation:

- Staff – who comprises the organisation's workforce?

- Skills – how skilled are these workers?

- Style – how do organisational leaders inspire their colleagues?

- Shared values – how does the organisation demonstrate its core values?

Use of McKinsey 7S model

The model can be used to:

- identify which elements need to be realigned to improve performance

- maintain alignment and performance during a period of change such as:

  - a restructuring

  - new systems implementation

  - a change in leadership

  - new processes.

6 Business Process Re-engineering (BPR)

6.1 What is BPR?

The discussion of BPR follows on from the value chain. As discussed, the value chain considers the way in which the various activities of an organisation work together to add value. How these **activities function and inter-relate constitute an organisation's processes**. This **process perspective is the emphasis of BPR**.

BPR is the **fundamental rethinking and radical redesign of business processes** to achieve **dramatic improvements** in **critical, contemporary measures of performance**, such as cost, quality, service and speed. Improved customer satisfaction is often the primary aim.

Illustration 7 – IBM and BPR

Prior to re-engineering, it took IBM Credit between one and two weeks to issue credit, often losing customers during this period.

- On investigation it was found that performing the actual work only took 90 minutes. The rest of the time (more than seven days!) was spent passing the form from one department to the next.

- The solution was to replace specialists (e.g. credit checkers) with generalists – one person (a deal 'structurer') processes the entire application from beginning to end.

- Post re-engineering, the process took only minutes or hours.

> ### Test your understanding 7
>
> A business process is a series of activities that are linked together in order to achieve given objectives. For example, materials handling might be classed as a business process in which the separate activities are scheduling production, storing materials, processing purchase orders, inspecting materials and paying suppliers.
>
> **Required:**
>
> Suggest ways in which materials handling might be re-engineered.

6.2 The influence of BPR on the organisation

BPR cuts across traditional departmental lines in order to achieve more efficient delivery of the final product or service.

- This **change to a process view** will require a change in **culture** with a move towards **process teams** rather than functional departments.

- Employees will need to **retrain** in order to gain additional skills.

- The change will require **communication and leadership** from senior management.

- BPR results in more **automation and greater use of IT/IS** to integrate processes. (The rise of BPR in the 1990s coincided with the widespread adoption of new IT systems based on personal computers, networks and the internet.)

6.3 Does BPR improve organisational performance?

Advocates of BPR would argue that **organisational performance will improve**:

- BPR **encourages a long-term strategic view** by asking questions about how core processes can be honed in order to achieve corporate goals more effectively.

- BPR **revolves around customer needs**; the fulfilment of which is vital for **sustaining competitive advantage**.

- Re-engineered processes often allow **workers more autonomy** to make decisions, allowing a greater degree of **flexibility to make decisions to reflect customers' needs** and should also **improve motivation**.

  This increased autonomy and flexibility should make a **process cheaper** and more responsive to customer needs by stripping away the peripheral activities and bureaucratic layers that sometimes emerge from excessive focus on functional boundaries.

- BPR can help reduce organisational complexity and reduce costs by **eliminating unnecessary activities or combining several jobs into one**.

  Staff will be re-organised into multi-disciplinary teams creating **overhead savings**.

However, the approach does have a number of **weaknesses** which may make it ill-suited to an organisation. BPR may produce a quick fix to perceived problems but at a long-term cost. Practical problems include:

- **Additional costs** associated with, for example, investment in **new information systems** or **retraining of staff** to work in unfamiliar roles.

- A **decline in morale** due to **staff cuts** and a **perception that BPR is all about cost cutting**.

- **Staff may feel devalued when their current role is fundamentally changed** with a re-organisation into new teams with different goals and expectations.

- BPR often **strips out different layers of middle management**. This may lead to a **loss of co-ordination and communication**.

- BPR commonly utilises **outsourcing**; using a third party provider for elements of production. However, this may have **adverse consequences on quality and flexibility** and so any decision to outsource should be considered carefully.

- **In many cases, business processes were not redesigned but merely automated**; this is not BPR.

- BPR may be considered a **backward-looking** approach. It takes what has happened in the past and seeks to improve it, but with limited regard for what will happen in the future.

Illustration 8 – The continued relevance of BPR

The Covid-19 pandemic resulted in a major global health threat. The research community responded to the outbreak, focusing their efforts on producing an effective vaccine. Part of this effort required individuals to participate in clinical trials. A major criticism was the lack of co-ordination and collaboration across the research community. Ideally, data should be published and shared with the entire community but this was not the case, rather processes were carried out in the same way that they had always been.

In fact, what should have been utilised to address this lack of co-ordination and collaboration is BPR. Processes for dealing with personal privacy, data security and data standardisation have become increasingly sophisticated over the past 10 years and it would have been possible to re-engineer the process so that the data from different clinical trials is centralised in one place. The hope is that lessons have been learned and that BPR would ensure future clinical trials can utilise a research data sharing platform.

6.4 The influence of BPR on systems development

The organisation may need to invest in specialised systems to ensure they can adequately monitor and control performance:

- For example, the organisation may establish a shared database accessible by all parts of the multidisciplinary team.

- The system should be updated in real time.

- The system should be capable of producing both financial performance data (e.g. cost information) and non-financial performance measurement data (e.g. regarding quality).

- The system must be capable of providing teams with budgetary information and performance data for their particular area of concern.

- The system may be integrated with that of its stakeholders, e.g. suppliers' systems.

The reward system (for example, the payment of a bonus) should be aligned to the achievement of the new performance measures. In addition, the basic part of the remuneration may also increase to reflect the increased skills base, autonomy and responsibility of employees.

Chapter summary

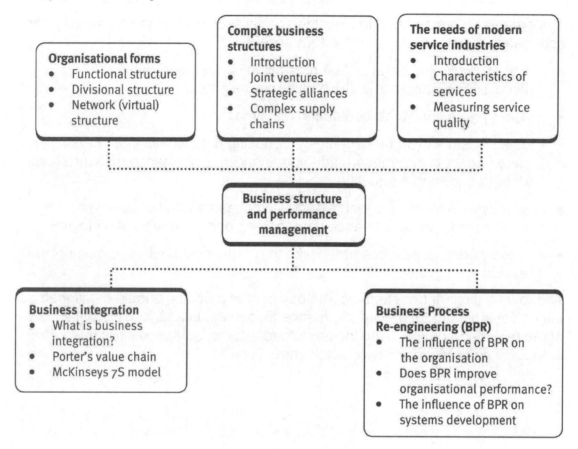

Organisational forms
- Functional structure
- Divisional structure
- Network (virtual) structure

Complex business structures
- Introduction
- Joint ventures
- Strategic alliances
- Complex supply chains

The needs of modern service industries
- Introduction
- Characteristics of services
- Measuring service quality

Business structure and performance management

Business integration
- What is business integration?
- Porter's value chain
- McKinseys 7S model

Business Process Re-engineering (BPR)
- The influence of BPR on the organisation
- Does BPR improve organisational performance?
- The influence of BPR on systems development

Test your understanding answers

Test your understanding 1

Company A

Given that business units are in unrelated markets, there is likely to be more devolved management, with the use of divisional performance measures and reliance on the measurement systems, particularly financial reporting, for control.

Company B

- There is a need for a high level of interaction between business units, so senior management control is more important, whether in terms of standardisation or detailed operational targets.

- The performance measurement system may aid communication between managers and provide a common language.

Test your understanding 2

Tutor tip: Splitting your answer into the measurement and management sections is a good start. You can break it down further by separating employees, strategic partners and other issues.

Performance measurement problems at Callisto

In a virtual organisation such as Callisto, performance measurement can be difficult due to the fact that key players in the business processes and in the supply chain are not 'on site'. Callisto has the problem of collecting and monitoring data about its employees working from home and the outsourcing partners.

Tutor tip: This identifies the key issue relating to the 'virtual' nature.

At Callisto, there is a reliance placed on information technology for handling these remote contacts. Collecting and monitoring performance should therefore be done automatically as far as possible. A large database would be required that can be automatically updated from the activities of the remote staff and suppliers. This will require the staff and supplier systems to be compatible.

Tutor tip: Another specific issue relating to virtual organisations that has been linked to information regarding Callisto. This paragraph goes further than just identifying the issue and explains the implications.

Employees

The employees can be required to use software supplied by Callisto and in fact, at Callisto, they use the internet to log in remotely to its common systems. Although this solution requires expenditure on hardware and software, it is within the control of management.

> **Tutor tip:** Part of 'assessing' the difficulty may involve explaining why it is not too much of an issue – so here identifying the fact that Callisto still have control over their employees.

Even with reviews of system logs to identify the hours that staff spend logged in to the systems, there is still the difficulty of measuring staff outputs in order to ensure their productivity. These outputs must be clearly defined by Callisto's managers, otherwise there will be disputes between staff and management.

> **Tutor tip:** Again, the implication of the problem has been described.

One further outstanding issue is the need to ensure that such communication is over properly secured communication channels, especially if it contains customer or financial data. There are likely to be significant penalties if data protection regulations are breached, not to mention the reputational impact.

Strategic partners

The strategic partners, such as RLR, will have their own systems. A problem for Callisto is that there is disagreement over the measurement of the key SLAs. In order to resolve such disputes, lengthy reconciliations between Callisto's and RLR's systems will have to be undertaken otherwise there are no grounds for enforcement of the SLAs which represent Callisto's key control over the relationship.

> **Tutor tip:** The implication has been explained with specific reference to information in the scenario. This ensures your answer is not just a generic 'textbook' answer.

The solution would be for the partners to agree a standard reporting format for all data that relates to the SLAs which would remove the need for such reconciliations.

> **Tutor tip:** Part of 'assessing' a difficulty may involve thinking about how it can be resolved.

Finally, there is the problem that Callisto and the partner organisation may have differing objectives – the obvious conflict over price between supplier and customer being one. However, at Callisto, this is being addressed by the use of detailed SLAs which both organisations can use to develop performance measures such as inventory levels and delivery times.

Performance management problems at Callisto

Tutor tip: Performance management goes a step further than merely measuring output and considers how improvements can be made.

Employees

The performance management of employees is complicated due to the inability of management to 'look over their shoulder' since they are not present in the same building. However, employees will enjoy the advantages of homeworking, such as lower commuting times, more contact with family and greater flexibility in working hours. The disadvantages are the difficulties in measuring outputs mentioned above and ensuring motivation and commitment.

Tutor tip: This nicely combines an identification of the problem, the implications of the problem along with an upside to the situation.

The motivation and commitment can be addressed through suitable reward schemes which would have to be tied to agreed outputs and targets for each employee. Work could be divided into projects where the outputs are more easily identified and pay/bonuses related to these.

Tutor tip: Further assessment of the problem considers the possible solutions.

Strategic partners

When managing the performance of the strategic partners it is crucial that there is a balance between consideration of security and control issues and encouraging a positive and collaborative relationship.

Tutor tip: This introduces the difficulty faced regarding performance management of strategic partners.

One difficulty which may arise concerns confidentiality as the partners will have access to commercially sensitive information about customers' locations and suppliers' names and lead times. Callisto must control access to this information without affecting the relationship. Leakage of such data will have a detrimental effect on the company's reputation. However interface between the organisations can create wasteful activity if there is not an atmosphere of trust. At Callisto, this is illustrated by the problem of reconciliation of performance data.

Tutor tip: The problem is further explained and the possible implications considered.

It is also important to consider reliability where the partner is supplying a business critical role (as for RLR with Callisto) such that it would take considerable time to replace such a relationship and affect customer service while this happened.

Finally Callisto must carefully consider profit sharing. The collaborative nature of the relationship and the difficulty of breaking it combine to imply that it will be in the interest of both parties to negotiate a contract that is motivating and profitable for both sides. For Callisto, the business aim is to increase volume and this will require customer loyalty so the quality of service is important.

Tutor tip: The 'difficulty' identified here is how to determine the appropriate split of profit between Callisto and its partners.

Test your understanding 3

- The percentage of satisfied patients which could be measured by using the number of customer complaints or via a patient survey.

- The time spent waiting for non-emergency operations which could be measured by reference to the time elapsed from the date when an operation was deemed necessary until it was actually performed.

- The number of successful operations as a percentage of total operations performed which could be measured by the number of remedial operations undertaken.

- The percentage of total operations performed in accordance with agreed schedules which could be measured by reference to agreed operation schedules.

- The standards of cleanliness and hygiene maintained which could be measured by observation or by the number of cases of hospital bugs such as MRSA.

- The staff to patient ratio which could be measured by reference to personnel and patient records.

- The responsiveness of staff to requests of patients which could be measured via a patient survey.

Test your understanding 4

1   Sales staff to make the original sale.

2   Delivery staff to arrange delivery.

3   Accounts staff chasing up payment if invoices are overdue.

4   Customer service staff if there is a problem with the product.

Possible problems include:

- delivery staff may be unaware of any special delivery requirements agreed by the sales staff

- accounts staff may be unaware of any special discounts offered

- aggressive credit controllers could damage sales negotiations for potential new sales

- credit controllers might not be aware of special terms offered to the client to win their business

- customers may resent having to re-explain their circumstances to each point of contact

- customer service may be unaware of the key factors in why the client bought the product and hence not prioritise buying.

Customer service could be improved by having one customer-facing point of contact.

Test your understanding 5

Firms following a cost leadership strategy have found that outsourcing to China, say, has cut costs considerably, even after taking into account distribution costs.

Differentiators have, on the whole, found that they have saved costs without compromising quality. Thus the apparent conflict between low cost production and high quality branding has not been a problem. Furthermore the perceived quality of Chinese garments is rising with some manufacturers claiming that quality is higher than in older European factories.

Note: Commercial awareness – given that many firms do it, be wary of criticising the approach too heavily. They must have their reasons.

Test your understanding 6

Introduction

Generally, the value chain is a model of business integration showing the way that business activities are organised. This model is based around activities rather than traditional functional departments (such as finance). A key idea is that it is activities which create value and incur costs. The activities are split into two groups: primary ones which the customer interacts with directly and can 'see' the value being created and secondary ones which are necessary to support the primary activities. By identifying how value is created, the organisation can then focus on improving those activities through its performance measurement system.

Context – competitive strategy

If KGA is going to adopt a strategy of differentiation as recommended, then it needs to ensure that all aspects of the value chain are coordinated to support this.

In particular the following issues are relevant:

- There is a risk that the cheaper range could undermine the brand perception as the inherent quality will be lower than the hand-built models. Whether this is a significant risk is unclear as the cheaper models may still offer exceptional sound quality compared to rival products within their price range. If there is a risk, then it might be worth considering using a different brand strategy for them.

- Non value-added activities should be discontinued. In particular, excessive spending on clean room and extraction processes seems unnecessary as it does not add to the perceived quality of the amplifiers and does not appear to be valued by customers.

- Activities that are vital for the high sound quality – sourcing NOS components, being hand built and tested by craftsmen and the publicity gained from being used by famous guitarists – need to be strengthened and consolidated.

Performance management – establishing CSFs and KPIs

Based on the above analysis, KGA will need to establish a system of CSFs and KPIs, which could include the following:

CSF	Comment	KPIs
Securing sufficient volumes of high quality NOS components	The NOS components are a vital part of the final sound quality for the hand built amplifiers.	• Number of each component in stock • % returns back to suppliers due to quality problems • Lead times by component and supplier
Ensuring build and sound quality of top of the range amplifiers	KGA's success is underpinned by the sound quality of its amplifiers. If this suffers for any reason then customers will by competitors' offerings instead.	• % rejected by quality control • % requiring reworking or repair • Average scores in online reviews • Staff turnover of master craftsmen
Meeting sponsored guitarists' needs	Many customers are drawn to KGA products because they see guitar heroes using the products. If these guitar players chose to use different brands then sales would drop and the brand be undermined.	• Turnaround time on repairs and servicing • No (%) of returns • Time taken to build new equipment for them
Effective website sales and marketing	The website is seen as key to new growth.	• No of hits • Average length of visit • % of hits that translate into sales • Average purchase value • % down time

Note: Only two KPIs are required for each CSF.

Performance management – MIS issues

Another feature of the value chain is the idea of a chain. This is the thought that value is built by linking activities and so there must be a flow of information between the different activities and across departmental boundaries. In performance management terms, this will affect:

- information systems which will have to ensure good communication across functional boundaries and

- job descriptions and reporting hierarchies as these will have to reflect activities.

The chain does not stop at the organisation's boundaries. This is likely to be obvious to KGA given the importance of supply chain management but the value chain will allow the organisation to focus on those relationships on which value most depends.

Specifically for KGA, the value chain would emphasise the importance of supplier management to obtain suitable NOS components, leading through to operations in the form of testing and matching components, resulting in finished amplifiers.

Test your understanding 7

In the case of materials handling, the activity of processing purchase orders might be re-engineered by:

- integrating the production planning system with that of the supplier (an exercise in supply chain management (or SCM)) and thus sending purchase orders direct to the supplier without any intermediate administrative activity

- joint quality control procedures might be agreed thus avoiding the need to check incoming materials. In this manner, the cost of material procurement, receiving, holding and handling is reduced.

Information systems and developments in technology

Chapter learning objectives

Upon completion of this chapter you will be able to:

- assess the need for businesses to continually refine and develop their management accounting and information systems if they are to maintain or improve their performance in an increasingly competitive and global market

- evaluate the compatibility of management accounting objectives and the management accounting information systems

- discuss the issue of data silos and the problems they present for the accounting function

- discuss the integration of management accounting information within an overall information system, for example the use of enterprise resource planning systems

- evaluate whether the management information systems are lean and the value of the information that they provide (e.g. using the 5 Ss)

- evaluate the external and internal factors (e.g. anticipated human behaviour) which will influence the design and use of a management accounting system

- discuss the principal internal and external sources of management accounting information, their costs and limitations

- demonstrate how the information might be used in planning and controlling activities, e.g. benchmarking against similar activities

- demonstrate how the type of business entity will influence the recording and processing methods

- discuss how IT developments may influence management accounting systems (e.g. unified corporate databases, process automation, the internet of things, RFIDs, cloud and network technology)

- explain how information systems provide instant access to previously unavailable data that can be used for benchmarking and control purposes and help improve business performance (e.g., through the use of artificial intelligence (AI), enterprise resource planning, knowledge management and customer relationship management systems and also, data warehouses)

- discuss the development of big data and its impact on performance measurement and management, including the risks and challenges it presents

- discuss the impact of big data and data analytics on the role of the management accountant

- demonstrate and evaluate different methods of data analysis (e.g. descriptive, diagnostic and predictive analytics)

- discuss the use of alternative methods of data analytics (e.g. text, image, video and voice analytics and sentiment analysis)

- discuss the ethical issues related to information collection and processing (e.g. the use of 'black box' algorithms and large-scale data collection and mining)

- justify the need to assess the characteristics of quality in management information systems.

PER

One of the PER performance objectives (PO13) is to plan business activities and control performance, making recommendations for improvement. Another PER performance objective (PO22) is data analysis and decision support. Working through this chapter should help you understand how to demonstrate these objectives.

KAPLAN PUBLISHING

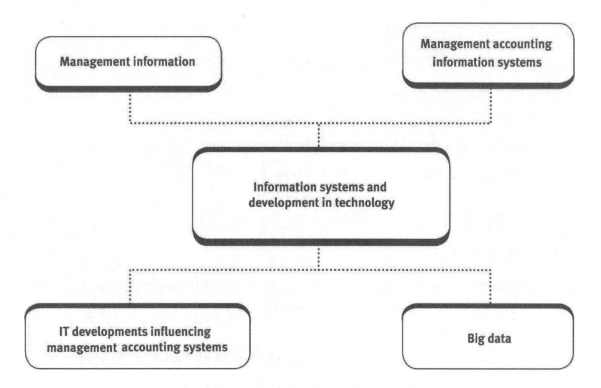

1 Introduction

Once an organisation has set its objective and targets (syllabus area A), it will need to design effective systems to capture the information required to monitor the organisation's progress with performance measures (syllabus area B).

Managers need access to good information in order to be able to effectively plan, direct and control the activities that they are responsible for. In this chapter, we consider the important role of information systems in collecting, monitoring and reporting performance management information.

The first part of this chapter focuses on management information and on the development and importance of an effective management accounting information system.

The chapter then goes on to look at some IT developments and discusses how advancements in technology have enabled organisations to better measure and control performance and to improve performance.

The final part of the chapter discusses the development of big data and data analytics and its impact on the role of the management accountant. It discusses the methods of data analysis and data analytics and some of the ethical issues involved.

2 Common knowledge

Chapter 7 builds on the following knowledge from PM:

- Information and data
- Big data
- Data analytics
- Management information systems (MIS)

3 Management information

3.1 Introduction

As mentioned above, managers need access to **good information** for **planning**, **decision-making** and to **control** the organisation effectively.

This information will help managers to:

- **forecast** future performance in order to plan ahead and set budgets.
- monitor an organisation's performance using **performance measures.**
- use **benchmarking** to evaluate the organisation's activities.

3.2 Characteristics of good information

We have said that we need good information but what makes information good? One way of looking at the qualities of 'good' information is to use the acronym 'accurate'. This is explained using the illustration below.

Illustration 1 – Characteristics of 'good' information
An important type of information produced for management will be performance reports (output reports).
These may be in the form of overall performance reports (e.g. monthly management accounts) or be more specific and tailored to the manager in question, e.g. an inventory report for a production manager.
The performance reports produced for management from an information system should allow the organisation to run the business effectively both today and in the future and should include '**good**' information.
The characteristics of good information can be summarised using the **acronym 'ACCURATE'**.

Characteristic	Explanation
Accurate	For example, figures should add up and there should be no typos.
Complete	The reports should include all the information that is needed by the readers of the report and should be aligned to the overall objectives of the report and mission/objectives of the organisation.
Cost < benefit	The benefit of having the information must be greater than the cost of providing it.
Understandable	The readers of the report must be able to understand the contents and use the contents to fulfil their needs. Presentation should be clear and in line with best practice.
Relevant	Information that is not needed by the reader(s) of the report should be omitted. Information overload can be a huge problem and can detract from the usefulness of the report. The problem of information overload may be overcome using, for example, drill-down reports (provide users with the capability to look at increasingly detailed information about a particular item) and exception reports (which are only triggered when a situation is unusual or requires management action).
Adaptable	The output reports should have the capability of being adapted to meet the needs of the user or the organisation. (**Note**: The 'A' can also be for '**A**ccessible' meaning that the information is accessible via the appropriate channel of communication (verbally, via report, via email etc.) and is reported to the relevant person.)
Timely	The information should be provided when needed and should not be provided too frequently (this can result in information overload and the cost of providing the information exceeding the benefit).
Easy to use	Information should be presented in a form recommended by the industry or organisation's best practice. It should not be too long (to prevent information overload) and it should be sent using the most appropriate communication channel to ensure user needs are met.

Note: The design of a good performance report will be discussed in detail in Chapter 8.

3.3 Sources of information

Information will be assembled from a range of **internal** and **external** sources:

Internal sources of information

Examples	Advantages	Disadvantages
Accounting records, e.g. sales ledger Payroll information Production data, e.g. number of rejected units Sales and marketing data, e.g. market research results	• Known origin, increasing likelihood information is accurate • Should be up to date • Should meet the needs of the organisation • Should be easier and cheaper to gather than external information	Too narrow a focus on internal information may limit competitiveness and performance, it is also important to consider external information.

External sources of information

Examples	Advantages	Disadvantages
Supplier information, e.g. product prices Customer information, e.g. feedback Internet, newspapers, journals, e.g. information on competitors The government, e.g. interest rates, taxation policy	As mentioned, too narrow a focus on internal data will limit competitiveness and performance. To compete effectively in the modern business environment it is also important to consider the external environment and therefore external sources of information.	• May not be accurate. Can we rely on the data? • May not be up to date • It is not tailored to the organisation and so may not meet their exact needs • It may be costly and difficult to gather, e.g. competitor information or customer feedback.

As mentioned, the sources have their advantages and limitations but **both** will be **important** and **necessary**.

3.4 Types of information

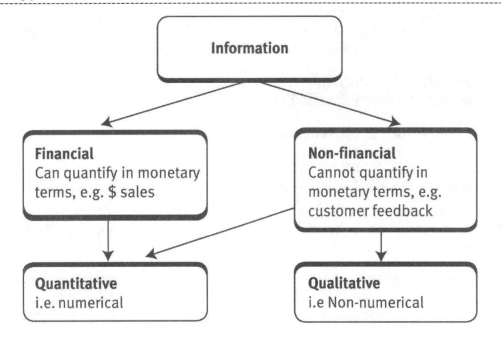

The above diagram shows a summary of the different types of information. Performance management will require a range and balance of all of these types.

Note: Financial information will be covered in Chapter 10, non-financial information will be covered in Chapter 13 and qualitative and quantitative information will be discussed in Chapter 8.

4 Management accounting information systems

4.1 Introduction

 A **management accounting information system** is an information system (IS) capable of producing performance and control information that is consistent with the objectives of the management accountant.

 Illustration 2 – Uses of management accounting information

Management accounting information may be used in the following ways:

- To **assess the performance** of the business as a whole or of individual divisions or products

- To **value inventories**

- To **make future plans** – the information may assist in making future business plans, e.g. development of new products or expansion into new markets

- To **control the business** – for example, through variance reporting and corrective action

> • To **make decisions** – for example, through the provision of summary information (this can be used to make strategic decisions) or through the provision of more detailed information (this can be used to make tactical and operational decisions).

The system should produce quality information, consistent with the characteristics of 'good' information (section 3.2).

Management information systems (MIS)

 Management information system are systems used to produce information to allow managers to make effective decisions.

Therefore, a management accounting information system is simply a MIS that produces information to allow **management accountants** to make effective decisions.

A MIS converts internal and external data into useful information which is then communicated to managers at all levels and across all functions to enable them to make timely and effective decisions for planning, directing and controlling activities.

4.2 Types of MIS

Type of MIS	Explanation
Transaction processing system (TPS)	A TPS is mainly used by operational managers to make decisions. It records all the daily transactions (for example, payroll or purchases) of an organisation and summarises them so they can be reported on a routine basis.
Decision support system (DSS)	A decision support system aids managers in making decisions. The system accesses (usually from a data warehouse) and manipulates data (using data mining and analytical tools) to predict the consequences of a number of possible scenarios and the manager then uses their judgement to make the final decision. (**Note**: data warehouses, data mining and data analytics are discussed later in this chapter).
Expert system	Expert systems consist of a database holding specialist knowledge, for example, on law and taxation, and allow non-experts to interrogate them for information, advice and recommended decisions. Can be used at all levels of management.
Executive information system (EIS)	An EIS gives senior executives access to internal and external information. Information is presented in a flexible, user-friendly, summarised form with the option to 'drill down' to a greater level of detail.

Illustration 3 – DSS

A supermarket chain is planning to start selling its goods online, but is uncertain of whether it is appropriate for the organisation.

A DSS would gather information about the company itself – does it have the resources to start selling online?

It will also provide information about the online groceries market, such as the size of the market and who the competitors are.

The DSS will then present this information in a way that is easy to understand, helping the management to make the decision.

Illustration 4 – EIS

A typical report from an EIS would combine many types of data on the same screen and make it easier for senior management to understand the performance of the business.

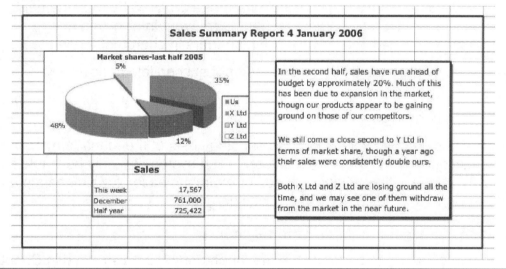

Test your understanding 1

CB publishing is considering the impact of a new system based on an integrated, single database which would support an executive information system (EIS) and a decision support system (DSS). A network update would allow real time input of data.

Required:

Evaluate the potential impact of the introduction of the new system on performance management.

Test your understanding 2
Required: Discuss the factors that need to be considered when determining the capacity and development potential of a management information system.

4.3 The design and development of management accounting IS

Factors influencing design

- As discussed, a management accounting IS is a system capable of producing performance and control information that is consistent with the objectives of the management accountant. Therefore, when designing the management accounting IS, a key consideration is ensuring this is achieved and that the information produced is 'good' information.

- It is important to define the areas of control within the organisation and the individuals who are responsible for those areas. The management accounting IS should ensure that the relevant information is communicated and flows to the managers in charge of those areas.

- The system should be reliable and not susceptible to downtime.

- The system should be user friendly. Otherwise, it will not be accepted within the organisation or may result in inefficiencies.

- The design, development and ongoing costs of the management accounting IS must be considered. The system will only be viable if the cost is less than the benefit so, for example, ease of maintenance and upgrade will be an important consideration.

Quality management information systems

The role of quality in performance management will be discussed in Chapter 14. However, one aspect of quality that is relevant to this chapter is the need for a quality management information system.

There is no one definition of a quality management information system but features could include:

- **Functionality** – the system should perform the task it was designed for, e.g. does it produce information that is relevant and adaptable to the needs of the user?

- **Reliability** – the system should not be susceptible to downtime and the output should be accurate, timely and complete.

- **Usability** – the system should be easy to use and understandable.

- **Build quality** – ease and cost effectiveness of the system build, maintenance and upgrade.

Note: Many of the features of 'good' information have been included in the above points.

Lean MIS

In the exam, you may be asked to evaluate if the MIS is lean. A lean approach (**Note**: this will be discussed further in Chapter 14) would aim to **identify and eliminate waste in the MIS** and improve the efficiency of the flow of information to users. The system should be simplified but also improved as a result. Relating this back to the discussion above, a lean approach may be one aspect of having a quality system in place.

A lean MIS aims to get the right thing to the right place at the right time, first time. The MIS should:

- only produce a report if it **adds value**

- only produce a report for the **people who need them**

- should produce information that is **accurate, presented clearly** and can be **retrieved easily**

- be capable of **real time** information processing

- **eliminate waste**, such as data duplication

- be **flexible** enough to adapt to the changing needs of the organisation or to ad hoc requirements

- be **continually improved**, for example regular user meetings should be held to discuss requirements.

Note: Many of the points which will be discussed in Chapter 8, section 2 on the design of a good performance report are also relevant here and can be referred back to when answering a question on lean MIS.

The 5 Ss

The 5 Ss concept is often associated with lean principles and has the aim of creating a workplace (but more specifically, here, a MIS) which is in order.

5 Ss	Example of application to MIS
Structure (sometimes called **sort**)	The IS should be structured and ordered in such a way so that user-friendly information can be accessed quickly by those who require it and that it fulfil their needs.
Systemise (sometimes called **simplify**)	The system should be arranged for ease of use; for example, at Toyota, key information is communicated to all employees on the factory floor using large television screens. The IS should improve efficiency and accuracy by arranging items for ease of use and eliminating duplication.
Sanitise (sometimes called **scan**)	This could involve removing duplicated data or obsolete data (such as old customers or inventory items that are no longer used) or only producing reports for the people who need them and/or are authorised to receive them.
Standardise	This could involve, for example, establishing an optimum standard for producing output reports and then applying this consistently.

Self-discipline (sometimes called **sustain**)	Motivating employees to continually perform the above four Ss will also continuously improving the information systems.

Student accountant article: visit the ACCA website, www.accaglobal.com, to review the article on 'Lean enterprises and lean information systems'.

4.4 The importance of IS integration

Introduction

Collaboration and **co-ordination** is a vital element of performance management and organisational success. If we take as an example an organisation with a functional structure, the accounting (finance) function, and the management accountants within it, will not work in isolation. Instead, they will:

- **Work with and alongside the other functions** in the organisation as a business partner. For example, they will work with the operations function to establish an appropriate set of KPIs, measure and report performance to those people who need this information in the organisation and externally, control performance by helping to develop solutions to any operational problems or areas for improvement identified.

- Take an active **leadership role** working alongside and with senior management and the CEO to lead key initiatives that support organisational goals, execute and fund strategies set by the CEO and liaise effectively with internal and external stakeholders.

Illustration 5 – Collaboration between operations function and accounting function

The operations function will identify CSFs for its supply chain and may establish that it is critical to achieve a high level of quality, minimal level of waste and to reduce supply chain costs.

The function will use techniques such as TQM, Kaizen, lean and JIT (discussed in Chapter 14) to optimise its performance in these areas.

KPIs will be used to indicate whether or not the CSFs are being achieved and the **finance function will work with the operations function** to establish appropriate KPIs. So, for example:

- Defect/error rate, % product returns, amount spent on warranties will be used in a TQM environment

- Target costs will be used in a Kaizen environment

- Waste measurement and lean techniques will go hand in hand

- Inventory measurement will be important in a JIT environment

- % returns, reuse/recycling of returns will be used to monitor and measure the effectiveness of a reverse logistics strategy.

The above discussion is important in the context of this chapter because it highlights the importance of collaboration and co-ordination between the different areas of the organisation (internal stakeholders) and with external stakeholders (e.g. investors, suppliers and customers) for performance management and organisational success.

If we relate this to our discussion of IS, it is therefore important that IS (and the information produced by them) do not exist in isolation but rather the **IS in the organisation should be connected and integrated**.

Data silos

 A data silo is when data exists in separate areas of the organisation or in separate IS and does not connect up with or integrate with other organisational data or information systems.

The **issues of data silos** are as follows:

- The data silo may result in duplicated information. This is inefficient and therefore costly and it also increases the risk that information will be inaccurate or outdated (or not 'good'). In the context of the accounting function, its role in performance management will be made much more difficult, time consuming, costly and potentially less effective because of these data silos.

- The data in question may be held in just one silo. This creates a barrier to the collaboration and co-ordination that is required for performance management since:

    - Information is inaccessible or invisible to other systems or users, e.g. there is a separate system for accounting, HR, operations etc.

 Illustration 6 – Separate systems in public sector organisations

The NHS (National Health Service) is the publicly funded healthcare system in the UK (United Kingdom). It provides free healthcare at the point of access and, since its inception in 1948, it has often been heralded as the world's best healthcare system.

However, it is not without its problems, one of which is the existence of data silos. Legacy systems combined with a lack of capital available for investment, the complexity of the organisation and concerns about sharing of information and data privacy, have resulted in this data silo issue. The impact of this issue is negative in terms of the quality of patient care, patient outcomes and, on an organisational level, the efficiency and effectiveness of the NHS.

     –   Different parts of the business start to work independently, perhaps prioritising their own needs and objectives at the cost of the organisation's overall mission and objectives (this is dysfunctional behaviour). For example, the operations function may prioritise low cost suppliers but to the detriment of quality, customer satisfaction and long-term performance improvement.

     –   Even if users identify a need to access other information and to co-ordinate with other users, this process will be slow, time consuming and costly.

So how can an organisation **overcome the issue of data silos**? Data silos occur naturally as organisations grow but the problem can be overcome through the **adoption of new technology** and by **changing the organisation culture** and processes to encourage the sharing of information. The good news is that technology now exists, and is available and accessible to organisations, to overcome this issue. Examples of the technology available include **cloud and network technology**, **data warehouses**, **unified corporate databases** and **enterprise resource planning systems**. An important consideration when investing in new technologies is to ask the question as to whether or not the technology will help to address any data silos that exists.

Note: The technologies listed above are discussed in the next section of this chapter. However, it may be helpful to your understanding at this stage to review the illustration below.

> **Illustration 7 – Integration of management accounting information within an overall IS**
>
> Rather than the management accounting information existing in isolation in its own system, it would make sense to integrate the system with all the other separate systems within the organisation (e.g. operations, HR and sales and marketing).
>
> This single system is known as an **Enterprise Resource Planning (EPR) system**. It is an example of a **unified corporate database** and allows users to access the same information, to see an overall picture of performance and helps inform business decisions.
>
> **Note**: Unified corporate databases and ERP systems will be discussed in greater depth in Section 5 and much of what is covered in Section 5 can be used to answer a question on data silos.

4.5 The importance of continuous change

In order to maintain or improve performance in an increasingly competitive and global market, a business needs to continually refine and develop its management accounting and information systems. If not, they will become out of date and will not fit into the current circumstances of the organisation

There are many reasons why the management accounting and information systems need to change. Some example of these reasons are discussed below:

Reason for change	Explanation
New technology	Technology developments should be embraced by the organisation and viewed as an opportunity to better manage and measure performance and as a way to drive competitive advantage (IT developments will be explored in the remainder of this chapter).
Increased competition	More and better information is required to compete successfully in what is often a highly unpredictable and competitive marketplace.
Business growth and/or change in structure	As discussed, many organisations have grown in size. For example, one change is the development of multinational, divisionalised organisations with operations and processing centres in several countries. This has resulted in a need to: – consolidate systems to, say, one type of accounting software – integrate the management accounting system with the organisation's other information systems (ERP systems) – to perhaps consolidate all of the management accounting activities to one site (called a shared service centre).
Customers' expectations	The management accounting and IS must reflect the changing needs of the customer.
Changing expectations of shareholders and other stakeholders	Organisations are now expected to produce a wide range of information to satisfy the diverse needs of its stakeholders. Shareholders are becoming increasingly aware of the need for organisations to demonstrate, for example, good sustainability practices (discussed in Chapter 4). The IS may need to change to capture the information required.
New accounting developments	Developments such as ABC and ABM (Chapter 5) or the use of EMA (Chapter 4) may result in an adaption of the IS to capture and analyse the required information.

Adapting management accounting and information systems for technological developments

Some technological developments will effectively update existing systems and improve their capability. These have been termed **core modernisation tools** and are considered mainstream. Examples include cloud technology and data visualisation (these will be discussed in Section 5).

Other developments will deliver new capabilities, pushing the management accountant's role and the organisation forward. These are referred to as **exponentials** and include, for example, advanced data analytics (section 6). An organisation that is an early adopter of such technologies may gain competitive advantage over its rivals.

Test your understanding 3

Lead times are becoming increasingly important within the clothing industry. An interesting example of a company going against the conventional wisdom is Zara International:

- Zara produces half of its garments in-house, whereas most retailers outsource all production. Although manufacturing in Spain and Portugal has a cost premium of 10 to 15%, local production means the company can react to market changes faster than the competition.

- Instead of predicting months before a season starts what women will want to wear, Zara observes what is selling and what is not and continuously adjusts what it produces on that basis. This is known as a 'design-on-demand' operating model.

- Rather than focusing on economies of scale, Zara manufactures and distributes products in small batches.

- Instead of using outside partners, Zara manages all design, warehousing, distribution, and logistics functions itself.

- The result is that Zara can design, produce, and deliver a new garment to its 600-plus stores worldwide in a mere 15 days.

By comparison, a typical shirt manufacturer may take 30 days just to source fabric and then a further ten days to make the shirt. For some firms overall lead time could be between three and eight months from conception to shelf.

Required:

Comment on the importance of IT systems to Zara's competitive strategy.

5 IT developments influencing management accounting systems

5.1 Introduction

In this section, we will look at the technology driven changes facing organisations today.

The following IT developments will be discussed:

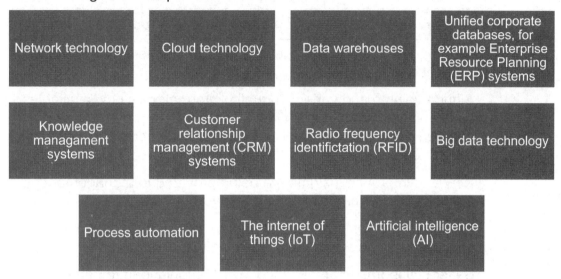

Although you are **not expected to be IT experts**, you should consider that these developments whilst presenting their own risks and challenges for organisations, also **present organisations with the opportunity to improve performance**, for example:

- through their **influence on management accounting systems** (e.g. cloud and network technology)

- by **providing instant access to previously unavailable data** that can be used for benchmarking and control purposes, to help improve organisational performance (e.g. customer relationship management systems).

It is worth noting that although there are many benefits relating to the different IT developments, that different **organisations will have different needs, priorities and budgets and these factors will influence the extent to which the developments are adopted**. For example:

- A small organisation with a functional structure may prioritise investment in network, cloud and unified corporate database technology, to improve efficiency, collaboration and co-ordination.

- A manufacturing organisation may prioritise investment in process automation, where as a service organisation may prioritise a customer relationship management (CRM) system.

Test your understanding 4

Required:

Discuss, with examples, the impact of recent IT developments on management accounting and on business performance.

Implications for managing and measuring performance

There are many implications of these IT developments for performance management and measurement. These include:

- A huge volume and variety of quality information is now available to organisations, often in real-time. This should improve planning, decision-making and control and can help drive competitive advantage.

- New and improved insights are being provided to management as a result of better processing and analysis of data.

- Timely information can be easily accessed by managers and employees in a way that fulfils their individual requirements.

- Better collaboration and sharing, which should lead to better team working within organisations (and across organisations with business partners) and a focus on goal congruence.

Impact on the role of the management accountant

- The role of the management accountant has traditionally been to assemble information and provide some analysis of this information to organisations to help them to plan and control their activities, and to make decisions. Much of this information was financial in nature. IT developments have meant that this traditional role is somewhat redundant with huge amounts of both financial and non-financial information being produced and shared easily in real-time and even analysed to provide some insight into its impact.

- Management accountants, however, should view this as an opportunity and not a threat. Their unique combination of traditional technical accounting skills plus business, people, leadership and digital skills (all underpinned by the ethical code they work within) means that they are well placed to refocus their efforts on the aspects of accountancy that are less easily automated; interpreting and analysing information and providing recommendations. The role of the management accountant is now more as a consultant or advisor to organisations, in relation to strategic development, decision-making and value creation.

Student accountant article: visit the ACCA website, www.accaglobal.com, to review the two articles on 'Developments in IT and the impact on performance management'.

5.2 Network technology

 A **network** is a group of two or more computer systems linked together.

A network should **facilitate the transfer of information** between different parts of the organisation.

Most organisations connect their computers together in local area networks (LANs), enabling them to share data (for example, via email) and to share devices such as printers. Wide area networks (WANs) are used to connect LANs together, so that computer users in one location can communicate with computer users in another location.

Some examples of networks are the **internet**, **intranets** and **extranets**.

Network technology

Internet

One of the best examples of a network is the internet, which connects millions of people all over the world. It is a global system of interconnected networks carrying a vast array of information and resources.

Intranet

This is a private network contained within an organisation. It allows company information and computing resources to be shared among employees.

Extranet

This is a private, secure extension of an Intranet. It allows the organisation to share information with suppliers, customers and other business partners.

Connecting to a network could result in many benefits for performance management. For example, by connecting to the internet an organisation's communication with key stakeholders will be improved and it may be possible to share data with organisations which could assist in a benchmarking exercise.

However, the use of networks by an organisation may provide additional opportunities for the spread of viruses and possibly open the network to hackers.

Note: All of the other developments discussed below will utilise this network technology.

Illustration 9 – The internet and management information

An internet site that allows customers to place orders online can provide the following useful management accounting information:

Data	Use
Customer details	For delivery purposes; also to build up a record of customer interests and purchases.
Product details accessed and products bought	For delivery purposes; also to build up patterns such as products that are often bought together.
Value of products bought	Sales accounting and customer profiling.
Product details accessed no product bought	Other items that the customer might be interested in. Why were they not bought? Has a rival got better prices?
Date of purchase	Seasonal variations; tie in with special offers and advertising campaigns.
Time of purchase	Some websites might be particularly busy at certain times of the day. Why that pattern? Avoid busy times when carrying out web-site maintenance.
Delivery method chosen	Most Internet sellers give a choice of delivery costs and times. Analysis of this information could help the company to increase its profits.

The use of intranets to enhance performance

HI is a large importer of cleaning products; HI has its head office situated in the centre of the capital city. This head office supports its area branches; a branch consists of an area office and a warehouse. The branches are spread geographically throughout the country; a total of seven area branches are supported.

Currently each HI area office and warehouse supports and supplies its own dealers with the required products. When stocks become low they place a Required Stock Form (RSF) with head office. On receipt of the RSF, head office despatch the goods from their central warehouse to the appropriate area office. When the central warehouse becomes low on any particular item(s) HI will raise purchase orders and send them to one of their many international suppliers.

Typically, each area office has its own stock recording system, running on locally networked personal computer systems (PCs). RSFs are e-mailed to head office.

Required:

How would the introduction of an Intranet enhance performance within HI?

Solution:

An Intranet could provide an excellent opportunity for HI to link all the areas in a number of ways: i.e. allowing access to a central database would be a substantial improvement on the current system, where updates are faxed or e-mailed to head office. This may possibly lead to the development of an integrated database system.

An automatic stock replenishment system could be introduced for the branches, replacing RSFs. If some branches were short of specific items and other branches had ample stocks, then movement between branches may be possible. Currently head office may order goods from suppliers when the organisation has sufficient stocks internally.

Dissemination of best practice throughout the organisation can be encouraged and savings in terms of printing and distributing paper based manuals, catalogues and handbooks. All the current internal documentation can easily be maintained and distributed.

The Intranet would enable the establishment of versatile and standard methods of communication throughout the company.

The Intranet could encourage group or shared development, currently several area offices have their own IT systems working independently on very similar projects.

An Intranet could also enable automatic transfer of information and data i.e. the quarterly figures could be circulated. Monthly returns of business volumes could be calculated on an as required basis. Information can be provided to all in a user-friendly format.

5.3 Cloud technology

 Cloud computing is defined as the delivery of on-demand computing resources – everything from applications to data centres – over the internet.

The basic idea and application of cloud computing sees users log in to an account in order access, manage and process files and software via remote servers hosted on the internet. This replaces the traditional method of owning and running software locally on a computer or networked server.

There are two main types of cloud setups:

- **Public cloud** hosted by a third-party company. Specialist companies sell their cloud computing services to anyone over the public internet who wishes to purchase them.

- **Private cloud** sees IT services provided over a private infrastructure, typically for the use of a single organisation. They are usually managed internally also.

Illustration 10 – Amazon, cloud computing services

Amazon's market value broke the $1 trillion mark in 2018. A large contributor to this was the continued growth of Amazon Web Services (AWS). They are the market leader in cloud computing, controlling a third of the market in an industry expected to be worth over $145bn in 2022. Their customers range from individuals to government agencies.

Significantly, their AWS business supports operations of other core areas of Amazon's business including e-commerce, Amazon prime video & music and the Amazon home assistant. This is a gateway to the 'internet of things' another marketplace projected to grow significantly in the coming years.

Features of cloud computing

Advantages	Disadvantages
Flexibility and scalability – Cloud computing allows simple and frequent upgrades allowing access to the latest systems developments. A company doesn't become laden with expensive hardware and software that quickly becomes obsolete. This allows organisations to evolve and change, to adapt to new opportunities and working practices.	**Organisational change** – Working methods and roles need to be modified to incorporate a move to cloud computing. It may also lead to job losses, primarily in IT support and maintenance roles.
Cost efficient – Limited IT maintenance costs and reduced costs of IT hardware, sees capital expenses and fixed costs become operating expenses. Cloud technology also allows pay as you go computing, with charges based on what a company actually needs.	**Contract management** –The cloud provider will immediately become a very significant supplier. Managing this relationship, monitoring performance and ensuring contractual obligations will introduce new challenges and costs.
Security – Cloud services like any outsource provider are specialists. The security and integrity of their systems is fundamental to their business model and will be a strategic priority. Disaster recovery and backups are built in.	**Security, privacy & compliance** – Whilst cloud providers will be specialists, they are bigger targets for malicious agents. This can threaten the security of sensitive information. Additionally compliance with data regulations is placed largely in the hands of a third party.

Advantages	Disadvantages
Flexible working – The increase in remote and home working is supported by cloud computing and the ability to access your 'desktop' from any location.	**Reliance** – More so than with a standard outsource arrangement, the reliability of the cloud service provider is essential. Often the entire provision of information systems fundamental to the operation of a business is passed to this third party.
Environment – Less waste from disposal of obsolete technology. More efficient use of scarce resources.	

Illustration 11 – Hacking into a public cloud

A Chinese hacking group nicknamed 'Red Apollo' launched one of the largest ever sustained global cyber espionage campaigns. Rather than targeting companies directly, it targeted cloud service providers, attempting to use their networks to spread spying tools to a wide number of companies in 15 different countries. This indirect approach demonstrates a new level of maturity in cyber espionage, and is increasingly common.

Using cloud technology for management accounting systems

In terms of **performance management** cloud based management accounting systems will allow managers to access performance management information:

- anytime using a laptop, smartphone or tablet

- that is relevant to their own needs, for example a mixed visual and numeric output of timely, relevant and accurate information

- that can be shared with other managers across the organisation and at different levels and perhaps with external stakeholders, thus enhancing collaboration and improving the speed and quality of decision making.

However, despite the advantages of using cloud technology for management accounting systems the realisable cost savings and flexibility need to be carefully considered.

5.4 Data warehouses

 A data warehouse is a:

- first and foremost a **database:** data is combined from multiple and varied sources (internal and external) into one comprehensive, secure and easily manipulated data store.

- **data extraction tool:** data can be extracted from the database to meet the individual user's needs.

- **decision support system:** data mining is used to analyse the data and unearth unknown patterns or correlations in data.

Advantages and disadvantages of data warehouses

The advantages and disadvantages of data warehouses are as follows:

Advantages	Disadvantages
• Reduced duplication since data should only be stored in one place.	• Cost of buying, developing and maintaining the system and of staff training.
• Reduced storage of data and hence reduced storage cost.	• System failure will be more catastrophic.
• Improved data integrity due to additional focus to ensure that this one set of data is 'good'.	• A security breach could be more catastrophic.
• Flexibility to meet individual needs. For example, allows extraction of relevant data only, in the right format and in the right amount of detail.	
• Aligned across the entire organisation.	
• Instant access to data leading to quicker decisions.	
• May be able to link to suppliers' and customers' systems.	

Illustration 12 – Influence of IT on Sainsbury

Sainsbury, the UK supermarket giant, has a data warehouse with information about purchases made by the company's eight million customers.

Transactional details are tied to specific customers through the company's Nectar loyalty programme, producing valuable information about buying habits.

Initial analysis of the information quickly showed Sainsbury's how ineffective its traditional mass-mailing approaches were – where large numbers of coupons were widely distributed in an attempt to get customers through its doors. Rather than buying more, many customers would cherry-pick the specials and go to its competitors for other items. This meant many advertising campaigns were running at a loss.

Since those initial findings, a concerted focus on timely data analysis and relevant marketing has helped Sainsbury to design far more effective direct marketing campaigns based on customers' actual purchasing habits.

In one campaign designed to increase the value of customers' shopping baskets, Sainsbury's analysed purchases and identified the product category from which each customer purchased most frequently. A coupon for that category would then be sent, along with five other coupons for areas in which it was hoping to boost sales – to encourage customers to buy other types of products. The response rate was 26%, a tremendous amount in retail.

Data mining

This is the analysis of data contained within a data warehouse to unearth relationships between them.

Illustration 13 – Data mining relationships

Data mining results may include:

- **Associations** – when one event can be correlated to another, for example beer purchasers buy peanuts a certain percentage of the time.

- **Sequences** – one event leading to another event, for example a rug purchase followed by a purchase of matching curtains.

- **Classifications** – profiles of customers who make purchases can be set up.

These relationships can be used to help an organisation focus on the things that the customer enjoys and desires. Marketing can be targeted to a group of customers and the organisation will focus on the more profitable product offerings.

5.5 Unified corporate databases

 A unified corporate database is an **organisational wide database**. It allows all users to access the same information, to see an overall picture of performance and helps inform business decisions.

Note: It addresses the issue of data silos (discussed in section 4.4).

Enterprise resource planning (ERP) systems

An ERP system is an **example of a unified corporate database**. Rather than data existing in isolation in different parts of the business, it integrates the data from many aspects of operations (for example, manufacturing, inventory, distribution, invoicing and management accounting) and support functions (such as human resource management and marketing) into **one single system**.

Benefits to the organisation:

- Senior managers have access to all of the data in one place, rather than information being spread among separate systems.

- Aids the management decision making process due to decision support features.

- Assists the free flow of information, often in or close to real-time, between all functions and improved communication and collaboration between departments.

- Identification and planning of the use of resources across the organisation to ensure customers' needs are fulfilled.

- Less duplication of data, which means that less time is wasted entering information into two or more systems and reconciling information from different systems.

- Can be extended to incorporate supply chain management (SCM) and customer relationship management (CRM) software, thus helping to manage connections outside the organisation.

Software companies like SAP, Oracle, PeopleSoft and Baan have specialised in the provision of ERP systems across many different industries.

How ERP systems impact the role of the management accountant

The introduction of an ERP system has the potential to have a significant impact on the work of management accountants.

- The use of an ERP system causes a substantial reduction in the gathering and processing of routine information by management accountants.

- Instead of relying on management accountants to provide them with information, managers are able to access the system to obtain the information they require directly via a suitable electronic access medium.

- An ERP system performs routine tasks that not so long ago were viewed as an essential part of the daily routines of management accountants, for example perpetual inventory valuation.

- Therefore, if management accountants are not to be diminished then it is of necessity that they should seek to expand their roles within their organisations:

  - Management accountants should view this as an opportunity.

  - The emphasis of their work will be less on the routine assembly of information and more on analysing the information to gain insights that will help to develop solutions that will impact strategic plans, budgets and performance measures.

  - Management accountants will no longer work largely in isolation but will work with others from across the organisation to drive organisational transformation that improves performance.

5.6 Knowledge management systems

What is knowledge?

Knowledge is an important organisational resource. There is a difference between:

- **Data** – raw, unprocessed facts

- **Information** – processed, organised and meaningful data (should be 'good' information)

- **Knowledge** – an application of a cognitive process to the information so that it becomes useful.

There are **two broad types** of knowledge:

- **Explicit knowledge** – is knowledge that the company knows it has, for example customer information.

- **Tacit knowledge** – is personal knowledge and expertise held by people within the organisation that has not been formally documented, for example knowledge gained through the experiences of employees within the organisation.

What is knowledge management?

Knowledge management is the process for the acquisition, sharing, retention and utilisation of knowledge.

In what is increasingly referred to as a knowledge-based economy, it is evident that sufficient management attention should be given to this valuable organisational asset.

Organisations hold a huge volume and variety of information in different systems and people and therefore a knowledge management strategy is needed to unlock the value of this asset and improve organisational performance.

An important part of this strategy will involve a technology-based solution (a knowledge management system).

Knowledge management systems (KMS)

IT is seen as a key element in the solution to effective knowledge management.

 Knowledge management systems refer to any type of IT that helps to capture, store, retrieve and use knowledge to enhance the knowledge management process.

There are **two categories** of KMS:

- **Codified based systems** – Include formal, technical knowledge such as tax rules or law.

- **Personalisation based systems** – Employees input their knowledge so that this can be shared with others within the organisations.

Examples of KMS include:

- **Groupware** – refers to technology designed to help people collaborate. Examples include email, file sharing technology and video/audio conferencing.

- **Intranets and extranets** (as discussed in Section 5.2).

- **Data warehouses and data mining** (as discussed in Section 5.4).

- **Decision support systems (DSS)** (as discussed in Section 4.2).

- **Content management systems** – these make it easier to create content (for example, using templates), to edit content, to track changes allowing for version control and allow for collaborative and parallel work on content.

- **Document management systems** – often part of a content management system. They assist with, for example, the indexing and retrieval of documents.

The role of the management accountant

The knowledge management systems discussed (such as data warehouses) may actually result in a lack of focus in knowledge management as most of the systems do not help distinguish data and information from useful and relevant knowledge.

Therefore, although technology is an important part of knowledge management, it may simply increase the volume and management of unfocused data and analysed information if **appropriate people skills and organisational processes focused on the conversion of this data/information into knowledge are not established**.

It would seem appropriate for the training of management accountants to change to reflect the increased importance of managing the knowledge resource within the organisation.

Management accountants need to be trained not just in technology-based approaches to knowledge management, but also people-based and process-based approaches. They will play an important role in knowledge management through:

- making explicit the link between effective knowledge management and improved organisational performance
- acting as a knowledge champion
- focusing on the better utilisation of an organisation's existing knowledge base.

The implications of knowledge management for performance management

Knowledge and performance form a closed loop since:

- the more knowledge the people in the organisation have, the better they perform by applying this knowledge to their work
- the organisation's people then learn from this performance increasing knowledge further.

This drives continuous performance improvement.

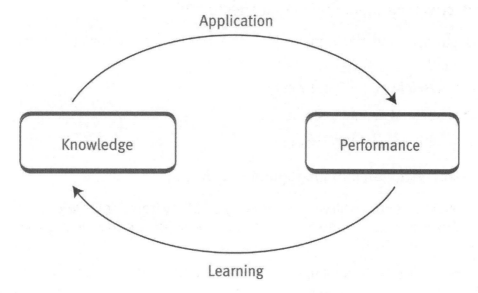

Link between knowledge management and performance management

The link is three fold:

- Performance measures (using appropriate KPIs) and benchmarking shows where performance of a team or unit is weak or strong.

- Targets should be set based on the findings of this exercise. The targets should be achievable but go beyond the current knowledge of the team or unit, encourage them to seek the knowledge to deliver the goal.

- Knowledge management is the enabler and helps to close the gap. The strong performers (as a source of knowledge) can help the weaker performers (as a user of the knowledge). Knowledge management systems can assist with the process of closing the gap.

5.7 Customer relationship management (CRM) systems

What is customer relationship management?

 Customer relationship management (CRM) is the process the organisation uses to:

- identify, attract and win new customers

- retain existing customers

- entice past customers back.

Customer relationship management systems

 Customer relationship management (CRM) systems refer to the technology that is used to gather the information needed to achieve the above (i.e. CRM).

CRM systems range from simple spreadsheets and databases containing information about the customer to more complex online applications which are fully integrated with the organisation's other systems.

Illustration 14 – Data use and CRM

By harnessing technology and building a profile on customers, even small independent restaurants are incorporating data driven **customer relationship management (CRM)** in driving repeat custom.

Rather than taking a booking and it being a one-time only transaction, a restaurant will collect data such as an email address and/or phone number when taking this booking. This will then be used to create a new customer profile.

In addition, they will look at what the type of booking it is i.e. couple, group, family as well as the time and date of the booking. They may even try to find out if it is a special occasion which could also be used for future marketing.

The **data** collection continues as once the profile is established what food you order and the drinks you have will also be added to the profile giving them an insight into what you like and what in future may prompt you to return.

Then with all this data collected if the restaurant notices that you are a fairly regular customer and you haven't visited for some time.
A marketing email can be generated; this can be tailored to hit the specific data held in your profile. For instance if every time you visit you order the same starter the email may contain a picture of this dish to whet your appetite as well as offering a complimentary starter on your next visit. This may well be enough to convince you to make that next booking.

The **building blocks of a typical CRM system** are as follows:

- Most CRM systems are based on a database (often in the cloud and maybe integrated with social media) that collects information about the organisation's customers.

- Appropriate tools are used to unlock the value and to analyse the information in the database. Any gap between current performance and desired performance (perhaps established through a benchmarking exercise) should be identified.

- A performance improvement strategy is established for applying this analysis to better meet the needs of current and prospective customers. Relevant KPIs will be set.

- The CRM system should allow collection of ongoing performance data to ensure that the strategy is effective and that any necessary control action can be taken.

Illustration 15 – Possible features and benefits of a CRM system

A CRM system can include the following features:

Feature	Benefits
A central database that is accessible by all employees to view and update customer data.	Improved customer service, loyalty and retention.
Analysis of customer data including customer segmentation (existing and potential customers).	Improved marketing campaigns through customised targeting.
Customer web-based ordering.	Reduced order cost and customer service cost.
Identifying and tracking potential customers.	A wider customer base and more focused prospect tracking.
Reports generated with up-to-date information including revenue forecasting and trend analysis.	Better and more timely decision making.

5.8 Radio frequency identification (RFID)

Organisations can use small radio receivers to tag items and hence to keep track of their assets. It can be used for a variety of purposes, for example:

- to track inventory to retail stores

- to tag livestock on farms

- to track the location of doctors in a hospital.

Illustration 16 – RFID

Many clothing retailers began the phased rollout of item-level radio frequency identification (RFID) tags 20 or so years ago following extensive testing of the technology. Stock accuracy has improved and stores and customers have commented on the more consistent availability of sizes in the pilot departments.

The tags allow staff to carry out stocktaking 20 times faster than bar code scanners by passing an RFID reader over goods. At the end of each day, stock on the shop floor will be scanned and the data collected will be compared with information in a central database containing each store's stock profile, to determine what products need to be replaced. This has led to improved sales through greater product availability.

The introduction of RFID can bring about a number of **benefits**:

- Information on the location and quantity of items can be provided in real time meaning that less time is spent looking for items.

- This information should be more accurate since it will be less reliant on physical checks.

- Performance reporting should improve due to the provision of real time information.

- Control should be easier. This is firstly due to the provision of real time information and, secondly, since the location and quantity of items will be known, the risk of theft and obsolescence will be reduced.

The benefits must outweigh the costs. **Costs** will include the cost of hardware, software, ongoing running and maintenance costs and training costs.

5.9 Process automation

 Process automation is the technology enabled automation of business processes previously carried out by human workers. This can be entire processes or elements therein.

Repetitive, low skilled manual tasks (such as data entry) that add minimal value to the end users of the information are most likely to be automated by process automation software. This:

- is done quickly,

- to a consistent and high quality standard and

- without errors and with less wastage.

This will reduce costs and free up the time and resource of human workers for higher level, and arguably more rewarding and more interesting, value adding activities.

Developments in technology are now enabling **more complex activities** to be automated and process automation is therefore becoming increasingly significant to an organisation.

 Illustration 17 – Process automation

Traditional process automation – The traditional idea of process automation is that of a machine carrying out a simple repetitive task, replacing a job that would have been done by hand or in a semi-automated fashion. This type of automation is everywhere and has driven industrialisation, through the ability to produce ever higher volumes of products, with fewer problems and at less cost.

Modern process automation – Increasingly automation and process automation are focusing upon complex business areas, which were previously thought to be beyond the limits of technology.

Big data and the internet of things generate huge amounts of data; data analytics transforms this into useful information that supports artificial intelligence (see the discussion that follows) and machine learning. Essentially process automation is becoming smarter and can make decisions using reasoning, language and learned behaviour.

Illustration 18 – Process automation and customer contact centres

Customer contact centres are an area that many businesses are keen to automate. It is a business function deemed to be relatively low skilled in comparison to other business processes, but is an area that customers value so must be handled with care.

This was evidenced by the wave of contact centres being moved overseas to countries with lower labour costs in the 1990s/2000s driven by the aim of achieving cost savings. Customers were however, often dissatisfied with the level of service received resulting in a large number of companies ultimately bringing their contact centres back to the home country.

Companies were still keen to realise cost savings in this area but required a new approach to doing so. Developments in technology have led to significant improvements in process automation, contact centres are now typically heavily automated using the technology in conjunction with humans. The use of automation has been designed to use workers time more efficiently, through redesigning and streamlining processes as well as fully automating simple tasks and processes.

Developments in voice recognition technology and the ability of artificial intelligence allows contact centre calls to be answered robotically, they will typically ask the nature of the call, then place this on the right track. Many calls can be handled fully autonomously for instance making payments or tracing orders. Callers who do require a contact centre operative will then begin the security process, this will then interrogate the system to bring the customer and case information up on the operatives screen before they even speak.

Data capture and analytics are also used to monitor and understand call types, monitoring for new or emerging trends and suspicious or potentially fraudulent activity. This will enable workers to be more prepared and trained specifically to deal with high risk call types.

All of these improvements have led to both cost savings and service improvements through more targeted and efficient use of contact centre workers time, seeing them specifically used on activities where value can be added.

5.10 Internet of things

 The internet of things describes the network of smart devices with inbuilt software and connectivity to the internet allowing them to constantly monitor and exchange data.

They are an increasingly significant area of big data (section 6).

Illustration 19 – Devices connected to the internet of things (IoT)

Essentially anything with an on off switch can become a 'smart' device and be connected over the internet. This allows them to talk to us, applications and each other, which is at the core of their functionality.

Common devices currently connected as part of the internet of things include:

- **Smart meters** and home control devices which allow control of heating, electricity and hot water.

- **Doorbells and security;** these talk to your smart device. A live connection is established if the doorbell is pressed or the motion sensors activated, allowing immediate interaction.

- **Wearable tech** such as smart watches and fitness trackers capture and record an array of data to monitor and record your fitness.

- **Home appliances** such as smart lights, fridges, washing machines, ovens etc... the connectivity built in allows remote access and control of these devices, for instance turnings your lights on if you're out at night can be done using a smart phone.

- **Cars;** the computer systems used to control cars are increasingly sophisticated. They track and monitor thousands of parameters on every journey. This capability is central in the continued pursuit of autonomous vehicles.

- **Transport and infrastructure;** smart motorways are a common feature in many countries with traffic sensors monitoring the flow and build-up of traffic and responding to provide extra lanes or activate temporary speed limits.

- **Manufacturing equipment and plant;** monitoring of business assets facilitates efficient utilisation, it allows continual live feedback to track performance and flag maintenance requirements earlier.

The ability to make virtually any asset a business owns and operates into a 'smart' asset by building in some relevant sensors and internet connectivity can lead to some very useful data. It should facilitate better business planning, resource allocation and will help to optimise processes, minimise expenditure and give advanced warning of potential issues.

Illustration 20 – The internet of things at Rolls-Royce

Rolls-Royce, manufacturer of aircraft engines, has embraced the capabilities of the **internet of things** and **big data** and this has fundamentally changed their business model.

Rolls-Royce engines are manufactured with hundreds of sensors built in throughout the engine unit. These sensors produce constant live data which is fed back to systems engineers at centres across the globe. Any anomalies are immediately flagged and the engineers can make an assessment from the vast array of data available as to the best course of action. Preventative maintenance can be scheduled much earlier than would ordinarily be possible and can be planned for the most convenient and cost effective time and location.

AI is anticipated to replace the human intervention over time as its capability and reliability improves, the stakes are very high when it comes to aircraft engines so there is no room for error.

This new way of monitoring the performance of their engines has facilitated design improvements for new models and has led to an entirely new business model in how Rolls-Royce 'sell' their engines. Customers are now charged per hour of use of an engine and have a package called total care that covers all maintenance and upkeep of the engines.

The growth in the **internet of things** often termed '**smart technology**' is fuelled by improvements in broadband connectivity and the development of 4G communication networks. As governments look to roll out the next generation 5G networks, connectivity will be improved further. Coupled with the fact that people and businesses are increasingly comfortable with the idea and operation of this smart technology, it is anticipated that the internet of things will continue grow, becoming increasingly central to how we live and work as new and innovative applications for the technology emerge all the time.

5.11 Artificial intelligence

Artificial Intelligence (AI) is an area of computer science that emphasises the creation of intelligent machines that work and react like human beings.

What is Artificial Intelligence (AI)?

A common definition from Kaplan and Haenlein describes AI as a **"system's ability to correctly interpret external data, to learn from such data, and to use those learnings to achieve specific goals and tasks through flexible adaptation".** This is often considered in the context of human-type robotics but reaches much further than this, and is set to transform the way we live and work.

An **algorithm** is a sequence of instructions to perform a computation or solve a problem.

The term algorithm includes simpler sets of rules as well as more advanced **AI or machine learning code**.

Early applications of AI included expert systems (as discussed in Section 4.2).

Some of the more advanced activities and skills AI can now master, and therefore present huge opportunity for developers and companies alike, include:

- Voice recognition

- Planning

- Learning

- Problem solving.

 Illustration 21 – AI

Companies such as **Apple** and **Amazon** have developed and marketed voice recognition systems, either to be built into an existing product (such as Apple with its **Siri** system) or developed new products whose main function is voice recognition (such as Amazon and '**Alexa**').

A further simple example is that of Facebook, and its process of recommending new friends for users to connect with.

There are many, more complex examples of AI, but a common factor to both the simple and the more involved is machine learning.

Machine learning

Machine learning is a **subset of AI** where effectively **AI computer code is built to mimic how the human brain works**.

The machines can **'learn' from their experience**, rather like humans do and therefore provide **more accurate output than traditional AI** which has a general level of intelligence but can't think and learn like humans.

It essentially uses probability based on past experiences through data, events and connections between events. The computer then applies this learning to a given situation to give a fact driven plausible outcome. If the conclusion the computer reaches turns out to be incorrect this will act to add more experience and enhance its understanding further, so in future the same mistake will not be repeated.

Essentially machine learning algorithms detect patterns and learn how to make predictions and recommendations rather than following explicit programming instruction. The algorithms themselves then adapt to new data and experiences to improve their function over time.

Illustration 22 – AI and accountancy

AI and **machine learning** are anticipated to lead to significant impacts on the future of accountancy. **Process automation** as discussed above, will be enhanced by AI enabling automated reasoning making automation more flexible and capable of dealing with complexity.

AI enables computers and machines to exhibit higher level, human style learning. A system can interpret data correctly and over a period of time continually learn to interpret data better by understanding the differences between its interpretations and the actual outcomes.

Although AI techniques such as machine learning are not new, and the pace of change is fast, widespread adoption in business and accounting is still in the relatively early stages.

Increasingly, we are seeing systems that are producing outputs that far exceed the accuracy and consistency of those produced by humans. In the short to medium term, AI brings many opportunities for accountants to improve their efficiency, provide more insight and deliver more value to businesses. In the longer term, AI brings opportunities for much more radical change, as systems increasingly carry out decision-making tasks currently done by humans.

AI, no doubt, will contribute to substantial improvements across all areas of accounting, equipping accountants with powerful new capabilities, as well as leading to the automation of many tasks and decisions.

Examples include:

- Using machine learning to code accounting entries and improve on the accuracy of rules-based approaches, enabling **greater automation** of processes

- Improving **fraud detection** through more sophisticated, machine learning models of 'normal' activities and better prediction of fraudulent activities

- Using machine learning based **predictive models** to forecast revenues

- Improved analysis of unstructured data, including contracts and emails.

Despite the opportunities that AI brings, it does not replicate **human intelligence**. The strengths and limits of this different form of intelligence must be recognised, and users need to build an understanding of the best ways for humans and computers to work together.

6 Big data

6.1 What is big data?

There are several definitions of big data. The most common refer to:

 Extremely large collections of data that may be analysed to reveal patterns, trends and associations.

 Data collections so large that conventional methods of storing and processing that data will not work.

The ability to harness these vast amounts of data will transform our ability to understand the world and will lead to huge advances, for example, in understanding customer behaviour, foiling terrorist attacks, preventing diseases and pinpointing marketing efforts.

Organisations may view the ability to extract valuable information from big data as a strategic capability and perhaps even a CSF. Extracting the value from this information will, however, require investment in technologies, processes and governance.

Illustration 23 – Big data in everyday life

The sheer volume of data we produce on a daily basis is vast and increasing all the time. It largely goes unnoticed as much of it we produce incidentally as we live our lives. Yet companies are desperate to collect this data as they hope to gain unique insights and information that could deliver a crucial advantage over their rivals.

If you consider a hypothetical morning routine for instance; woken up by your smartphone alarm, you pick it up to silence it before having a look at emails or messages received overnight.

Realising its a little cold you ask your smart home assistant to turn the heating up a few degrees and maybe even turn the lights on. As it's the weekend you decide to turn the TV on, digital of course, constantly firing data back to the service provider. What programme are you watching, how long do you watch for? Which adverts do you watch?

Next up you decide to have a quick browse on social media, a few likes and shares, time spent watching videos and clicking on an interesting advert or two, all adds a little more to this 'gold mine' of data.

So without even leaving bed we have already generated multiple types of data. Not to mention the smart meter that is monitoring the power usage of all this technology and continually harvesting this data.

A quick drive to the shops will see the computer used to control all modern cars collect a wide array of data about the performance and condition of the car, both the cars sat-nav and your smart phone will be communicating data about your location and what the driving conditions are like on the roads you travel down. Monitors in traffic lights and in the roads themselves as well as cameras along the way will also track vehicles passing with data being used for traffic monitoring and surveillance.

You then pull up and park, the car park records your number plate and updates its information on the number of available spaces.

As you enter the shop your footfall is logged, the way we navigate the store, what causes us to stop and pick up certain items, all of this is of huge value to retailers so increasing attention is devoted to trying to capture this data to gain valuable insight.

Our card payment is logged by the provider as we pay for the basket of shopping, the contents of which is recorded and matched to our loyalty card profile which contains all of our shopping history as well as our profile info. This can be used to better understand customers, their habits and how they may be changing, what people want and when they buy it, what was the weather like when these purchases were made? And did this influence your choices?

Data on stock movements will also be generated, which is vital to the supply chain and inventory management systems of stores; these are often almost entirely automated.

So from this simple example, without any deliberate actions or specific intent a surprisingly large amount of different data has been generated by one individual. If you multiply this across billions of different people doing their own morning routine, the result is a truly vast amount of data.

6.2 The characteristics of big data – the 5Vs

Big data is **characterised** by the 5Vs

Volume Considers the amount of data fed into the organisation	• Does the organisation have the resources available to store and manage this data? • Or does it have the financial resources required to invest in or upgrade IT/IS?
Velocity Considers the speed that data is fed into the organisation	• Are systems able to capture and process 'real time' data? • Does the organisation have the skills to provide timely analysis of this data?
Variety Considers the various formats of data received	• Are systems compatible and capable of accepting various forms of data? • Legally, is the data owned by the organisation or by the third party?
Veracity Considers the reliability of the data being received	• Can the organisation challenge data received from third parties? • Is the data received fully representative of the whole data population?
Value Considers the potential for data to add value to the organisation (i.e. cost must be less than benefit)	• Can the organisation harness the potential value of all of the volumes of fast-moving data of different variety and veracity? • For example, using big data tools to improve efficiency, identify new opportunities, provide customers with better products and services and predict future patterns of behaviour.

Illustration 24 – Volume and big data

Organisations now hold huge volumes of data. For example:

- A **supermarket** will have a data store of all purchases made, when and where they were made, how they were paid for and the use of coupons via loyalty cards swiped at the checkout.

- An **online retailer** will have a data store of every product looked at and bought and every page visited.

- **Mobile phone providers** will have a data store of texts, voice mails, calls made, browsing habits and location.

- **Social media companies**, such as Facebook, will have a data store of all the postings an individual makes (and where they were made), photos posted and contacts.

In order to perform meaningful analysis of this volume of data, organisations will require large investment, new skills and deliberate focus on big data.

Illustration 25 – Variety and big data

Big data can include much more than simply financial information. It includes non-financial data, other organisational data which is operational in nature, as well as other internal and external information.

This data can be both structured and unstructured in nature:

- **Structured data**: Deliberately produced and collected for a specific purpose and therefore exhibits a clear, standard structure. For example, a bank will hold a record of all receipts and payments (date, amount and source) for a customer.

- **Unstructured data**: Captured passively without a clear purpose. Its format is non-standard and highly variable. For example, social media posts and 'likes'.

Test your understanding 5

Facebook

Facebook was launched in February 2004 and now has over 2 billion active monthly users. This includes over 80 million fake profiles. Every day 500,000 new users are added as the social media site's growth continues.

Every 60 seconds Facebook's users upload over 100,000 photographs, post over 250,000 status updates and generate over 4 million "likes". In total, this creates 4 petabytes of new data every day.

Facebook uses sophisticated analytical tools to measure this data to create a detailed insight into the activity of its users. This allows their advertisers to target specific audiences using precise segmentation tools.

In addition to analysing this internal data, Facebook also has the capability to identify other websites that a user has visited by tracking cookies located on their individual device. Computer IP addresses and mobile phone tracking technology can even identify a user's location.

As a result of this focused advertising strategy almost 1% of users that view an advert will usually click on the links provided and visit the corresponding website. Approximately 20% of all website visits in USA now come via Facebook.

This success creates over $1 million of advertising revenue for the company every three months. Facebook is now one of the ten most valuable companies in the world.

Required:

Using the 5Vs of big data, explain the challenges that big data creates for Facebook.

6.3 The impact of big data on performance management and measurement

Understanding the potential value of data and its significance to an organisation presents a real opportunity to gain unique insight. This can be used to improve performance management and measurement and potentially gain competitive advantage over rivals.

Business consultants McKinsey, summarised the following benefits an organisation can realise from effective big data management:

- **Fresh insight and understanding** – Seeing underlying patterns through the intelligent use of data can reveal patterns and insight into how a business operates, revealing issues that they may not have known existed.

- **Performance improvement** – Data, processed and sorted into relevant management information in real time, can lead to significant operational gains and improved decision making and resource utilisation.

- **Market segmentation and customisation** – Refining customer groups into ever more specific segments and understanding the want and needs of those groups can lead to increased personalisation and customisation of products and services.

- **Decision making** – Real time information that is relevant can lead to faster decisions and decisive advantage over competitors.

- **Innovation** – Existing products can be improved from understanding the features and elements that customers enjoy and use. This can also lead to the development of whole new products.

- **Risk management** – Risk management and control are vital in the effective running of any organisation. The use of data can enhances all stages of the risk management process.

> **Illustration 26 – Examples of how big data is used**
>
> - **Consumer facing organisations** monitor social media activity to gain insight into customer behaviour and preferences. This source can also be used to identify and engage brand advocates and detractors, and assess responsiveness to advertising campaigns and promotions.
>
> - **Sports teams** can use data of past fixtures to track tactics, player formations, injuries and results to inform future team strategies.
>
> - **Manufacturing companies** can monitor data from their equipment to determine usage and wear. This allows them to predict the optimal replacement cycle.
>
> - **Financial institutions** such as banks and insurance companies use data analytics for fraud analysis whilst credit card companies use analytics to manage collection.

- **Politicians** are using social media analytics to establish where they have to campaign the hardest to win the next election.

- **Educational institutions** use data from student tests and assessments to reveal patterns and performance levels, helping to adapt courses and teaching methods.

- **Humanitarian agencies**, such as the United Nations, use phone data to understand population movements during relief operations and outbreaks of disease, meaning they can allocate resources more efficiently and identify areas at risk of new disease outbreaks.

More examples of big data in the real world

UPS's delivery vehicles are equipped with sensors which monitor data on speed, direction, braking performance and other mechanical aspects of the vehicle. This information is then used to optimise maintenance schedules and improve efficiency of delivery routes saving time, money and reducing wastage.

Data from the vehicles is combined with customer data, GPS information and data concerning the normal behaviour of delivery drivers. Using this data to optimise vehicle performance and routes has resulted in several significant improvements:

- Over 15 million minutes of idling time were eliminated in one year. This saved 103,000 gallons of fuel.

- During the same year 1.7 million miles of driving was eliminated, saving 183,000 gallons of fuel.

It is widely reported that **Walmart (Asda)** tracks data on over 60% of adults in the US. Data gathered includes online and in store purchasing pattern, Twitter interactions and trends, weather reports and major events. This data, according to the company, ensures a highly personalised customer experience. Walmart detractors criticise the company's data collection as a breach of human rights and believe the company uses the data to make judgements and conclusions on personal information such as sexual orientation, political view and even intelligence levels.

Tesco has sophisticated sensors installed on all refrigeration units to monitor the temperature at regular intervals and to send the information over the internet to a central data warehouse. The data collected is used to identify units that are operating at temperatures that are too low (resulting in energy wastage) or too high (resulting in potential stock obsolescence and a safety risk). Engineers can monitor the data remotely and can then visit the store to rectify any problem that is identified. Previously, store managers may have overlooked a problem or only identified a problem once it had escalated into something more serious.

Netflix has over 100 million users worldwide. The company uses information gathered from analysis of viewing habits to inform decisions on which shows to invest in. Analysing past viewing figures and understanding viewer populations and the shows they are likely to watch allows the analysts to predict likely viewing figures before a show has even aired. This can help to determine if the show is a viable investment.

Test your understanding 6

MC is a mobile phone network provider, offering mobile phones and services on a range of different tariffs to customers across Europe. The company enjoyed financial success until three years ago but increasing competitive pressure has led to a recent decline in sales. There has also been an increase in the level of complaints regarding the customer service provided, and the company's churn rate (number of customers leaving the company within a given time frame) is at an all-time high.

Required:

Discuss how big data could help drive the strategic direction of MC company.

6.4 Risks associated with big data

As discussed, big data has the potential to positively impact performance management and measurement. However, it also presents a number of risks and challenges.

- The **availability of skills** to use big data systems, which is compounded by the fact that many of the systems are rapidly developing and support is not always easily and readily available. There is also an increasing need to combine data analysis skills with a deep understanding of the industry being analysed and this need is not always recognised.

- The **security of data** is a major concern in the majority of organisations and if the organisation lacks the resources to manage data then there is likely to be a greater risk of leaks and losses. There can be a risk to the data protection of organisations as they collect a greater range of data from increasingly personal sources (for example, Facebook). Current laws and regulations on the storage of personal information must be complied with to avoid legal action and/or reputational damage.

- It is important to recognise that just because something can be measured, this does not necessarily mean it should be. There is a risk that **valuable time is spent measuring relationships that have no organisational value**.

- **Incorrect data** (poor veracity) may result in incorrect conclusions being made. For example, data collected from social media may not be accurate.

- The nature of much of the data means that there is a risk that it will become **outdated and irrelevant very quickly** resulting in the need to constantly monitor databases.

- There may be **technical difficulties** associated with integrating existing data warehousing and, for example, Hadoop systems.

- The **cost** of establishing the hardware and analytical software needed. In addition, there will be a need to constantly **update** or **maintain** it in order to achieve competitive advantage.

6.5 Big data analytics

 Data analytics is the process of **collecting**, **organising** and **analysing** large sets of data (big data in the context of this discussion) to discover patterns and other information which an organisation can use for future decisions.

Collection of data
Organisations have access to greater quantities of data available from a number of internal and external sources.

Organisation of data
Once the data has been captured it needs to be organised and stored for future use, often using data warehousing facilities.

Analysis of data
Data mining software uses statistical algorithms to discover correlations and patterns to create useful information.

 Illustration 27 – Big data analytics

Google analytics provides organisations with a range of information and analysis about visitors to the organisation's website.

A fee is paid to Google by the organisation and in return Google Analytics install a tracking code on the organisation's website. When visitors use the website the tracking code is activated on the visitor's browser:

- This collects a large amount of information about the visitor and their visit.

- Google Analytics uses this as the basis of its analysis and reporting.

- Data collection and analysis can be standardised or customised.

The volume of data as well as its importance to modern organisations is increasing exponentially. Therefore, being able to make sense of this data quickly and concisely and in an accessible and user-friendly manner has seen rapid growth too.

 Data visualisation allows large volumes of complex data to be displayed in a visually appealing and accessible way that facilitates the understanding and use of the underlying data.

A common type of data visualisation technique is **dashboards**. Dashboards contain summarised information, typically showing a small number of KPIs. They allow managers to see the big picture quickly, focusing on the CSFs. They may also contain 'drill-down' facilities that aid more detailed understanding and analysis.

Note: Data visualisation will be discussed further in Chapter 8, section 3.

> ### Illustration 28 – Big data analytics and internet based companies
>
> The digital revolution has resulted in a huge increase in internet-based companies and a switch by consumers to buying online.
>
> In terms of performance management, internet based companies must focus on **measuring the online experience** including:
>
> - **Customer acquisition** – getting visitors to the company website and converting visits to sales (conversion rate).
>
> - **Customer retention** – persuading customers to return and buy again.
>
> - **Customer extension** – selling additional products/services to customers.
>
> Vast amounts of data (big data) are recorded from visitors to the organisation's website and value is extracted from this big data by the process of big **data analytics**:
>
> Examples of **reports produced as a result of big data analysis** include the following:
>
> - **Audience reports** providing information about website visitors such as the percentage return customers, customer location (for example, to ascertain growth markets) and a host of demographic information such as age/ gender (for example, to link such factors to customer conversion rates).
>
> - **Acquisition reports** show how visitors arrived at the website (for example, via a web search engine or clicking on an advertisement) and the effectiveness of the different methods used to attract visitors.
>
> - **Behaviour reports** analyse what visitors actually do while on the website. One performance measure would be 'bounce rate' which shows customers who arrive at the website but don't interact further (for example, they move onto another site). A high bounce rate will correlate with poor visitor conversion rates.

6.6 Data analysis methods

In the exam, you may be asked to demonstrate and evaluate the different methods of data analysis. There are a number of methods available for data analysis. The methods can be used individually but are commonly used collectively:

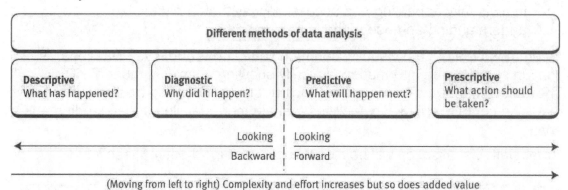

Each of these methods is explained in more detail below:

Data analysis method	Description
Descriptive	• The starting point of the data analysis process. Uses **current and historical data** to identify trends and relationships. • Answers the question '**What has happened?**' • Data is collected, organised and presented in a way that makes it easily understood and turns it into valuable 'good' information (see illustration 29). • Includes **simple statistical tools** such as the calculation of averages and percent changes, and **basic statistical software** (such as Microsoft Excel) to highlight trends in data to produce **visualisations** such as line graphs, bar charts and pie charts. **Advantages** – A quick and easy way to report on performance, communicating changes over time and identifying patterns and trends that can then be analysed further. **Disadvantages**: • Does not help understand why something happened and what will happen in the future, to inform future decisions. • The creation of 'good' information relies on the accuracy of the historic data.

Diagnostic	• **Analysis** of the data (financial and non-financial, internal and external) to **find connections between the different sets of data** to understand why the trends and relationships identified by descriptive analysis have developed.
	• Helps answer the question '**Why did it happen?**'
	• Involves the use of **statistical software tools** and a **variety of techniques** including:
	– **Data drilling**, for example, drilling down into summary sales information to understand which products are showing increased/decreased sales.
	– **Data mining** to unearth unknown patterns and correlations in the data and gain insight into how the data can be used (see illustration 30).
	– **Time series analysis** to analyse data and establish any underlying trend and seasonal variations (see discussion later on in Section 6.6).
	– **Regression analysis** (see discussion later on in Section 6.6).
	Advantages:
	• Helps organisations to understand the range of factors – internal and external – which affect outcomes and which have the greatest impact, so that managers can focus on these when developing initiatives to optimise performance.
	• Relatively quick and easy compared to the other two methods below.
	Disadvantages:
	• More complex and time consuming than descriptive analysis (the first method).
	• Does not help understand what will happen in the future, to inform future decisions.
	• The creation of 'good' information relies on the accuracy of the historic data.

Predictive	• Uses the results from the methods above to answer the question 'What will happen next?'
	• This informed projection uses **historical and current data** to predict how things may unfold in particular areas of the business, allowing organisations to develop initiatives to enhance performance.
	• May use **analysis techniques for forecasting** such as **linear regression models**, **time series**, **expected values** or **standard deviation** and **other techniques** such as **decision trees** or **simulations** (see discussion later on in Section 6.6).
	Advantages:
	• Helps forecast possible future events and the likelihood of those events, which in turn should improve forecasts.
	• Informs effective future business strategy.
	• Helps improve many areas of the business including planning, target setting or unnecessary risk taking (see illustration 31).
	Disadvantages:
	• More complex and time consuming than the methods above.
	• Relies on the accuracy of historic data and its ability to forecast future events.
	• Based on probabilities, these may not be completely accurate.
Prescriptive (Note: this is included as a separate type of data analysis but can also be included and discussed as part of predictive analysis. Credit will be given for either approach in APM answers.)	• Combines predictive analysis with **AI** and **machine learning algorithms** to anticipate what, when and, importantly, why something might happen.
	• Uses all the available data to determine the optimum outcome (i.e. it answers the question '**What action should be taken?**') for a variety of business decisions, for example:
	– capital rationing decisions
	– replacement analysis
	– identifying the optimal balance of finance.

Advantages:

- Invaluable insights to help make the best business decisions.

- Can consider multiple decisions and variables to identify optimum decisions.

- AI and machine learning reduces the scope for human error.

Disadvantages:

- As with predictive analysis, it relies on the accuracy of historic data and its ability to predict future events.

- Creating reliable models is complex and requires specialist data scientist skills (see section 6.9).

- The most complex and time consuming of the methods.

Organisations are likely to use data analytics software (such as Microsoft Power BI, Tableau or Qilk Sense) to facilitate their analysis. Although the detailed modelling and analysis takes place in the software, accountants need to be able to interpret the information provided in the software; for example, assessing whether patterns or trends identified seem realistic. In the APM exam, the focus of the question scenario will not be on the details of the analysis software itself, but on how organisations can use the information provided by the software to help make business decisions to improve performance.

Illustration 29 – Descriptive analysis and demand trends

Supermarkets use loyalty cards and debit/credit card data to build up a customer profile; identifying what customers buy, how much they spend and how loyal they are. This knowledge can then help shape decision-making (for example, about future product offerings) and can be used for individual and collective marketing.

Illustration 30 – Data mining

Supermarkets may use data mining to unearth unknown patterns and correlations in customer's loyalty card and debit/credit card information. For example, in the United Kingdom, a customer buying pizza on a Friday or Saturday evening also buys alcohol more than 60% of the time. This information allows supermarkets to develop effective cross-promotions and to take other simple steps, such as stocking pizza and beer next to one another.

Illustration 31 – Predictive analysis and performance management

Predictive analysis can help improve many areas of a business including:

- **Efficiency** – for example of inventory forecasting.

- **Customer service** – an organisation can gain a better understanding of who its customers are and what they want, so that recommendations can be tailored to the individual customer.

- **Fraud detection and prevention** – it helps organisations identify patterns and changes.

- **Risk reduction** – for example, detecting possible IT security issues requiring further investigation or detecting if valuable employees are thinking of leaving the organisation and persuading them to stay.

Illustration 32 – Examples of prescriptive analysis

- **In GPS technology** – recommends the optimal route based on, for example, traffic and road closures.

- **Manufacturing** – improves equipment maintenance.

- **Healthcare** – improves patient care by evaluating factors such as rates of readmission and the cost effectiveness of procedures.

- **Pharmaceutical testing** – identifying the best testing and patient groups for clinical trials.

Note: You will be familiar with the techniques discussed below from PM. These will be recapped here. In APM, it is unlikely that you will have to carry out the calculations that would take place in the analysis software. Rather you may be expected to have the business knowledge and commercial acumen to interpret the results of data analytics (for example, a set of regression calculations), including having an understanding of the modelling assumptions and what decisions can justifiably be made based on the analysis.

Linear regression models

 Linear regression is a statistical technique that attempts to identify the factors that are associated with the change in the value of a key variable.

The variable that the business is trying to predict is called the **dependent** variable (e.g. sales volume or total cost), and the factors that have an impact are called the **independent** variables (e.g. time or volume of activity).

The technique quantifies the relationship between the dependent variable and the independent variable (so can be used for **diagnostic analysis**). If there is a strong relationship (correlation) between the variables, regression analysis can reliably be used to forecast, e.g. future sales (so can be used for **predictive analysis**).

Regression analysis is a technique for estimating the line of best fit given a series of data.

 Linear regression equation

The equation of a straight line is:

$$y = a + bx$$

where y = dependent variable
a = intercept (on y-axis)
b = gradient
x = independent variable

and $b = \dfrac{n\Sigma xy - \Sigma x \Sigma y}{n\Sigma x^2 - (\Sigma x)^2}$

where n = number of pairs of data

and $a = \bar{y} - b\bar{x}$

The line of best fit can be used to make a forecast (e.g. of sales or costs) for inclusion in the budget.

 Illustration 33 – Linear regression

X Co is forecasting its sales for the four quarters of 20X5. It has carried out a linear regression exercise on its past sales data and established the following:

   $a = 20$

   $b = 0.7$

The equation of the regression line is therefore:

   $y = 20 + 0.7x$

When x is number of the quarter and y is the sales value in $000s.

The equation can be used to calculate the sales for each of the quarters in 20X5.

		$000
Quarter 1	y = 20 + (0.7 × 1) =	20.7
Quarter 2	y = 20 + (0.7 × 2) =	21.4
Quarter 3	y = 20 + (0.7 × 3) =	22.1
Quarter 4	y = 20 + (0.7 × 4) =	22.8

The **advantages** of regression analysis are:

- Models are simple to use and easily explained to non-financial managers.

- Models can be used to predict the impact of changes in estimates (e.g. sales volumes being higher than predicted).

However, there are also some **limitations**:

- There will not always be a linear relationship between variables and outcomes.

- Linear models may identify spurious relationships as they do not consider the difference between correlation and causation.

- Will be less meaningful if the data collected is inaccurate.

Time series forecasting

Linear regression analyses the relationship between variables using a 'line of best fit', assuming a linear trend. However, this type of simple linear relationship alone as the basis of forecasts will not be realistic if there are seasonal variations within the data.

- Time series analysis can establish not only underlying **trends** but also **seasonal variations** within the data.

- The trend and seasonal variation can then be used together to help make predictions about the future.

In addition to the trend and seasonal variation components, a time series will also include **cyclical variations** (medium-term to long term influences usually associated with the economy) and **residual or random variations** (caused by irregular items, which cannot be predicted, such as a fire or flood). We are only really interested in the first two components of time series, the trend and any seasonal variations, when we are looking to forecast for a budget as the cyclical variations are too long term and residual variations are too unpredictable.

Illustration 34 – Sales forecasting using time series analysis

A company will forecast its quarterly sales units for a new product by using a formula to predict the base sales units and then adjusting the figure by a seasonal index.

The formula is $BU = 4,000 + 80Q$

Where BU = Base sales units and Q is the quarterly period number.

The seasonal index values are:

Quarter 1	105%
Quarter 2	80%
Quarter 3	95%
Quarter 4	120%

> ### Question
>
> Identify the forecast increase in sales units from Quarter 3 to Quarter 4.
>
> ### Answer
>
> | Sales in quarter 3 (Q = 3) | | |
> |---|---|---|
> | Base = 4000 + (80 × 3) | = | 4,240 |
> | Seasonal adjustment | | 95% |
> | Actual sales | = | 4,028 |
> | Sales in quarter 4 (Q = 4) | | |
> | Base = 4000 + (80 × 4) | = | 4,320 |
> | Seasonal adjustment | | 120% |
> | Actual sales | = | 5,184 |
> | Overall increase in sales | = | 5,184 – 4,028 = 1,156 units |

A major **advantage** of time series analysis is that forecasts are based on clearly understood assumptions and forecasting accuracy may improve with experience.

However, the **disadvantages** of time series analysis are:

- There is an assumption (as with all forecasting techniques) that what has happened in the past is a reliable guide to the future.

- There is an assumption that a straight line trend exists and that seasonal variations are constant.

Expected values

Expected values were discussed in Chapter 3. An important part of predictive analytics is that it doesn't simply forecast possible future outcomes, it also identifies the likelihood of those events happening. If the probabilities of potential outcomes are available, then the expected value can be calculated.

Expected values can be useful to evaluate alternative courses of action. The organisation should choose the alternative that has the most beneficial expected value.

Standard deviation

When analysing sets of data, it can often be useful to calculate the average (mean) value. However, looking at an average value could be misleading when the distribution of values in the data set is skewed, or the distribution contains outliers.

Standard deviation measures how clustered or dispersed a data set is in relation to its mean. A low standard deviation tells us that data is clustered around the mean and therefore the data is accurately characterised by the mean.

Decision trees

 A **decision tree** is a diagrammatic representation of a multi-decision problem, where all possible courses of action are represented and every possible outcome of each course of action is shown.

Note: The examining team will not expect candidates to prepare a decision tree.

 Illustration 35 – Decision trees

The example below shows the four different NPVs (net present values) that are predicted to occur based on one decision (the size of the investment) and one variable (economic conditions).

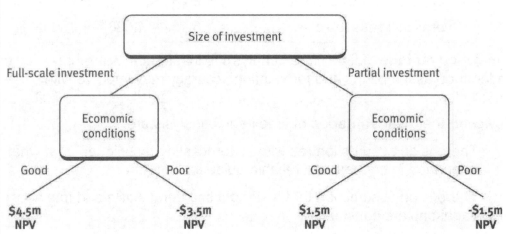

The technique can be used to show the impact of multiple decisions or variables. The following shows the impact of changes to two different variables; economic conditions and cost of materials.

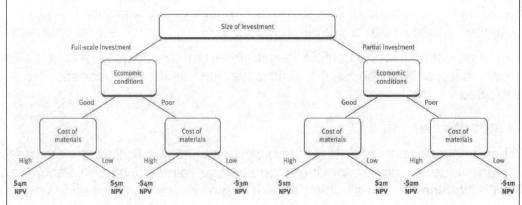

Probabilities and expected values could be used to evaluate the decision tree.

Simulation (Monte Carlo simulation)

One of the most valuable forms of predictive analysis is **'what-if' analysis**, which involves changing variables or factors to see how these changes will affect the outcome.

Sensitivity analysis considers the effect of changing one variable at a time. **Simulation** improves on this by looking at the impact of many variables changing at the same time.

Using mathematical modelling it produces a distribution of the possible outcomes from the project. The probability of different outcomes can then be calculated.

 Simulation

A business is choosing between two projects, project A and project B. It uses simulation to generate a distribution of profits for each project.

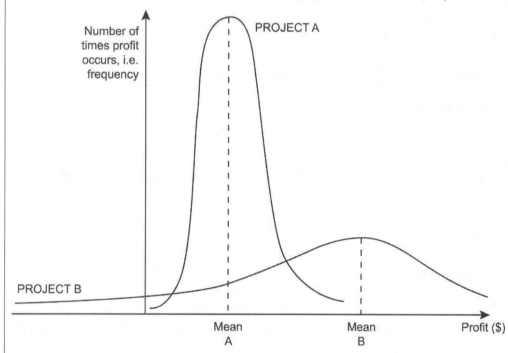

Required:

Which project should the business invest in?

Solution:

Project B has a higher average profit but is also more risky (more variability of possible profits).

However, if the business would prefer to minimise its exposure to risk, it would take on project A. This has a lower risk but also a lower average return.

Project A has a lower average profit but is also less risky (less variability of possible profits).

There is no correct answer. All simulation will do is give the business the above results. It will not tell the business which is the better project.

If the business is willing to take on risk, they may prefer project B since it has the higher average return.

6.7 Alternative methods of data analytics

The data analysis methods discussed above will use data in a variety of different **structured and unstructured** forms, both **financial and non-financial** in nature and from both **internal and external** sources.

Some of the non-financial data sources include text, images, video and voice. The alternative methods of data analytics discussed below can help to identify patterns and trends in these different types of data. In the exam, you may be asked to describe these forms and to discuss their application to the scenario.

Text analytics

Existing text (for example, from emails or social media posts) is translated into quantitative data to uncover trends or valuable insights. For example, an organisation may have a customer support team on Twitter that uses text analytic applications (for example, on customers' short written feedback, questions or other comments) to identify any issues or opportunities.

Image analytics

This is the extraction of useful information from (mainly digital) images. Image analysis technology has a variety of uses. For example:

- It can be as simple as reading a barcode in a retail environment.

- It can speed up airport traffic through the use of sophisticated fingerprint or iris recognition and the use of scanners to virtually unpack bags and check the contents.

Video analytics

This can be used in two main ways:

- Historical video content is analysed to gain insight. For example, when is customer presence in a shop at its peak and what is the age/gender distribution of customers?

- Real-time video monitoring to gain valuable insights. For example, in order to better understand major traffic events, the New York Department of Transportation uses real-time video analytics to detect traffic jams, monitor weather patterns, identify parking violations and more. The cameras capture the activities, process them and send real-time alerts to city officials.

Voice analytics

Voice analytics software can be used to automatically identify and analyse speech including words and phrases.

- There are multiple simple and established uses such as its use to recognise phone speech when a customer books train tickets, cinema tickets or pays for a carpark.

- More sophisticated uses, such as call centres using voice analytics to gain valuable insights into why each call was made; determining what types of call are being received and exactly what customers require when they call. This can help the organisation to monitor performance and identify areas that need improvement (for example, product quality). It can also help the organisation to understand the topics which are important to customers to help them build stronger relationships with customers.

Sentiment analysis (opinion mining)

This is the process of determining the emotional tone behind a series of words to gain understanding of attitudes, opinions and emotions. For example:

- **Text** on a website in the form of customer opinions may be analysed to determine if it is positive, neutral or negative. For example, 'I really like the new design of your website' would be classed as positive, where as 'The product arrived late resulting in a very disappointed son on his birthday' can help the organisation to identify areas for improvement.

- **Voice** based sentiment analysis can be used. For example, in a call centre, customer voice data is analysed using the tone, pitch and frequency of the customer's voice, to reveal which call agent responses evoke positive customer emotions.

6.8 Ethical issues associated with information collection and processing

Introduction

The amount of personal data available to and used by organisations (for example, using the different data analytics techniques discussed above) means that the privacy, sensitivity and security of this data are very significant considerations in modern business.

When considering the way in which an organisation handles technology and data, ethical and social considerations are important for the following reasons:

- A company that handles technology and data in an ethical way will give investors confidence

- Customer confidence in data security is vital in the digital age and is an important element of brand confidence

- Consumers feel safer dealing with companies that are proactive and responsible in its use of data

- Employees are attracted to companies that exhibit a strong ethical stance when it comes to how it uses technology and data

- Ethical handling of technology and data helps ensure long-term sustainability of an organisation through stakeholder confidence and trust

- It demonstrates a proactive awareness of the risks associated with data and technology

Data ethics

 Data ethics encompasses the moral obligations of gathering, protecting and using personally identifiable information and how it affects individuals.

The following are **key issues to consider when collecting and analysing data**:

- **Ownership**: It is unlawful and unethical to collect someone's personal data without their consent. The organisation must ask permission to do so, for example by asking users to agree to the company's terms and conditions.

- **Transparency**: Individuals have the right to know how the organisation plans to collect, store and use the information. For example, organisations may have a written policy on how cookies are used and should allow individuals to access this information so they can decide whether to accept the cookies or decline them.

- **Intention**: Organisations need to establish why they need the data and should only collect and store necessary data.

- **Outcomes**: Even when intentions are good, the outcomes of data analysis can cause inadvertent harm to individuals (see discussion on 'The ethics of big data, AI and algorithms' in Section 6.8).

In APM it is important to consider whether there are sufficient controls over the way the data is captured, stored and used, to ensure the process is ethical and that it avoids bias as far as possible.

General Data Protection Regulation (GDPR)

GDPR was introduced in 2018 and applies to countries in the European Union (EU) and to the United Kingdom (UK). The legislation details the following principles about data:

- Used fairly, lawfully and transparently

- Used for specified, explicit purposes

- Used in a way that is adequate, relevant and limited to only what is necessary

- Accurate and, where required, kept up to date

- Kept for no longer than is necessary

- Handled in a way that ensures appropriate security. Including protection against unlawful or unauthorised processing, access, loss, destruction or damage.

Illustration 36 – Facebook and Cambridge Analytica scandal

Facebook received a £500,000 fine for its role in the Cambridge Analytica scandal. The fine was the maximum available under the data protection legislation in place at the time (prior to the introduction of GDPR legislation).

Facebook was found to have breached data protection legislation by allowing third party app developers access to users data without sufficiently clear and informed consent. They also failed to make suitable checks on apps and developers using the platform.

What was the Cambridge Analytica scandal?

A third party app designed as a personality quiz collected the data of 87 million Facebook users without their knowledge or explicit consent. This data was then sold on to third parties, one of whom was Cambridge Analytica.

They then used this data to profile voters in the US election based on personality and psychology before targeting advertising which took advantage of this information.

Around 1 million UK users' data was obtained in the scandal.

Corporate digital responsibility

Corporate digital responsibility (CDR) is a relatively new concept which extends the idea and ethos of **corporate social responsibility** (**CSR**) to the digital world.

CDR involves a commitment to protecting both customers and employees and ensuring that new technologies and data are used both productively and wisely.

CDR strategy

The development of a **CDR strategy** is increasingly common in modern business and would include the following **5 key areas**:

- **Digital stewardship**, using data in a responsible and secure way that is in line with customers and employees expectations of what is reasonable

- **Customer expectations** around data use and the need for transparency are increasing. The ability to opt in and be rewarded for sharing data empowers the consumer

- **Giving back** means that companies can share data in a benevolent way to help society. For example, a bank with knowledge of financial information could help to inform a customer's choices to improve their financial management, even if it meant a loss of overdraft or credit card fees. Additionally, a pharmaceutical company sharing clinical trial data with university researchers for no gain

- **Data value** is becoming increasingly apparent to customers as well as businesses, so the need to reward and incentivise customers to give more data will become the norm

- **Digital inclusion** is about ensuring all members of society have the skills, tools and ability to access the online digital world, and are not left behind through lack of education or opportunity. Businesses need to be proactive to help and support users and reduce barriers and obstacles.

The ethics of big data, AI and algorithms

As discussed, organisations are collecting and using increasing amounts of (big) data. It is important that the organisation act in an ethical way when collecting, processing and using the data provided.

Illustration 37 – Ethics and big data

An organisation should use the data it collects fairly and without bias. One use of big data is individualised marketing. However, this potentially excludes some customers from particular offers or price categories.

For example, in the United Kingdom (UK) almost a sixth of energy customers have been with their suppliers for more than a decade. Energy companies are legally obliged to tell its existing customers if they are on the cheapest tariff for their particular circumstances but do not need to include tariffs only available via third parties; these include tariffs offered on price comparison websites and these are often only available to new customers. The consequence is that existing customers may end up paying more for their energy because they do not have access to the cheaper energy tariffs that are only marketed to and available for new customers.

The ethics of big data should also be considered in the context of AI and machine learning technology.

Illustration 38 – The ethics of artificial intelligence (AI)

AI has the capability to transform lives for the better but also raises certain ethical issues. These include amongst many others:

- **Unemployment** – for example, what happens to delivery drivers' jobs if self-driving vehicles become widely available?

- **Inequality** between the owners of AI driven companies making the money and the impact on employees of other companies where AI is used to drastically cut the workforce.

- **Discrimination** – AI systems are created by humans who can be biased and judgmental, for example with regards to race. Therefore, it can't always be trusted to be fair or neutral.

- **How it is used** – for example, is it ethical to use AI to monitor employees working from home/remotely? Another example would be is it ethical to use military AI capable of deadly force in modern warfare?

Microsoft is one of a number of high profile technology companies to lay down a voluntary set of ethical principles surrounding its use of AI. It recognises that AI is an area of technology that presents some of the most challenging ethical questions. Its **AI principles** are as follows:

- **Fairness** – AI systems should treat all people fairly

- **Reliability & safety** – AI systems should perform reliably and safely

- **Privacy & security** – AI systems should be secure and respect privacy

- **Inclusiveness** – AI systems should empower everyone and engage people

- **Transparency** – AI systems should be understandable

- **Accountability** – AI systems should have algorithmic accountability

The use of AI and machine learning algorithms (traditionally programmed by humans but increasingly self-learning) applied to the data sources can give the organisation valuable insights and new opportunities. Algorithms produce an outcome or answer that organisations and people may rely on for making a decision. However, **most algorithms do not explain how they arrived at that answer**. These are known as **'black box' algorithms**.

Illustration 39 – The ethics of AI and black box algorithms in recruitment

AI can be used to streamline the recruitment process, enabling hiring companies to assess many more applicants by analysing and interpreting a huge volume of candidate data quickly and cost effectively. However, caution must be applied here, because the basis of the selection decisions must be legally defensible. Inherent bias in automated systems for hiring can result in a legal nightmare.

In one high profile example, Amazon developed an AI recruiting tool that went back and analysed 10 years of employment applications in order to create a system that automatically identified characteristics of high performing employees and against those standards, scored new candidates. The tool made headlines when it was determined that the algorithm favoured male candidates due to societal influences such as gender bias and wage gaps in technology jobs.

Organisations need to implement a **robust strategy to manage such risks, minimising the risk of, for example, human bias or technical flaws** within the algorithm.

One way to gain public trust is to use **explainable AI**. This generates an audit trail alongside the answer, showing the working of the algorithm and explaining how the answer is arrived at.

 Explainable AI emphasises the role of the algorithm not just for providing an output, but for also sharing with the user, supporting information on how it reached the conclusion. Furthermore, the idea is for this information to be available in a human-readable way, rather than being hidden in code.

This is becoming increasingly important as the use of algorithms and AI becomes more commonplace, powerful and continues to evolve.

6.9 Big data and the role of the management accountant

Introduction

Big data and big data analytics will have an impact on the role of the management accountant, presenting both opportunities and challenges.

Technology has facilitated the ability to sort and analyse data to produce meaningful information far quicker than before, initially through the use of spreadsheet and database software but now more so through the use of sophisticated digital technology, such as the use of AI and machine learning algorithms applied to data sources to give insight, or the use of advanced data visualisation tools.

The role of finance professionals has evolved over a number of decades from the traditional idea of 'bean counters' to a more strategic value adding position. **Management accountants will need a broader skills set combining technical (traditional accounting and finance skills) and professional skills (including business, people, leadership and digital skills), all underpinned by ethics, integrity and professionalism.** Employers should be willing to invest in upskilling them and employees should continue to learn as the areas evolve.

Skills needed by management accountants in current and future roles

Competency	Explanation
Technical skills	The management accountant will be required to **apply accounting and finance skills**. Technical skills will enable the management accountant to collect, store, process and analyse information (including big data) to be shared with various stakeholders. As discussed previously, activities such as data collection and processing are increasingly automated.
Business skills	**Understanding of the business and the environment** is crucial to effective decision-making and the ability to transform organisational data into insight for use by the business and its functions to create and preserve value. Management accountants will increasingly require good **knowledge of big data sources, analytical skills** and **judgement**.
People skills	Management accountants will need people skills (including emotional intelligence, resilience, diversity and inclusion) and the **ability to communicate**. They will work alongside other parts of the organisation as a partner, collaborating to generate insight into big data to influence decisions and improve performance.
Leadership skills	Management accountants increasingly **occupy a central position in an organisation**, understanding and questioning numbers and information given. Leadership skills will centre on **team building, coaching** and **mentoring, driving performance** and **change management**, and the **ability to motivate and inspire**.

Digital skills	Includes, for example, **understanding information and data** in a digital environment, **data strategy and planning**, planning/use of **data analytics** and applying existing/developing new **data visualisation** tools.
	Digital skills are **essential for the management accountant**, from basic digital literacy through to deeper expertise of, for example, cloud computing or data analytics.
	If management accountants are to remain relevant, they **need to keep pace with advances in technology**.
	As well as being a standalone skill, digital skills also permeate through the other four skill areas.

These competencies will be underpinned by **ethics**, **integrity** and **professionalism**.

Potential roles for the management accountant

Role	Description
Data manager	Data analytics technology will allow data to be processed in a user friendly, often visual manner in real-time, supporting decision making and contributing to a shift in the role of the management accountant from reactive and analytical (a focus on the past, on financial data and on traditional variance analysis) to proactive and predictive (a focus on the future).
	The management accountant is in an ideal position to:
	• **Establish the areas the organisation should be monitoring** since they have a holistic view of the organisation and its existing IS. For example, they should be aware of performance measures (metrics) collated by organisations such as Google Analytics and be able to explain and interpret them. Knowledge of big data and data analytics will be considered a key skill for any management accountant.
	• **Working with data scientists** (see below) **to ensure that this information is being collected and used**.
	• Using their business knowledge and commercial acumen to **report back to senior managers** with meaningful commercial analysis and recommendations in order to create value. For example, calculating the profit per product or per customer, recommendations for controlling market spend, recommendations for improved inventory management or production planning.

Working with and alongside data scientists	**Data scientists** are individuals with the ability to extract meaning from and interpret data, which requires both tools and methods from statistics and machine learning.
	Data science is a very new field. It is an amalgam of data experts with a background in mathematics, statistics, programming and computer science. Organisations looking to capitalise on **big data** using **data analytics** are increasingly employing specialist data scientists.
	In this data driven world it is important to maintain a coherent commercial, business focus to the work being undertaken by data scientists, this is where **management accountants** are ideally situated to take the lead. Partnering with data scientists to ensure the work they undertake is deliberate and targeted with clear objectives to ultimately support or enhance the business. Management accountants should also act to translate insights gained back to the wider business in a practical and commercial way.
	Essentially **management accountants will act as an interface between the business functions and the data scientists**; they are uniquely positioned to do so for the following reasons:
	• All activities have a financial consequence so the management accountant is central to an organisation with a unique understanding of the overall business picture.
	• The information produced is already trusted, typically audited and grounded in factual accounting reality.
	• The management accounting function and the information produced provide the basis of performance management across the business.
	• Finance is based on rational and measurable information. Management accountants have credibility and ethical guidelines which underpin their objectivity and rigour in decision making.
Data champion	The management accountant may act as a big data champion. The board can influence the culture at a high level and the management accountant can cascade that influence throughout the organisation.

Finance business partner	Effective collaboration will be needed across functions to harness the value of big data. Management accountants may be embedded within functional departments of the organisation rather than operating from a central accounts department. The objective is to provide real-time support and analysis to improve the operational performance of the functional department.
	The role of the management accountant brings them into contact with all aspects of the organisation, meaning that they are well positioned to partner with business managers, IT professionals and data experts to support performance improvement. The management accountant will put rigour and credibility around the information used.

Student accountant article: visit the ACCA website, www.accaglobal.com, to review the articles on:

- 'Big data 1: What is big data?'
- 'Big data 2: How companies use big data'
- 'Data analytics and the role of the management accountant'
- 'Data analytics: Part 1 – Types of data analytics'
- 'Data analytics: Part 2 – Methods of data analytics and ethical issues in data analysis' and
- 'Forecasting with data'.

Chapter summary

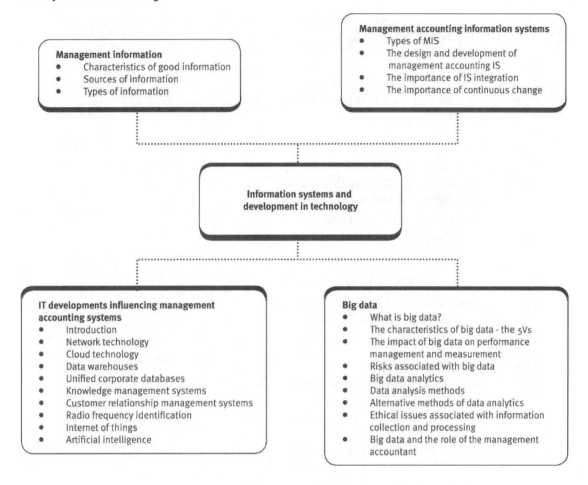

Management information
- Characteristics of good information
- Sources of information
- Types of information

Management accounting information systems
- Types of MIS
- The design and development of management accounting IS
- The importance of IS integration
- The importance of continuous change

Information systems and development in technology

IT developments influencing management accounting systems
- Introduction
- Network technology
- Cloud technology
- Data warehouses
- Unified corporate databases
- Knowledge management systems
- Customer relationship management systems
- Radio frequency identification
- Internet of things
- Artificial intelligence

Big data
- What is big data?
- The characteristics of big data - the 5Vs
- The impact of big data on performance management and measurement
- Risks associated with big data
- Big data analytics
- Data analysis methods
- Alternative methods of data analytics
- Ethical issues associated with information collection and processing
- Big data and the role of the management accountant

Test your understanding answers

Test your understanding 1

Advantages	Disadvantages
• Benefit of real time data input and access.	• Cost of real time data input.
• Improved decision making, for example the EIS should allow drill-down access of data to operational level but presentation of data should be based on the KPIs of the company.	• Cost of linking the EIS to new, external data sources.
	• Cost of implementation and training.
• The EIS will link to external data sources thus reducing the risk of ignoring issues from the wider environment.	• Risk that the system does not work properly or that training is inadequate.
	• Increased security threat since the data is only held in one place.
• The database will reduce/eliminate the problem of data redundancy since data is only held in one place.	• Potential information overload, especially for senior management.
• Improved data integrity. Data is only held in one place and therefore time and effort will be taken to ensure it is of high quality.	

Note: Some of these ideas will be discussed and explored later on in this chapter.

Test your understanding 2

A management information system can be developed to varying levels of refinement. Specifically:

- **Reporting frequency** – information can be collected and reported with varying levels of frequency, for example, the management accounting system of a manufacturer can report actual production costs on a daily, weekly, monthly or even annual basis.

- **Reporting quantity and level of detail** – information can be collected and reported at varying levels of detail e.g. in absorbing overheads into product costs one can use a single factory overhead absorption rate (OAR) or one can operate a complex ABC system. The information requirements of the latter are far more elaborate than those of the former.

- **Reporting accuracy and back-up** – subtle qualitative factors can be incorporated into information systems at varying levels, e.g. information can be rigorously checked for accuracy or a more relaxed approach can be adopted.

Broadly, **the more refined the MIS** is, then **the more expensive it is** to establish and operate. The organisation has to decide if the increased benefits outweigh the increased costs.

Test your understanding 3

IT systems are critical to Zara's short lead times.

Zara needs comprehensive information in the following areas:

- which garments are selling, at what price points and in what quantities – key information will relate to both Zara stores and those of competitors

- detailed product specifications for these garments to enable design of new products

- compatibility between reporting and design software systems

- supply chain management

- order and delivery systems.

Test your understanding 4

- IT developments, such as networks and databases, provide the opportunity for instant access to management accounting information.

- It is possible to directly access and manipulate information from both internal and external sources.

- Information is relatively cheap to collect, store and manipulate.

- Many of the modern forms of management accounting have been developed in conjunction with IT systems, for example it may be difficult to run a meaningful ABC system without IT support.

- Data mining techniques can be used to uncover previously unknown patterns and correlations and hence improve performance.

Test your understanding 5

Facebook faces enormous challenges due from the big data being analysed and its ability to meet those challenges will determine the company's sustainable competitive advantage.

Volume

Facebook has billions of active monthly users, creating huge volumes of data every day. It is therefore crucial that the company has expansive data warehouse facilities available to cope with it colossal volume of data created.

Velocity

Every 60 seconds Facebook's users upload over 100,000 photographs and post over 250,000 status updates. Therefore, Facebook needs to have the facilities available to capture this data which is occurring at an immense speed.

Variety

Internal data includes photographs, status updates and "liked" pages. In addition to this Facebook captures external data from user's devices and location tracking technology. Therefore, they need to have the capabilities of integrating all of this information which has come from a variety of sources.

Veracity

Capturing external data may create difficulties verifying the trustworthiness of information collected. There are also 80 million fake profiles which create data that may not have a legitimate use.

Value

Facebook need to harness the potential value of all of the volumes of fast-moving data of different variety and veracity.

Test your understanding 6

Big data management involves using sophisticated systems to gather, store and analyse large volumes of data in a variety of structured and unstructured formats. Companies are collecting increasing volumes of data through everyday transactions and marketing activity. If managed effectively this can lead to many business benefits although there are risks involved.

A company like MC will already collect a relatively large amount of data regarding its customers, their transactions and call history. It is likely that a significant proportion of their customers are also fairly digitally engaged and therefore data can be gathered regarding preferences and complaints from social media networks. This will be particularly useful to MC as they have seen an increase in complaints and have a high churn rate so engaging with customers will be highly beneficial.

Recent competitive pressure has led to a decline in sales and so MC need to consider the strategic direction which is most appropriate for them to improve performance.

Analysing the large amounts of data available to them will inform decisions on areas such as:

- The type of handsets currently most in demand and therefore the prices required when bundling with tariffs; Main areas of complaint and therefore the areas of weakness which need to be resolved

- Which types of communication are most popular (for example data, call minutes, text messages) to ensure the tariffs have the right combinations

- Usage statistics for 'pay as you go' customers, to drive the most appropriate offers and marketing activity

- Most popular competitor offerings with reasons.

Performance reports for management

Chapter learning objectives

Upon completion of this chapter you will be able to:

- discuss the difficulties associated with recording and processing data of a qualitative nature

- evaluate the output reports of an information system in the light of:

    - best practice in presentation;

    - the objectives of the report/organisation;

    - the needs of the readers of the report; and

    - avoiding the problem of information overload

    - the use of presentation techniques such as data visualisation

- advise on common mistakes and misconceptions in the use of numerical data used for performance measurement

- discuss the difficulties in interpreting data on qualitative issues.

PER

One of the PER performance objectives (PO12) is to apply different management accounting techniques is different business contexts to effectively manage and use resources. Another PER performance objective (PO22) is data analysis and decision support. Working through this chapter should help you understand how to demonstrate these objectives.

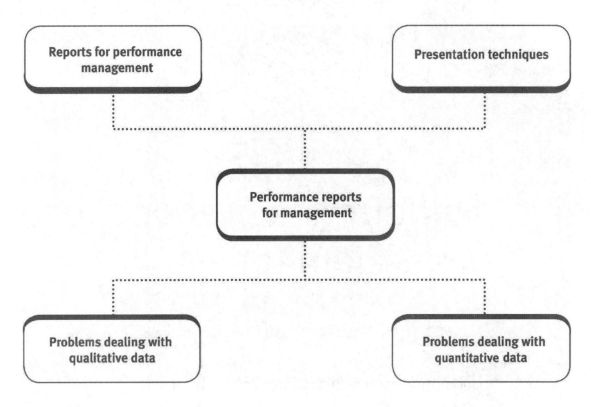

1 Introduction

In the previous chapter we discussed the managers' requirement to access 'good' information in order to be able to effectively plan, direct and control the activities that they are responsible for.

An important component of this good information will be the performance reports produced for management. The output reports produced from a management information system might include overall performance reports for managers (e.g. a monthly management account report) or they may be more specific and tailored to the manager in question, e.g. an inventory report may be produced for the production manager. Importantly, the performance reports need to be tailored to suit the needs of the users of those reports. The qualities of a good performance report are discussed in the first part of this chapter.

The chapter then moves on to discuss data visualisation. This was touched upon in Chapter 7 and is also relevant here since it can be used to present the information in the performance report in a user friendly and accessible way.

The final part of the chapter focuses on the types of information, firstly looking at the common mistakes and misconceptions that people make when using numerical data for performance measurement and then secondly the chapter discusses qualitative information. Qualitative information is highly subjective and hard to pin down and is therefore often ignored to the detriment of the quality of the performance report. However, although it is difficult to record and process data of a qualitative nature these factors still need to be considered when making a decision.

2 Reports for performance management

2.1 Introduction

The design of a **performance report** (sometimes called an **output report** or provided in the form of a **performance dashboard**) has been examined regularly in APM.

Before discussing what makes a good performance report, it is worth noting that performance means different things to different organisations and therefore there is no single correct way of measuring or presenting performance. For example, a profit-seeking organisation may be interested in sales growth or gross margins where as a charity may be interested in the efficient and effective use of its funds. In addition, within a single organisation different aspects of performance will be examined at different times.

2.2 Designing a good performance report

When designing a good performance report there are four key considerations:

1   What is the purpose of the report?

2   Who is the audience for which the report is being produced?

3   What information is needed (as a result of points 1 and 2 above)?

4   What layout is suitable?

Each of these will be examined in turn.

(**Note**: Although this is a useful list of considerations, it is important to tailor your points to the scenario given in the exam. Do not be constrained by this list; some of the above points may be less relevant to a given scenario and/or other considerations may need to be taken into account).

2.3 Purpose

A common mistake in performance reports is that the focus is primarily on profit. However, successful performance (and therefore, successful performance reporting) depends on the achievement of the organisation's individual mission and objectives and should not solely focus on profit or financial measures (this may be a theme in the question scenario).

The performance report should reflect the mission and objectives with performance measures clearly showing if the mission and objectives are being achieved.

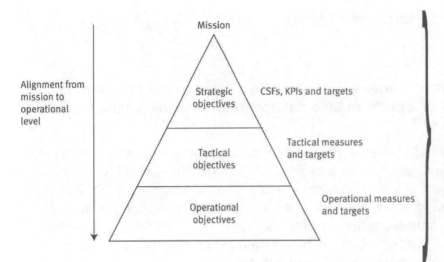

In addition, different aspects of performance may need to be reported on at different times and therefore the performance report should be flexible to meet the changing needs of the organisation.

2.4 Audience

In the exam, the audience of the report will most **often** be the **board of directors** or the **organisation's managers** but it could also be any other stakeholder such as owners, government, those in charge with governance or the local community.

The **audience of the report may range from**, for example:

- **skilled and experienced senior managers** who will be sophisticated enough to understand the information without much detailed explanation and will generally be interested in strategic level, summarised performance reporting (perhaps with the option to 'drill down' to the detailed performance at the other levels)

- to, say, the **local community** who may have fewer skills and require further explanation.

It is important to consider the scenario given in the exam to determine whether the right amount and type of information (for example, operational versus strategic) has been given and whether the layout and terminology used in the report is appropriate.

Care must be taken to ensure that the performance report contains 'good' information (Chapter 7, section 3.2), i.e. is it relevant to the needs of the user, is it easy to use, is it understandable and is it adaptable to their needs etc?

2.5 Information

The information provided must:

- match the purpose of the performance report (as discussed in section 2.3)

- aid comparison, for example over time or to an appropriate benchmark

- comprise both internal information and external information (such as external benchmarks)

- should focus on areas in which the organisation is performing both well and not so well and

- provide a balanced picture of the organisation's financial and non-financial performance.

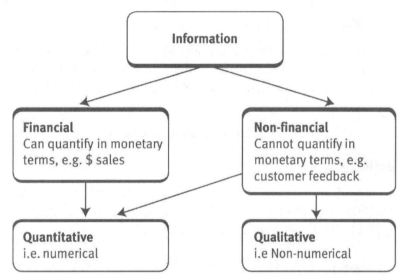

Considering this final point, a common theme in exam questions is that the organisation's performance report focuses solely on **financial** performance. Although important in the short-term, the sole focus on financial performance may be detrimental to the achievement of the organisation's mission and objectives in the long-term and will not fully capture the performance of the organisation.

Non-financial factors focusing on areas such as customer satisfaction, product innovation, sustainability and employee productivity will be equally as important. (**Note**: Non-financial performance indicators will be discussed in Chapter 13).

Some of this non-financial information may be **quantitative** (i.e. can be expressed in numerical terms, such as volume of sales or number of complaints) but much of this information will be **qualitative** (non-numerical, such as customer satisfaction or innovation). This qualitative information is highly subjective and hard to pin down and is thus often ignored to the detriment of the quality of the performance report. (**Note**: Quantitative and qualitative information are explored in more detail later on in this chapter).

2.6 Layout

The layout of the report needs to be relevant to the needs of the user and help the user quickly understand the important amounts, results, the key trends and the reasons for these.

Information overload is a common theme in exam questions. Too much information can:

- detract from the usefulness of the report for the user and/or
- can hide the facts.

Rather than solely including a large volume of figures, the figures could be complemented through the inclusion of:

- graphs, charts or other visual displays making the performance report easily understandable and easy to use.

- narrative explanation drawing attention to important matters and causes. The commentary should accurately represent performance and should not, for example, omit the bad news or be selective or misleading in its coverage.

- an option to 'drill-down' to a greater level of detail.

Question practice

The question below is an extract from a past exam question. Take the time to complete and review this question. It will help to give you a broader understanding of some of the areas covered above.

Test your understanding 1

Metis is a restaurant business in the city of Urbanton. Metis was started three years ago by three friends who met at university while doing courses in business and catering management. Initially, their aim was simply to 'make money' although they had talked about building a chain of restaurants if the first site was successful.

The three friends pooled their own capital and took out a loan from the Grand Bank in order to fit out a rented site in the city. They designed the restaurant to be light and open with a menu that reflected the most popular dishes in Urbanton regardless of any particular culinary style. The dishes were designed to be priced in the middle of the range that was common for restaurants in the city. The choice of food and drinks to offer to customers is still a group decision amongst the owners.

Other elements of the business were allocated according to each owner's qualifications and preferences. Bert Fish takes charge of all aspects of the kitchen operations while another, Sheila Plate, manages the activities in the public area such as taking reservations, serving tables and maintaining the appearance of the restaurant. The third founder, John Sum, deals with the overall business issues such as procurement, accounting and legal matters.

Competition in the restaurant business is fierce as it is easy to open a restaurant in Urbanton and there are many competitors in the city both small, single-site operations and large national chains. The current national economic environment is one of steady but unspectacular growth.

The restaurant has been running for three years and the founders have reached the point where the business seems to be profitable and self-sustaining. The restaurant is now in need of refurbishment in order to maintain its atmosphere and this has prompted the founders to consider the future of their business. John Sum has come to you as their accountant looking for advice on aspects of performance management in the business. He has supplied you with figures outlining the recent performance of the business and the forecasts for the next year (see the performance report below). This table represents the quantitative data that is available to the founders when they meet each quarter to plan any short-term projects or initiatives and also, to consider the longer-term future. Bert and Sheila have often indicated to John that they find the information daunting and difficult to understand fully.

Metis Performance Report

	Actual 20X0 ($)	Actual 20X1 ($)	Actual 20X2 ($)	Forecast 20X3 ($)	Latest quarter to 31 March 20X2 (Q4 20X2) ($)	Previous quarter (Q3 20X2) ($)
Revenue						
Food	617,198	878,220	974,610	1,062,180	185,176	321,621
Wine	127,358	181,220	201,110	219,180	38,211	66,366
Spirits	83,273	118,490	131,495	143,310	24,984	43,394
Beer	117,562	167,280	185,640	202,320	35,272	61,261
Other beverages	24,292	34,850	38,675	42,150	7,348	12,763
Outside catering	9,797	13,940	15,470	16,860	2,939	5,105
Total	979,680	1,394,000	1,547,000	1,686,000	293,930	510,510
Cost of sales						
Food	200,589	284,422	316,748	345,209	60,182	104,527
Wine	58,585	83,361	92,511	100,821	17,577	30,528
Spirits	21,651	30,807	34,189	37,261	6,496	11,283
Beer	44,673	63,566	70,543	76,882	13,403	23,279
Other beverages	3,674	5,228	5,801	6,323	1,102	1,914
Outside catering	3,135	4,461	4,950	5,395	941	1,634
Total	332,307	472,845	524,742	571,891	99,701	173,165
Gross profit	647,373	921,155	1,022,258	1,114,109	194,229	337,345
Staff costs	220,428	313,650	348,075	379,350	66,134	114,865

Other operating costs						
Marketing	25,000	10,000	12,000	20,000	3,000	3,000
Rent/ mortgage	150,800	175,800	175,800	193,400	43,950	43,950
Local property tax	37,500	37,500	37,500	37,500	9,375	9,375
Insurance	5,345	5,585	5,837	6,100	1,459	1,459
Utilities	12,600	12,978	13,043	13,173	3,261	3,261
Waste removal	6,000	6,180	6,365	6,556	1,591	1,591
Equip' repairs	3,500	3,658	3,822	3,994	956	956
Depreciation	120,000	120,000	120,000	120,000	30,000	30,000
Building upgrades				150,000		
Total	360,745	371,701	374,367	550,723	93,592	93,592
Manager salary	35,000	36,225	37,494	38,806	9,373	9,373
Net profit/ loss before interest and corporate taxes	31,200	199,579	262,322	145,230	25,130	119,515
Net margin	3.2%	14.3%	17.0%	8.6%	8.5%	23.4%

Required:

Critically assess the existing performance report and suggest improvements to its content and presentation. **(12 marks)**

Professional marks will be awarded for the demonstration of skill in communication, analysis and evaluation, scepticism and commercial acumen in your answer. **(4 marks)**

(Total: 16 marks)

Student accountant article: visit the ACCA website, www.accaglobal.com, to review the article on 'Performance reports'.

3 Presentation techniques

The growing significance of data has seen a rise in the importance of being able to access and understand the data in clear, concise way. This is where data visualisation fits in (this was touched on briefly in Chapter 7, section 6.5).

 Data visualisation allows large volumes of complex data to be displayed in a visually appealing and accessible way that facilitates the understanding and use of the underlying data.

Data visualisation is an **enabling technology that complements data analytics** by facilitating user friendly and accessible presentation of key data.

Essentially it aims to remove the need for complex extraction, analysis and presentation of data by finance, IT and data scientists. It puts the ability to find data in to the hands of the end user, through intuitive, user-friendly interfaces.

The most common use of data visualisation is in creating a **dashboard** to display the **key performance indicators (KPIs)** of a business in a live format, thus allowing immediate understanding of current performance and potentially prompting action to correct or amend performance accordingly.

An effective data visualisation tool should consider the four factors discussed in Section 2 (i.e. purpose, audience, information needed and layout).

> ### Illustration 1 – Data visualisation tools
>
> The tools of today's market leaders **Tableau** and **Qlik**, go far beyond the simple charts and graphs of Microsoft Excel. Data is displayed in customisable, interactive 3D formats that allow uses to manipulate and drill down as required. Central to data visualisation is understanding and ease of use, the leading companies in the field look to make data easier and more accessible for everyone.

Key benefits of data visualisation

- **Accessible** – traditional spreadsheets and financial reports can be both difficult to understand and unappealing to look at. Modern data visualisation graphics and dashboards are designed to be user friendly and intuitive putting the ability to find data in the hands of the end user (rather than relying on, say, finance or IT experts)

- **Real time** – synchronising real time data with data visualisation tools gives live up to date numbers in a clear, informative style. This allows quicker response to business changes rather than waiting for weekly or monthly reports

- **Performance optimisation** – the immediacy and clarity of the information being displayed supports better decision making and proactive, efficient utilisation of resources as problems are identified promptly

- **Insight and understanding** – (as discussed in Chapter 7, section 6) big data presents a real opportunity for organisations to gain unique insight and understanding. However, the value of big data will only be unlocked through a combination of effective data analytics and data visualisation. Combining data and visualising it in a new way can lead to improved understanding and fresh insights about the cause and effect relationships that underpin performance.

Illustration 2 – Visualisation, key performance indicators

Companies are increasingly using **dashboards** (a collection of key infographics displayed together) to display key performance indicators to staff in real time and to flag areas requiring improvement in order to hit the pre-determined targets and drive success. This instant feedback allows for action to be taken quickly to highlight and fix potential problems.

For instance, an IT service desk within a business will use key performance indicator dashboards to monitor and display performance for all staff and the department as a whole.

Metrics such as the number of support tickets logged, time taken to open support tickets, time taken to resolve support tickets and customer satisfaction would all be displayed clearly using graphics.

If performance in any of the areas is falling below target levels the graphics will clearly display this, prompting action to resolve the poor performance.

4 Problems dealing with quantitative data

As discussed, quantitative data is data that can be expressed in numerical terms. It will form a **significant and important part of a performance report**. The quantitative data is **often the most reliable data** available because:

- it is commonly generated and controlled by the organisation's internal systems

- using easily quantified data (such as invoice values)

- and may be additionally monitored and controlled by the organisation's external auditors.

However, although this data is important and useful, there are a **number of common mistakes and misconceptions that people make when using numerical data for performance measurement**. These include the following:

Collection of data and failure to understand the underlying samples

An organisation often uses sampling to collect data and establish statistics.

However, it is difficult, costly and time consuming to collect a sample that is big enough to be representative of the whole population. For example, a divisional manager may claim 90% customer satisfaction, but this is misleading if, say, only ten out of five thousand customers were consulted.

Similarly, it is also difficult to collect a random sample. For example, any samples that are self-selecting are notoriously unreliable, such as the scores on websites where customers can post feedback and rate products; these may be distorted by false positives paid for by sellers or false negatives paid for by rivals.

Failing to look for underlying causes

For example, an internet retailer may report that the number of hits to their website has increased by 50% over the last two weeks. This does not seem as impressive if it turns out that the manager has advertised some heavily discounted products.

Looking at figures in isolation

Continuing the previous example, rather than focusing on one number in isolation, a better approach to assess internet sales might be to consider number of hits, what % of customers then bought something and the average purchase value.

Data processing

Care should be taken when processing data. For example, when choosing an average to report, the mean can be skewed by extreme values (however, the mode and median also have limitations).

Presentation of data

The choice of, say, graph or chart may be inappropriate. For example, a graph may indicate dramatic changes but only because of the scale chosen.

Failing to evaluate figures using a suitable comparator or benchmark

A manager may report an increase in sales of 20% on the last year but this may indicate poor performance if the market grew by 30% over the same period.

Failing to understand percentages

Suppose quality control reject rates increase from 5% to 6% of total items made. This should be reported as a 20% increase but some managers may state that rejects have only increased by 1%.

It may also be misleading to quote a percentage figure, rather than an absolute figure. For example, a business may boast that eating one of its yogurts every day results in a 50% reduction in a certain disease. However, looking at the absolute figures this decrease is only from a two in a million chance of catching the disease to a one in a million chance.

Selective use of figures

Detailed performance measurement often reveals a mixed picture but, unless KPIs are set in advance, some managers may select only the positive indicators, thus omitting the bad news, when reporting performance. For example, a manager may boast about revenue growth but fail to report a reduction in profit.

Confusing correlation and causality

Suppose a new manager has invested heavily in their division and, at the same time, revenues have increased. It is very easy to assume that the increase in revenue was caused by the investment, whereas it may be due to a different cause altogether, such as an up run in the economy.

In **summary**, numerical data is an important tool for performance measurement and management in an organisation. However, in order to use it optimally, the organisation must take great care when determining:

- what numerical data to collect, i.e. the source and quantity, and

- how this is analysed and

- how the analysed data is presented and used.

In addition, as discussed in section 2.5, it is also important to use qualitative data alongside this quantitative data.

Student accountant article: visit the ACCA website, www.accaglobal.com, to review the article on 'Common mistakes and misconceptions in the use of numerical data used for performance measurement'.

5   Problems dealing with qualitative data

 Qualitative information is information that cannot normally be expressed in numerical terms (whereas quantitative information can).

It is difficult to record and process data of a qualitative nature but qualitative factors still need to be considered when making a decision.

Test your understanding 2
Required:
A company is considering replacing its current products with a new range which will use different production techniques. What qualitative issues will it need to consider?

Problem 1: Qualitative information is often subjective in nature

Qualitative information is **often in the form of opinions**, for example, those of:

- **Employees** – who will be affected by certain decisions which may impact the nature of their role, threaten their continued employment, or cause them to need re-training

- **Customers** – who will have opinions about the organisation's products/services. They will be interested to know about new products, but will want to be assured that service arrangements, etc. will continue for existing products

- **Suppliers** – who will have opinions about the terms of the supplier arrangement and will want to be aware of the entity's plans, e.g. a move to a just-in-time (JIT) environment.

Such opinions must be collected and co-ordinated into meaningful 'good' information.

Illustration 3 – Dealing with qualitative data

Here are some examples of qualitative effects.

- The impact of a decreased output requirement on staff morale is something that may be critical but it is not something that an information system would automatically report.

- The impact of a reduction in product range may have a subtle impact on the image that a business enjoys in the market – again something that an information system may not report.

The fact that qualitative information is often in the **form of opinions presents a problem** since the information is **subjective** in nature. For example, in assessing quality of service, customers have different expectations, priorities and needs and so are unlikely to be consistent in their judgements.

Solution to problem 1

One way to reduce the effect of subjectivity is to look at **trends** in performance since the biases will be present in each individual time-period but the trend will show relative changes in quality.

Another method for overcoming the problems of dealing with qualitative information is to **transform it into quantitative information** (for example, by applying a 1 to 5 scale when assessing customer satisfaction). However, it will never escape from the problem of being judgemental and subjective; the **interpretation into a single measure is also problematic.** For example, a customer may rate their level of satisfaction as 4 but this does not indicate which elements of the customer is satisfied or dissatisfied with or one customer's perception and interpretation of a scoring system may be different to that of another customer.

Alternative methods of **data analytics**, e.g. text and voice analytics and sentiment analysis were discussed in Chapter 7, section 6.7. These methods can be used to unlock the potential value of qualitative data (e.g. customer opinions posted on social media) and to transform it into useful information for performance management.

Problem 2: Qualitative information may be incomplete

Another common **problem** in using and interpreting qualitative data is that the **data may be incomplete.** For example, when trying to understand the opinions of or gather feedback from employees or customers, the organisation may rely on the individual being willing or motivated to share their opinion or to provide feedback. Therefore, the qualitative information gathered will often be from a sample of the population only and may not be representative of all employees' or customers' opinions.

Solution to problem 2

The organisation needs to find a way to **encourage the individual to provide their opinion** (for example, a customer may be entered into a free prize draw for completing a satisfaction survey). Again, this solution will come at a cost.

Problem 3: Lack of management familiarity and/or inadequate information systems

A lack of management familiarity with qualitative information or poor understanding of the importance of considering qualitative factors can make recording, processing and interpreting qualitative data difficult.

Information systems are often set up to in a way that accurately and reliably generates, monitors and controls the production of quantitative (often financial) data but is unable to generate the required qualitative information. The source of the qualitative information may be from internal sources (which are perhaps not subject to adequate checks or controls) or from external sources (which can't always be relied on to produce 'good' qualitative information).

Solution to problem 3

May be overcome using, for example, employee training, systems upgrades or additional checks and controls of the qualitative data (but this will be at a cost).

Test your understanding 3

Moffat commenced trading on 01/12/X2, it supplies and fits tyres and exhaust pipes and services motor vehicles at thirty locations. The directors and middle management are based at the Head Office of Moffat.

Each location has a manager who is responsible for day-to-day operations and is supported by an administrative assistant. All other staff at each location are involved in the fitting and servicing operations.

The directors of Moffat are currently preparing a financial evaluation of an investment of $2 million in a new IT system for submission to its bank. They are concerned that sub-optimal decisions are being made because the current system does not provide appropriate information throughout the organisation. They are also aware that not all of the benefits from the proposed investment will be quantitative in nature.

Required:

(a) Explain the characteristics of **three** types of information required to assist in decision-making at different levels of management and on differing timescales within Moffat, providing two examples of information that would be appropriate to each level.

(b) Identify and explain **three** approaches that the directors of Moffat might apply in assessing the **qualitative** benefits of the proposed investment in a new IT system.

(c) Identify **two qualitative** benefits that might arise as a consequence of the investment in a new IT system and explain how you would attempt to assess them.

Tutor tip:

When planning and writing up your answer, consider the following:

- Make sure that you include the most important, relevant and crucial points relating to the requirement.

- Link information from different parts of the scenario.

- Show your ability to prioritise points and avoid repeating points.

- Address the requirements as written.

- Structure and present your answer in a professional manner.

- Express points clearly, factually and concisely.

Keep this checklist in your mind when attempting other questions. It will help you to maximise the **professional skills** marks you earn.

Chapter summary

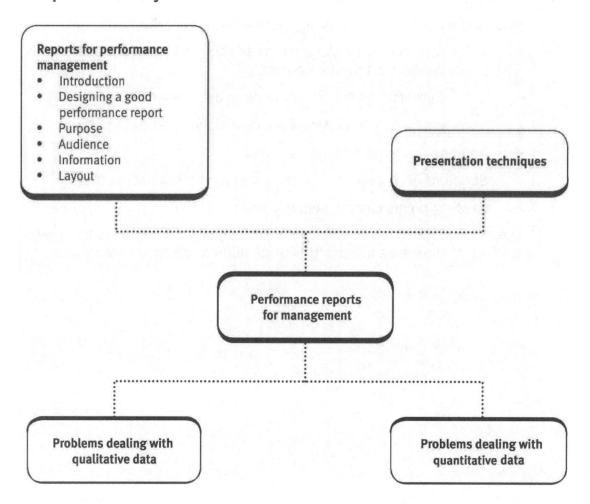

Test your understanding answers

Test your understanding 1

Current performance report

The existing performance report has some good elements and many weaknesses. The current report shows clearly the calculation of profit and the profit margin from the business and shows how this has changed over the past three years along with a forecast of the next year. There is also a breakdown of the performance in the last two quarters which gives a snapshot of more immediate performance. The report breaks revenue and costs into product categories and so might allow a review of selling and procurement activities.

However, there are a number of weaknesses with the existing report. Firstly, the report only clearly answers the question 'what was the profit?' The owners have indicated that their aim is to 'make money' and it is possible that making money and profit may not be entirely compatible in the short term. For example, there are no cash measures of performance on the report. These are likely to assume greater importance given the planned improvements and any long-term expansion of the business. The owners might wish to consider refining their long-term goal in order to make it a more precise statement.

The current report does not present its information clearly. There is too much unnecessary information (e.g. the detail on operating costs). The style of presentation could easily be confusing to a non-accountant as it shows a large table of numbers with few clear highlights. The use of more percentage figures rather than absolute numbers may help (e.g. gross margins, change on comparative period percentages). Also, the numbers are given to the last $ where it would probably be sufficient to work in thousands of dollars.

The current report does not break down conveniently according to the functional areas over which each owner-manager has control. It summarises the overall build-up of profit but, for example, it cannot be easily used to identify performance of the service staff except indirectly through growth in total revenue. In order to improve this aspect of the report, the critical success factors associated with each functional area will need to be identified and then suitable performance measures chosen. For example, Sheila's area is customer-facing and so a measure of customer satisfaction based on number of complaints received or changes over time in average scores in customer surveys would be helpful. Bert's area is kitchen management and so staff efficiency (measured by number of meals produced per staff hour) and wastage control (measured by gross margin) may be critical factors. In your own financial and legal areas, costs are mostly fixed and so absolute measures such as the cost of capital may be helpful. In the area of procurement, purchasing the appropriate quality of food and drink for the lowest price is critical and so a gross margin for each product category would aid management.

The timescales reported in the current format are possibly not helpful for quarterly meetings. The existing report shows evidence of seasonality in the large change between Q3 and Q4 performance (42% fall in revenue). The figures for two years ago may not be particularly relevant to current market conditions and will not reflect recent management initiatives. It may be useful to consider reporting the last quarter's monthly performance giving comparative figures from the previous year and drop the use of the detailed 20X0 and 20X1 figures in favour of just supplying net profit figures for those years in order to give an overview of long-term performance.

The current report does not give much benchmark data to allow comparisons in order to better understand the results. It would be helpful to have budget figures for internal comparison and competitor figures for an external comparison of performance. Such external data is often difficult to obtain although membership of the local trade association may give access to a suitably anonymised database provided Metis is willing to share its data on the same basis.

Finally, the current document only reports financial performance. I have already indicated that this may not be sufficient to capture the critical factors that drive the business. A restaurant will be judged on the service and quality of its products as well as its pricing. It would be an improvement to include this style of reporting although gathering reliable data on these non-financial areas is more demanding.

Professional skills

As you plan and write up your answer, consider how to maximise the professional skills marks awarded. Examples of how these marks may be earned are as follows:

- **Communication**: Style language and clarity – answer is easy to follow and with more than a negligible amount of content (use of headings and sub-headings would also have been useful here).

- **Analysis and Evaluation**: Reasoned assessment of the existing performance report and appropriate use of the data to support the discussion.

- **Scepticism**: Recognition of the failings of the report including, as part of the recommendation, information that is missing or is required.

- Commercial acumen: **Recommendations of improvements are practical and plausible in the context of the company situation.**

Test your understanding 2

- The impact on and the views of employees. Any decision which affects working practices will have a morale effect on employees. Some decisions, such as to close a department, will have a greater effect than others, for example an increase in production, but both will affect employees.

- The impact on and opinion of customers who will be affected by any decision that changes the finished product or its availability. For example, the deletion of a product will force customers to choose an alternative item.

- Suppliers will be affected by changes to production which require different raw materials or delivery schedules. For example, an increase in production may cause the supplier to increase production of the raw material.

- The response of competitors. Any decision to changes in product specification or pricing will affect competitors who will then choose whether or not to respond.

- The impact on demand for scarce resources. A change in production as a result of the decision may alter the demand for individual resources and the result of the decision may alter availability.

- Any social and environmental effects.

Test your understanding 3

Information and Investment – Moffat

(a) The management of an organisation need to exercise control at different levels within an organisation. These levels are often categorised as being strategic, tactical and operational. The information required by management at these levels varies in nature and content.

Strategic information

Strategic information is required by the management of an organisation in order to enable management to take a longer term view of the business and assess how the business may perform during the period. The length of this long term view will vary from one organisation to another, being very much dependent upon the nature of the business and the ability of those responsible for strategic decisions to be able to scan the planning horizon.

Strategic information tends to be holistic and summary in nature and would be used by management, when for example, undertaking SWOT analysis.

In Moffat strategic information might relate to the development of new services such as the provision of a home-based vehicle recovery service or the provision of 24hr servicing. Other examples would relate to the threats posed by Moffat's competitors or assessing the potential acquisition of a tyre manufacturer in order to enhance customer value via improved efficiency and lower costs.

Tactical information

Tactical Information is required in order to facilitate management planning and control for shorter time periods than strategic information. Such information relates to the tactics that management adopt in order to achieve a specific course of action. In Moffat this might involve the consideration of whether to open an additional outlet in another part of the country or whether to employ additional supervisors at each outlet in order to improve the quality of service provision to its customers.

In Moffat the manager at each location within Moffat would require information relating to the level of customer sales, the number of vehicles serviced and the number of complaints received during a week. Operational information might be used within Moffat in order to determine whether staff are required to work overtime due to an unanticipated increase in demand, or whether operatives require further training due to excessive time being spent on servicing certain types of vehicle.

Operational information

Operational information relates to a very short time scale and is often used to determine immediate actions by those responsible for day-to-day management.

Perhaps the preferred approach is to **acknowledge the existence of qualitative benefits and attempt to assess them in a reasonable manner acceptable to all parties including the company's bank**. The financial evaluation would then not only incorporate 'hard' facts relating to costs and benefits that are qualitative in nature, but also would include details of qualitative benefits which management consider exist but have not attempted to assess in financial terms. Such benefits might include, for example, the average time saved by location managers in analysing information during each operating period.

(b) One approach that the directors of Moffat could adopt would be to **ignore the qualitative benefits** that may arise on the basis that there is too much subjectivity involved in their assessment.

The problem that this causes is that the investment will probably look unattractive since all the costs will be included in the valuation where as significant benefits and savings will have been ignored. This approach lacks substance and would not be recommended.

An alternative approach would involve **attempting to attribute values to each of the identified benefits that are qualitative in nature**. Such an approach will necessitate the use of management estimates in order to derive the cash flows to be incorporated in a cost benefit analysis. The problems inherent in this approach include gaining consensus amongst interested parties regarding the footing of the assumptions from which estimated cash flows have been derived. Furthermore, if the proposed investment does take place then it may well prove impossible to prove that the claimed benefits of the new system have actually been realised.

Alternatively, the management of Moffat could attempt to express qualitative benefits in specific terms linked to a hierarchy of organisational requirements.

For example, qualitative benefits could be categorised as being:

1　Essential to the business.

2　Very useful attributes.

3　Desirable, but not essential.

4　Possible, if funding is available.

5　Doubtful and difficult to justify.

(c)　One of the main qualitative benefits that may arise from an investment in a new IT system by Moffat is the **improved level of service to its customers in the form of reduced waiting times** which may arise as a consequence of better scheduling of appointments and inventory management. This could be assessed via the introduction of a questionnaire requiring customers to rate the service that they have received from their recent visit to a location within Moffat according to specific criteria such as adherence to appointed times, time taken to service a vehicle, cleanliness of the vehicle and attitude of staff.

Alternatively a follow-up telephone call from a centralised customer services department may be made by Moffat personnel in order to gather such information.

Another qualitative benefit may arise in the form of competitive advantage. **Improvement in customer specific information and service levels may give Moffat a competitive advantage**.

Likewise **improved inventory management may enable costs to be reduced** thereby enabling a 'win-win' relationship to be enjoyed with customers.

Human resource aspects of performance management

Chapter learning objectives

Upon completion of this chapter you will be able to:

- advise on the relationship of HR management to performance measurement (performance rating) and suitable remuneration methods

- advise on the link between the achievement of the corporate strategy and the management of human resources (e.g. through the Building Block model)

- discuss and evaluate different methods of reward practices, including the potential beneficial and adverse consequences of linking reward to performance measurement

- discuss the accountability issues that might arise from performance measurement systems

- assess the statement; 'What gets measured, gets done' in the context of performance management

- demonstrate how management style needs to be considered when designing an effective performance measurement system (such as Hopwood's management styles).

PER

One of the PER performance objectives (PO3) is to contribute to the wider business strategy of your organisation through your personal and team objectives. You should identify innovative ways to improve organisational performance – which may include making or recommending business process changes and improvements.

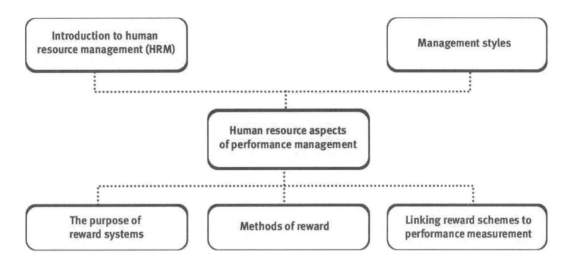

Student accountant articles: visit the ACCA website, www.accaglobal.com to review the articles on:

- Reward schemes

- Human resource management and the appraisal system and

- Reward schemes for employees and management.

1 Introduction

This chapter looks at the link between human resource management and performance measurement and how management style needs to be considered when designing an effective performance measurement system.

It considers the impact of the employee reward system on the behaviour of employees and on the performance of the organisation as a whole.

It also discusses the accountability issues that might arise from performance measurement systems.

2 Introduction to human resource management (HRM)

2.1 Definition of HRM

 HRM is the strategic and coherent approach to the management of an organisation's most valued assets: the people working there that individually and collectively contribute to the achievement of its objectives for sustainable competitive advantage.

HRM includes the recruitment, selection and induction of employees, the development of policies relating to human resources (e.g. reward systems), the management and development of employees (e.g. through training and development and through performance measurement and the appraisal system) and the termination of employees.

The **scope of HRM is wide**. In APM, the **focus is on performance measurement and reward practices**.

2.2 Importance of human resources

An organisation uses HRM to ensure that it has the **correct people** in place to **fulfil its strategic and operational objectives**.

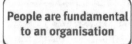

Strategic significance – the creation and fulfilment of the strategy relies on the skills, knowledge and creativity of the people	**Operational significance** – successful completion of a task relies on having employees with appropriate skills and abilities to carry out their work

Illustration 1 – The link between HRM and the achievement of strategic objectives

Some examples of the link between HRM and strategy are as follows:

- If competitive advantage is sought through a strategy of **differentiation,** HRM needs to ensure that:

  – high quality, skilled staff are recruited

  – that these staff are given the freedom to be creative and innovate

  – that a culture of service and quality is prevalent

  – and that rewards are geared towards long-term success and beyond short-term financial measures and are aligned with the strategic goals of the organisation.

- On the other hand, if a strategy of cost **leadership** was pursued, then HRM needs to focus on:

  – recruiting low skilled workers

  – providing repetitive, simple tasks

  – minimising staff numbers

  – providing strict controls

  – and focusing appraisals and rewards on short-term cost measures.

Human resource management has grown in importance from the traditional view of the personnel department, whose role was primarily seen as that of hiring and firing employees. Today, **employees** are seen less as an expensive necessity but as a **strategic resource** that **may provide the organisation with competitive advantage**.

Illustration 2 – Importance of human resources

In service industries, such as restaurants, employees have direct contact with customers. Having employees that are friendly and helpful has a large impact on how customers will view the business. Teams must be passionate about delivering an amazing guest experience to each and every customer and they should be provided with the right tools and training to deliver this brilliant experience.

2.3 HRM and performance management

Performance management is essentially about **managing the performance of the organisation's human resources**. Any controllable improvement or decline in an organisation's performance is usually due to human behaviour.

Human behaviour can be influenced through the use of the following:

- **Performance measures and targets**

  In Chapter 1, we introduced the concept **'what gets measured, gets done'** and considered how performance measures and targets can be an effective way to **motivate** staff to achieve the organisation's objectives.

  A typical process should include the following stages:

  – Select suitable performance measures and **set targets** which are relevant to the employee's responsibilities.

  – Use the chosen measures to monitor staff performance.

  – **Appraise** staff on the basis of whether they have achieved their targets and **feedback** on their performance.

  Feedback of performance extends the concept 'what gets measured, gets done' to the idea **'what gets measured and fed back, gets done well'**

- **Reward systems**

  A further way to motivate staff to achieve optimal performance is to

  offer rewards to incentivise staff to succeed.

  – Offer rewards to **incentivise** staff to succeed.

  This additional offer of a financial or non-financial incentive then takes us to one final theory which is **'what gets rewarded, gets repeated'**.

Based on these approaches for managing human performance, the remaining sections of this chapter will consider:

- How the organisation's **management style** affects the choice of performance measures/targets that are used to motivate, monitor and appraise staff.

- How to design effective **reward systems** to incentivise staff to succeed in meeting their targets.

3 Management styles

Hopwood identified three distinct management styles of performance appraisal. The style needs to be considered when designing an effective performance measurement system.

Style	Advantages	Disadvantages
Budget constrained: The manager's performance is primarily evaluated upon the basis of their ability to continually meet the budget on a **short-term** basis. The manager will receive unfavourable feedback from their superior if, for instance, their actual costs exceed the budgeted costs, regardless of other considerations. Short-term financial performance is measured using, say, ROCE or annual gross profit.	• Should ensure short-term targets are met. • May be more motivating for some employees who find it easier to focus on the short-term and will be motivated if their rewards are aligned to the achievement of short-term targets.	• Short-termism (for example, cost cutting). • Stress for employees and difficult working relationships. • Lack of flexibility. • Stifles ingenuity. • Can result in manipulation of data.
Profit-conscious: The manager's performance is evaluated on the basis of their ability to increase the performance of the unit's operations in relation to the **long-term** purposes of the organisation. Measures of long- term profitability will be used. For example, the net present value (NPV) of a project over its entire life may be used when making decisions.	• Gives flexibility to go 'off plan' if justifiable and should help in meeting long-term profitability targets. • Less job related pressure, manipulation of data and better working relationships than compared to budget-constrained. • May motivate and help retain employees if rewards are linked to the achievement of long-term profitability targets.	• Loss of short-term control (resulting in, for example, cash flow issues). • May ignore non-financial aspects such as ESG issues, customer satisfaction or innovation.

Non-accounting:	• Focus is on causes (e.g. customer satisfaction) rather than effects (profitability), all of which will contribute to long-term success.	Financial implications of behaviour may be neglected (both short-term and long-term).
The budgetary information plays a relatively unimportant part in the superior's evaluation of the manager's performance. Little emphasis on financial performance, looking instead at **non-financial** aspects and how these drive **long-term** performance.	• Targets may be more meaningful and motivating to staff and may help to attract and retain staff.	
Non-financial measures such as customer satisfaction, employee morale, energy/water usage or innovation may be used.	• Less job-related pressure, manipulation of data and better working relationships than compared to budget-constrained.	

4 The purpose of reward systems

 A **reward system** refers to all the monetary, non-monetary and psychological payments that an organisation provides for its employees in exchange for the work they perform.

There are a **number of purposes** of reward systems:

- **To assist in the achievement of strategic objectives**. The reward system offered to employees should ideally include a method (the different methods will be covered in section 5) that motivates the employee to achieve the organisation's objectives. The alignment of objectives was discussed in Chapter 1. This idea can now be expanded upon to include employee objectives:

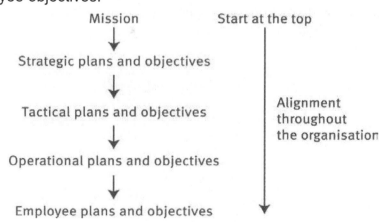

As we have already discussed:

– **'What gets measured, gets done'**, i.e. if an employee knows that they are being assessed on the achievement of pre-agreed targets (performance measures), they are more likely to work hard to achieve these.

– **'What gets measured and fed back, gets done well'**, i.e. if an employee knows that their performance is being measured and fed back to, for example their manager, they are more likely to work hard to achieve the objectives set.

– **'What gets rewarded, gets repeated'**. Importantly, the employee should feel that they are being rewarded for the achievement of the objectives set, otherwise they will not be motivated to work hard to achieve current and future objectives.

A robust review and appraisal system may need to be in place in order to ensure the above.

> ### Illustration 3 – Alignment of goals
>
> The reward scheme should support the organisation's goals and must be consistent with its strategy. For example, the UK supermarket Waitrose has a strategy of differentiation. Staff receive generous pay and benefits which are linked to the achievement of certain skills and pre-agreed targets. The supermarket, Lidl, on the other hand has a strategy of cost leadership. It has a simple reward scheme offering fairly low wages as staff are less skilled and new staff are easy to recruit and need little training.

- To ensure the **recruitment** and **retention** of appropriately **skilled** and **experienced staff**. A desirable reward scheme can help to attract and retain the best employees to an organisation and can act as a source of competitive advantage.

- To provide a **fair and consistent basis for rewarding employees**.

- To **motivate staff** and maximise performance. The reward scheme should serve to motivate staff. Motivated staff will be more productive and more likely to work towards achieving the organisation's goals and targets.

Vroom's expectancy theory

Vroom believed that people will be motivated to do things to reach a goal if they believe in the worth of that goal and if they can see that what they do will help them in achieving it. **Vroom's expectancy model is stated as:**

Force = valence × expectancy

where:

Force = the strength of a person's motivation.

Valence = the strength of an individual's desire for an outcome.

Expectancy = the probability that they will achieve that outcome.

Note: This is a useful theory for enhancing your understanding of motivation but you are not expected to know the model when answering APM questions.

Reward schemes and employee motivation

A well known theory of motivation is Maslow's hierarchy of needs.

Maslow stated that people's wants and needs follow a hierarchy. As employees become progressively more highly paid, monetary rewards become less important as other needs such as recognition and an ability to achieve one's potential become more important.

Note: This is a useful theory for enhancing your understanding of motivation but you are not expected to know the model when answering APM questions.

- To **reward performance** through promotion or progression.
- To **control salary costs**.
- To **comply with legal requirements and ethical obligations**.

Illustration 4 – Reward systems and ESG issues

ESG issues (discussed in Chapter 4) will not be fully embraced and executed with as much precision as are the more commonly measured functions such as sales and staff management until it is built into the performance appraisal and reward systems for a company's employees. For example, Johnson and Johnson measures its employees on both their functional performance as well as their performance against the organisation's well respected ethical stance.

 Illustration 5 – Reward systems and ethics

Awarding huge salaries and large bonuses to the senior executives of big companies may be seen as unethical when the economy is in recession and there is a climate of job cuts and pay freezes. However, others would argue that in order for a company to survive and thrive, the best senior executives must be attracted and retained. Therefore, executives must be offered a competitive and attractive reward package.

- To ensure the employees' attitude to risk is aligned with that of the organisation (see discussion in Chapter 3, section 5 on the risk appetite of employees and managers).

Note: In the exam, you may be asked to assess how effectively a proposed or existing reward scheme meets the objectives of reward schemes. Questions will often focus on how well the scheme supports the organisation's strategic goals. In questions such as these, many of the general points covered in Section 6.1 can be drawn upon. In addition, one performance measurement system that makes the link between the achievement of corporate strategy and the management of human resources in the **Building Block model**. This is a useful model to use when framing your answer in APM. The model will be covered in detail in Chapter 13.

Poorly designed reward schemes could create several risks, including:

Strategic risk	If the reward scheme is not aligned to the organisation's goals, the result may be a failure to attract and retain the employees needed for organisational success.
Behavioural risk	If the reward scheme is not aligned to the required employee behaviours, the result may be rewarding inappropriate or unproductive behaviour.
Financial risk	The cost of the reward scheme outweighs the benefits, leading to an overall reduction in profit.
Legal and ethical risk	Non-compliance with legal/regulatory requirements or societal/ethical expectations can result in employee claims, regulatory action and/or reputational damage.

KAPLAN PUBLISHING

5 Methods of reward

Employee rewards fall into four categories:

5.1 Basic pay

- The minimum amount that an employee receives for working in an organisation.

- Determined in a number of ways such as market rates or job evaluation.

- Hourly rates or fixed annual salaries may be paid.

- May be supplemented by other types of remuneration.

Advantages	Disadvantages
• Easy to administer. • Basic employee needs taken care of. • A competitive rate of basic pay can assist in attracting and retaining the best employees.	• Does not motivate employees to achieve strategy (no alignment to strategic goals). • Does not motivate employees to improve performance.

5.2 Benefits

A wide range of rewards other than wages or pensions, such as company cars or health insurance.

Advantages	Disadvantages
• Can be tailored to the individual employee. • Can be less expensive than basic or performance-related pay. • Can be used as a tool to attract and retain the best employees. • Can compensate for lower rates of basic or performance-related pay.	• Employees may not want the benefits offered. • Does not motivate employees to achieve strategy (no alignment to strategic goals). • Additional cost of providing the benefits. • Can be complicated to administer.

5.3 Executive share options schemes

Gives directors the right to purchase shares at a specified exercise price after a specified time-period in the future.

Advantages	Disadvantages
• Should align management and shareholder interests, because the directors have an interest in ensuring the share price increases over time. • Can assist in attracting and retaining the best directors. • Can encourage risk-averse directors to take positive action to increase the value of the company. • Can compensate for payment of a lower salary or benefits. • Can be a tax-efficient way of remunerating directors.	• Can encourage risk-seeking behaviour in the hope of increasing the value of the options. • Costly and time consuming to administer. • It may give directors an incentive to manipulate share price (see note below), particularly if a large number of options are due to be exercised.

Important note: The potential for the 'manipulation' of data is discussed above and in a number of subsequent chapters. In the exam, exercise caution when including this as part of your answer. Accounting data is not simple to manipulate; there are checks and balances and audit requirements in place. 'Manipulation', if it does exist, would more likely be in the form of the accounting method used or policy changes than fraud.

Executive share options schemes

An executive share option scheme (ESOS) gives directors the right to purchase shares at a specified exercise price after a specified time-period in the future.

The options will normally have an exercise price that is equal to, or slightly higher than, the market price on the date that the options are granted.

If the price of the shares rises so that it exceeds the exercise price by the time the options can be exercised, the directors will be able to purchase shares at lower than their market value.

The time-period that must pass before the options can be exercised is generally a few years. If the director leaves during that period the options will lapse.

5.4 Performance-related pay

Pay is based on the level of performance achieved. Types of performance-related pay include:

- **Individual performance-related pay** – a pay rise or bonus is given to an employee on achievement of pre-agreed objectives or based on the assessment by a manager. Advantages include the ability to align individual objectives with organisational goals and the controllability of rewards by the employee. However, such schemes may result in a lack of teamwork and in tunnel vision (sole concentration on areas which are measured and rewarded).

- **Group performance-related pay** – rewards are based on the achievement of group targets. Encourages teamwork but may not be seen as fair by employees.

- **Profit-related pay** – part of the employee's remuneration is linked to organisational profit. Can motivate employees to increase company profit and increase loyalty but may lead to short-termism and lack of motivation if employees feel they have no control over organisational profit.

- **Commission** – for example, used for sales staff and is based on a percentage of their sales. Can motivate staff but may lead to short-termism and manipulation of results.

- **Piecework schemes** – a price is paid for each unit of output. Often viewed as a fair system but quality control will be required.

- **Knowledge contingent pay** – for example, an accountant may receive a bonus or pay rise on passing their ACCA exams.

Advantages	Disadvantages
• Motivates employees to achieve strategy, if aligned to this.	• Can be subjective and inconsistent.
• Motivates employees to improve performance.	• Can be viewed as unfair if based on team/company performance.
• Can be used as a tool to attract and retain the best employees.	• Stressful for employee if they rely on this pay for basic needs (e.g. in the case of commission).
• Can compensate for lower rates of basic pay or less attractive benefits.	• Can be complicated to administer.

6 Linking reward schemes to performance measurement

6.1 Introduction

As discussed in section 5, part of the employee's reward (e.g. a bonus or pay rise) may be performance-related and linked to the achievement of pre-agreed objectives.

It is important that appropriate objectives and targets (performance measures) are set for the employee. Targets should be **SMART**:

SMART criteria	Explanation
Specific	The target should be specific and not vague. For example, a HR manager in an organisation may be given a specific target of 'recruiting three new people to the marketing team by the end of June', rather than a vague objective of 'recruiting employees needed'.
Measurable	The achievement of the target should be measurable. If we relate this to the previous example, it is easy to measure if three new people are recruited to the marketing team by the end of June.
Attainable	Employees may be unmotivated if they consider targets are very difficult or impossible to achieve, e.g. '50% increase in gross profit in the next year' may be seen as impossible. (However, it is worth noting that the same may be true if targets are too easy to achieve.) Targets should be discussed and agreed between the employee and, for example, their line manager.
Relevant	Relevant to the organisation's overall objective, e.g. if the organisation has an objective of 100% quality then an individual production worker may be set a target to produce products with zero defects.
Time-bound	Targets should also be time-bound. In the example above, the target for recruitment is the end of June.

In addition to being SMART, targets set for employees should be:

- **Controllable** – the individual will be unmotivated if they feel they can't control the target set and are held accountable for such targets. For example, a production worker may not be responsible for defects if poor quality materials are purchased. This can be a significant issue if profit-related pay or group-related pay (section 5.4) are used.

- **A prioritised, small set** – employees will be overwhelmed and hence unmotivated if they are set a large number of targets. A small number of prioritised, SMART, controllable targets is desirable.

- **Fair and consistent** – applied fairly and consistently to employees who have similar roles and similar levels of performance.

- **Sufficiently rewarded** – the level of reward should be sufficient to motivate employees to achieve targets now and in the future.

6.2 Beneficial and adverse consequences of linking reward to performance measures

Benefits of linking reward to performance measures	Potential problems of linking reward to performance measures
• By aligning the organisation's KPIs to a reward scheme, it is clear to all employees that employee performance creates organisational success and they will be more motivated to work towards this success.	• Employees will not be motivated if they consider targets are not SMART, prioritised, controllable or if there are a large number of targets.
• Following on from this point, the reward scheme should be affordable; the reward is only given if the employee achieves the pre-agreed objectives and since these are aligned with the achievement of the organisation's objectives this should, in theory, create the resources required to reward the employee.	• Employees may become unmotivated if they feel they are not rewarded for the achievement of a target or they were penalised financially for circumstances outside of their control. For example, an employee may have achieved their quality target but did not receive a reward because the company's annual performance was poor.
• Targets that are SMART, controllable, small in number, prioritised and rewarded will be considered fair and consistent, giving individuals an incentive to achieve a good performance level since they know that this will be rewarded.	• Employees may become highly stressed if a significant proportion of their income is performance related.
• Effective schemes also attract and retain the employees valuable to an organisation.	• Employees may prioritise the achievement of their reward, which may impact their risk appetite. Employees may become too cautious and risk averse or conversely they may take bigger risks.
• By rewarding performance, an effective scheme creates an organisation focused on continuous improvement ('what gets rewarded, gets repeated').	• If the targets are not aligned to the organisation's overall objectives, employees will have an extra incentive towards dysfunctional behaviour, i.e. making decisions that are not in the best interests of the business.
	• It may be difficult to decide if targets should be based on individual, team, division or group performance.

There are **many ways in which poorly designed performance measurement can result in wrong signals and dysfunctional behaviour**. These include the following problem areas:

- **Misrepresentation** – 'creative' reporting to suggest that a result is acceptable. For example, a manager may report that 98% of customers were 'satisfied' or 'more than satisfied' with the level of service. However, on further investigation it may be found that feedback was only sought from a small selection of customers.

- **Gaming** – is deliberate distortion of performance in order to achieve the rewarded goals. For example, a manager may decide to cut divisional investment to boost divisional return on investment (and their reward) but this may result in a long-term fall in profits.

- **Sub-optimisation** – if the areas measured are not optimally chosen, performance is only driven by the measured factors and the outcome will not be the best possible for the organisation. For example, a focus on winning new customers may result in a reduced focus on the satisfaction of existing customers.

- **Misinterpretation** – failure to recognise the complexity of the environment in which the organisation operates. For example, looking at the financial aspects of performance a manager may be assessed as performing well. However, on further investigation it may be discovered that non-financial factors such as customer satisfaction are less favourable and therefore performance has been misinterpreted.

- **Short-termism (myopia)** – measures chosen are short-term in nature, leading to the neglect of longer-term objectives. Financial measures such as return on capital employed (ROCE) may lead to short-termism. The use of a mix of financial and non-financial measures may lead to an improved focus on long-term success.

- **Tunnel vision** – an undue focus on stated performance measures and a consequent lack of resources being applied to unmeasured areas. For example, an undue focus on ROCE to the detriment of employee satisfaction due to their needs, for say training or competitive remuneration, not being met.

- **Measure fixation** – excessive focus on certain behaviours in order to achieve specific performance indicators which may not be effective. For example, an excessive focus on cost cutting to the detriment of quality and long-term performance.

- **Ossification** – an unwillingness to change the performance measurement scheme once it has been set up, especially when it shows that good or adequate results are being achieved. The example of customer surveys being sent to only a select group of customers is also relevant here.

A number of actions might be taken in order to minimise the impact of imperfections that may exist within the performance measurement system. These methods will be explored in later chapters.

Question practice

The question below is an extract from a past exam question. Make sure that you take the time to attempt the question and review the answer.

Test your understanding 1

Lincoln & Lincoln Advertising (LLA) is an advertising agency based in Veeland, which is a large well-developed country considered to be one of the wealthiest in the world. LLA operates out of three regional offices (North, East and West) with its head office functions based in the East offices. The business offers a wide range of advertising services:

Strategic: Advising on an overall advertising campaign (mix of advertising channels and overall themes)

Buying: Advising and buying advertising space (on television, radio, websites and in newspapers and magazines); and

Creative: Designing and producing specific adverts for the customers' use.

The company is one of the three largest agencies in Veeland with many years of experience and many awards won. Competition in advertising is fierce, as advertising spending by businesses has suffered recently during a general economic downturn. Most new business is won in tender competitions between different advertising agencies.

Remuneration policy and regional offices

There are broadly five grades of staff at each regional office. The following is an outline of their remuneration packages. (The head office staff are treated separately and are not part of this exercise.)

Senior management

All staff at this level are paid a basic fixed salary, which reflects industry norms over the last few years, plus a bonus dependent on the net income of their office.

Creative staff

The 'creatives' are on individual packages which reflect the market rates in order to recruit them at the time that they were recruited. Some are fixed salary and some have a fixed element plus a bonus based on their office's revenues.

Buying staff

The buyers are paid a fixed salary plus a bonus based on the prices for advertising space that they negotiate compared to the budgeted cost of space. The budget is set by the finance team at head office based on previous years' experience and their forecast for supply and demand in the year in question.

Account management staff

Account management handles relationships with clients and also develops new clients. They are paid a fixed market-based salary.

Administration staff

These staff are paid the market rate for their jobs as a fixed salary based on hours worked.

Required:

Using the information provided, evaluate LLA's remuneration policy, recommending changes as appropriate. **(10 marks)**

Tutor tip:

As a professional accountant of the future, you need to have the right **blend of professional and technical skills**. This question is a great opportunity for you to develop both of these skill sets. To gain a good mark in the exam, you must apply your technical knowledge in the context of the scenario and address the specifics of the requirement in a professional manner. Take particular notice of the verb used.

One of the professional skills is 'Analysis and Evaluation' and this will be included in all APM questions. This question requires you to 'evaluate' and 'recommend'. Therefore, to maximise your mark you need to carefully assess the situation in a balanced way, taking each of the staff levels in turn, using professional judgement as a sound basis for the recommendations made.

Chapter summary

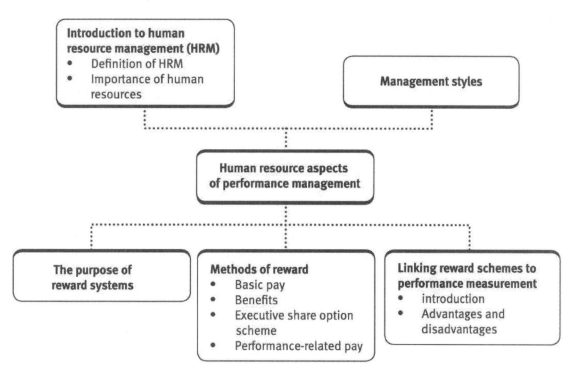

Introduction to human resource management (HRM)
- Definition of HRM
- Importance of human resources

Management styles

Human resource aspects of performance management

The purpose of reward systems

Methods of reward
- Basic pay
- Benefits
- Executive share option scheme
- Performance-related pay

Linking reward schemes to performance measurement
- introduction
- Advantages and disadvantages

Test your understanding answers

Test your understanding 1

Remuneration packages

Generally, using industry norms as a basic benchmark will help to ensure that staff are kept broadly happy, although it will not motivate them to outperform their peers.

Taking each of the staff levels in turn:

Senior management

Their basic salary reflects historic norms and the bonus should motivate performance. It is notable that no account is taken of the different economic conditions that each office may find itself in and so there may be resentment from those in offices where the general economy is doing poorly to those who are in a region with good performance and so profits are growing easily. It may be worthwhile trying to benchmark the performance of each office against its regional competitors, although it can be hard to obtain such detailed information.

Creative staff

The creatives' packages are set when recruited. This could lead to a loss of motivation, especially for those who get only a fixed salary. If a bonus is paid, then it is currently based on revenue and not profits and so there is no mechanism to control costs on projects with these employees. There will be tension between the need for imaginative ideas and cost efficient ones. Overall, it is likely that each staff member should have a personalised package with a performance element that would be based on the assessment of a superior manager. In order to maintain some sense of objectivity, the criteria that the manager might use to judge performance should be agreed across the firm and could include, primarily, winning new business in tender competitions and, secondarily, winning industry awards.

Buying staff

The packages for the buying staff appear to be based on appropriate performance, although the setting of such targets depends heavily on the expertise of the finance team and, as they are based in the East office, they may lack the local knowledge to set the budget accurately. It may be wise to maintain the bulk of the buyers' remuneration as a fixed salary element as a result.

Account management staff

It is surprising that this group of client-facing staff are not paid on performance. It would seem that their performance could be directly measured by client retention and new business won, so it would be common for such staff to have a high percentage of their remuneration based on performance and not be wholly fixed. Measures such as numbers of clients and total client revenues would be appropriate for these posts.

Administration staff

This is a common method of remuneration for these types of jobs and in line with the general market. A small bonus based on the overall performance of the firm may help to create a culture of loyalty throughout the business. It is unlikely to be efficient to set individual targets for such employees, given that there will probably be a large number of them.

Financial performance measures in the private sector

Chapter learning objectives

Upon completion of this chapter you will be able to:

- demonstrate why the primary objective of financial performance should be primarily concerned with the benefits to shareholders

- discuss the appropriateness of, and apply different measures of performance, including:

    - Gross profit and operating profit

    - Return on Capital Employed (ROCE)

    - Earnings Per Share (EPS)

    - Earnings Before Interest, Tax, Depreciation and Amortisation (EBITDA)

    - Net Present Value (NPV)

    - Internal Rate of Return and Modified Internal Rate of Return (IRR, MIRR)

- discuss why indicators of liquidity and gearing need to considered in conjunction with profitability

- compare and contrast short and long run financial performance and the resulting management issues

- assess the appropriate benchmarks to use in assessing performance.

PER

Three of the PER performance objectives are:

–   Monitor performance (PO14)

–   Business advisory (PO21) and

–   Data analysis and decision support (PO22).

Working through this chapter should help you understand how to demonstrate these objectives.

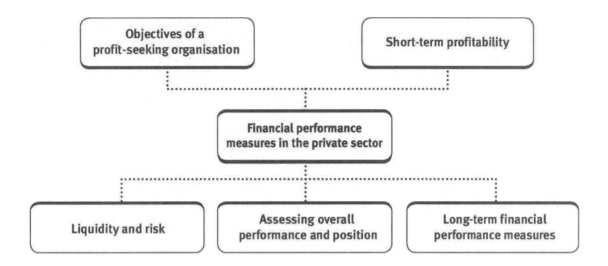

1 Common knowledge

Chapter 10 builds on your knowledge of financial performance measures from PM.

2 Introduction

In the exam, you may be required to look at performance measures in a variety of contexts. In this chapter, we focus on the principal measures used by the private sector. The emphasis will be on financial measures (non–financial measures will be reviewed in Chapter 13).

3 The objectives of profit-seeking organisations

3.1 Maximising shareholder wealth

- The primary objective of financial performance in a profit-seeking organisation is to maximise shareholder wealth.

- This is based on the argument that shareholders are the legal owners of a company and so their interests should be prioritised.

- Shareholders are generally concerned with the following:
  - current earnings
  - future earnings
  - dividend policy
  - relative risk of their investment.

A common theme in exam questions is that the organisation's performance report focuses solely on **financial** performance. Although important in the short-term, the sole focus on financial performance may be detrimental to the achievement of the organisation's mission and objectives in the long-term. **Non-financial** factors, focusing on areas such as customer satisfaction, product innovation, sustainability and employee productivity, will be equally as important.

However, although the sole focus should not be on financial performance, an **evaluation of financial performance remains important** and will be covered in **this chapter**.

Test your understanding 1

Required:

What will be the primary objective of a commercial bank? What might be some of its subsidiary or secondary objectives?

Objectives according to Drucker

Peter Drucker has suggested that profit-seeking organisations typically have objectives relating to the following:

- market standing
- innovation
- productivity
- physical and financial resources
- profitability
- manager performance and development
- worker performance and attitude
- public responsibility.

3.2 The relationship between profits and shareholder value

Rather than focusing on achieving higher profit levels, **companies are under increasing pressure to look at the long-term value of the business**. This is due to the following factors:

- Research has suggested a poor correlation between shareholder return and short-term profitability
- Investors are increasingly looking at long-term value
- Reported profits may not be comparable between companies.

3.3 How to measure the long-term value of a business

As discussed in section 3.1, the sole focus on financial performance may be detrimental to the achievement of the organisation's mission and objectives in the long-term. One approach to measuring the long-term value of a business is to focus on both financial performance (this chapter) and non-financial performance (Chapter 13).

Another example of an approach to measuring long-term value to shareholders is **value based management** (VBM). A VBM approach aligns the strategic, operational and management processes to focus management decision making on what activities create wealth for shareholders (VBM will be explored in more detail in Chapter 11).

3.4 Financial performance measures

This chapter is concerned with measuring:

*   the **financial performance of the organisation as a whole**

*   the **performance of the key projects**.

Chapter 11 will cover **divisional performance** and **Chapter 13** will cover **non-financial performance**.

Importantly:

*   Although most of these indicators will be familiar to you from PM, there will be a different emphasis in APM questions.

*   A common mistake of APM candidates is that they throw every indicator that they can remember at a problem in an uncritical fashion. APM is all about the critical approach. It is about selecting from the range of indicators that you know from PM and using those that are most appropriate to the scenario.

*   It is also important that the indicators are not calculated in isolation (this will be meaningless). Instead, they should be compared to, for example, a previous period or an appropriate benchmark, such as a competitor or to an industry average, or to any targets set.

*   Finally, the examining team will not only expect you to calculate the numbers but to also give performance management advice based on what you have calculated.

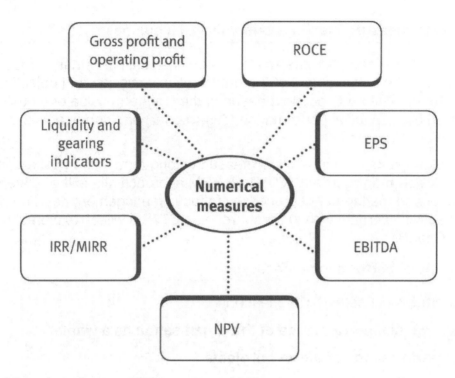

Each of these measures will be reviewed in turn.

4 Short-term profitability

4.1 Gross and operating profit

Despite concerns over the poor correlation between profit and shareholder value, many business use gross or operating profit based targets. This is primarily for the following reasons:

- The information is readily available internally as it is needed for statutory reporting

- It makes comparisons between companies easier as they also have to produce statutory reports

- Most managers feel they understand it

- The profit measures do not include variables, such as tax or interest charges, which management have little control over and therefore, these measures are useful if managers are set targets to achieve based on either profit figure.

The gross profit margin and operating profit margin are often calculated:

> **Gross profit margin = (Gross profit ÷ Sales) × 100%**
>
> **Operating profit margin = (Operating profit ÷ Sales) × 100%**

The **relative pros and cons** of using gross compared with operating profit are as follows:

Gross profit	Operating profit
• Focusses purely on whether the process of making and selling products is profitable – i.e. does the price cover the manufacturing cost, before considering selling, distribution and admin costs.	• Also considers selling, distribution and admin costs, so indicates whether gross profit is sufficient to cover wider costs.
• Useful for highlighting product profitability issues – for example, if gross profit has fallen, is this due to cost rises, pressure to drop prices or a mixture of both? Management response will depend on the underlying causes.	• Useful for highlighting wider cost efficiency issues – for example, a division may have improving gross profit but worsening operating profit indicating underlying good products but poor control over distribution and/or admin.
For short-term decision making it could be argued that **contribution** would be a more useful metric.	

4.2 Return on capital employed (ROCE)

ROCE is a key measure of **profitability**. It shows the operating profit that is generated from every $1 of assets employed.

$$\text{ROCE} = \frac{\text{Operating profit}}{\text{Capital employed}} \times 100$$

Capital employed = total assets less current liabilities <u>or</u> total equity plus long-term debt.

It is important to **be guided by the exam question**:

• If the operating profit is not given in the question, use the profit figure that is closest to it or the one you are asked to use.

• Capital employed may be based on net book value (NBV), gross book value or replacement cost.

• Capital employed may be the average figure (if information for two periods is given), the figure at the start of the period (if an average can't be calculated) or the figure at the end of the period (if this is all that is given in the question or the question states that this figure should be used).

Evaluation of ROCE

A high ROCE is desirable. An increase in ROCE could be achieved by:

- Increasing operating profit, for example through an increase in sales price or better control of costs.

- Reducing capital employed, for example through the repayment of its debt.

Advantages	Disadvantages
• Easy to calculate. • Figures are readily available. • Measures how well a business is utilising the funds invested in it. • Often used by external analysts/investors.	• Research shows a poor correlation between ROCE and shareholder value. • ROCE can be improved by cutting back investment – this may not be in the company's long-term best interest. • Differences between the companies being compared (e.g. different accounting policies or industries) may make comparison less meaningful. • Can be distorted by accounting policies.

Test your understanding 2

	Company A	Company B
	$	$
Operating profit	20,000	1,000,000
Sales	200,000	2,000,000
Capital employed	100,000	10,000,000

Required:

For companies A and B, which of the following statements are true?

1 Company A has a higher ROCE than Company B.

2 Company B has a higher ROCE than Company A.

3 Company A is more profitable than Company B.

4 Company A is better utilising the funds invested in it than company B.

Choose:

A 1, 3 and 4

B 2 only

C 1 and 4

D None of these

4.3 Earnings per share (EPS)

EPS is a measure of the profit attributable to each ordinary share.

$$EPS = \frac{\textbf{Profit after tax less preference dividends}}{\textbf{Weighted average number of ordinary shares in issue}}$$

As per other ratios, for EPS to be meaningful, it must be set in context:

- Is EPS growing or declining over time?

- Is there likely to be significant dilution of EPS?

- Is it calculated consistently?

Advantages	Disadvantages
• Easily understood by shareholders. • Calculation is precisely defined by accounting standards. • Figures are readily available. • Often used as a performance measure between companies, sectors, periods within the same organisation.	• Research shows a poor correlation between EPS growth and shareholder value. • Accounting treatment may cause ratio to be distorted.

Test your understanding 3

A company's share capital is as follows:

Ordinary shares ($1 each) $6,000,000

9% Preference shares $1,000,000

The company made profits before tax of $5,500,000. Corporation tax on this is calculated as $2,100,000.

Required:

Calculate the company's EPS.

4.4 EBITDA

EBITDA is **E**arnings **B**efore **I**nterest, **T**ax, **D**epreciation and **A**mortisation (and write-offs such as goodwill)

Advantages	Disadvantages
• It is a measure of underlying performance since it is a proxy for cash flow generated from operating profit. • Tax and interest are excluded. These are externally generated and therefore not relevant to the underlying success of the business. • Depreciation and amortisation represent a write-off of expenditure over a number of years and are therefore not relevant when examining the performance of a particular year. • Easy to calculate. • Easy to understand.	• Despite its advantages, there remains a poor correlation to shareholder wealth. • Comparison between organisations is difficult due to potential differences in accounting policies and the calculation of an absolute figure. • It ignores changes in working capital and their impact on cash flow. • It fails to consider the amount of non-current asset replacement needed by the business. • It can easily be manipulated by aggressive accounting policies related to income recognition and capitalisation of expenses.

4.5 Other profitability measures

Measure	Calculation
Return on equity	Profit after tax ÷ Average shareholders' equity
Asset turnover	Sales ÷ Capital employed
Dividend cover	PAT ÷ Total dividend
Dividend per share	Total dividend ÷ Number of shares
Dividend yield	(Dividend per share ÷ Current share price) × 100%
P/E ratio	Share price ÷ Earnings per share
Earnings yield	(Earnings per share ÷ Share price) × 100%
Return on equity	Net profit after tax ÷ Average shareholders' equity

Note: Other additional measures of profitability are return on investment (ROI), residual income (RI) and economic value added (EVA). These will be discussed in Chapter 11.

5 Liquidity and risk

5.1 Liquidity indicators

Liquidity the ability of the company to meet its short-term liabilities using its current assets, which can readily (or hopefully quickly) be turned into cash.

There is often a trade-off between liquidity and profitability. Companies can be highly profitable but get into trouble when they run out of cash (overtrading).

Therefore, liquidity needs to be considered alongside profitability when appraising a company's financial situation.

Measure	Calculation
Current ratio	Current assets ÷ Current liabilities
Acid test or quick ratio	(Current assets – inventories) ÷ Current liabilities
Inventory period	(Ave. value of inventory ÷ Cost of sales) × 365
Raw material period	(Ave. value of raw materials ÷ Purchases) × 365
WIP period	(Ave. value of WIP ÷ Cost of sales) × 365
Finished goods period	(Ave. value of finished goods ÷ Cost of sales) × 365
Receivables period	(Ave. receivables ÷ Sales) × 365
Payables period	(Ave. payables ÷ Purchases) × 365

5.2 Risk indicators

These ratios measure the ability of the company to meet its long-term liabilities:

Financial gearing

The financial gearing ratio measures the financial risk and reflects the organisation's ability to service its long-term debt.

> **Financial gearing = (Long-term debt + Preference share capital/Shareholder funds) × 100% <u>or</u>**
>
> **Financial gearing = (Long-term debt + Preference share capital/ Long-term debt + Preference share capital + Shareholder funds) × 100%**

Note: This is sometimes shortened to D/E or D/D+E where D = debt (i.e. long-term debt plus preference share capital) and E = equity (i.e. shareholder funds).

A high level of financial gearing indicates a higher level of financial risk since the organisation is less able to finance its long-term debt (and pay preference dividends) if profits fall.

Operational gearing

Operational gearing measures the level of business risk relating to how fluctuations in sales volume might lead to falling profits as fixed costs are not covered. A high level of operational gearing indicates a higher level of business risk.

There are a number of definitions including the below:

> **Operational gearing = (Contribution/PBIT)**

If the contribution is large but PBIT is low then fixed costs are only being marginally covered, and a small loss of revenue due to reduced sales volumes could lead to losses.

Note: It is difficult to measure operational gearing precisely because most costs have both fixed and variable elements. However, costs can normally be classified into one or other of the categories based on their general expected behaviour.

Interest cover

Interest cover indicates the ability of a company to pay interest out of profits generated.

> **Interest cover = (PBIT/Interest charges)**

A low interest cover indicates that the company may have difficulty financing its debts (and paying dividends) if profits fall.

6 Assessing overall financial performance and position

The following question considers a combination of profitability, liquidity and risk.

Test your understanding 4

AK is a privately owned manufacturing company and has been experiencing difficulties.

Required:

You have been asked to assess the current position of AK using appropriate performance measures:

	20X6	20X5
	$000	$000
Receivables	5,200	3,120
Inventory	2,150	2,580
Cash	350	1,350
	———	———
Total current assets	7,700	7,050
Non-current assets	14,500	14,500
Total payables	4,500	3,150

Sales	17,500	16,625
Operating costs	14,000	12,950
Operating profit	3,500	3,675
Earnings	2,625	2,756

There are 2.5 million shares in issue.

6.1 Assessing performance and giving performance management advice

As discussed, the examining team will expect you to be able to assess and comment on the financial performance of an organisation using a range of appropriate measures. In the APM exam, it is more important that you can give performance management advice rather than just being able to calculate a long list of ratios.

Additional example on assessing financial performance

BPG is a Telecommunications company that commenced trading in 20X1 in the country of Brean. In 20X6 it created a similar division in the country of Portlet.

Required:

Assess the financial performance of BPG and its operations in Brean and Portlet during the years ended 20X8 and 20X9. Using the data provided below.

Note: you should highlight any information that would be required to make a more comprehensive assessment of financial performance.

Summary Income Statements

	20X9 Brean $000	20X9 Portlet $000	20X9 Company $000	20X8 Brean $000	20X8 Portlet $000	20X8 Company $000
Revenue	14,400	2,900	17,300	14,040	1,980	16,020
Salaries	4,450	1,340	5,790	4,125	1,185	5,310
Consumables	2,095	502	2,597	1,950	380	2,330
Other operating costs	2,921	695	3,616	2,754	620	3,374
	9,466	2,537	12,003	8,829	2,185	11,014
Marketing	2,456	600	3,056	2,092	480	2,572
Interest			850			900
Depreciation and amortisation	400	160	560	400	100	500
	2,856	760	4,466	2,492	580	3,972
Total costs	12,322	3,297	16,469	11,321	2,765	14,986
Profit/(loss)	2,078	(397)	831	2,719	(785)	1,034

Statement of financial position

	20X9 Brean $000	20X9 Portlet $000	20X9 Company $000	20X8 Brean $000	20X8 Portlet $000	20X8 Company $000
Assets						
Non-current assets	9,000	1,600	10,600	8,000	1,000	9,000
Current assets	4,550	1,000	5,550	5,000	800	5,800
Total assets	13,550	2,600	16,150	13,000	1,800	14,800
Shareholders' equity			9,150			7,800
Long term borrowings			4,000			4,500
Current liabilities	2,400	600	3,000	2,000	500	2,500
			16,150			14,800

Solution:

Company		20X9	20X8
ROCE =	PBIT/D+E	12.8%	15.7%
EBITDA =	EBITDA	2,241	2,434
Gearing =	D/E	43.7%	57.7%
or gearing =	D/D+E	30.4%	36.6%

Each operation

		20X9 Brean	20X9 Portlet	20X8 Brean	20X8 Portlet
Sales margin =	Profit/revenue (%)	14.4	(13.7)	19.4	(39.6)
Non-current asset turnover =	Revenue/non-curr assets	1.6	1.8	1.76	1.98

	Brean	Portlet	Company
% Revenue growth	2.6	46.5	8
% Profit growth	(23.6)	49.4	
% Increase in costs:			
Salaries	7.9	13.1	
Marketing	7.4	32.1	
Operating costs	6.1	12.1	

The turnover in Brean has increased by 2.6% whilst in Portlet turnover has increased by 46.5% which is excellent since the business only commenced trading in 20X6. The overall growth amounted to 8% which is an acceptable level.

The profits in Brean are down by nearly 24% whilst in Portlet the loss has fallen by 49%. Portlet will need to make further growth in sales and monitor costs in order to become more profitable.

The costs within Brean have risen by 8% for salaries, 7% for marketing and 6% for operating costs yet sales have only increased by 2.6%.

The costs within Portlet have risen substantially more than in Brean. Marketing for example has risen by 32%. This may be due to the fact that this is a necessary cost to develop the growth in revenue within the newly established operation.

Salaries and operating costs have risen by between 12 and 13%, yet sales have increased by 46%. These costs should be monitored as the business grows further.

The EBITDA has fallen by 8% from $2,434,000 to $2,241,000 and ROCE has also fallen from 13.1% to 10.4%. This is not a very good sign for the company.

The non-current asset utilisation ratios of Brean show a decrease from 20X8 to 20X9. Portlet also shows a decrease from 2 to 1.8, this is less surprising given that the operation has only recently been established. Portlet is clearly in a rapid growth phase hence the need for investment in non-current assets.

It would be useful to have previous years data for Brean to observe longer term trends for revenue and costs. Data for Portlet from its first year of operation in 20X6 would enable a complete picture to be taken.

Competitor information would allow us to establish the market share and establish how well the operations are performing in comparison to competitors.

It is clear that long-term borrowings have decreased from 20X8 to 20X9 and that BPG has sufficient cash flow to repay some of the debt finance. However, it would be useful to have a breakdown of working capital for each operation.

It would also be useful to have future market and financial projections for Brean and Porlet, which should reflect the actual results in 20X8 and 20X9.

Budgeted data would be useful to see if they have managed to meet the targets set.

Additional question practice

Test your understanding 5

Water Supply Services (WSS) and Enterprise Activities (EA) are two wholly-owned subsidiaries of Aqua Holdings. You have recently qualified as an accountant and have joined the finance team of Aqua Holdings at headquarters. Your finance director is not satisfied with the performance of these two subsidiaries and has asked you to prepare a report covering the following issues:

1   The profitability of the two subsidiaries.

2   The competence of the EA manager to make financial decisions.

3   The consequences of having a common management information system serving both companies.

The finance director has also provided you with the following background information on the two companies:

WSS

The company holds a licence issued by the government to be the sole supplier of drinking water to a large town. The business necessitates a considerable investment in infrastructure assets and is therefore highly capital intensive. To comply with the licence the company has to demonstrate that it is maintaining guaranteed service standards to its customers. WSS is extensively regulated requiring very detailed annual returns concerning costs, prices, profits and service delivery standards. The government enforces a price-capping regime and therefore the company has limited freedom in tariff determination – the government will normally only sanction a price increase following a demonstrable rise in costs.

EA

In contrast to WSS, EA operates in a very competitive market offering a plumbing service to domestic properties. The business has the following characteristics:

- rapidly changing market conditions

- a high rate of new entrants and business failures

- occasional shortages of skilled plumbers

- fluctuating profits.

In addition to this background information you also have summarised income statements and statements of financial position for the last two years for both companies.

Water Supply Services

Summary income statement

	Year	
	20X9	20X8
	$m	$m
Turnover	31	30
Less: Staff costs	3	2
General expenses	2	2
Depreciation	12	9
Interest	5	5
Profit	9	12

Summary statement of financial position

	Year	
	20X9	**20X8**
	$m	$m
Non-current assets	165	134
Current assets	5	6
Total assets	170	140
Current liabilities	(3)	(6)
Debentures	(47)	(47)
Net assets	120	87
Shareholders' equity	120	87

Enterprise activities – summary income statement

	Year	
	20X9	**20X8**
	$m	$m
Turnover	20	35
Less: Staff costs	5	6
General expenses	10	10
Materials	3	6
Depreciation	1	1
Profit	1	12

Summary statement of financial position

	Year	
	20X9	**20X8**
	$m	$m
Non-current assets	22	22
Current assets	13	12
Total assets	35	34
Current liabilities	(4)	(4)
Net assets	31	30
Shareholders' equity	31	30

Required:

Prepare an extract from the report discussing the comparative financial performance of Water Supply Services and Enterprise Activities from the above financial statements. Your report extract should incorporate an assessment of the potential limitations of undertaking such a comparison.

Tutor tip:

A requirement such as this could be part of a Section A question. These questions will always contain 10 **professional marks**, covering all four professional skills. This is a significant number of marks and therefore practising producing professional answers is key. For example, in this question you can maximise your '**Communication**' marks as follows:

- Appropriate format and structure, i.e. use headings and sub-headings. Single sentences or short bullet points are not appropriate; paragraphs are required.

- Style, language and clarity, i.e. tone should be appropriate for the finance director, answer should be easy to follow and to understand and, importantly, CBE tools should be used appropriately (meaning that calculations or tables of data are included in a spreadsheet where as written work is included in the word processing software).

- Effectiveness of communication, i.e. content of the report is relevant and tailored to WSS and EA.

Practising questions will help to embed a professional mindset into how you approach your answers so that by the time you get to the exam it becomes automatic and you are able to easily pick up the professional skills marks as you work through the technical requirements.

7 Long-term financial performance measures

7.1 Introduction

Short-term financial performance measures (i.e. those covered in section 4.1 to 4.8) are used for the following:

- Control purposes, e.g. variance analysis is carried out comparing actual and budgeted results and investigating any differences.

- Determining rewards – rewards may be linked to the achievement of short-term targets.

- Assessing the quality of past decisions and assessing the impact of decisions yet to be made.

7.2 Problems of using short-term targets to appraise performance

A focus on short-term performance (and the measurement of a manager's performance based on short-term results) can threaten a company's ability to create long-term value for its shareholders.

Managers may feel the pressure to achieve short-term targets (such as a target ROCE or gross profit margin) and, as a result make decisions that are not in the best interests of the organisation overall (i.e. there is a **lack of goal congruence**). For example:

- Investment in new assets is cut. This may lead to a short-term boost in profits but long-term profitability may suffer as a result of old, and potentially inefficient, assets being used.

- The development and training budget may be cut to boost short-term profitability. However, employees are a vital resource for many organisations and a lack of investment in this area could lead to a loss of competitive advantage and a resultant fall in long-term profits.

7.3 Steps to reduce short-termism

- **Use financial and non-financial measures:** These should focus manager's attention on long-term financial performance. Methods such as the balanced scorecard can be used (these methods will be discussed in Chapter 13).

- **Switch from a budget-constrained style:** A switch should be made to a profit-conscious or non-accounting style (management styles were covered in Chapter 9). Both of these approaches have a more long-term focus.

- **Share options:** If these are given to management they should focus their attention on improving share price and hence long-term performance.

- **Bonuses:** These should be linked to profits over timescales greater than one year.

- **NPV and IRR:** Should be used to appraise investments. Discounted cash flow techniques recognise the future economic benefits of current investments.

- **Reduce decentralisation:** This should increase central control and reduce the problem of dysfunctional behaviour (however, this also comes with its own drawbacks).

- **Value-based techniques:** Focus on the key drivers of shareholder wealth. These techniques can be incorporated and will be discussed in more detail in Chapter 11.

7.4 Should a short-term approach ever be taken?

It is generally accepted that a focus on long-term performance is superior. However, there are some situations when it is important to measure the achievement of short-term targets and to link rewards to these targets.

The best example of this would be an organisation which is fighting to survive. It is only by overcoming short-term hurdles and building short-term profits that long-term survival (and profitability) can be achieved. Cash flow measures may be more important than profit measures at this stage.

7.5 Appraising long-term projects

We will now review some of the techniques that are available for appraising long-term projects. These include:

- Net present value (NPV)
- Internal rate of return (IRR)
- Modified internal rate of return (MIRR).

7.6 Net present value (NPV)

Net present value (NPV) represents the increase or decrease in the value of an organisation today as a result of accepting the project being reviewed.

Decision rule: any project that generates a positive NPV is viable.

> **NPV = present value of the future cashflows – investment**

The present value of the future cash flows can be calculated by either:

- Using the NPV spreadsheet function
- Multiplying all future cash flows by a discount factor based on the cost of capital of the organisation.

The NPV spreadsheet function uses the following formula:

> **=NPV(rate,values)**
>
> rate = cost of capital (i.e. 12% = 0.12)
>
> values = the cell references of the future cash flows (from T1 onwards)
>
> Then **deduct the value of the investment** to get the NPV.

Advantages	Disadvantages
• Strong correlation with shareholder value.	• Difficult to calculate/understand.
• It considers the time value of money.	• It does not easily allow two projects of very different sizes to be compared.
• Risk can be allowed for by adjusting the cost of capital.	• It is based on assumptions about cash flows, the timing of those cash flows and the appropriate cost of capital.
• Cash flows are less subject to manipulation and subjective decisions than accounting profits.	• Many firms use NPV for investment appraisal and then switch to profit-based measures to motivate managers.
• Considers all project cash flows.	
• Superior measure to IRR for mutually exclusive projects.	

Test your understanding 6

Oracle invests in a new machine at the beginning of Year 1 which costs $15,000. It is hoped that the net cash flows over the next five years will correspond to those given in the table below:

Year	1	2	3	4	5
Net cash flow ($)	1,500	2,750	4,000	5,700	7,500

Required:

(i) Calculate the NPV assuming a 15% cost of capital.

(ii) Calculate the NPV assuming a 10% cost of capital.

(iii) Draw a conclusion based on your findings.

Sensitivity analysis calculates the percentage change in a variable, for example sales volume, that would have to occur before the original investment decision is reversed, i.e. the project NPV changes to $0.

$$\text{Sensitivity} = \frac{\text{NPV}}{\text{PV of flows under consideration}} \times 100$$

Test your understanding 7

JDL manufactures a range of solar panel heating. They have recently developed the new Environmental Friends (EF) solar panel. The directors of JDL recently spent $20,000 on market research, the findings of which led them to believe that a market exists for the EF panels.

The finance director of JDL has gathered relevant information and prepared the following evaluation relating to the proposed manufacture and sale of the EF solar panels:

1 Sales are expected to be 2,700 units per annum at a selling price of $3,000 per unit.

2 Variable material, labour, and overhead costs are estimated at $1,580 per unit.

3 In addition, a royalty of $250 per unit would be payable to EF for the use of their brand name.

4 Fixed overheads are estimated at $900,000 per annum. These overheads cannot be avoided until the end of the year in which the EF solar panels is withdrawn from the market.

5 An initial investment of $7 million would be required. A government grant equal to 50% of the initial investment would be received on the date the investment is made. No tax allowances would be available on this initial investment. The estimated life cycle of the EF solar panels is six years.

6   Corporation tax at the rate of 30% per annum is payable in the year in which profit occurs.

7   The cost of capital is 12%.

Required:

(a)   Calculate the net present value (NPV) of the EF solar panels proposal and recommend whether it should be undertaken by the directors of JDL.

(b)   Using sensitivity analysis, estimate by what percentage each of the under-mentioned items, taken separately, would need to change before the recommendation in (a) above is varied:

   (i)   Initial outlay of $3,500 (i.e. initial investment of $7,000 minus grant of $3,500).

   (ii)   Annual contribution.

(c)   Comment on THREE factors other than NPV that the directors of JDL should consider when deciding whether to manufacture the EF solar panels.

(d)   Explain the term 'benchmarking' and briefly discuss the potential benefits that JDL can obtain as a result of undertaking a successful programme of benchmarking.

Note: This question is included as a recap of the NPV technique (covered in other ACCA exams). It is unlikely in an APM question that you will be asked to prepare detailed calculations similar to those shown in requirements (a) and (b).

7.7   Internal rate of return (IRR)

When presented with uncertainty about the cost of capital, some managers prefer to assess projects by reference to the IRR.

Internal rate of return (IRR) represents the break-even cost of capital of the project (i.e. the discount rate when the NPV would be nil).

Decision rule: the project should be accepted if the IRR is greater than the firm's cost of capital.

The IRR of a project can be calculated by either:

•   Using the IRR spreadsheet function

•   Using the interpolation method (this method only provides an estimate of the IRR, so ideally the IRR spreadsheet function should be used).

The IRR spreadsheet function uses the following formula:

=IRR(values)

values = the cell references of all of the cash flows (from T0 onwards)

The interpolation method uses the following formula:

$$IRR = L + \frac{NPVL}{NPVL - NPVH} \times (H - L)$$

where:

L = lower cost of capital

H = higher cost of capital

NPVL = the NPV at the lower cost of capital

NPVH = the NPV at the higher cost of capital

> ### Test your understanding 8
>
> Oracle invests in a new machine at the beginning of Year 1 which costs $15,000. It is hoped that the net cash flows over the next five years will correspond to those given in the table below:
>
> | Year | 1 | 2 | 3 | 4 | 5 |
> |---|---|---|---|---|---|
> | Net cash flow ($) | 1,500 | 2,750 | 4,000 | 5,700 | 7,500 |
>
> **Required:**
>
> Calculate the IRR of the project.

7.8 Modified internal rate of return (MIRR)

One drawback of IRR is that it is possible to get multiple rates of return.

MIRR eliminates this possibility.

Modified internal rate of return (MIRR) represents the actual return generated by a project.

The MIRR assumes that funds will be reinvested at the investor's required return (cost of capital).

Decision rule: the project should be accepted if the MIRR is greater than the firm's cost of capital.

The MIRR of a project can be calculated by either:

- Using the MIRR spreadsheet function

- Using formula.

The MIRR spreadsheet function uses the following formula:

=MIRR(values,finance rate,reinvest rate)

values = the cell references of all of the cash flows (from T0 onwards)

finance rate = cost of capital (i.e. 12% = 0.12)

reinvest rate = cost of capital (unless a specific reinvestment rate is given)

Alternatively, there are several formulas which can be used to calculate MIRR, but the simplest is to use the following:

$$MIRR = \left[\frac{PV_R}{PV_I}\right]^{1/n} \times (1 + r_e) - 1$$

where:

PV_R = the present value of the 'return phase' of the project (i.e. cash inflows)

PV_I = the present value of the 'investment phase' of the project (i.e. cash outflows)

n = the life of the project in years

r_e = the firm's cost of capital

Test your understanding 9

Oracle invests in a new machine at the beginning of Year 1 which costs $15,000. It is hoped that the net cash flows over the next five years will correspond to those given in the table below:

Year	1	2	3	4	5
Net cash flow ($)	1,500	2,750	4,000	5,700	7,500

Required:

Calculate the MIRR of the project, assuming that the company's cost of capital and reinvestment rate are both 10% per annum.

Chapter summary

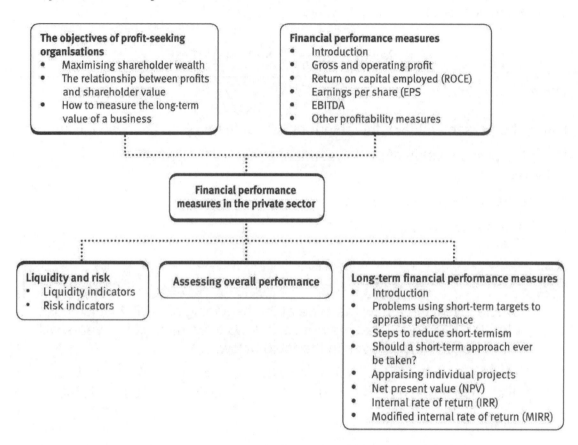

Test your understanding answers

Test your understanding 1

A bank's primary objective will be **profit maximisation** for the benefit of the shareholders.

Secondary objectives may include:

- market share
- customer satisfaction
- revenue growth
- employee satisfaction.

Test your understanding 2

Answer is C.

Company A has a ROCE of 20% ($20k ÷ $100k) compared with only 10% for Company B ($1m ÷ $10m). A higher ROCE means that the company is better at utilising the funds invested in it.

Test your understanding 3

Profits before tax	$5,500,000
Less tax	$2,100,000
Less preference dividends (9% × 1,000,000)	$90,000
	———————
Earnings	$3,310,000
	———————
Number of ordinary shares	6,000,000

EPS = (Profit after tax, – preference dividends)/Weighted average number of ordinary shares in issue

= $3.31 m/6m

= 55.2 cents

Test your understanding 4

	20X6	20X7
Current ratio	7,700 ÷ 4,500 = 1.7	7,050 ÷ 3,150 = 2.2
Acid test ratio	5,550 ÷ 4,500 = 1.2	4,470 ÷ 3,150 = 1.4
Receivable days	(5,200 ÷ 17,500) × 365 = 108 days	(3,120 ÷ 16,625) × 365 = 68 days
Inventory days	(2,150 ÷ 14,000) × 365 = 56 days	(2,580 ÷ 12,950) × 365 = 73 days
Asset turnover	17,500 ÷ 17,700 = 1.0 times	16,625 ÷ 18,400 = 0.9 times
ROCE	(3,500 ÷ 17,700) × 100 = 19.8%	(3,675 ÷ 18,400) × 100 = 20.0%
EPS	2,625 ÷ 2,500 = 1.05	2,756 ÷ 2,500 = 1.10

The company has high receivables, low inventories, a low cash balance and high trade payables.

The philosophy is to chase sales by offering lax trade credit to customers, while attempting to maintain adequate liquidity by taking extensive credit from suppliers.

This is a risky policy since it involves the risk of:

- long-standing receivables balances going bad

- discouraging potential customers since low inventory means an increased risk of goods being out of stock.

The low cash balance means that unexpected expenditures cannot be paid for out of cash. Specific funds would have to be organised.

The high trade payables will upset the suppliers; they may even stop supply until the balance outstanding is paid.

Test your understanding 5

Summary of financial ratios

	WSS		EA	
	20X9	**20X8**	**20X9**	**20X8**
Profitability (W1)				
ROCE	8.4%	12.7%	3.2%	40.0%
Profit margin	45.2%	56.7%	5.0%	34.3%
Asset utilisation	18.6%	22.4%	64.5%	116.7%
Liquidity				
Current ratio	1.7	1.0	3.25	3.0
Risk				
Gearing (W2)	39.2	54.0	0	0
Growth				
Turnover	3.3%		(42.9%)	
Profit	(25%)		(91.7%)	
Capital employed	24.6%		3.3%	

Comments on ratios

Both companies have shown a significant fall in profits. The ratios show that this is due to both a reduction in margins and falling asset utilisation. Capital employed has grown (especially for WSS) and it may be that this extra investment needs more time to generate additional profit.

EA has witnessed a dramatic reduction in sales. Costs seem to be largely fixed as these have only fallen by 17%. Turnover for the regulated monopoly appears to be more stable.

Financial risk (gearing) is high in WSS (although no comparisons with similar companies are available), but the gearing ratio has fallen in the year. High gearing magnifies the effect of volatile turnover on profit. Although it would seem EA has high operating gearing (fixed to total costs), this is somewhat compensated by the fact that it has no financial gearing.

Liquidity for both companies has improved, although no benchmarks against respective industry averages are available.

Limitations:

Accuracy of the figures – are the two years under review representative?

Short versus long term – longer-term trends would be useful. Certain events in 20X9 (i.e. expenditure on fixed assets) will reduce short-term performance but fuel longer-term growth (and profit).

The two companies cannot really be compared – one is a regulated monopoly, the other has to compete in a competitive market based on the perception of its products, quality and value for money. As such, comparison may be better carried out using industry benchmarks.

Profitability can only be fully appraised when compared against required returns of the shareholders. This, in turn, reflects the perceived risks they take when investing in each company. This may be lower for a regulated monopoly, and thus ROCEs lower, although the monopoly does have a higher level of gearing.

Workings:

(W1) **Profitability ratios (20X9 shown)**

	WSS	EA
ROCE*	14/167 × 100 = 8.4%	1/31 × 100 = 3.2%
Profit margin	14/31 × 100 = 45.2%	1/20 × 100 = 5.0%
Asset utilisation	31/167 × 100 = 18.6%	20/31 × 100 = 64.5%

*Note: profit before interest used as the objective is to measure internal efficiency rather than return to external shareholders.

(W2) **Gearing ratios (20X9 shown)**

	WSS	EA
Debt/Equity	47/120 = 39.2	0

Test your understanding 6

(i)(ii) NPV (using spreadsheet function)

	A	B	C	D	E
1	Year	Cash flows			
2	0	-15,000			
3	1	1,500			
4	2	2,750			
5	3	4,000			
6	4	5,700			
7	5	7,500			
8	NPV @ 15%	-1,998			
9	NPV @ 10%	192			

Formula:

NPV @ 15%: =NPV(0.15,B3:B7)+B2

NPV @ 10%: =NPV(0.10,B3:B7)+B2

(iii)   If the company's cost of capital is 10% the project would be accepted, if it were 15% it wouldn't.

Alternative calculation

Year	Cash flow $	DF 15%	PV $	DF 10%	PV $
0	(15,000)	1.00	(15,000)	1.00	(15,000)
1	1,500	0.870	1,305	0.909	1,364
2	2,750	0.756	2,079	0.826	2,272
3	4,000	0.658	2,632	0.751	3,004
4	5,700	0.572	3,260	0.683	3,893
5	7,500	0.497	3,727	0.621	4,657
NPV			**(1,997)**		**190**

Test your understanding 7

(a)

	A	B	C	D	E	F	G	H
1	**All figures in $000**	**0**	**1**	**2**	**3**	**4**	**5**	**6**
2	Sales revenue		8,100	8,100	8,100	8,100	8,100	8,100
3	Variable costs		-4,266	-4,266	4,266	4,266	-4,266	-4,266
4	Royalties		-675	-675	-675	-675	-675	-675
5	Fixed costs		-900	-900	-900	-900	-900	-900
6	**Cash inflow from operations**		**2,259**	**2,259**	**2,259**	**2,259**	**2,259**	**2,259**
7	Tax payable (30%)		-678	-678	-678	-678	-678	-678
8	Initial investment	-7,000						
9	Government grant	3,500						
10	**Net cash flow**	**-3,500**	**1,581**	**1,581**	**1,581**	**1,581**	**1,581**	**1,581**
11	**NPV**	**3,000**						

Formula:

=NPV(0.12,C10:H10)+B10

(b) (i)

$$\text{Sensitivity} = \frac{\text{NPV}}{\text{PV of initial outlay}} \times 100$$

$$= \frac{3,000}{3,500} \times 100$$

= 85.7% i.e. the initial outlay would have to increase by 85.7% before decision is reversed

(ii)

	A	B	C	D	E	F	G	H
1	**All figures in $000**	**0**	**1**	**2**	**3**	**4**	**5**	**6**
2	Sales revenue		8,100	8,100	8,100	8,100	8,100	8,100
3	Variable costs		-4,266	-4,266	4,266	4,266	-4,266	-4,266
4	**Contribution**		**3,159**	**3,159**	**3,159**	**3,159**	**3,159**	**3,159**
5	Tax payable (30%)		-948	-948	-948	-948	-948	-948
6	**Net cash flow**		**2,211**	**2,211**	**2,211**	**2,211**	**2,211**	**2,211**
7	**Total present value**	**9,090**						

Formula:

=NPV(0.12,C6:H6)

Sensitivity = NPV/PV of contribution = 3000/9090 = 33% i.e. the annual contribution would have to decrease by 33% before the project was rejected.

(c) Factors that should be considered by the directors of JDL include:

- How the cash flows are estimated. How accurate they are requires detailed consideration.

- The cost of capital used by the finance director might be inappropriate. For example if the EF solar panels proposal is less risky than other projects undertaken by JDL then a lower cost of capital should be used.

- How strong is the EF brand name? The directors are proposing to pay royalties equivalent to 8% of sales revenue during the six years of the anticipated life of the project. Should they market the EF solar panels themselves?

- Would competitors enter the market and what would be the likely effect on sales volumes and selling prices?

Note: Only three factors were required.

(d) Benchmarking is the use of a yardstick to compare performance. The yardstick for benchmarking is based on best in class.

A major problem facing the management of JDL lies in the accessing of information regarding the activities of a competitor firm that may be acknowledged to display best practice. Internal benchmarking i.e. using another function within the same firm as the standard can help in the avoidance of the problems of information access, but that clearly limits the scope of what can be achieved. The most common approach is process benchmarking, where the standard of comparison is a firm which is not a direct competitor but is best in practice for a particular process or activity.

The objective is to improve performance. This is best achieved by means of the sharing of information which should prove of mutual benefit to both parties to the benchmarking programme. As a result of receiving new information each party will be able to review their policies and procedures. The very process of comparing respective past successes and failures can serve as a stimulus for greater innovation within each organisation.

To evaluate the performance JDL they need to establish a basis for targets which reflects the performance of an organisation which displays 'Best Practice'. As a direct consequence of a comparison of existing standards with the 'Best Practice' organisation, managers can focus upon areas where improvements can be achieved and evaluate measures to help attain those improvements.

A principal benefit that will be derived by JDL as a result of undertaking a successful programme of benchmarking will be the identification of areas where cost savings are possible. Hence the levels of cost of sales and operating expenses can be reduced leading to increased profitability.

Test your understanding 8

IRR (using spreadsheet function)

	A	B	C	D	E
1	Year	Cash flows			
2	0	−15,000			
3	1	1,500			
4	2	2,750			
5	3	4,000			
6	4	5,700			
7	5	7,500			
8	IRR	10.4%			

Formula:

=IRR(B2:B7)

<u>Alternative calculation</u>

NPV @ 10% = 192 as per TYU 6

NPV @ 15% = (1,998) as per TYU 6

$$\text{IRR} = 10\% + \frac{192}{192 + (1,998)} \times (15\% - 10\%) = 10.4\%$$

Test your understanding 9

MIRR (using spreadsheet function)

	A	B	C	D	E
1	Year	Cash flows			
2	0	−15,000			
3	1	1,500			
4	2	2,750			
5	3	4,000			
6	4	5,700			
7	5	7,500			
8	MIRR	10.3%			

Formula:

=MIRR(B2:B7,0.10,0.10)

KAPLAN PUBLISHING

Alternative calculation

Year	Cash flow $	DF 10%	PV $
1	1,500	0.909	1,364
2	2,750	0.826	2,272
3	4,000	0.751	3,004
4	5,700	0.683	3,893
5	7,500	0.621	4,657
PV of inflows			**15,190**

$$\text{MIRR} = \left[\frac{15,190}{15,000}\right]^{1/5} \times (1 + 0.10) - 1 = 10.3\%$$

Divisional performance appraisal and transfer pricing

Chapter learning objectives

Upon completion of this chapter you will be able to:

- discuss the appropriateness of, and apply different measures of performance, including:
    - Residual Income (RI)
    - Economic Value Added (EVA™)
- describe, compute and evaluate performance measures relevant in a divisionalised organisation structure including ROI, RI and Economic value added (EVA™)
- discuss the need for separate measures in respect of managerial and divisional performance
- discuss the circumstances in which a transfer pricing policy may be needed and discuss the necessary criteria for its design
- demonstrate and evaluate the use of alternative bases for transfer pricing
- explain and demonstrate issues that require consideration when setting transfer prices in multinational companies
- evaluate and apply the value-based management approaches to performance management
- discuss the problems encountered in planning, controlling and measuring performance levels, e.g. productivity, profitability, quality and service levels, in complex business structures.

PER

Three of the PER performance objectives are:

– Monitor performance (PO14)

– Business advisory (PO21) and

– Data analysis and decision support (PO22).

Working through this chapter should help you understand how to demonstrate these objectives.

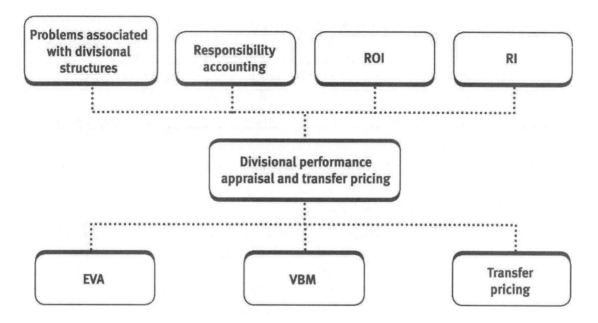

1 Common knowledge

Chapter 11 builds on the following knowledge from PM:

- Divisional performance measurement.
- Transfer pricing.

2 Introduction to divisional performance management

Business structure (including divisional structures) was covered in Chapter 6. A feature of modern business management is the practice of splitting a business into semi-autonomous units with devolved authority and responsibility. Such units could be described as divisions, subsidiaries or strategic business units (SBUs) but the principles are the same.

This chapter will review some of the methods available for appraising divisional performance. Before looking at these methods, the problems associated with divisional structures, the concept of responsibility accounting and the types of responsibility centre, will be reviewed.

The chapter then covers the value-based management approach to performance management and how this might help to address some of the issues of short-termism already discussed.

The chapter concludes with a discussion of transfer pricing, focusing on why a transfer price may be needed and considerations when setting a transfer price.

3   Problems associated with divisional structures

Before looking at the methods for divisional performance appraisal it is worth noting that, although potentially beneficial (as discussed in Chapter 6), divisional structures may result in a number of **problems**:

- **Co-ordination** – How to co-ordinate different divisions to achieve overall corporate objectives.

- **Goal congruence** – There is a potential loss of control; managers will be motivated to improve the performance of their division, possibly at the expense of the larger organisation.

- **Controllability** – Divisional managers should only be held accountable for those factors that they can control. The performance of a division's manager must be appraised separately to the performance of the division. It may be difficult to determine exactly what is and what is not controllable.

- **Inter-dependence of divisions** – The performance of one division may depend to some extent on others, making it difficult to measure performance levels.

- **Head office costs** – Whether/how head office costs should be reapportioned.

- **Transfer prices** – How transfer prices should be set as these effectively move profit from one division to another.

Illustration 1 – Inter-dependence of divisions

Suppose division A makes components that are subsequently used in division B to make the finished item that is then sold to customers. The following are examples of areas where the performance of B will be affected by problems in A.

- **Productivity** – Suppose some staff in division A are ill, slowing down the supply of components to division B. This will slow down division B as well, unless adequate inventories are held.

- **Profitability** – Suppose the transfer pricing system includes an element of actual cost. Cost overruns in A would be passed on to B.

- **Quality** – Poor quality work in A will ultimately compromise the quality of the finished product.

- **Service levels** – Customer queries to B could involve A's component in which case they need to be re-directed. Division A may not be as customer-focused as B, compromising customer goodwill.

4 Responsibility accounting

Responsibility accounting is based on the principle of **controllability**. Managers should only be made accountable and be assessed on those aspects of performance they can control, whereas a division should be assessed in relation to its overall performance. (**Note**: This relates back to the discussion of rewards in Chapter 9).

For example, expenditure relating to the division (such as marketing, legal or audit fees) but agreed by head office rather than the divisional manager, should be treated as an uncontrollable cost and therefore excluded in the calculation of performance measures for the divisional manager.

The controllability principle may result in the **establishment of different performance measures for the division and its manager**.

Illustration 2 – Performance measurement for a division and a divisional manager

Consider the following information about a division's revenue and costs for the last year:

	$m	
Revenue	1,058	
Variable costs (controlled by divisional manager)	(572)	
Fixed costs (controlled by divisional manager)	(274)	
Controllable operating profit	**212**	Use this profit to assess divisional manager
Marketing campaign agreed by head office (divisional manager does not control)	(56)	
Traceable operating profit	**156**	Use this profit to assess division
Apportioned head office costs for central marketing, HR, IT and finance	(86)	
Divisional operating profit	**70**	Use this profit when comparing performance of the division to that of an external competitor (see note)

Note: If the division was a separate company it would have to incur some of the apportioned head office costs for itself. As such, when comparing divisional performance to that of an external competitor, the divisional operating profit figure (i.e. $70m) should be used. This is a minor point but is worth noting.

In practice, **it can be difficult to establish which items are controllable and which are uncontrollable**. For example, an increase in supplier's prices may be seen as something that the divisional manager cannot control. However, it could be argued that the cost is controllable since the divisional manager may be able to change the source or type of supply.

Types of responsibility centres

Divisions may be classed as responsibility centres. There are three types of responsibility centre. Depending on the type of responsibility centre, the divisional manager will be responsible for, and held accountable for costs, revenue, investment or a combination of these.

When assessing divisional performance it is vital that the measures used match the type of responsibility centre:

Type of responsibility centre (division)	Description	Performance measurement
Cost centre	Division **incurs costs** but has **no revenue** stream.	Divisional managers should be assessed on performance measures that focus on: • costs, e.g. cost ratios and variances • relevant non-financial measures, for example based on productivity or efficiency.
Profit centre	• Division has both **costs and revenue**. • Manager **does not** have the authority to make **investment** decisions.	Divisional managers should be assessed on performance measures that focus on: • costs, revenues and profit, e.g. profitability ratios and cost/sales variances • relevant non-financial measures, for example based on customer satisfaction.
Investment centre	• Division has both **costs and revenue**. • Manager **does** have the authority to **invest** in new assets or dispose of existing ones.	Divisional managers should be assessed as for profit centre plus on their investment decisions using: • return on investment (ROI) • residual income (RI) • economic value added (EVA) ROI, RI and EVA are discussed in more detail below.

Student accountant articles: visit the ACCA website, www.accaglobal.com, to review the article on 'Divisional performance management'.

5 Return on investment (ROI)

5.1 What is ROI?

ROI is the divisional equivalent of ROCE. It shows the operating profit that is generated for every $1 of assets employed.

$$\text{ROI} = \frac{\text{Operating profit}}{\text{Capital employed}} \times 100$$

Decision rule: If ROI > cost of capital (required return), then accept the project or appraise the division as performing favourably.

What profit and capital employed figures should be used?

If ROI is used to appraise the performance of the divisional manager then (as discussed in the previous section) only the controllable elements of operating profit and capital employed should be included. If ROI is used to appraise the performance of the division, the traceable profit figure should be used (as per illustration 2). However, if divisional performance is being assessed in relation to the performance of an external competitor the divisional profit figure should be used (see illustration 2).

In addition, refer back to the points discussed in Chapter 10, section 4.3 on ROCE; these points are also applicable when calculating ROI.

5.2 Advantages and disadvantages of ROI

Advantages	Disadvantages
• Widely used and accepted since it is in line with ROCE which is frequently used to assess overall business performance. • As a relative measure it enables comparisons to be made with divisions or companies of different sizes.	• May lead to dysfunctional decision making (see below). • Increases with age of asset if net book values (NBVs) are used (see below). • It is not aligned to the corporate objective of maximising total shareholders' wealth. • Differences between the internal divisions being compared or between the division and the external company it is being compared to (e.g. different industries, different accounting policies or differences in capital employed figures such as average or year-end), may make comparisons less meaningful.

• It can be broken down into secondary ratios for more detailed analysis, i.e. profit margin and asset turnover.	• Exclusion from capital employed of intangible assets, such as brands and reputation. • It may encourage the manipulation of profit and capital employed figures to improve results and, for example, to obtain a bonus payment.

Dysfunctional decision making

There is a risk that if ROI is used as a performance measure, management may only take decisions which will increase divisional ROI, regardless of wider corporate benefits. The test your understanding below illustrates the problem of dysfunctional behaviour.

Test your understanding 1

Managers within MV are appraised on the ROI of their division. The company's cost of capital is 15%.

Jon, a divisional manager, has the following results:

	$
Annual profit	30,000
Investment	100,000

Within his division, the purchase of a new piece of equipment has been proposed. This equipment would cost $20,000, would yield an extra $4,000 of profit per annum and would have many other non-financial and environmental benefits to the division and the company as a whole.

Required:

Will Jon invest in the new equipment? Is this the correct decision for the company?

Age of assets

The ROI will increase with the age of the asset. This may encourage divisional managers to hold onto old, and potentially inefficient, assets rather than investing in new ones. The test your understanding below illustrates this problem.

Test your understanding 2

McKinnon Co sets up a new division in Blair Atholl investing $800,000 in fixed assets with an anticipated useful life of 10 years and no scrap value. Annual profits before depreciation are expected to be a steady $200,000.

Required:

You are required to calculate the division's ROI for its first three years based on the opening book value of assets. Comment on your results.

This issue also reduces the validity of comparisons between different divisions since the relative age of the assets will impact the divisional ROI.

6 Residual income

6.1 Introduction

The problems of dysfunctional behaviour and holding onto old assets can be addressed by using residual income (RI) to appraise divisional performance.

6.2 What is residual income (RI)?

	$
Operating profit	X
Less imputed interest (capital employed × cost of capital)	(X)
RI	**X/(X)**

Decision rule: if the RI is positive:

* accept the project or

* appraise the division as performing favourably.

What profit and capital employed figures should be used?

If RI is used to appraise the performance of the divisional manager then (as discussed in section 4) only the controllable elements of operating profit and capital employed should be included. If ROI is used to appraise the performance of the division, the traceable profit figure should be used (as per illustration 2). However, if divisional performance is being assessed in relation to the performance of an external competitor the divisional profit figure should be used (see illustration 2).

In addition, refer back to the points discussed in Chapter 10, section 4.3 on ROCE; these points are also applicable when calculating RI.

6.3 Advantages and disadvantages of RI

Advantages	Disadvantages
• It reduces the problems of ROI, i.e. dysfunctional behaviour and holding onto old assets and encourages decision making consistent with the logic of NPV (considered the best method of investment appraisal). • Interpreting the result is simple; if the RI is positive then the division is generating a return above that required by the finance providers. • The cost of financing a division is brought home to divisional managers. • Different cost of capitals can be applied to different divisions based on their risk profiles.	• It does not always result in decisions that are in the best interests of the company, for example it does not fully eliminate the issue of short-termism or holding onto old assets. (EVA is a superior measure to RI in this respect). • An absolute measure is calculated so this does not facilitate comparisons between divisions since the RI is driven by the size of the divisions and their investment. • It is difficult to decide upon an appropriate cost of capital. • Differences between the internal divisions being compared or between the division and the external company it is being compared to (e.g. different industries, different accounting policies or differences in capital employed figures such as average or year-end), may make comparisons less meaningful. • It may encourage the manipulation of profit and capital employed figures to improve results and, for example, to obtain a bonus payment (as for ROI).

6.4 Comparison of ROI and RI

Test your understanding 3

Division Z has the following financial performance:

Operating profit	$40,000
Capital employed	$150,000
Cost of capital	10%

Required:

Would the division wish to accept a new possible investment costing $10,000 which would earn an annual operating profit of $2,000 if the evaluation was on the basis of:

(a)   ROI

(b)   RI?

Is the division's decision in the best interests of the company?

Test your understanding 4

KM is considering a new project and has gathered the following data:

The initial investment is $66 million which will be required at the beginning of the year. The project has a three year life with a nil residual value. Depreciation is calculated on a straight-line basis.

The project is expected to generate revenue of $85m in year 1, $90m in year 2 and $94m in year 3. These values may vary by 6%.

The direct costs will be $50m in year 1, $60m in year 2 and $70m in year 3. These may vary by 8%.

Cost of capital may also vary from 8% to 10% for the life of the project.

Use the written down value of the asset at the start of each year to represent the value of the asset for the year.

Required:

Prepare two tables for:

(a)   the best outcome and

(b)   the worst outcome

showing the annual operating profit, residual income and return on investment for each year of the project and the NPV. Ignore tax.

7   Economic value added

7.1   What is economic value added (EVA)?

- EVA is a measure of performance similar to RI. However, it addresses some of the disadvantages of RI (and ROI), such as the impact of different accounting policies.

- Adjustments are made to financial profits and capital to truly reflect the economic value generated by the company for its shareholders.

- It is a measure of performance that is directly linked to shareholder wealth.

- It is important to note that EVA **can be used to appraise organisation-wide performance** (and is therefore relevant to the discussion in Chapter 10) **as well as divisional performance**.

Calculating EVA

	$
Net operating profit after tax (NOPAT)	X
Less:	
Adjusted value of capital employed at beginning of the year × WACC	(X)
EVA	**X/(X)**

Decision rule: a positive EVA is favourable, since the organisation is providing a return greater than that required by the providers of finance.

7.2 Adjustments required to operating profit and capital employed

	Change to operating profit	Change to capital employed
Depreciation and non-current assets	**Add** back depreciation. **Deduct** economic depreciation which reflects the true value of assets during the period.	Adjust value to reflect economic depreciation and not accounting depreciation. In addition, adjust value to reflect replacement cost of non-current assets rather than the net book value.
Provisions	**Add** increase in provisions in the period, e.g. debt provisions, deferred tax provisions. **Deduct** reduction in provisions in the period. These represent over-prudence in the financial accounts.	**Add** back the value of provisions in the period.
Non-cash expenses	**Add** back since they do not represent cash paid and may be as a result of profit manipulation and not real costs.	**Add** to retained profit at the end of the year.
Interest paid net of tax, i.e. interest × (1 – tax rate)	Interest payments are taken into account in WACC.	
Expenditure on advertising, research and development and employee training	**Add** back, i.e. capitalise the entire expense. These are value building expenditures. **Deduct** amortisation for the period (if mentioned).	**Increase** capital employed at the end of the year. **Increase** capital employed in respect to similar add backs in previous year's investments.

Note: Only a small number of adjustments will be required in the exam. Calculations will be relatively straightforward; the focus of the requirement will be on applying EVA and discussing it in the context of the scenario.

Summary NOPAT calculation

	$
Controllable operating profit	X
Add:	
accounting depreciation	X
increase in provisions	X
non-cash expenses	X
advertising, research and development and employee training costs	X
Deduct:	
economic depreciation	(X)
decrease in provisions	(X)
amortisation of advertising, research and development and employee training	(X)
tax paid plus tax relief on interest (interest × tax rate)	(X)
= NOPAT	**X**

7.3 What is the WACC?

WACC = (proportion of equity × cost of equity) + (proportion of debt × post tax cost of debt)

For example, suppose that a company is 60% financed by equity which has a cost of 10% pa and 40% financed by debt which has an after tax cost of 6%

WACC = (0.60 × 0.10) + (0.40 × 0.06) = 0.084 therefore 8.4%

7.4 Evaluation of EVA

EVA assesses the value created by managers, so is a more appropriate tool for measuring performance than a profit based measure. However, it is not without its drawbacks.

Advantages	Disadvantages
EVA is better aligned (than ROI or RI) with the company's objective of maximisation of shareholder wealth.	Requires numerous adjustments to profit and capital employed figures which can be cumbersome. (The full version requires more than 100 adjustments to the information in the financial statements).
The adjustments made mean the measure is closer to cash flow than to accounting profit avoiding the distortion of results by the accounting policies in place (as can happen with ROI and RI).	Its complexity may be poorly understood by managers who, as a result, may be less likely to achieve targets for EVA.

Using economic depreciation and the replacement cost of non-current assets should make it less attractive for divisional managers to delay replacing old assets (a disadvantage highlighted for ROI and RI).	Some of the adjustments in the NOPAT calculation may be difficult to measure (for example, economic depreciation).
The cost of financing a division is brought home to the division's manager (as with RI).	Does not facilitate comparisons between divisions since EVA is an absolute measure (as is RI). If comparisons are made then differences, for example in industry types, may make comparisons less meaningful.
Long-term value-adding expenditure can be capitalised, removing any incentive that managers may have to take a short-term view.	There are many assumptions made when calculating the WACC, making its calculation difficult and potentially inaccurate. In addition, the WACC may change over time. For example, fluctuations in interest rates may impact the cost of debt or changes in business risks may impact the cost of equity. Finally, the WACC is for the company as a whole whereas the cost of capital chosen when calculating RI can reflect the risk of the division.
Interpreting the result is simple (as with RI); if the EVA is positive then the division is generating a return above that required by the finance providers.	Based on historical data whereas shareholders are interested in future performance.

KAPLAN PUBLISHING

Rationale behind the required adjustments for EVA

Accounting adjustments

Stern Stewart argues that profits calculated in accordance with financial reporting principles do not reflect the economic value generated by the company and so need adjusting.

There are three main reasons for these adjustments:

1   To convert from accrual to cash accounting.

2   Spending on 'market building' items such as research, staff training and advertising costs should be capitalised to the extent that they have not been in the financial statements. Stern Stewart believes that financial reporting standards are too strict in this regard, and discourage managers from investing in items that bring long-term benefits.

3   Unusual items of profit or expenditure should be ignored.

This can result in 160 adjustments being necessary in calculating NOPAT. The APM examining team will test only the most common adjustments, which are as follows:

1   Expenditure on promotional activities, research and development and employee training should be capitalised where they generate long-term benefit.

   Marketing activities for long-term benefit generate future value for the business, so are added back to profit and should also be added to capital employed in the year in which the expenses were incurred. This also means any prior year expenditure is also added in to capital employed.

2   The accounting depreciation charge is replaced with a charge for economic depreciation.

   Economic depreciation reflects the true change in value of assets during the period, unlike accounting depreciation. If no detail is given on economic depreciation then candidates should assume that accounting depreciation represents a reasonable approximation for it.

3   Items such as provisions, allowances for doubtful debts, deferred tax provisions and allowances for inventory should be added back to capital employed.

   These are considered to represent over-prudence on the part of financial accountants, and this understates the true value of capital employed. Any expenses or income recognised in the income statement in respect of movements in such items should also be removed from NOPAT.

> 4   Non-cash expenses should be added back to profits, and to capital employed.
>
> Non-cash expenses are correctly added back to profit as such costs are treated as unacceptable accounting adjustments on a cash-based view.
>
> 5   The tax charge.
>
> The tax cost should be the amount paid adjusted for lost tax on interest and not the adjusted amount of tax charged in the accounts. These "cash taxes" are calculated as follows:
>
> Cash taxes = tax charge per income statement − increase (add reduction) in deferred tax provision + tax benefit of interest
>
> **Note:** no further adjustments are made in respect of the tax on the other items adjusted for during the calculation of NOPAT.

Test your understanding 5

Division B has a reported operating profit of $8.4 million, which includes a charge of $2 million for the full cost of developing and launching a new product that is expected to generate profits for 4 years.

The company has an after tax weighted average cost of capital of 10%.

The operating book value of the division's assets at the beginning of the year is $60 million, and the replacement cost has been estimated at $75 million.

Assume the tax charge is $0.

Required:

Calculate division B's EVA.

Student accountant articles: visit the ACCA website, www.accaglobal.com, to review the two articles on 'Economic value added versus profit-based measures of performance'.

8   Value-based management

This is a slight aside but it is worth covering here since it follows on from our discussion of ROI, RI and EVA.

8.1   Introduction

Being able to apply and evaluate alternative views of performance measurement and management is an important capability for APM. Value-based management (VBM) is one such approach to performance management (other examples include the balanced scorecard (Chapter 13) and activity-based management (Chapter 5)).

As mentioned in the previous chapter, businesses (and the divisions within them) are under increasing pressure to look at the long-term value of the organisation since this is what investors will be interested in.

Traditionally, profit-based measures, such as ROCE/ROI, EPS or net profit margin, were used to measure performance. The source of this information was the company's annual financial statements and therefore the measures were short-term and backward looking.

More recently it has been recognised that there is a limited link between 'maximising profits' and the company's overall goal of 'maximising shareholder wealth'. For example, in Section 5.2 we said that one of the disadvantages of using ROI (divisional equivalent of ROCE) to measure performance is dysfunctional decision making.

8.2 What is VBM?

 VBM is an approach to management whereby the company's strategy, objectives, culture and processes are aligned to help the company focus on the key drivers of shareholder wealth and hence the maximisation of this value.

VBM is an approach which takes the interests of the shareholders as its primary focus.

It begins from the view that the value of a company (and hence shareholder wealth) is measured by its **discounted cash flows**. The idea being that value is only created when companies generate returns which beat their cost of capital.

To measure performance under VBM a **single, overall organisational metric** is established, such as EVA. Then '**value drivers**' are identified. These are activities **linked to long-term shareholder value** that:

- managers can influence and control
- cascade throughout all levels of the organisation and across all divisions
- link to the objectives for managers and staff
- cover both financial and non-financial areas of performance.

Illustration 3 – Value drivers at Waitrose & Partners

Waitrose & Partners is a British supermarket selling high quality groceries and wine. It has established that **employee satisfaction** and **employee training** are value drivers and that these have a direct impact on **customer satisfaction**. Customer satisfaction, in turn, directly impacts **customer retention**. Improved customer retention will then (combined with revenue per customer) positively affect **revenue**, which will directly impact **operating profit**.

These value drivers move upwards from operational to tactical and then strategic level and cover financial and non-financial areas.

Each level of management will be able to link its activities to one or more of these value drivers.

8.3 Measuring value

VBM is based on the idea that the value of a company is the total value of its discounted cash flows. This can be measured using the following techniques:

- **NPV** – (as per Chapter 10) this is the PV of all the cash inflows less the PV of all the cash outflows.

- **Shareholder value analysis** – this is the application of a discounted cash flow technique to valuing the whole business rather than a single potential investment.

Shareholder value analysis (SVA)

SVA is an application of discounted cash flow techniques to valuing the whole business rather than a potential investment.

One problem in the estimation of future values is that theoretically the cash flows go to infinity. A practical way to resolve this is to take free cash flows for a few years into the future (the 'competitive advantage period') and then estimate the residual value of the organisation using either some market multiple or book value. The valuation of the company and hence the individual shares can be directly derived from the SVA.

One criticism of the above is that the estimation of the terminal value is subjective. There is a problem in determining how many years' cash flows can be realistically projected into the future and therefore at which point the terminal value should be calculated. However, all valuation methods depend upon estimating future dividends, earnings or cash flows and hence they all contain some element of subjectivity.

Alternative approach

However, EVA is often used as an alternative to measure discounted cash flows because it also considers cash flows and financing costs.

- **EVA** – this is often the primary measure used in VBM. A positive EVA indicates value creation while a negative one indicates destruction.

- **Market value added** (**MVA**) – this is the accumulated EVAs generated by an organisation since it was formed.

Market value added (MVA)

MVA is the value added to the business by management since it was formed, over and above the money invested in the company by shareholders and long-term debt holders. A positive MVA means value has been added and a negative MVA means value has been destroyed.

MVA can effectively be seen as the accumulated EVAs generated by an organisation over time. As such, it should be highly correlated with EVA values. If year after year, a company has a positive EVA then these will add up to give a high MVA.

8.4 Implementing VBM

The implementation of VBM will involve **four steps**:

- **Step 1: Strategy development.** A strategy is developed with the overall objective of maximising shareholder wealth, measured using a single overall metric. Value drivers are then defined at all organisational levels and for all divisions.

- **Step 2: Performance targets created**. Performance targets (both short-term and long-term and financial and non-financial) are defined for those value drivers established in step 1. The targets must be aligned to one another and to the overall organisational metric, for example EVA.

- **Step 3: Operational plans**. The performance targets assigned in step 2 are assigned to specific employees, for example a divisional manager. Operational plans are then defined to help the employee achieve their individual target.

- **Step 4: Performance measures**. Performance metrics and reward systems are created that are compatible with these targets. As discussed, these will be a combination of short-term and long-term targets and financial and non-financial targets. Staff at all levels of the organisation should be motivated to achieve the new targets set.

8.5 VBM evaluation

Advantages	Disadvantages
VBM focuses on value as opposed to profit and is therefore aligned with the company's overall goal of maximisation of shareholder wealth.	Requires a cultural shift with new objectives, performance metrics and reward schemes impacting employees at all levels. Staff may require training to overcome any unfamiliarity and to understand some of the complexities of VBM (for example, EVA).
VBM is long-term and forward looking.	Shareholders may need to be educated to understand this performance management system.
Value drivers are established and aligned at all levels of the organisation and across all business units.	A change adept organisational culture plus commitment and leadership from the board is required in order to motivate employees to change.
Controllable targets are created and assigned to specific employees.	It may be difficult to identify the value drivers.

Specific plans are created to help the employee achieve their targets.	The MIS may need to be adapted (at a cost) to capture the new information required, for example non-financial measures established.
Performance metrics (financial and non-financial) and rewards systems are created that are compatible with these targets and that motivate employees.	Can become a costly and fruitless exercise in valuing everything but actually changing nothing in regards to the new processes required.

Note: Since EVA and NPV are two of the key measures used in VBM, the advantages and disadvantages of these will also be relevant here.

Student accountant article: visit the ACCA website, www.accaglobal.com, to review the article on 'Demystifying value-based management'.

Question practice – EVA and VBM

Take the time to review and attempt the scenario-based question below. It contains an exam standard EVA calculation and it also requires an explanation of VBM.

Test your understanding 6

EcoHomes is an innovative company that was born from the demand of customers for high quality, bespoke homes at affordable prices. The company is based in the country of Geeland and is divided into three geographical areas; North, East and West. The company's mission is 'to make environmentally sound homes available to the general public in a way that ensures accessibility and quality of the product'.

EcoHomes is an off-site timber frame manufacturer, producing the shell of the house in their state of the art factory using sustainably sourced, certified timber. The controlled environment assures customers of the best quality available. EcoHomes prides itself on being a 'one-stop shop' providing the customer with a full design and build and a fixed price quotation which includes all the planning, demolition, ground works, house build and landscaping.

EcoHomes is starting to lose market share and its key goal of 'being the number one bespoke house builder in Geeland' is starting to slip away. The fall in market share is primarily due to the entry of two new competitors into the market. The first of these, Dream Homes, provides cutting edge house designs and premium quality builds (but at prices to match). The second new competitor, Bespoke Homes 4all, undercuts EcoHomes on price but is not able to provide the same quality, design, build or finish.

EcoHomes has just released a profit warning for the first quarter of the current year, 20X2. This has caused the board to reconsider its position and to take action to address the changed environment. Some cost cutting has already begun, such as the commencement of a voluntary redundancy programme and the introduction of a pay freeze for all employees. However, the board recognises that it will need to take more radical steps to fully address the issues it is facing.

EcoHomes has traditionally used EPS and ROCE to quantify shareholder value. The CEO understands that a number of EcoHomes' rivals are now using a value-based management (VBM) approach to performance management and they think that it may be a useful development for EcoHomes given the tough competitive environment. Financial data for EcoHomes for the last two years is provided in appendix 1. The CEO has come to you to advise him on the implications of a switch to VBM.

Appendix: Financial data for EcoHomes

	20X1	20X0
	$m	$m
Operating profit	130	110
Interest	20	18
Profit before tax	110	92
Tax @ 25%	27.5	23
Profit after tax	82.5	69

Further information is as follows:

1   The allowance for doubtful debts was $6 million at 1 January 20X0, $5 million at 31 December 20X0 and $7 million at 31 December 20X1.

2   Research and development costs of $10 million were incurred during each of the year's 20X0 and 20X1 on a new project, Project Light which is part completed. These costs were expensed in the income statement.

3   At 1 January 20X0, the company had completed another research project, Project Glass. Total expenditure on this project was $30 million, none of which had been capitalised in the financial statements. The product developed by Project Glass went on sale on 1 January 20X0. The product has a two year lifecycle and no further sales of this product are expected after 31 December 20X1.

4   The company incurred non-cash expenses of $0.3 million in both years.

5   Capital employed was $670 million at 1 January 20X0 and $740 million at 1 January 20X1.

> 6 The pre-tax cost of debt was 5% in each year. The estimated cost of equity was 12% in 20X0 and 14% in 20X1. The rate of corporation tax was 25% in both years.
>
> 7 The company's capital structure was 60% equity and 40% debt.
>
> 8 There was no provision for deferred tax.
>
> **Required:**
>
> Write a report to the CEO of EcoHomes addressing the following:
>
> (a) Perform an assessment of EcoHomes using economic value added (EVA). Briefly comment on the results of your calculations.
>
> **(14 marks)**
>
> (b) Evaluate the use of value-based management (VBM) approaches to performance management. **(7 marks)**
>
> Professional marks will be awarded for the demonstration of skill in communication, analysis and evaluation, scepticism and commercial acumen in your answer. **(5 marks)**
>
> **(Total: 26 marks)**

9 Transfer pricing

9.1 Introduction

 The **transfer price** is the price at which goods or services are transferred from one division to another within the same organisation.

Characteristics of a good transfer price

There are a number of necessary criteria to consider when designing a transfer pricing policy:

- **Goal congruence** – the transfer price that is negotiated and agreed upon by the buying and selling divisions should be in the best interests of the company overall.

- **Fairness** – the divisions (commonly, either profit or investment centres) must perceive the transfer price to be fair since the transfer price set will impact divisional profit and hence performance evaluation.

- **Autonomy** – the system used to set the transfer price should seek to maintain the autonomy of the divisional managers. This autonomy will improve managerial motivation.

- **Bookkeeping** – the transfer price chosen should make it straightforward to record the movement of goods or services between divisions.

- **Minimise global tax liability** – multinational companies can use their transfer pricing policies to move profits around the world and thereby minimise their global tax liability.

9.2 Commonly used transfer prices

Marginal cost	Market price
If the supplying division is operating with spare capacity, the marginal cost will represent the relevant cost to the supplying division of providing the goods or services.	In a perfect market, this would represent any opportunity cost to the supplying division and the price which the receiving division would pay to an external supplier.
But the transfer will provide no contribution to the supplying division to contribute to the division's fixed costs and profit.	However, market prices may vary over time which would mean that the transfer price frequently needs to be changed.
Cost-plus pricing	**Adjusted market price**
his provides an opportunity for the supplying division to charge a mark-up on their costs so that the transfer price can contribute to covering their fixed costs or earning a profit.	The market price is adjusted for any costs which would usually be incurred on external sales but are not required on internal transfers (e.g. marketing costs or delivery costs).
Determining the mark up can be subjective and may make the transfer price more expensive than external suppliers' prices.	However, establishing the value of any internal cost savings can become complicated and time-consuming.

9.3 The general rules for setting transfer prices

Scenario 1: There is a perfectly competitive market for the product/service transferred

> **Optimum transfer price = adjusted market price**

A perfect market means that there is only one price in the market, there are no buying and selling costs and the market is able to absorb the entire output of the primary division and meet all the requirements of the secondary division.

Practical considerations when using the market price:

- As mentioned, if a perfectly competitive market exists for the product, then the market price is the best transfer price.

- However, care must be taken to ensure the division's product is the same as that offered by the market (for example, quality and delivery terms are the same). If not, an adjusted market price should be used.

- In addition, the market price should be adjusted for costs not incurred on an internal transfer, for example, delivery costs and marketing costs.

If scenario 1 does not exist, then scenarios 2 or 3 should be applied.

Scenario 2: The selling division has surplus capacity

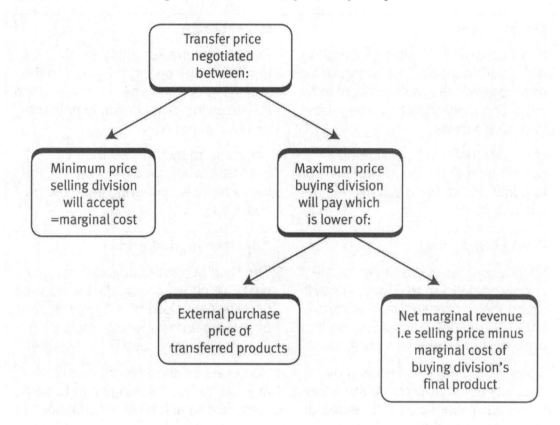

Scenario 3: The selling division does not have any surplus capacity

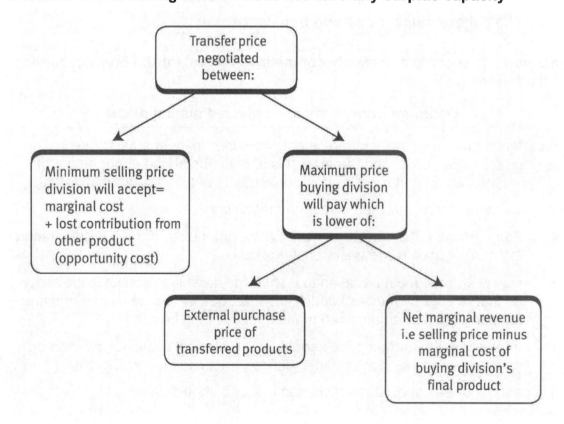

Practical considerations when using a cost based approach (scenarios 2 and 3)

- The cost may:

    - be the **marginal cost**. As mentioned in scenario 2, this will be the **very minimum the selling division will accept**. This will be **preferred by the buying division**, i.e. they will consider the price to be fair.

    - include the **opportunity cost**. If there is **no spare capacity in the selling division** (scenario 3), the opportunity cost should be added to the marginal cost.

    - be the **full cost**. Used in place of the marginal cost and this will be **preferred by the selling division** in both scenarios 2 and 3, i.e. they will consider the price to be fair since it will also include any fixed costs incurred. The selling division may negotiate that this is used instead of the marginal cost.

    - be the **standard cost or actual cost**. The standard cost should be used rather than actual cost to avoid inefficiencies being transferred from the selling division to the buying division and to aid planning and budgeting.

- The **selling division will want to recognise an element of profit** on its transfer (since it will most probably be a profit/investment centre). Therefore, the final transfer price may be set at **cost** (as per the discussion above) **+ % profit**. This approach would be preferred by the selling division but not the buying division.

- **'Fairness'** is one of the key characteristics of a good transfer price and it is clear from the above discussion that negotiation will be required between the selling division (who will want to charge the highest price possible) and the buying division (who will want to pay the least amount possible) before reaching a mutually agreeable transfer price.

    Two alternative approaches that may be perceived as fair by both the buying and the selling divisions are:

    - **marginal cost plus a lump sum (two-part tariff)**. The selling division transfers each unit at marginal cost (favoured by the buying division) and a periodic lump sum charge is made to cover fixed costs (thus keeping the selling division happy).

    - **dual pricing**. The selling division records one transfer price (e.g. full cost + % profit) and the buying division records another transfer price (e.g. marginal cost). This will be perceived as fair by both divisions but will result in the need for period-end adjustments in the accounts and is therefore less than ideal.

Illustration 4 – Practical methods of transfer pricing

Manuco has been offered supplies of special ingredient Z at a transfer price of $15 per kg by Helpco, which is part of the same group of companies. Helpco processes and sells special ingredient Z to customers external to the group at $15 per kg. Helpco bases its transfer price on total cost-plus 25% profit mark-up. Total cost has been estimated as 75% variable and 25% fixed.

Required:

Discuss the transfer prices at which Helpco should offer to transfer special ingredient Z to Manuco in order that group profit maximising decisions may be taken on financial grounds in each of the following situations.

(a) Helpco has an external market for all its production of special ingredient Z at a selling price of $15 per kg. Internal transfers to Manuco would enable $1.50 per kg of variable packing cost to be avoided.

(b) Conditions are as per (i) but Helpco has production capacity for 3,000 kg of special ingredient Z for which no external market is available.

(c) Conditions are as per (ii) but Helpco has an alternative use for some of its spare production capacity. This alternative use is equivalent to 2,000 kg of special ingredient Z and would earn a contribution of $6,000.

Solution

(a) Since Helpco has an external market, which is the opportunity foregone, the relevant transfer price would be the external selling price of $15 per kg. This will be adjusted to allow for the $1.50 per kg avoided on internal transfers due to packing costs not required, i.e. the transfer price is $13.50 per kg.

(b) In this situation Helpco has no alternative opportunity for 3,000 kg of its special ingredient Z. It should, therefore, offer to transfer this quantity at marginal cost. This is variable cost less packing costs avoided = $9 – $1.50 = $7.50 per kg (note: total cost = $15 × 80% = $12; variable cost = $12 × 75% = $9). The remaining amount of special ingredient Z should be offered to Manuco at the adjusted selling price of $13.50 per kg (as above).

(c) Helpco has an alternative use for some of its production capacity, which will yield a contribution equivalent to $3 per kg of special ingredient Z ($6,000/2,000 kg). The balance of its spare capacity (1,000 kg) has no opportunity cost and should still be offered at marginal cost. Helpco should offer to transfer: 2,000 kg at $7.50 + $3 = $10.50 per kg; 1,000 kg at $7.50 per kg (= marginal cost); and the balance of requirements at $13.50 per kg.

Test your understanding 7

X, a manufacturing company, has two divisions: Division A and Division B. Division A produces one type of product, ProdX, which it transfers to Division B and also sells externally. Division B has been approached by another company which has offered to supply 2,500 units of ProdX for $35 each.

The following details for Division A are available:

	$
Sales revenue:	
Sales to division B @ $40 per unit	400,000
External sales @ $45 per unit	270,000
Variable costs @$22 per unit	(352,000)
Fixed costs	(100,000)
Profit	218,000

External sales of Prod X cannot be increased, and division B decides to buy from the other company.

Required:

(a) Calculate the effect on the profit of division A.

(b) Calculate the effect on the profit of company X.

Test your understanding 8

A company operates two divisions, Able and Baker. Able manufactures two products, X and Y. Product X is sold to external customers for $42 per unit. The only outlet for product Y is Baker.

Baker supplies an external market and can obtain its semi-finished supplies (product Y) from either Able or an external source. Baker currently has the opportunity to purchase product Y from an external supplier for $38 per unit. The capacity of division Able is measured in units of output, irrespective of whether product X, Y or a combination of both are being manufactured.

The associated product costs are as follows:

	X	Y
Variable costs per unit	32	35
Fixed overheads per unit	5	5
Total unit costs	37	40

Required:

(a) Using the above information, provide advice on the determination of an appropriate transfer price for the sale of product Y from division Able to division Baker under the following conditions:

(i) when division Able has spare capacity and limited external demand for product X

(ii) when division Able is operating at full capacity with unsatisfied external demand for product X.

(b) The design of an information system to support transfer pricing decision making necessitates the inclusion of specific data. Identify the data that needs to be collected and how you would expect it to be used.

Question practice

Take the time to review and attempt the scenario-based question below. It contains a more challenging transfer pricing calculation and also requires an explanation of transfer pricing.

Note: The examining team will expect you to be able to demonstrate and evaluate the use of alternative bases for transfer pricing but will not be interested in testing very detailed or complicated calculations. Therefore, do not spend too much time focusing on lots of different transfer pricing calculations.

Test your understanding 9

The Thornthwaite division is a member of the Kentmere group, and manufactures a single product, the Yoke.

It sells this product to external customers, and also to Froswick, another division in the group. Froswick further processes the Yoke and then sells it on to external customers.

The divisions have the freedom to set their own transfer prices, and also to choose their own suppliers.

The Kentmere group uses Residual Income (RI) to assess divisional performance, and each year it sets a target RI for each division. The group uses a cost of capital of 12%.

Each divisional manager receives a salary, plus a bonus equal to that salary for hitting its RI target.

There has recently been much discussion at board level about the impact of internal transfers and their impact on reported performances. In part this was prompted by a comment from a retired shareholder, Mr Brearley, at the recent shareholder meeting. He said that he had read a lot in the press about bonus schemes and their dysfunctional impact on corporate performance. The directors want to know whether or not Kentmere has any such issues.

The managers of both divisions have provided you with the following information for the next quarter (quarter 3):

Thornthwaite division

Budgeted information for quarter 3:
  Maximum production capacity 200,000 units
  External demand 170,000 units
  External selling price $45
  Variable cost per unit $30
  Fixed production costs $2,500,000
  Capital employed $6,000,000
  Target RI $250,000

Froswick division

Froswick has found an external supplier willing to supply Yokes at a price of $42 per unit.

Required:

(a) Froswick requires 50,000 Yokes. Calculate the transfer price that Thornthwaite would set to achieve its target RI.   **(6 marks)**

(b) What prices should Thornthwaite set in order to maximise group profits? Explain the basis of your calculations.   **(4 marks)**

(c) Is Mr Brearley correct to be concerned about the bonus scheme? Draft some briefing notes for the board so that they can prepare their response, including supporting calculations and suggested improvements to the transfer pricing and bonus policies.

(10 marks)

(Total: 20 marks)

Tutor tip:

If you have not done so already, this may be a good time to answer a question using the Exam Practice Platform available on the ACCA website (refer to the final chapter of the Study Text for details). Using this platform will help you to develop good exam technique which in turn should help improve your **professional skills mark**. As a general rule, use the excel software for any calculations, workings or tables of data and use the word software for written answers (calculations can be referenced here). Remember, you can cut and paste from the question exhibits and requirements; this is a great way to save time, to use the scenario information and to ensure you address the specifics of the requirement.

9.4　International transfer pricing

Almost two thirds of world trade takes place within multinational companies. Transfer pricing in multinational companies has the following complications:

Taxation

The selling and buying divisions will be based in different countries. Different taxation rates in these countries allows the manipulation of profit through the use of transfer pricing. However, an organisation should consider if trying to minimise the tax liability in this way would be legal or ethical.

Illustration 5 – Taxation and transfer pricing

Rosca Coffee is a multinational company. Division A is based in Northland, a country with a tax rate of 50%. This division transfers goods to division B at a cost of $50,000 per annum. Division B is based in Southland, a country with a tax rate of 20%. Based on the current transfer price of $50,000 the profit of the divisions and of the company is as follows:

	Division A $	Division B $	Company $
External sales	100,000	120,000	220,000
Internal transfers to div B	50,000	–	50,000
Fixed and variable costs	(70,000)	(40,000)	(110,000)
Transfer costs from div A	–	(50,000)	(50,000)
Profit before tax	80,000	30,000	110,000
Profit after tax	40,000	24,000	64,000

Rosca Coffee want to take advantage of the different tax rates in Northland and Southland and have decided to reduce the transfer price from $50,000 to $20,000. This will result if the following revised profit figures:

	Division A $	Division B $	Company $
External sales	100,000	120,000	220,000
Internal transfers to div B	20,000	–	20,000
Fixed and variable costs	(70,000)	(40,000)	(110,000)
Transfer costs from div A	–	(20,000)	(20,000)
Profit before tax	50,000	60,000	110,000
Profit after tax	25,000	48,000	73,000

Conclusion: the manipulation of the transfer price has increased the company's profits from $64,000 to $73,000.

Artificial attempts at reducing tax liabilities could, however, upset a country's tax authorities. Many tax authorities have the power to alter the transfer price and can **treat the transactions as having taken place at a fair arm's length price** and revise profits accordingly.

Remittance controls

- A country's government may impose restrictions on the transfer of profits from domestic subsidiaries to foreign multinationals.

- This is known as a 'block on the remittances of dividends' i.e. it limits the payment of dividends to the parent company's shareholders.

- It is often done through the imposition of strict exchange controls.

Test your understanding 10

Required:

Discuss how a multinational company could avoid the problem of blocked remittances.

Protectionist measures

A country's government may introduce a range of protectionist measures to protect local manufacturers from competition from imported goods. For example, **import tariffs** imposed on the value of imported components would increase the organisation's costs and may make the products less competitive than those of domestic organisations.

Organisations may consider charging a lower price on international transfers compared to domestic competitors. However, a country's government may require all transfers to be at arm's length price to try to protect local manufacturers by restricting companies from importing goods into a country.

Exchange rates

Differences in currency between the buying and selling country may result in a number of difficulties:

- Planning and budgeting is more difficult if the transfer price varies over time due to exchange rate movements.

- The price may change over time, which may affect the divisions' decisions to buy or sell.

- Divisional managers may require an adjustment to the transfer price to reflect exchange rate movements. Otherwise, their performance is assessed on factors outside of their control. This adjustment would make calculating and recording the transfer price more complex and may make it harder for managers to understand.

Student accountant article: visit the ACCA website, www.accaglobal.com, to review the article on 'Transfer pricing'.

Chapter summary

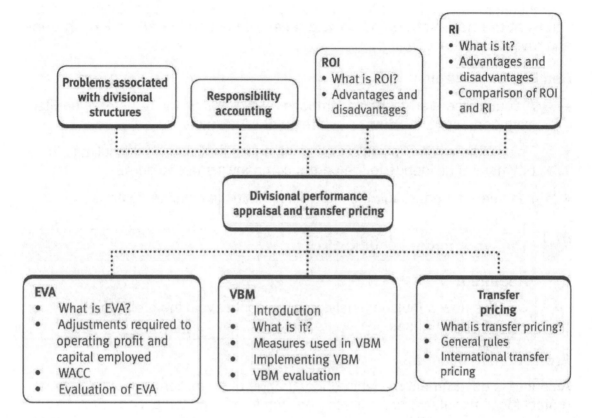

Test your understanding answers

Test your understanding 1

	Before	After	Investment
Profit ($)	30,000	34,000	4,000
Investment ($)	100,000	120,000	20,000
ROI	30%	28%	20%

- Jon's decision – from a personal point of view, the ROI of Jon's division will go down and his bonus will be reduced or lost as a result. Therefore, Jon will reject the investment.

- However, the new equipment has a ROI of 20%. This is higher than the company's cost of capital (required return) of 15% and therefore Jon should accept the new investment.

Conclusion: dysfunctional behaviour has occurred.

Test your understanding 2

Year	Opening book value of assets	Annual book depreciation	Closing value of assets	Pre-dep'n profits	Post dep'n profits	ROI
	$000	$000	$000	$000	$000	
1	800	80	720	200	120	15%
2	720	80	640	200	120	17%
3	640	80	560	200	120	19%

Conclusion: The ROI increases, despite no increase in annual profits, merely as a result of the book value of assets falling. Therefore, the divisional manager will be rewarded for holding onto old, and potentially inefficient, assets.

Test your understanding 3

(a) **ROI**

Current ROI = ($40k/$150k) × 100	26.7%
ROI with new investment = ($42k/$160k) × 100	26.3%
ROI of the new investment = ($2k/$10k) × 100	20%

Decision: The division would not accept the investment since it would reduce the division's ROI.

However, this is not in the best interests of the company since the ROI (20%) is greater than the company's cost of capital (10%).

(b) **RI**

Current RI = $40k – (10% × $150k)	$25k
RI with new investment = $42k – (10% × $160k)	$26k

Decision: The division would accept the investment since it generates an increase in RI of $1,000.

This decision is in the best interests of the company.

Test your understanding 4

(a) **Best outcome**

	Year 1	Year 2	Year 3
RI and ROI	$m	$m	$m
NBV @ start of year	(66.0)	(44.0)	(22.0)
Revenue (add 6%)	90.1	95.4	99.6
Less direct cost (minus 8%)	(46.0)	(55.2)	(64.4)
Net cash flow	44.1	40.2	35.2
Less depreciation	(22.0)	(22.0)	(22.0)
Operating profit	**22.1**	**18.2**	**13.2**
Less imputed interest @ 8%	(5.3)	(3.5)	(1.8)
RI	**16.8**	**14.7**	**11.4**
ROI	**33.5%**	**41.4%**	**60.0%**

NPV @ 8% discount factor

Timing	CF	DF	PV
t_0	(66.0)	1.000	(66.0)
t_1	44.1	0.926	40.8
t_2	40.2	0.857	34.5
t_3	35.2	0.794	28.0
NPV			**37.3**

(b) **Worst outcome**

RI and ROI	Year 1	Year 2	Year 3
	$m	$m	$m
NBV @ start of year	(66.0)	(44.0)	(22.0)
Revenue (minus 6%)	79.9	84.6	88.4
Less direct cost (add 8%)	(54.0)	(64.8)	(75.6)
Net cash flow	25.9	19.8	12.8
Less depreciation	(22.0)	(22.0)	(22.0)
Operating profit	**3.9**	**(2.2)**	**(9.2)**
Less imputed interest @ 10%	(6.6)	(4.4)	(2.2)
RI	**(2.7)**	**(6.6)**	**(11.4)**
ROI	**5.9%**	**−5.0%**	**−41.8%**

NPV @ 10% discount factor

Timing	CF	DF	PV
t_0	(66.0)	1.000	(66.0)
t_1	25.9	0.909	23.5
t_2	19.8	0.826	16.4
t_3	12.8	0.751	9.6
NPV			**(16.5)**

Test your understanding 5

NOPAT

	$m
Controllable operating profit	8.4
Add back items that add value: development costs	2
Deduct amortisation of development costs ($2m ÷ 4 years)	(0.5)
NOPAT	9.9

Adjusted value of capital employed

	$m
Opening book value of assets	60
Adjustment to reflect the replacement cost of assets ($75m − $60m)	15
Adjusted value of capital employed	75

EVA

	$m
NOPAT	9.9
Less: adjusted value of capital employed × WACC ($75m × 10%)	(7.5)
EVA	**2.4**

Test your understanding 6

REPORT

To: CEO

From: A accountant

Date: April 20X2

Subject: EVA calculation and evaluation of VBM

Introduction

This report performs an assessment of EcoHomes using economic value added (EVA) and evaluates the use of value-based management as a tool for managing performance.

(a)   **EVA calculation**

(W1) **Calculation of NOPAT**

	20X1 $m	20X0 $m
Operating profit	130	110
Add research costs expensed (Project Light)	10	10
Less amortisation of prior year expenses (Project Glass)	(15)	(15)
Add increase in allowance for doubtful debts	2	(1)
Add non-cash expenses	0.3	0.3
Less cash taxes (W3)	(32.5)	(27.5)
NOPAT	94.8	76.8

(W2) Calculation of adjusted capital employed at 1 January

	20X1 $m	20X0 $m
Capital at 1 January per statement of financial position	740	670
Add allowance for bad and doubtful debts	5	6
Add capitalisation of research and development (Project Light)	10	
Add capitalisation of research and development (Project Glass)	15	30
Add non-cash expenses incurred during 20X0	0.3	
Adjusted capital employed at 1 January	770.3	706

(W3) Calculation of net tax

	20X1 $m	20X0 $m
Tax charge per income statement	27.5	23
Add tax relief on interest (interest × 25%)	5	4.5
Cash taxes	32.5	27.5

(W4) Weighted average cost of capital (WACC)

20X1: (60% × 14%) + ((40% × 5% × (1 – 25%)) = 9.9%

20X0: (60% × 12%) + ((40% × 5% × (1 – 25%)) = 8.7%

EVA = NOPAT – (WACC × adjusted capital employed)

20X1: 94.8 – (9.9% × 770.3) = **$18.54 million**

20X0: 76.8 – (8.7% × 706) = **$15.38 million**

Conclusion:

EVA is positive in both 20X0 and 20X1 showing that EcoHomes is adding value in both periods. The EVA increased by 20.5% year on year from $15.38 million in 20X0 to $18.54 million in 20X1. This is particularly pleasing given the level of competition within the industry. However, it will be necessary to closely monitor the EVA to ensure that there is no reduction in the figure in 20X2.

(b) Evaluation of value-based management

Value-based management (VBM) is an approach to management whereby the company's strategy, objectives and processes are aligned to help the company focus on the key drivers of shareholder wealth and hence the maximisation of value.

Traditionally, EcoHomes used the financial measures of ROCE and EPS to quantify shareholder value. However, neither of these measures directly correlates with the market value of the company (shareholder value).

VBM takes the interests of shareholders as its primary objective. EVA is the primary measure used, (other methods include NPV, market value added and shareholder value analysis). A positive EVA indicates value creation (as in 20X0 and 20X1 in EcoHomes) while a negative one indicates destruction. EVA is consistent with net present value (NPV). Maximisation of EVA will create real wealth for shareholders.

Although EVA is calculated using the profit figure, the profit is adjusted in order to bring it closer to a cash flow measure of performance which is less affected by various accounting adjustments such as depreciation. Long-term value added expenditure can be capitalised, removing any incentive that managers may have to take a short-term view.

EVA will also bring the cost of financing home to EcoHomes' managers.

A major disadvantage of VBM measures such as EVA, compared to say EPS or ROCE, is the unfamiliarity and complexity of the calculation. Staff will need to be trained and shareholders educated in order to overcome this.

Another disadvantage of EVA is the large number of assumptions made when calculating the WACC. It should also be remembered that calculations such as EVA are based on historical data whereas shareholders are interested in future performance.

Note: marks would be awarded for other relevant points.

Professional skills marks

Communication:

- Report format and structure – use of headings, sub-headings and introduction

- Style, language and clarity – appropriate tone of report response, presentation of calculations (use excel spreadsheet in the CBE).

Analysis and Evaluation:

- Appropriate use of data to perform suitable calculations to support discussion and draw conclusions on Ecohomes' performance

- Comprehensive evaluation of the use of VBM.

Scepticism:

- Recognition of the need to monitor the EVA and of the challenges, as well as the benefits, of using VBM.

Commercial acumen:

- Effective use of examples drawn from across the scenario information and other practical considerations related to the context to illustrate the points being made.

Test your understanding 7

(a)   Division A will lose the contribution from internal transfers to Division B. Contribution foregone = 2,500 × $(40 − 22) = $45,000 reduction.

(b)

	$ per unit
Cost per unit from external supplier	35
Variable cost of internal manufacture saved	22
Incremental cost of external purchase	13

Reduction in profit of X   = $13 × 2,500 units
= $32,500

Test your understanding 8

(a)   (i)   The transfer price should be set between $35 (minimum price Able will sell for) and $38 (maximum price Baker will pay). Able has spare capacity, therefore the marginal costs to the group of Able making a unit is $35. If the price is set above $38, Baker will be encouraged to buy outside the group, decreasing group profit by $3 per unit.

(ii)   If Able supplies Baker with a unit of Y, it will cost $35 and they (both Able and the group) will lose $10 contribution from X. Therefore, the minimum price able will sell for is $45. So long as the bought-in external price of Y to Baker is less than $45, Baker should buy from that external source.

(b)   The following are required.

–   Marginal costs (i.e. unit variable costs) and incremental fixed costs for various capacity levels for both divisions.

–   External market prices if appropriate.

–   External bought-in prices from suppliers outside the group.

–   Opportunity costs from switching products.

–   Data on capacity levels and resource requirements.

Test your understanding 9

(a) We must assume that Thornthwaite can divert sales away from existing customers, as it only has 30,000 units of spare capacity. This may not be possible because of existing contractual arrangements, or the adverse impact on goodwill and future sales.

Target Residual Income = $250,000.

Charge for capital employed = $6,000,000 × 12% = $720,000.

So, required profit = 250 + 720 = $970,000

As fixed costs are $2,500,000, the required contribution is 2,500 + 970 = $3,470,000

If we transfer 50,000 units to Froswick, we can sell 150,000 units externally at a contribution of (45 – 30) = $15/unit.

So, contribution from external sales = 150,000 × $15 = $2,250,000

We therefore require contribution of 3,470 – 2,250 = $1,220,000 from internal transfer of 50,000 units. Contribution required per unit = $1,220,000/50,000 = $24.40 per unit.

Therefore transfer price Thornthwaite would set = 24.4 + 30 = $54.40.

(b) The transfers should be made on an opportunity cost basis.

Thornthwaite has spare capacity of 30,000 units, and since the variable cost of production is less than the price at which Froswick can buy in from an external supplier, it should use this capacity.

The transfer price should be at least equal to Thornthwaite's marginal cost of $30, but less than the external price that Froswick can buy in at of $42.

Once this spare capacity has been used up, we do not want Thornthwaite to turn away external customers paying $45/unit as this would only save $42/unit from Froswick buying in. Hence, when there is no spare capacity the transfer price should be set at the external selling price of $45/unit. This would encourage Froswick to buy in externally.

Summary

Transfer 30,000 units at >marginal cost of $30 (but less than the buy-in price of $42).

Set a transfer price of $45 for units in excess of 30,000, to encourage Froswick to buy externally.

(c) **Briefing notes on the potential dysfunctional effect of the bonus scheme at Kentmere**

The first thing to note is that the bonus is material – the divisional manager can double his/her pay by hitting the RI target. It is likely that this will influence decisions that the manager takes.

A decentralised structure encourages local managers to optimise their own reported performance. They are not necessarily that concerned with corporate performance overall, especially as this is not linked to their rewards. This may well encourage dysfunctional behaviour since a decision that looks good for an individual division may not be in the best interests of the company overall. This is indeed the case here.

We can use the figures given to illustrate this:

If Thornthwaite sets the transfer price calculated of $54.40, Froswick will exercise its right to buy from the external supplier at a price of $42. This is clearly dysfunctional as Thornthwaite could have used its spare capacity to manufacture 30,000 units internally at a marginal cost of $30/unit.

This causes a net cost to the group of $30,000 \times (30 - 42) = $360,000$.

Using the opportunity costs for the transfer price as calculated in part (b) would avoid this dysfunctional behaviour, but would of course mean that Thornthwaite misses its RI target.

Improvements to transfer pricing policy

A transfer pricing policy should have the following attributes:

- The transfer price should motivate the correct decision for the company as a whole.
- It should preserve the local autonomy rather than being imposed.
- It should provide a margin to both parties.
- It should be simple to operate and understand.

Clearly our current system, whilst being simple, does not meet these criteria. Allowing Thornthwaite to set the transfer price means that it will seek to meet its own objectives, which will in turn mean that Froswick rejects the transfer and buys from outside. This is dysfunctional and causes a loss to the group as a whole.

One solution would be to use a two – part system. Goods could be transferred at marginal cost during the period, with a lump sum period end recharge to cover Thornthwaite's fixed costs and to allocate profit. This would require Head Office intervention as the two divisions would clearly disagree on what the lump sum should be!

Improvements to the bonus scheme

The problem with the current bonus scheme is that it is based on the achievement of a single target figure, which it seems can readily be manipulated by setting a higher transfer price. It provides a classic example of "what you measure is what you get", and so dysfunctional behaviour results.

We need a scheme that encourages a corporate view rather than a parochial divisional view, so Thornthwaite's bonus should be linked to the overall Company performance and not its own result. This in turn means that it should incorporate measures like quality, efficiency improvements and staff welfare.

This is more difficult, because as models such as Fitzgerald and Moon's Building Blocks tell us, rewards should be based on principles such as clarity, motivation and controllability. A divisional manager may feel that overall company performance is outside their direct control, and lacks the necessary clarity.

So, in conclusion Mr Brearley is correct to be concerned. There are fundamental weaknesses in linking the bonus to a single measure, and particularly one that can be manipulated by adjusting the transfer price.

Test your understanding 10

Blocked remittances might be avoided by means of:

- increasing transfer prices paid by the foreign subsidiary to the parent company (see below)

- lending the equivalent of the dividend to the parent company

- making payments to the parent company in the form of:

  - royalties

  - payments for patents

  - management fees and charges

- charging the subsidiary company additional head office overheads.

Note: The government of the foreign country might try to prevent many of these measures being used.

Performance management in not-for-profit organisations

Chapter learning objectives

Upon completion of this chapter you will be able to:

- highlight and discuss the potential for diversity in objectives depending on organisation type

- discuss the difficulties in measuring outputs when performance is not judged in terms of money or an easily quantifiable objective

- discuss the use of benchmarking in public sector performance (league tables) and its effects on operational and strategic management and client behaviour

- discuss how the combination of politics and the desire to measure public sector performance may result in undesirable service outcomes e.g. the use of targets

- assess 'value for money' service provision as a measure of performance in not-for-profit organisations and the public sector.

PER

One of the PER performance objectives (PO14) is to measure and assess departmental and business performance. Working through this chapter should help you understand how to demonstrate that objective.

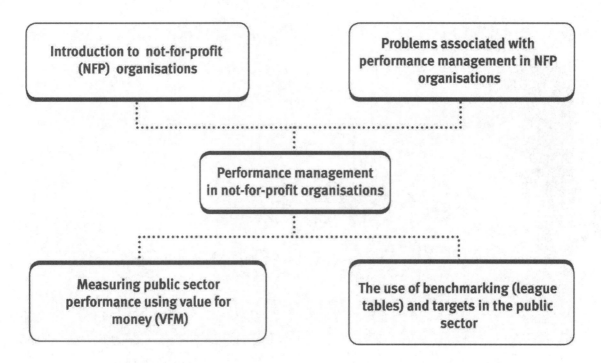

1 Common knowledge

Chapter 12 builds on your knowledge of not-for-profit organisations from PM.

2 Introduction to not-for-profit (NFP) organisations

NFP organisations include private sector and public sector organisations:

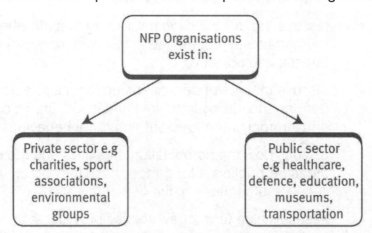

NFP organisations display the following characteristics:

- Most do not have external shareholders and hence an underlying financial objective, typically to maximise profit in order to **maximise shareholder wealth**, is **not the primary objective**.

- Instead, NFP organisations exist primarily to **maximise the benefit to beneficiaries**. Their objective normally includes some social, cultural, philanthropic, welfare or environmental, dimension that would not be readily provided in their absence.

United Kingdom Ministry of Defence (UK MOD)

The UK MOD is a government department that encompasses the UK's three armed forces; the Royal Navy, Army and Royal Air Force.
Its primary objective is to **defend the UK and its interests and to strengthen international peace and stability**.

The Football Association (FA)

The FA is the NFP governing body of football in England. Its primary objective is to **make football a positive and inclusive experience for everyone involved in the game**.

Oxfam

Oxfam is a group of 20 individual charitable organisations. Its primary objective is **to help create long lasting solutions to the injustice of poverty**.

3 Problems associated with performance management in NFP organisations

The characteristics of NFP organisations result in a unique set of challenges in managing performance. The main problems associated with managing performance in NFP organisations are:

- Non-quantifiable costs and benefits
- Assessing the use of funds
- Multiple and diverse objectives
- The impact of politics on performance measurement.

These problems will be explored below, together with some possible solutions for overcoming each problem and for assessing performance in an optimum manner.

3.1 Problem: Non-quantifiable costs and benefits

Many of the costs incurred and benefits arising in NFP organisations are non-quantifiable in monetary terms.

Why are the costs and benefits non-quantifiable?

There are a number of reasons:

- **No readily available scale exists**

  No readily available scale exists for measuring the costs and benefits associated with NFP organisations.

Illustration 2 – Non-quantifiable costs and benefits

Non-quantifiable benefits

A number of years ago, the British government scrapped admission charges to some of the country's most famous museums and galleries. The policy has attracted tens of millions of extra people to the nation's great artistic and cultural collections. Subjects such as history, art and geography have been enlivened by being able to go to a museum or gallery and see and touch the exhibitions. However, it is difficult to quantify the benefits.

Non-quantifiable costs

A hospital has decided to save money by using a cheaper cleaning firm. However, this decision may create problems in a number of areas:

- It may lead to the spread of infection.

- The general public may lose confidence in the quality of the cleaning.

- Medical staff may become demotivated because they are unable to carry out their work safely and effectively.

However, it is difficult to measure these costs.

Illustration 3 – How to trade off costs and benefits

The non-quantifiable nature of the costs and benefits, results in difficulty weighing up the relative costs against the benefit.

For example, suppose funds in a hospital are re-allocated to reduce waiting lists. The benefit would be the reduction in waiting time for those patients on the list. However, this may come at a cost to other patients who could face poorer quality of care due to the re-allocation of funds away from the service provided to them. It is difficult to weigh up if the waiting time saved is enough to compensate for any potential additional suffering.

- **Timescale problems**

  Benefits often accrue over a long time-period and therefore become difficult to estimate reliably. For example, a school may invest in additional sports facilities that will benefit pupils over many decades.

- **Negative externalities**

  A negative externality is a cost suffered by a third party as a result of an organisation's activities, for which no appropriate compensation is paid. For example, a council seeking the benefit of increased housing provision may grant planning permission for new houses to be built. The new residents will increase the number of cars on local roads, resulting in greater congestion and pollution, affecting other residents (i.e. this is a cost to the residents, a negative externality).

How to overcome the problem of non-quantifiable costs and benefits

One possible method for overcoming this problem is **cost benefit analysis (CBA)**.

- CBA attempts to quantify in financial terms the costs and benefits associated with a course of action.

- An overall net benefit would suggest that the course of action should go ahead where as an overall net cost would suggest that the course of action should not go ahead.

Illustration 4 – CBA

Suppose a local government department is considering whether to lower the speed limit for heavy goods vehicles (HGVs) travelling on a particular road through a residential area. The affected stakeholders may be identified as follows:

Stakeholder	Cost	Benefit
HGV operators	• Extra journey time • Potential speeding fines	Fewer accidents
Other road uses	• Extra journey times	Fewer accidents
Local residents	• Higher noise levels and pollution	Fewer accidents
Local authority	• Cost of new signs, speed cameras • Cost of enforcement	Fines collected

These costs and benefits then need to be quantified financially. For example:

Factor	How to measure
Cost extra journey time	• For HGV operators this can be quantified as additional wages, overtime premiums, additional fuel costs, etc. • For other road users we need to quantify how much people value their time. One way this can be done is by comparing the costs of different modes of transport (e.g. coach versus rail versus air) to see the premium travellers will pay to save time. • Another approach is to compare property prices as they get further away from train stations as this will in part reflect longer journey times.

Cost – higher noise levels	• Cost of installing double/triple glazing to reduce noise levels. • Difference in house prices between houses next to the busy road and those set further back.
Cost – higher pollution levels	• Cost of cleaning off soot and other pollutants. • Comparison of house prices near/away from main roads.
Benefit – fewer accidents	• Impact on insurance premiums for drivers. • For victims of accidents the value of not breaking a leg, say, or not being killed, is estimated in many ways, e.g. the present value of future earnings affected.

Once these have been quantified, it is relatively straightforward to compare overall costs and benefits to see the net impact on society and to make a final decision on lowering the speed limit for HGVs.

Another possible solution for addressing this problem is to **assess value for money (VFM)**. This is an important method for measuring performance in NFP organisations and is a common theme in exam questions. It will be discussed separately in section 4.

3.2 Problem: Assessing the use of funds

Many NFP organisations, particularly public sector organisations, in which the funding comes from the government, have strict constraints on the amount of funding they receive. They often do not generate revenue, instead they are allocated a fixed budget for spending within which they have to keep and cannot receive funding from elsewhere.

The funding should be put to the best use. However, it can be difficult to assess whether or not this is the case.

How to overcome the problem of assessing the use of funds

An assessment of the use of funds can be carried out using a VFM framework (section 4).

3.3 Problem: Potential conflict due to multiple and diverse objectives

As discussed, many NFP organisations do not have an objective of maximisation of shareholder wealth. Instead, they are seeking to satisfy the needs of a range of stakeholders resulting in multiple, and often diverse, objectives. These objectives may conflict.

Illustration 5 – Multiple and diverse objectives in a hospital

A hospital will have a number of different groups of stakeholders, such as patients, employees, the government and pharmaceutical firms. Each of these stakeholders will have their own objective(s) (resulting in multiple objectives) and these objectives may be quite varied (i.e. diverse in nature).

For example:

- **Employees** will seek a high level of job satisfaction. They will also aim to achieve a good work-life balance and this may result in a desire to work more regular daytime hours.

- **Patients** will want to be seen quickly and will demand a high level of care.

There is **potential conflict** between the objectives of the two stakeholder groups. For example, if hospital staff only work regular daytime hours then patients may have to wait a long time if they come to the hospital outside of these hours and the standard of patient care will fall dramatically at certain times of the day.

How to overcome the problem of multiple and diverse objectives

The problem of multiple and diverse objectives may be overcome as follows:

- **Prioritising** objectives – The NFP organisation should prioritise the needs of different stakeholder groups (stakeholder mapping, discussed in Chapter 4, could be used to determine the stakeholders to prioritise).

- Making **compromises** between objectives – An element of compromise should also be used so that the needs of all stakeholders are taken into account, to a greater or lesser degree.

The achievement of the established set of objectives can be measured using a **VFM** framework (section 4).

Illustration 6 – Prioritisation and compromise in a hospital

Following on from the previous illustration and the examples of employees and patients as two groups of stakeholders in a hospital, the hospital must prioritise the needs of different stakeholder groups. In this case, the standard of patient care would be prioritised above giving staff the regular daytime working hours that they would prefer. However, in order to maintain staff morale, an element of compromise should also be used. For example, staff may have to work shifts but will be given generous holiday allowances or rewards to compensate for this.

3.4 Problem: The impact of politics on performance measurement in the public sector

Public scrutiny of some sectors, such as health and education, make them a prime target for political interference.

Politicians may promise 'increased funding' and 'improved performance' as that is what voters want to hear, but it may result in undesirable outcomes.

Increased funding may:

- be available only to the detriment of other public sector organisations

- be provided to organisations in political hot-spots, not necessarily the places that need more money

- not be used as efficiently or effectively as it could be

- only be available in the short-term, as a public relations exercise to win votes but at a cost to long-term organisational objectives.

Improved performance may:

- be to the detriment of workers and clients

- come about as the result of data manipulation, rather than real results

- be a short-term phenomenon

- result in more funds being spent on performance measurement when it might better be used on improvements, e.g. hospitals under increasing pressure to compete on price and delivery in some areas may result in a shift of resources from other, less measurable areas, such as towards elective surgery and away from emergency services.

Note: League tables and targets are commonly used in the public sector as a method of managing and measuring performance. The use of these tools will be discussed in section 5.

> **Test your understanding 1 – Practice question on NFPOs**
>
> **Public versus private sector**
>
> The objective of a health authority (a public sector organisation) is stated in its most recent annual report as:
>
> > 'To serve the people of the region by providing high-quality health care within expected waiting times'.
>
> The mission statement of a large company in a manufacturing industry is shown in its annual report as:
>
> > 'In everything the company does, it is committed to creating wealth, always with integrity, for its shareholders, employees, customers and suppliers and the community in which it operates.'

> **Required:**
>
> (a) Discuss the main differences between the public and private sectors that have to be addressed when determining corporate objectives or missions. **(10 marks)**
>
> (b) Describe three performance measures which could be used to assess whether or not the health authority is meeting its current objective. **(3 marks)**
>
> (c) Explain the difficulties which public sector organisations face in using such measures to influence decision making. **(5 marks)**
>
> **(Total: 18 marks)**

4 Measuring public sector performance using value for money (VFM)

4.1 Introduction

As was briefly mentioned in Section 3, value for money (VFM) can be used to measure performance in NFP organisations.

VFM will be explained in section 4.3. A key component in assessing VFM is the use of non-financial performance indicators (NFPIs). Therefore, we will begin by discussing the importance of these NFPIs in NFP organisations.

4.2 NFPIs in NFP organisations

Financial performance measurement remains important to NFP organisations, e.g. to compare actual expenditure against budget or to compare a surplus/deficit of income over expenditure. This is particularly true of those NFP organisations that have strict constraints on the amount of funding they receive.

However, NFP organisations are different to profit seeking organisations. **NFPIs are particularly important for measuring performance in NFP organisations due to the following reasons**:

- NFP organisations **do not have the underlying financial objective to maximise profit** in order to maximise shareholder wealth, making financial indicators of performance less relevant.

- Many NFP organisations **do not have a revenue stream** (but instead have a fixed budget for spending within which they have to keep, as discussed in section 3.2) and it can be **difficult to define a cost unit** or to **quantify the benefits** (section 3.1). This makes traditional financial indicators, focused on revenue or costs or profit, less relevant or easy to use.

- As discussed in section 3.3, NFP organisations have **numerous stakeholders with multiple and often diverse objectives**. Many of these objectives are non-financial in nature and therefore NFPIs are required to measure performance.

- **Financial objectives are less relevant** in NFP organisations. For example, an organisation may exist to provide an essential public service and it would not be shut down purely due to the cost of provision. NFPIs are more relevant for measuring the achievement of the objectives of NFP organisations and capturing aspects of the organisation's mission that are fundamentally non-financial and subjective.

Test your understanding 2

Maple Council is concerned about the performance of Townend School, one of the schools within its jurisdiction and, in order to substantiate this concern, the Council's Education Department has collected the following information regarding the last two years.

	20X7	20X8
School Roll (no of pupils)	502	584
Number of teaching staff	22	21
Number of support staff	6	6
Number of classes	20	20
Possible teaching days in a year	290	290
Actual teaching days in a year	279	282
Total pupil absences (in pupil teaching days)	2,259	3,066
Total teaching staff absences (in pupil teaching days)	132	189
	$	$
Budgeted expenditure	2,400,000	2,600,000
Actual expenditure	2,200,000	2,900,000

The data has been sent to the council's finance department in which you work for analysis.

Required:

Calculate relevant performance measures for Townend School for each of the last two years.

Based on your calculations analyse the school's performance in terms of value for money and explain the possible management responses to your findings.

4.3 Assessing value for money (VFM) using the 3 Es

As discussed, in addition to measuring financial performance (such as actual expenditure against budget), NFP organisations need to monitor the quality of the resources they invest in, how efficiently they are using the resources available to them, and how well they are performing in relation to their key objectives.

In this respect, three important aspects of performance to measure are **economy**, **efficiency** and **effectiveness**; the so-called '**3 Es**'.

Achieving these 3 Es and finding an appropriate balance between them, will help an organisation ensure it is delivering good **value for money (VFM)**.

The 3 Es:		
Economy	**Efficiency**	**Effectiveness**
Are the appropriate quantity and quality of resources (inputs) bought at the lowest cost possible?	How well are the inputs (resources used) converted into outputs? This means optimising the process by which inputs are turned into outputs to maximise the output generated from the units of resource used.	How well do these outputs (actual results) help achieve the stated objectives of the organisation?

Appropriate **performance indicators** should be chosen for each E. As discussed in section 4.2, these will be a combination of financial and non-financial performance indicators.

Comparison should be made internally to historic performance and perhaps benchmarked against suitable external organisations.

The aim of VFM is to achieve an appropriate balance between the 3 Es but this can often be difficult to achieve. **Conflict** may arise, e.g. cost savings may emphasise 'economy' and potentially 'efficiency', rather than the 'effectiveness' of the service.

Sometimes a **fourth 'E'**, **equity**, is included when measuring VFM. This reflects the extent to which services are available to, and reach, the people they are intended for, and whether the benefits from the services are distributed fairly.

Test your understanding 3

Required:

Explain the meaning of economy, efficiency and effectiveness for a publicly funded school, incorporating specific examples and performance indicators for each of the 3 Es.

Student accountant article: visit the ACCA website, www.accaglobal.com, to review the article 'Value for money (VFM) and performance measurement in not for-profit organisations'.

5 The use of benchmarking (league tables) and targets in public sector performance

5.1 Introduction

Benchmarking (as discussed in Chapter 1) is undertaken by many public sector organisations.

The **results from a benchmarking** exercise can be used to **rank organisations in a league table,** with the various metrics from the exercise being presented and then summarised into an overall weighted average score.

 A **league table** is a chart or list that compares one organisation with another by ranking them in order of ability or achievement.

League tables have become a popular performance management tool in the public sector in recent years, for example in hospitals and schools.

Illustration 7 – The use of league tables in schools
Last year, the schools' league tables in the UK showed that London is the highest performing region in England at GCSE level (exams sat by students at the age of 16) with over 70% of pupils achieving the benchmark at GCSE of five 'good' passes including English and mathematics. This is a striking turnaround in the last 25 years or so. In 1997 only 29.9% of London pupils reached this level.

5.2 Advantages of benchmarking (league tables)

- Implementation **stimulates competition** and the **adoption of best practice**. As a result, the quality of the service should improve, resulting in both operational and strategic benefits.

- Monitors and ensures **accountability** of the providers. This accountability should serve as a source of motivation for the provider.

- **Relative performance** is easily compared and performance is **transparent**. This should motivate the provider and is beneficial for the user.

- League tables tend to be **readily available** and so can be used by consumers to make choices.

- Many different areas of performance can be summarised into **one weighted average score**, resulting in ease of use and acts as a focus for operational and strategic improvements.

5.3 Problems of using benchmarking (league tables)

- **Dysfunctional behaviour** – if targets are not aligned to the organisation's mission then managers may focus on achieving targets to the detriment of overall performance.

- League tables **only measure relative performance**. The best/worst performing organisation may still be performing unacceptably/acceptably in absolute terms.

- **Differences between the organisations in the league table** (for example, in location) are not accounted for. This may result in employees being held responsible for things over which they have no control.

- **Ranking** – what areas and weightings should be used in the scoring system to arrive at the ranking?

- The **quality of the information** will be dependent on the quality of data used to arrive at the weighted score. The data management systems in the public sector do not always provide quality data.

- **Poor results** may have a **negative impact on public trust** and **employee morale** and may lead to **users switching to alternative providers** resulting in a downward spiral in the quality of the service provided.

- **Encourages providers to focus on performance measures** (it becomes a measuring exercise) rather than the quality of the service (it does not become a learning exercise in improving operational and/or strategic performance). Many of the outcomes valued by society are not measurable but many of the performance indicators have been selected on the basis of what is practical rather than what is meaningful.

- Benchmarking **will not lead to improvements if pressure is not exerted by stakeholders**.

- The exercise is **costly and time consuming** and may not be considered a good use of limited public sector resource.

- Could encourage **creative reporting**.

Test your understanding 4

A government has decided to improve school performance by the use of league tables with schools assessed on the following:

- Percentage pass rates in examinations

- Absenteeism

It has been proposed that funding be linked to these measures.

Required:

Suggest some potentially negative outcomes of this system.

5.4   The use of targets in public sector organisations

Introduction

Countries such as the UK, Sweden and Australia have implemented the use of **performance measures and targets** to evaluate all aspects of public sector organisation performance.

 A **performance target** represents the level of performance that the organisation aims to achieve for a particular activity. Such targets should be consistent with the SMART criteria.

The results from the benchmarking process (discussed above) can be used to set attainment targets for public sector organisations such as schools, hospitals and the police force. Managers must explain any variance between actual performance and target and their rewards may be aligned to the achievement of these targets. The organisation should set a target for each of its objectives (and these in turn should be aligned to its mission).

Advantages and disadvantages of targets

Targets should act as an invaluable tool for improvement:

*   improving the efficiency and effectiveness of public expenditure

*   reducing overall expenditure

*   increasing accountability and transparency

*   increasing responsiveness to stakeholder needs

*   increased motivation of managers and staff if rewards are aligned to the achievement of the (controllable) targets set.

However, there are a number of issues associated with the use of targets:

*   **Central control** – most targets are set centrally by government and may focus too heavily on reducing costs to the detriment of quality provision. It may be more appropriate for targets to be established locally by professionals who are aware of the challenges faced in different parts of the country.

*   **Difficulty level** – targets that are too difficult tend to debilitate rather than motivate and those that are too easy lead to complacency.

*   **All or nothing** – not meeting the target can be seen as a sign of failure. However, if an aspirational target is set it may not be met but may still result in improvements and act as a motivator.

*   **Too many targets** – there is a tendency to set too many targets to try to measure every aspect of service delivery. However, a manager responsible for service delivery will be unable to concentrate on more than a handful of targets at any one time.

- **Targets not always appropriate** – it is not always appropriate to set targets, e.g. if the activity is not within the control of the person responsible for meeting the target or it is difficult to quantify the outputs of the organisation.

- **Cost** – the cost of setting the target and measuring performance may outweigh the benefit.

- **Lack of ownership of targets** – each target should have a named person who is accountable for the performance and achievement of the objective.

- **Gaming** – there may be a tendency for people to 'play the system' rather than using the targets as a tool for improvement, i.e. people want to look good rather than be good.

- **Conflict** – conflict between targets may occur, e.g. a reduction in the number of children on the Child Protection Register may coincide with an increase in child abuse cases.

Student accountant article: visit the ACCA website, www.accaglobal.com, to review the article 'Performance management in public sector organisations'.

Chapter summary

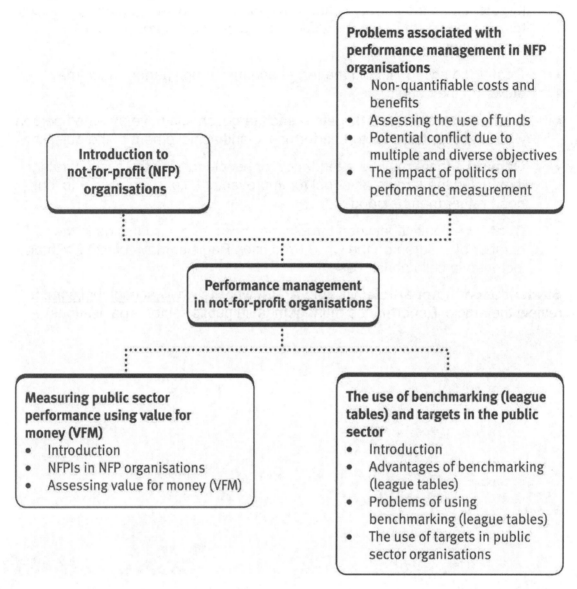

Test your understanding answers

Test your understanding 1 – Practice question on NFPOs

(a) The main differences between the public and private sector regarding corporate objectives are:

The objectives of a public sector body are usually set out in the Act of Parliament or legal document that brought the body into existence. They are therefore difficult to change, even as environmental conditions change around the body. The directors of a private sector body have more freedom in making up the objectives of the company as they go along, and can change the objectives rapidly in response to changing conditions.

The value of the output of a private sector body can be easily determined in an unbiased way, by looking at the sales revenue achieved. Such numbers can therefore be part of the objectives to be achieved. There is no easy way for determining the economic value of the output of a public sector body; placing a value on the achievements of a country's Navy last year is almost impossible.

The mission statement of the company in the question recognises the role of the company in having responsibilities to different groups of stakeholders: shareholders, customers, the community at large, etc. Some public sector bodies appear to ignore the interests of certain stakeholders; you might for example be able to think of bodies that appear to be run more for the employees of the body itself rather than the public it is supposed to be serving. Private sector bodies that ignore stakeholders go bust and leave the marketplace. Failing public sector bodies often are rewarded with greater slices of public money to finance their inadequacies.

Private sector companies can attract finance in a free marketplace if they wish to expand. Public sector bodies are constrained by short-term cash limits set by the government depending on the state of the public finances. This acts against the construction of long-term strategic plans in the public sector.

The public sector has historically had little understanding of capital as a scarce resource. In the objective quoted in the question for the health authority, there is no mention of giving value for money to the taxpayers who finance the services. Private sector companies have to give value for money to their shareholders; otherwise the shareholders will sell their shares and the share price will fall, making future capital issues more expensive.

(b) In terms of the health authority's current objective, three performance measures that could be used are:

Number of patients who survive serious surgery: this would give a measure of the quality of emergency health care provided, and could be calculated as an absolute figure and a percentage, and compared with the figures for the previous year and nationally.

Length of time (on average) before an ambulance arrives after an emergency call is made: this could be compared with the figure for the previous year and for other similar regions of the country.

Length of waiting list for serious operations, i.e. the average time period between a patient being recommended for an operation and the operation actually taking place: this figure could be compared with the figure for the previous year and with national figures.

(c) Decisions have to be made at both a local level (the tactical and operational decisions in running the public sector organisation) and a national level (mainly in terms of the amount of money to be made available to the service).

If insufficient funds have been made available to a health authority, the only way it can maintain standards is to let the waiting list increase. This might reflect badly on the local managers, but the responsibility for the problem really lies with the politicians who have decided to inadequately finance the organisation.

Similar problems exist in other public sector areas. Consider the police, for example. If they arrest more criminals, is this good or bad? Some people would say it is a good thing in that they are detecting more crime; others would say it is a failure of their crime prevention measures. If the statistical percentage of successful prosecutions brought was to be used as a performance measure, this might pressure the police to release on caution all those suspects against whom the police felt they did not have a watertight case. This is surely not in the public interest.

The recommended solution is for public sector organisations to rephrase their statements of objectives to bring more stakeholders into view, and then to construct a range of performance measures, which takes into account the wishes of each of these stakeholders.

Test your understanding 2

	20X7	20X8
Measure 1		
Possible pupil teaching days		
(school roll × possible teaching days in the year)	145,580	169,360
Actual pupil teaching days		
(school roll × actual teaching days in the year)	140,058	164,688
Actual to possible teaching days as a %	**96.2%**	**97.2%**
Measure 2		
Pupils absences as a % of total actual teaching days	2,259	3,066
	———	———
	140,058	164,688
	= 1.6%	**= 1.9%**
Measure 3		
Staff absences as a % of total actual teaching days	132	189
	———	———
	140,058	164,688
	= 0.1%	**= 0.1%**
Measure 4		
Pupil teacher ratio	502:22	584:21
	= 22.8:1	**= 27.8:1**
Measure 5		
Pupil to non-teaching staff ratio	502:6	584:6
	= 83.7:1	**= 97.3:1**
Measure 6		
Average class size	502	584
(school roll/number of classes)	———	———
	20	20
	= 25.1	**= 29.2**
Measure 7		
Budgeted expenditure per pupil	2,400,000	2,600,000
	———	———
	502	584
	= $4781	**= $4452**
Actual expenditure per pupil	2,200,000	2,900,000
	———	———
	502	584
	= $4382	**= $4966**

Comments

In certain circumstances, the schools performance has been fairly consistent over the two years. Staff and pupil absences as a percentage of total actual pupil teaching days have deteriorated marginally (but the fall may not merit investigation by management), whilst actual to possible total teaching days has shown a slight improvement (managers may investigate the reasons for this improvement and take steps to improve this figure further next year).

The major area of concern is the number of pupils on the school roll is roughly 16% higher than last year. This may have an impact on performance. Management must investigate the reasons for the increase and establish whether the trend is set to continue. Action may be taken if a link to a deterioration in performance is established, e.g. through the recruitment of more teaching staff, building additional classrooms and investing in extra resources such as IT resources and books. However, the increase in student numbers may actually indicate more efficient use of resources and hence value for money. Pupil to teaching staff, pupil to non-teaching staff, and average class size has worsened. Whether this is enough to effect the quality of provision is impossible to say without further investigation.

Expenditure per pupil has fallen but this is a function of the increased pupil numbers.

Overall, it is not really possible to arrive at a firm conclusion about the schools performance. This is partly due to a lack of data from the school, and partly because of a lack of data from other schools against which to compare it.

Test your understanding 3

Value for money for a school would comprise the three elements of economy, efficiency and effectiveness:

Economy – this is about balancing the cost with the quantity and quality of resources. Therefore, performance indicators (PIs) will focus on areas such as the cost of books, computers and teaching compared with the quality (factors such as the skills and experience of teaching staff) of these resources. It recognises that the organisation must consider its expenditure but should not simply aim to minimise costs, e.g. low cost but poor quality teaching or books will hinder student performance and will damage the reputation of the school.

Effectiveness – this measures the achievement of the organisation's objectives. PIs may focus on, for example:

- The % of students achieving a target grade or level of achievement.

- The % of staff and student absences.

Efficiency – this focuses on the efficient use of any resources acquired to achieve the desired results (outputs). For example, PIs may focus on:

- What is the utilisation of IT resources or books?

- What % of their working time do teaching staff spend teaching?

Test your understanding 4

- Children with special needs/disabilities may find it harder to gain school places as they may be perceived as having less chance of passing examinations reducing school performance and funding.

- Truants are likely to be expelled at the school's first realistic opportunity. This may result in the school performing better but only transfers the 'problem' somewhere else.

- Schools may focus on examination performance to the detriment of other educational goals, e.g. art, sports.

- Schools facing difficulties will receive less funding to help overcome those problems.

- There will be increased competitiveness and decreased collaboration between schools.

Non-financial performance indicators

Chapter learning objectives

Upon completion of this chapter you will be able to:

- evaluate how models such as SWOT analysis, PEST, Boston Consulting Group, balanced scorecard, Porter's generic strategies and 5 Forces may assist in the performance management process

- discuss the interaction of non-financial performance indicators with financial performance indicators

- identify and discuss the significance of non-financial performance indicators in relation to employees and product/service quality, e.g. customer satisfaction reports, repeat business ratings, customer loyalty, access and availability

- discuss the difficulties in interpreting data on qualitative issues

- discuss the significance of brand awareness and company profile and their potential impact on business performance

- advise on the link between achievement of the corporate strategy and the management of human resources (e.g. through the Building Block model)

- apply and evaluate the 'balanced scorecard' approach as a way in which to improve the range and linkage between performance measures

- apply and evaluate the 'performance pyramid' as a way in which to link strategy, operations and performance
- apply and evaluate the work of Fitzgerald and Moon that considers performance measurement in business services using building blocks for dimensions, standards and rewards.

PER

Three of the PER performance objectives are:

- Monitor performance (PO14)
- Business advisory (PO21) and
- Data analysis and decision support (PO22).

Working through this chapter should help you understand how to demonstrate these objectives.

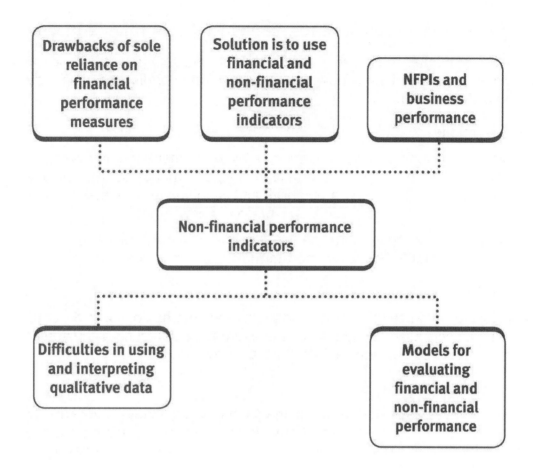

1 Common knowledge

Chapter 13 builds on your knowledge of the following topics from PM:

- Non-financial performance indicators (NFPIs)
- Balanced scorecard
- Building Block model.

2 Introduction

In Chapters 10 and 11 we looked at a wide range of financial performance measures. In order to fully appraise the performance of an organisation, and to understand if the best techniques are being used to drive its success, it is useful to use a range of financial performance indicators (FPIs) and non-financial performance indicators (NFPIs).

3   Drawbacks of sole reliance on financial performance measures

There are a number of problems associated with the sole use of FPIs to monitor performance (many of these have been touched upon or discussed already in Chapters 10 and 11):

Short-termism

Linking rewards to financial performance may tempt managers to make decisions that will improve short-term financial performance but may have a negative impact on long-term profitability and is not in the best interests of the organisation overall (i.e. there is a lack of **goal congruence**).

For example, a manager appraised using ROCE/ROI may decide to delay investment in order to boost the short-term profits of their division.

Internal focus

Financial performance measures tend to have an internal focus. In order to compete successfully it is important that external factors (such as customer satisfaction and competitors' actions) are also considered.

Do not convey the whole picture

The use of FPIs has limited benefit to the company since they do not convey the full picture regarding the factors that drive long-term success and maximisation of shareholder wealth, e.g. customer satisfaction, ability to innovate, quality, consideration of ESG issues, etc.

Backward looking

Financial performance measures are traditionally backward looking. This is not suitable in today's dynamic business environment. Organisations should be focusing on future performance and maximisation of long-term shareholder value.

Manipulation of results

Most managers will act in good faith and have an honest approach to performance management. However, in order to achieve target financial performance (and hence their reward), a small minority of managers may be tempted to manipulate results, e.g. costs recorded in the current year may be wrongly recorded in the next year's accounts in order to improve current year performance.

It is important to point out that NFPIs can also be open to manipulation by managers (in fact they may be even more open to manipulation due to their subjective nature). However, using a comprehensive range of FPIs and NFPIs should assist in achieving a true and fair view of organisational performance and any problems associated with manipulation of results should be minimised.

4 Solution = use financial and non-financial performance indicators

In order to overcome the problems discussed in section 3, a broader range of measures should be used.

The optimum system for performance measurement and control will include:

- Financial performance indicators (FPIs) – it is still important to monitor financial performance, e.g. using ROCE, EBITDA, EVA. These reveal the results of actions already taken.

- Non-financial performance indicators (NFPIs) – these measures will reflect the long-term viability and health of the organisation and will drive future financial performance.

As was touched upon in Chapter 10, the measures used should be tailored to the circumstances in the organisation (and therefore the scenario given in the exam).

The models used to evaluate financial and non-financial performance will be reviewed in detail in section 7.

Use of NFPIs

The following table gives examples of possible NFPIs:

Competitiveness	• Sales growth by product or service
	• Proportion new/repeat customers
	• Relative market share and position
Activity	• Sales units
	• Labour/machine hours
	• Number of material requisitions serviced
	• Number of accounts reconciled
Productivity	• Efficiency measurements of resources planned against consumed
	• Measurements of resources available against those used
	• Productivity measurements such as production per person or per hour or per shift
Product and service quality (discussed in more detail in section 5.3 and in Chapter 14)	• Number of quality issues relating to supplies
	• Number of customer complaints received about quality
	• Number of new accounts lost or gained as a result of quality
	• Rejections as a percentage of production or sales

5 NFPIs and business performance

5.1 Introduction

There are a number of areas that are particularly important for ensuring the success of a business and where the use of NFPIs play a key role. Three of these will be discussed in this section:

- The management of human resources

- Product and service quality

- Brand awareness and company profile.

Each of these will be reviewed in turn.

5.2 The management of human resources

As discussed in Chapter 9, today, employees are regarded as a strategic resource that may provide the organisation with competitive advantage.

FPIs will be an important part of measuring and monitoring the effectiveness of human resource management. For example, an organisation may measure the cost per employee hired, training and development costs or the cost of the reward system.

In addition, it will be important to have a range of **NFPIs** in place. These may include:

Example activity	Possible NFPI
Recruitment and selection	Time to fill a position
	Female to male ratio
Training and development	Training feedback
Performance management	Appraisals completed on time
	Appraisal action plan agreed and followed up
Motivation	Turnover rate
	Employee absenteeism
	Employee productivity
	Employee satisfaction scores
	Flexible working arrangements offered
Reward systems	Adherence to laws and regulations

5.3 Product and service quality

Problems with product or service quality can have a long-term impact on the business and they can lead to customer dissatisfaction and loss of future sales.

NFPIs are particularly useful when assessing product and service quality. The relative importance of different product/service quality characteristics, including value for money, performance, comparison with competitor's offerings, will vary from company to company and between customers. However, some typical NFPIs may focus on the following:

- The **quality of incoming supplies**, e.g. a sample of incoming supplies may be inspected to determine the level of quality.

- The **quality of work completed**. Again, a sample of output may be checked to verify the levels of quality.

- **Customer satisfaction**. One definition of quality is 'the ability of a product or service to meet the needs of the customer. Customer satisfaction, loyalty and repeat business go hand in hand and it is important to measure customer satisfaction, e.g. using customer surveys, level of repeat business, number and type of complaints about product/ service quality, availability of product/service.

Quality will be explored in more detail in Chapter 14.

Illustration 1 – Quality of service at Heathrow Airport

Heathrow Airport Holdings Limited owns and runs London Heathrow Airport, one of the world's busiest airports. It uses regular customer surveys for measuring customer perceptions of a wide variety of service quality attributes, including, for example, the cleanliness of its facilities, the helpfulness of its staff and the ease of finding one's way around the airport. Public correspondence is also analysed in detail, and comment cards are available in the terminals so that passengers can comment voluntarily on service levels received. Duty terminal managers also sample the services and goods offered by outlets in the terminals, assessing them from a customer perspective.

They check the cleanliness and condition of service facilities and complete detailed checklists which are submitted daily to senior terminal managers. The company has also a wealth of internal monitoring systems that record equipment faults and failures, and report equipment and staff availability. These systems are supported by the terminal managers who circulate the terminals on a full-time basis, helping customers as necessary, reporting any equipment faults observed and making routine assessments of the level of service provided by Heathrow Airport Holdings Limited.

Heathrow Airport Holdings Limited		
Quality characteristic	**Measures**	**Mechanisms**
Access	Walking distance/ease of finding way around	Surveys/operational data
Aesthetics	Staff appearance/airport appearance/quality of catering	Surveys/inspection
Availability	Equipment availability	Internal fault monitors
Cleanliness	Environment and equipment	Surveys/inspection
Comfort	Crowdedness	Surveys/inspection
Communication	Information clarity/clarity of labelling and pricing	Surveys/inspection
Competence	Staff efficiency	Management inspection
Courtesy	Courtesy of staff	Surveys/inspection
Friendliness	Staff attitude	Surveys/inspection
Reliability	Equipment faults	Surveys/inspection
Responsiveness	Staff responsiveness	Surveys/inspection
Security	Efficiency of security checks/number of urgent safety reports	Surveys/internal data

5.4 Brand awareness and company profile

Brand awareness is a general terms that describes how familiar (aware) consumers are of a brand. It is an indicator of the strength of a product's/service's place in the customers' minds.

A **company profile** is a written introduction to the company, focusing on its activities, mission, goals and strengths.

Developing and maintaining a brand and/or a company profile can be expensive. However, it can also **enhance performance** due to **customer loyalty**, which results in repurchasing and continued use of the product/service. The value of a brand and the strength of the company profile is based on the extent to which:

- it helps increase customer loyalty and attract new customers

- there is name awareness and awareness about the organisation and its activities in general

- it has perceived quality

- other attributes such as patents or trademarks.

A **range of FPIs and NFPIs** will assist in measuring the strength of the brand and its company profile.

FPIs may focus on areas such as:

- marketing spend against sales

- market share

- elasticity of demand to price (i.e. the change in demand as a result of a change in price) and

- profit margins compared to other companies that make similar products but with a brand strength that is much stronger/weaker.

NFPIs may focus on areas such as:

- customer awareness of the brand and of the company in general

- consumer opinions, for example on the quality of the product or service

- % repeat customers.

Test your understanding 1

Required:

How are the measures of product and service quality related to brand awareness and company profile?

6 Difficulties in using and interpreting qualitative data

In Chapter 8 we discussed the difficulties in recording and processing data of a qualitative nature and looked at how a business can deal with qualitative data.

Most NFPIs are in qualitative terms and, although this can present some challenges, should not be ignored. The notes in Chapter 8, section 5 should be referred back to since the points covered may be examined in the context of this chapter.

7 Models for evaluating financial and non-financial performance

7.1 Introduction

There are **three key models** that an organisation can use to evaluate its financial and non-financial performance.

- the balanced scorecard

- Fitzgerald and Moon's Building Block Model

- The performance pyramid.

Each one will be reviewed in turn but remember that questions may ask you to **compare and contrast the methods** rather than just discussing each one in isolation.

7.2 The balanced scorecard

What is the balanced scorecard?

The balanced scorecard was designed to be used as a strategic performance measurement and management framework.

It provides a **framework that can be utilised to develop a multi-dimensional set of performance measures for strategic control of the business**.

The balanced scorecard includes:

- **financial measures**, these reveal the results of actions already taken

- **non-financial measures**, these are drivers of future financial performance

- **external information** as well as **internal information**.

The balanced scorecard allows managers to look at the business from **four important perspectives**:

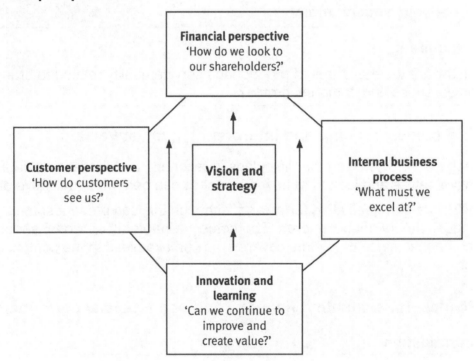

Within each of these perspectives, a business should seek to do the following:

- **Identify** a series of **goals** (**CSFs**, i.e. what are the vital areas where things must go right in order for the organisation to succeed and achieve its strategic objectives?) and

- **Establish** appropriate **measures** (**KPIs**, since 'what gets measured, gets done') **and targets**.

These **should be in line with the overall strategic objectives and vision** of the organisation (the vision and strategy form the central part of the balanced scorecard).

Illustration 2 – Examples of goals and measures

A balanced scorecard for an electronics company could include the following goals and measures:

	Goals (CSFs)	Measures (KPIs)
Customer perspective	Low cost	Benchmark cost vs competitor's cost
	High quality	% defects
	Responsive service	% on-time deliveries
Internal business processes perspective	Operational excellence	Production cycle time, rectification time, % of production completed on time and within budget
	Employee satisfaction	Staff turnover %
Innovation and learning	Innovation	% of income from new products
	Internal learning	Number of employee suggestions and % implemented, % of time spent on staff development
Financial perspective	Growth and development	Quarterly sales growth
	Survival	Cash flow
	Profitability	ROCE

It would be beneficial to rank the goals and measures in order of importance.

Required:

Using the four perspectives of the balanced scorecard, suggest some performance measures for a building company involved in house building and commercial property and operating in a number of different countries.

Implementing the balanced scorecard

There are four essential activities which have to be executed rigorously if the implementation of the balanced scorecard is to succeed:

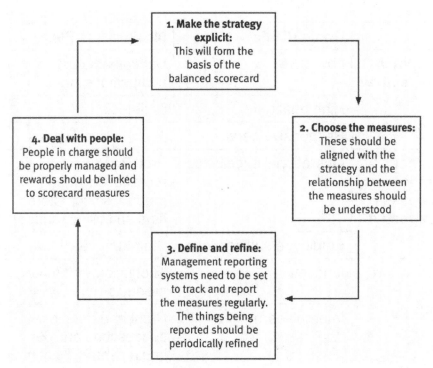

Steps involved in implementing the scorecard

1   **Make the strategy explicit**

The starting point in producing a balanced scorecard is identifying the strategic requirements for success in the firm. Typically, those strategic requirements will relate to products, markets, growth and resources (human, intellectual and capital).

For example, businesses like Dell may want to be low-cost producers achieving competitive advantage from selling undifferentiated products at lower prices than those of competitors, or a business may have a product development strategy to become a leader in technology and command a premium like Apple. Their strategy may also be to develop and maintain market share, like Microsoft, or their strategy may be to occupy the number-one or number-two position in their lines of business.

2   **Choose the measures**

Performance measures have to be selected that clearly relate to the achievement of the strategies identified in the earlier process. As has been seen throughout the discussion of performance measures in this text, the selection of appropriate indicators and measures is critical. The selected measures form the goals that management communicates to staff as being important. Those goals are what staff will strive to achieve. If the wrong goals are selected then the firm may find itself doing the wrong things.

The general problem is that performance measures that relate to limited parts of the business can be very prone to inducing dysfunctional behaviour. For example, a firm might minimise its inventory holding in order to meet some inventory holding target – but at the expense of total operating costs.

3 Define and refine

Management reporting systems and procedures need to be set up to track and report the measures regularly. This involves all the issues relating to the processing of data and the reporting of information discussed earlier in this text.

The precise requirements of reporting associated with the use of the balanced scorecard will make demands on both the management accounting and IT systems in an organisation. Fully satisfying those demands has a cost and sometimes compromises may have to be made in order to contain that cost.

All sorts of practical problems may be encountered in reporting on an indicator. For example, when reporting on revenue:

- How is revenue calculated and when is it recorded?
- Should it include the non-core business activity?
- Should revenue be reported under product, region or customer headings?
- How should interdivisional transactions be reported?

Operating the management accounting system associated with the balanced scorecard requires that the things being reported should be defined and periodically refined.

4 Deal with people

The balanced scorecard is an exercise in modifying human behaviour. It is its interaction with people that determines whether or not it will work.

Balanced scorecards can easily become a confusing mass of measures, some of which even contradict each other. There may be too many measures and action to achieve some of them may contribute to failure to achieve others. The measures may not always be prioritised.

To be effective, the measures contained in the scorecard should be limited in number, reasonably consistent and ranked in some order of priority. Further, performance measures should be aligned with the management structure. Career progression and remuneration should be appropriately linked to scorecard measure linked performance. Organisations which adopt a balanced scorecard but continue to reward managers on the basis of a narrow range of traditional financial measures are likely to be disappointed by the results.

Evaluation of the balanced scorecard as a performance management tool

Benefits of the balanced scorecard include:

- The balanced scorecard provides a balanced view of organisational performance in that:
    - it includes a mixture of financial measures (these reveal the results of actions taken) and non-financial measures (these drive future financial performance)
    - it covers internal and external matters.

- Although it focuses on the strategic level, a similar approach can be implemented at tactical and operational level. 'What gets measured, gets done', so if managers (at all levels) know they are being appraised on (and hopefully rewarded for achieving) various aspects of controllable performance, they will pay attention to these areas.

- Managers are unlikely to be able to distort performance, as bad performance is more difficult to hide if multiple measures are used.

- It is flexible; what is measured can be changed over time to reflect changing priorities.

- Success in the four key areas should lead to the long-term success of the organisation. It links the fulfilment of long-term and short-term objectives in each of these areas to the achievement of overall strategy and mission/vision because the balanced scorecard has the vision and strategy at its core. Other models do not make this link so explicit whereas the balanced scorecard does.

However, the balanced scorecard is not without its **problems**.

- It is **difficult to record and process data of a non-financial**, i.e. qualitative, **nature** (but it is still important to do so – see discussion in Chapter 8, section 5).

- **Information overload** due to the large number of measures that may be chosen. However, the creators of the balanced scorecard recommend that only a handful of measures are used.

- Potential **conflict between measures** (for example, profitability may increase in the short-term through a reduction in product development) which may result in managers not knowing which measures to focus on or they may simply focus on one measure and ignore the other.

- **Poor communication to employees/managers**. Organisations that adopt the balanced scorecard but continue to reward managers on the basis of a narrow range of traditional financial measures are likely to be disappointed with the results.

- **Lack of commitment by senior management** (for example, if they are sceptical about its benefits or consider it too difficult to implement) will lead to an inevitable failure of the scorecard.

- The **time** and **cost** involved in establishing suitable measures and in measuring the performance of all areas. IS may need to be upgraded in order to collect and process non-financial and external data.

- The **lack of some key perspectives**, such as ESG. To counter this, Tesco, for example, introduced a fifth perspective focusing on CSR.

- The **measures chosen may not align with the strategy and/or vision** of the organisation.

- **It tends to focus on the** strategic level.

Illustration 3 – The balanced scorecard and social and environmental aspects

One criticism (briefly mentioned above) of the way businesses use the balanced scorecard, is that it is linked to the delivery of traditional economic value (shareholder value) rather than considering the importance of CSR and sustainability (Chapter 4). As such, **some commentators have suggested the need to add social and environmental perspectives to the balanced scorecard**.

Others have argued that sustainability could be incorporated into the existing four perspectives since the overall vision and strategic objectives that form the central part of the balanced scorecard should include sustainability. For example:

- **Financial perspective** – has the financial impact of sustainability, e.g. achieving a target for recycling, been quantified?

- **Customer perspective** – have the interests of 'green' customers been taken into account?

- **Internal business process perspective** – have the environmental impacts of processes, e.g. water and energy usage, been considered?

- **Innovation and learning perspective** – do training and development programmes help promote sustainable values and culture?

Practical example of scorecard implementation

One example reported in management literature of how the balanced scorecard might be applied is the US case of Analog Devices (a semi-conductor manufacturer) in the preparation of its five-year strategic plan. Analog Devices had as its main corporate objective: 'Achieving our goals for growth, profits, market share and quality creates the environment and economic means to satisfy the needs of our employees, stockholders, customers and others associated with the firm. Our success depends on people who understand the interdependence and congruence of their personal goals with those of the company and who are thus motivated to contribute towards the achievement of those goals.'

Three basic strategic objectives identified by the company were market leadership, sales growth and profitability. The company adopted targets as follows:

Customer perspective

- Percentage of orders delivered on time: a target was set for the five-year period to increase the percentage of on-time deliveries from 85% to at least 99.8%.

- Outgoing defect levels: the target was to reduce the number of defects in product items delivered to customers, from 500 per month to fewer than 10 per month.

- Order lead time: a target was set to reduce the time between receiving a customer order to delivery from 10 weeks to less than three weeks.

Internal perspective

- Manufacturing cycle time: to reduce this from 15 weeks to 4 to 5 weeks over the five-year planning period.

- Defective items in production: to reduce defects in production from 5,000 per month to fewer than 10 per month.

Learning and innovation perspective

- Having products rated 'number one' by at least 50% of customers, based on their attitudes to whether the company was making the right products, performance, price, reliability, quality, delivery, lead time, customer support, responsiveness, willingness to co-operate and willingness to form partnerships.

- The number of new products introduced to the market.

- Sales revenue from new products.

- The new product sales ratio: this was the percentage of total sales achieved by products introduced to the market within the previous six quarters.

- Average annual revenues for new products in their third year.

- Reducing the average time to bring new product ideas to market.

Financial targets were set for revenue, revenue growth, profit and return on assets, but the idea was that the financial targets would flow from achieving the other targets stated above.

Analog Devices sought to adopt financial and non-financial performance measures within a single system, in which the various targets were consistent with each other and were in no way incompatible.

Question practice

The following question examines the balanced scorecard, amongst other areas, and effectively demonstrates the linkages between different performance management techniques. Take the time to attempt the question in full and learn from the answer.

Test your understanding 3

Jump is a listed business operating a chain of quality health clubs in a European country. The company has a strong reputation for the quality of its service but there are a number of other health clubs operating in the country and the market is fiercely competitive.

The country in which Jump is located is currently in recession. Consumer spending is falling throughout the economy and there is no immediate likelihood of a resumption of growth. Appendix 1 shows the financial data for Jump for the past two years.

Jump's Chief Executive Officer (CEO) has recently conducted a strategic review of the business in the context of the current economic recession. They have identified the following strategy as critical for Jump's success:

1   Focus on key customers.

2   Ensure Jump's offerings meet the needs of these customers.

3   Reduce/eliminate costs which do not address these needs.

4   Build for the future using a programme of sustainable development.

Jump recognises that it operates in a highly competitive environment and periodically monitors its share of the market and compares its prices with those of its competitors. The CEO has identified the need to operate a more systematic method of performance improvement. To this end, they believe that competitor benchmarking is necessary and has information that at least one of Jump's main competitors benchmark already.

Appendix 2 contains data analysing Jump and its two main competitors; Fitness Matters and Active First.

Appendix 1: Financial data in Euro (€) for Jump

	20X0	20X1
	€m	€m
Operating profit	51.9	42.7
Interest	4.2	6.1
Profit before tax	47.7	36.6
Profit for the year	37.2	26.3
EVA	20.6	7.2

	20X0	20X1
Average number of shares in issue	140 million	140 million

Stock market information:

Country's market index	1,020.7	704.3
Health club sector index	1,711.3	1,320.3
Jump's average share price	€1.22	€1.03

Appendix 2: Comparative data

	Fitness Matters		Active First		Jump	
	20X0	20X1	20X0	20X1	20X0	20X1
Revenue €m	246	239	521	508	483	522
Profit for the year €m	19.3	17.4	40.4	25.9	37.2	26.3
No. of health clubs	18	20	26	35	20	21
Market share	12.4%	12.2%	16.9%	15.6%	16.0%	16.0%
Revenue per health club €m	13.7	12.0	20.0	14.5	24.2	24.9

Required:

(a) Describe the different perspectives of the balanced scorecard showing how the new strategy as outlined by the CEO links to these perspectives. Recommend appropriate performance measures for Jump for each of the detailed points within the strategy. **(8 marks)**

(b) Assess the financial performance of the company using share price, EPS and EVA. Critically evaluate the use of these performance metrics and how they may affect management behaviour. **(11 marks)**

> (c) Prepare a report for the board on a benchmarking exercise using the information given in appendix 2.
>
> (i) Evaluate the benefits and difficulties of benchmarking in this situation.
>
> (ii) Evaluate the performance of Jump using the data given in the question. Conclude as to the performance of the company.
>
> **(13 marks)**
>
> Professional marks will be awarded for the demonstration of skill in communication, analysis and evaluation, scepticism and commercial acumen in your answer. **(7 marks)**
>
> **(Total: 39 marks)**

Student accountant article: visit the ACCA website, www.accaglobal.com, to review the article on 'Performance measures to support competitive advantage'.

7.3 The Building Block Model

Fitzgerald and Moon developed an approach to improving the performance measurement system in **service organisations**. It suggests that the **performance measurement system should be based on the three building blocks of dimensions, standards and rewards**.

Dimension
Competitiveness
Financial performance
Quality of service
Flexibility
Resource utilisation
Innovation

Standards
Ownership
Achievability
Fairness

Rewards
Clarity
Motivation
Controllability

Dimensions

The six different dimensions are the **CSFs for the business. Suitable metrics must be developed to measure each performance dimension.**

Dimensions fall into two categories:

*   **Downstream results** – competitiveness and financial performance and

*   **Upstream determinants** – quality of service, flexibility, resource utilisation and innovation.

It is the **upstream determinants that drive the future downstream results**. For example, quality service should contribute to future, long-term competitiveness and financial performance.

Dimension	Example of measure
Competitiveness	Relative market share
Financial performance	Turnover growth
Quality of service	Product reliability
Flexibility	Delivery time
Resource utilisation	Productivity
Innovation	New product numbers

Dimensions of performance

The table above identifies the dimensions of performance. The first two of these relate to downstream results, the other four to upstream determinants. For example, a new product innovation will not impact on profit, cash flow and market share achieved in the past – but a high level of innovation provides an indicator of how profit, cash flow and market share will move in the future. If innovation is the determinant of future performance, it is a key success factor.

Standards

The **standards are the targets set for the metrics (KPIs) chosen** from the dimensions measured. The standards set should have the following characteristics:

- **Ownership:** Managers who participate in the setting of standards are more likely to accept and be motivated by the standards than managers on whom standards are imposed.

- **Achievability:** An achievable, but challenging, standard is a better motivator than an unachievable one.

- **Fairness:** When setting standards across an organisation, care should be undertaken to ensure that all managers have equally challenging standards.

Rewards

Rewards are the **motivators for the employees to work towards the standards set**. Remember (from Chapter 9):

- 'what gets measured, gets done'

- 'what gets measured and fed back, gets done well'

- 'what gets rewarded, gets repeated'.

To ensure that employees are **motivated** to meet standards, the standards need to be **clear** (i.e. they should be SMART, prioritised and there should not be too many standards) (e.g. the target is to 'achieve four product innovations per year' rather than to simply 'innovate') and linked to **controllable** factors. The actual method of motivation may involve performance-related pay, a bonus or a promotion. The reward should be desirable in itself.

The building block model thus **makes an explicit link between achievement of the corporate strategy and the management of human resources**. In Chapter 9, we identified that this is one of the primary purposes of reward schemes. Therefore, if the exam question asks you to assess how effectively an existing or proposed reward scheme supports the organisation's goals, you can use the Building Block model as a framework; consider the principles of effective standards (ownership, achievability and fairness) and the principles of effective rewards (clarity, controllability and motivation).

Fitzgerald and Moon example

Fitzgerald and Moon applied to a Washing Machine retailer

Dimension = CSF	Flexibility – Customers can book a one hour delivery slot	Quality of service – Full installation offered, at a fixed price	Financial performance – e.g. ROCE
Standard = KPI	99% of deliveries are made within the delivery slot	All customers can request full installation, target for installation is less than 45 minutes	Target ROCE
Reward	Points for each on time delivery – leading to a bonus	% commission for installation staff for achieving target time set	Management ROCE related bonuses

Test your understanding 4

FL provides training on financial subjects to staff of small and medium-sized businesses. Training is at one of two levels – for clerical staff, instructing them on how to use simple financial accounting computer packages, and for management, on management accounting and financial management issues.

Training consists of tutorial assistance, in the form of workshops or lectures, and the provision of related material – software, texts and printed notes.

Tuition days may be of standard format and content, or designed to meet the client's particular specifications. All courses are run on client premises and, in the case of clerical training courses, are limited to 8 participants per course.

FL has recently introduced a 'helpline' service, which allows course participants to phone in with any problems or queries arising after course attendance. This is offered free of charge.

FL employs administrative and management staff. Course lecturers are hired as required, although a small core of technical staff is employed on a part-time basis by FL to prepare customer-specific course material and to man the helpline.

Material for standard courses is bought in from a group company, who also print up the customer-specific course material.

Required:

Suggest a measure for each of the six dimensions of the building block model.

Question practice

The question below is a useful question to attempt to ensure that you fully understand the building block model and that you can apply your knowledge in the context of the scenario.

Test your understanding 5

The Sentinel Company (TSC) offers a range of door-to-door express delivery services. The company operates using a network of depots and distribution centres throughout the country of Nickland. The following information is available:

1   Each depot is solely responsible for all customers within a specified area. It collects goods from customers within its own area for delivery both within the specific area covered by the depot and elsewhere in Nickland.

2   Collections made by a depot for delivery outside its own area are forwarded to the depots from which the deliveries will be made to the customers.

3   Each depot must therefore integrate its deliveries to customers to include:

(i)   goods that it has collected within its own area; and

(ii)   goods that are transferred to it from depots within other areas for delivery to customers in its area.

4   Each depot earns revenue based on the invoiced value of all consignments collected from customers in its area, regardless of the location of the ultimate distribution depot.

5   Depot costs comprise all of its own operating costs plus an allocated share of all company costs including centralised administration services and distribution centre costs.

6   Bonuses for the management team and all employees at each depot are payable quarterly. The bonus is based on the achievement of a series of target values by each depot.

7   Internal benchmarking is used at TSC in order to provide sets of absolute standards that all depots are expected to attain.

8   The Appendix shows the target values and the actual values achieved for each of a sample group of four depots situated in Donatellotown (D), Leonardotown (L), Michaelangelotown (M), and Raphaeltown (R). The target values focus on three areas:

(i)   depot revenue and profitability

(ii) customer care and service delivery; and

(iii) credit control and administrative efficiency.

The bonus is based on a points system, which is also used as a guide to the operational effectiveness at each depot. One point is allocated where the target value for each item in the Appendix is either achieved or exceeded, and a zero score where the target is not achieved.

Appendix: Target and actual value statistics for D, L, M and R for the Quarter ended 31 October 20X1.

Revenue and Profit Statistics:

	Revenue (1)		Profit (2)	
	Target	**Actual**	**Target**	**Actual**
	$m	$m	$m	$m
Company overall	200	240	30	32
Selected depots:				
D	16	15	2.4	2.3
L	14	18	2.1	2.4
M	12	14	1.8	2.2
R	18	22	2.7	2.8

Note: For the purpose of calculation of each depot's points it is essential that actual profit as a percentage of actual revenue must exceed the target profit (%).

Customer Care and Service Delivery Statistics:

Selected Depots:	Target	Actual			
		D	L	M	R
	%	%	%	%	%
Measure (% of total):					
(3) Late collection of consignments	2.0	1.9	2.1	1.8	2.4
(4) Misdirected consignments	4.0	4.2	3.9	3.3	5.1
(5) Delayed response to complaints	1.0	0.7	0.9	0.8	1.2
(6) Delays due to vehicle breakdown	1.0	1.1	1.4	0.3	2.0
(7) Lost items	1.0	0.6	0.9	0.8	1.9
(8) Damaged items	2.0	1.5	2.4	1.5	1.8
Credit Control & Administration Efficiency Statistics:					
(9) Average debtor weeks	5.5	5.8	4.9	5.1	6.2
(10) Debtors in excess of 60 days (% of total)	5%	?	?	?	?
(11) Invoice queries (% of total)	5%	1.1%	1.4%	0.8%	2.7%
(12) Credit notes as a % of revenue	0.5%	?	?	?	?

Other information:

	D	L	M	R
Aged Debtor analysis (extract):	$000	$000	$000	$000
Less than 30 days	1,300	1,500	1,180	2,000
31 – 60 days	321	133	153	552
Value of credit notes raised during the period ($000)	45	36	28	132

Note: TSC operates all year round.

Required:

Prepare a report for the directors of TSC which:

(a) contains a summary table which shows the points gained (or forfeited) by each depot. The points table should facilitate the ranking of each depot against the others for each of the 12 measures provided in the Appendix **(9 marks)**

(b) evaluates the relative performance of the four depots as indicated by the analysis in the summary table prepared in (a) **(5 marks)**

(c) assesses TSC in terms of financial performance, competitiveness, service quality, resource utilisation, flexibility and innovation and discusses the interrelationships between these terms, incorporating examples from within TSC; and **(10 marks)**

(d) critiques the performance measurement system at TSC. **(5 marks)**

Professional marks will be awarded for the demonstration of skill in communication, analysis and evaluation, scepticism and commercial acumen in your answer. **(7 marks)**

(Total: 36 marks)

Tutor tip:

Another great question to answer using the CBE Exam Practice Platform (see final chapter for details). Using the functionality of the CBE software in a variety of ways, e.g. to prioritise information within the questions exhibits, to organise and present answers in a manageable fashion or to use shortcuts (such as copy and paste and software functionality), you should be able to produce an answer in the **time given** and maximise both your **technical marks** and **professional skills marks**.

Evaluation of the building block model

The building block model has a number of **advantages**. The first four advantages discussed for the balanced scorecard are relevant for the building block model also. In addition:

- The dimensions differentiate between downstream results and upstream determinants.

- It is specifically tailored to and therefore useful for the service industry.

- It includes the building block 'standards' – the targets should motivate staff due to ownership, achievability and fairness.

- It includes the building block 'rewards' – the reward system should motivate staff due to it being clear and linked to controllable factors.

- Focusing on the three building blocks should help the organisation achieve its strategic objectives and mission.

However, it is not without its **drawbacks**. The first seven disadvantages discussed for the balanced scorecard are also relevant for the building block model. In addition:

- It is less suitable for non-service companies.

- It can be difficult to see how the building blocks link to the strategic objectives and mission. There is no explicit link in the building block diagram where as there is in the balanced scorecard diagram (this is one of the advantages of the balanced scorecard).

Student accountant article: visit the ACCA website, www.accaglobal.com, to review the article on 'Reward schemes'.

7.4 Performance pyramid

- The performance pyramid includes a hierarchy of financial performance measures and non-financial performance measures (these drive long-term performance). It aims to link the drivers of performance with the traditional financial results through the different layers of an organisation.

- It is based on the belief that each level of the organisation has different concerns but they must support each other in order to achieve the overall objective (vision) of the organisation. The elements of the pyramid are interrelated, and each level in the pyramid supports the one above it. For example, on-time delivery will result in increased customer satisfaction, which will eventually lead to greater market share and this will help to fulfil the corporate vision.

- Objectives cascade down the pyramid, i.e. the organisation begins by establishing its corporate vision. This is then translated into strategic, tactical and operational objectives. For example, a vision to increase shareholder wealth may be supported by a strategic financial objective to achieve a target EVA.

- The vision flows down through each layer generating appropriate measures which, in turn, support it. Measures flow up the pyramid so, for example, the measurement of on-time delivery can help the organisation in achieving customer satisfaction.

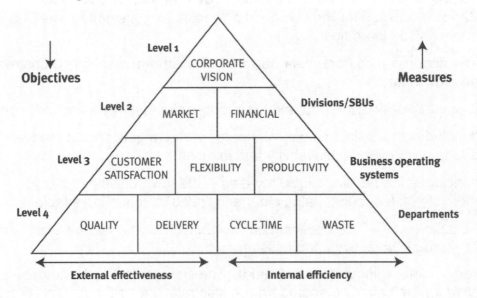

Level 1: At the top of the organisation is the corporate vision through which the organisation describes how it will achieve long-term success and competitive advantage.

Level 2: This focuses on the achievement of an organisation's CSFs and strategic objectives in terms of market-related measures and financial measures. The marketing and financial success of a proposal is the initial focus for the achievement of corporate vision.

Level 3: The marketing and financial strategies set at level 2 must be linked to the organisation's tactical objectives, i.e. the achievement of customer satisfaction, increased flexibility and high productivity at the next level. These are the guiding forces that drive the strategic objectives of the organisation.

Level 4: The status of the level 3 driving forces can be monitored using the lower level departmental indicators of operational performance, i.e. quality, delivery, cycle time and waste.

The left-hand side of the pyramid contains measures which have an external focus and which are predominantly non-financial. Those on the right are focused on the internal efficiency of the organisation and are predominantly financial.

Some of the terms in the pyramid are well understood but others are more specific to the model. For example:

- Flexibility indicates the business systems' ability to change in response to internal and external factors such as customers' needs.

- Cycle time relates to all the processes in the organisation from the credit cycle to product development to order processing.

- Waste is a general term relating to the optimal utilisation of the business's resources and elimination of non-value adding activities.

 Test your understanding 6

Required:

Suggest two measures (KPIs) for each of the three categories at the business operating systems level, i.e. customer satisfaction, flexibility and productivity.

Student accountant article: visit the ACCA website, www.accaglobal.com, to review the article on 'The pyramids and pitfalls of performance measurement'.

Evaluation of the performance pyramid

The performance pyramid has a number of **advantages**. The first four advantages discussed for the balanced scorecard are relevant here. In addition:

- **It is hierarchical** (the balanced scorecard and Building Block model are not), requiring senior managers to set objectives for each level of the organisation. The performance measures will then be specific to each level.

- **It is process focused**. It considers how processes combine to achieve the organisation's goals. Measures interact both horizontally (for example, cutting production cycle time should shorten delivery time) and vertically (for example, cutting production cycle time should increase productivity).

- **It recognises that financial and non-financial measures can support each other**. For example, improved flexibility should improve market position by meeting customer's needs, while also improving financial performance by increasing revenue and reducing fixed costs.

However, it is not without its **drawbacks**. The first six disadvantages discussed for the balanced scorecard are relevant here. In addition:

- The model is quite **complicated** making the **time and resources** required significant (perhaps more so than the other two models).

Chapter summary

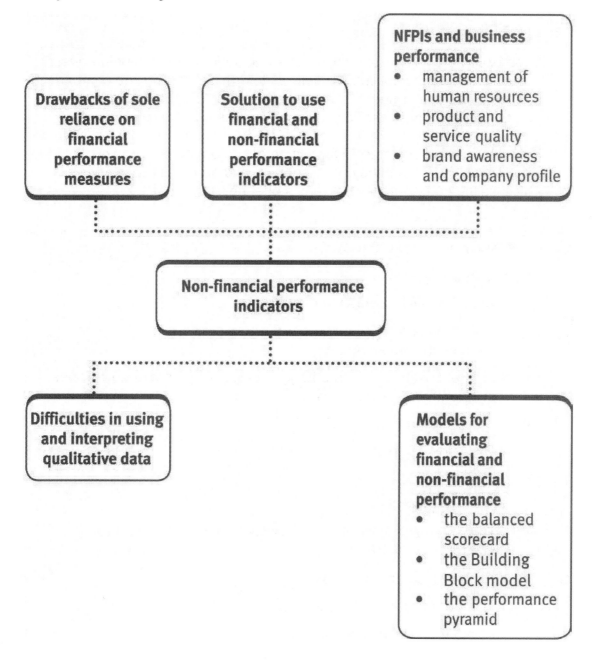

Drawbacks of sole reliance on financial performance measures

Solution to use financial and non-financial performance indicators

NFPIs and business performance
- management of human resources
- product and service quality
- brand awareness and company profile

Non-financial performance indicators

Difficulties in using and interpreting qualitative data

Models for evaluating financial and non-financial performance
- the balanced scorecard
- the Building Block model
- the performance pyramid

Test your understanding answers

Test your understanding 1

The experience of existing customers and their perception of the quality of the products or services will help to determine whether the company profile is positive or negative and whether or not the brand is perceived as favourable. This is particularly important for a high profile company, about which everyone will have an opinion whether or not they have any experience as a customer. This will be based on the opinions of customers with whom they have contact, and on press reports which discuss the quality of the company's offering.

Test your understanding 2

Financial perspective

- ROCE and RI – overall and by division.

- Operating and gross profit margins – overall and by product/customer/country.

- Different costs as a percentage of sales – e.g. labour costs/sales, sub-contractor costs/sales.

- Sales growth.

- Cash flow targets.

- Market share.

Customer perspective

- Percentage of scheduled targets met – especially whether contracts are finished on time.

- Percentage of repeat business.

- Number of complaints received.

- Number of new customers won.

- Percentage of apartments sold off-plan.

Internal business perspective

- Percentage of tenders won.

- Percentage of utilisation of fixed assets – vehicles, plant and machinery.

- Percentage of contracts with cost overruns.

- Cost overrun as percentage of budgeted cost.

- Employee productivity.

- For staffing, environmental and health and safety measures.

Innovation and learning perspective

- Number of patents established for new methods/technologies.

- Percentage of new materials used compared with total materials.

- Percentage of total revenue coming from new buildings using new structural innovations in their design.

Test your understanding 3

(a) The balanced scorecard allows managers to look at the business from four important perspectives:

Customer – how do our customers see us and how do we present ourselves to them?

Internal business process – what processes must we excel at in order to meet the needs of our customers and shareholders?

Innovation and learning – can we continue to improve and create value?

Financial – how do we look to our shareholders and how do we optimally serve their interests?

The new strategy focuses on four key areas which will address the balanced scorecard perspectives in different ways:

1   **Focus on key customers** – this will directly address the customer perspective but will also have implications for the other three perspectives.

In terms of appropriate performance measures, Jump should begin by segmenting the market, e.g. by age, gender, income or the family lifecycle. Jump should then analyse each segment in terms of profitability and changing market share and should then target the most profitable segment(s) of the market.

2   **Ensure Jump's offerings meet the needs of these customers** – this will directly address the customer perspective but may also result in a change in internal business processes and an increase in innovation and learning. This, in turn, should have a knock on impact on the financial perspective.

In terms of appropriate performance measures, from a customer perspective, Jump should monitor levels of customer satisfaction (e.g. via surveys) and repeat business. Internal business processes could be benchmarked against competitors or could be monitored internally, again through the review of customer satisfaction. Innovation and learning could be monitored by looking at the number of new products and staff training time, e.g. are target customers satisfied with a range of new aerobics classes offered and the competence of the staff leading these classes? The financial perspective could be monitored using, say, ROCE, EPS or profit margin.

3   **Cost cutting** – this focuses mainly on the internal business process perspective and seeks to focus the business on value added activities.

Appropriate performance measures may include efficiency savings generating by removing or reducing unnecessary processes or products.

4   **Build for the future using sustainable development** – the future focus ties into the innovation and learning perspective but may also have a knock on impact on the other three perspectives.

In terms of appropriate performance measures, Jump may monitor its energy efficiency.

(b)   **Assessment of financial performance**

The year on year performance has declined. EPS (W1) has fallen by 29% which would normally result in a fall in shareholder satisfaction. However, when reviewing the share price it would seem that Jump's shareholders would be encouraged by the company's future prospects. Although Jump's share price has fallen by 16% year on year, the market as a whole has fallen by 31% and more importantly the health sector has fallen by 23%.

Furthermore, even though Jump's EVA has fallen by 65% year on year it has remained positive so the company continues to create value for its shareholders.

(W1) **EPS**

	20X0	**20X1**
EPS = PAT ÷ average number of = shares in issue	€37.2m ÷ 140m = €0.266	€26.3m ÷ 140m = €0.188

Evaluation of performance metrics

	Advantages	Disadvantages
EPS	• Widely used measure. • Important to shareholders since relates to dividend growth.	• Based on accounting profit which is subject to manipulation. • Comparison is only between two years which can be misleading.
Share price	• Widely used by shareholders to monitor investments.	• Volatile. • Subject to fluctuations outside of manager's control. • Managers may be encouraged to make decisions which boost short term share price.
EVA	• Widely used and measured. • Adjustments are made to profit.	• Numerous adjustments to profit must be made.

Conclusion as to impact of metrics on management

Both EPS and share price may encourage managers to make decisions which improve short term financial performance but may impact on long term profitability. EVA aims to partially tackle this issue through the adjustment of accounting figures but the large number of adjustments can make this measure unwieldy.

(c) **To:** Board of Jump

From: A Accountant

Date: Today

Subject: Benchmarking performance

This report describes the benefits and problems associated with benchmarking the company's performance. Then, the performance of Jump and its two main competitors is calculated and evaluated.

Benchmarking is the use of a yardstick to compare performance. The yardstick, or benchmark, is based upon the best in class. Competitor benchmarking uses a direct competitor with the same or similar processes as the benchmark.

(i) **Advantages of benchmarking**

Improved performance

Benchmarking could be a key tool in enabling Jump to improve its performance and increase profitability in this highly competitive market. There should be improvements across all areas, e.g. quality, customer service.

Achievability

The improvements will be seen as achievable since the new methods have actually been used in another organisation. This should encourage managers and employees to buy-in to the change process.

Improved understanding of environmental pressures

The benchmarking process should enable Jump to get back in touch with the needs of its customers and to better understand its competitors. The industry is highly competitive and so this greater awareness will be essential for future success.

Eliminates complacency

Benchmarking can help Jump to overcome complacency and to drive organisational change.

Continuous improvement

Benchmarking can be carried out at regular intervals and can therefore drive continuous improvement in the business.

Disadvantages of benchmarking

Identifying best practice

It may prove difficult to identify the organisations that are best in class.

Cost

The actual benchmarking exercise will be costly for Jump. It is essential that the benefits of the exercise are greater than the associated costs.

Impact on motivation

If comparisons are unfavourable the information could have a negative impact on employee motivation and this would result in further inefficiencies.

Deciding which activities are to be benchmarked

This is a difficult process. Jump may not realise that there are better ways of doing things until they have seen their competitors carrying out certain processes.

Managers become too target driven

Benchmarking can result in managers becoming obsessed with hitting targets. This could sometimes be counterproductive.

Collection of data

The actual collection of data can be time consuming and costly.

Data may not be readily accessible for all areas of performance measurement and competitors may be unwilling to share details.

(ii) Comparing Jump to its competitors, it is clear that Jump has done well to increase its total revenue (8% increase) but this comes at the cost of a significant fall in profit compared with Fitness matters (Fitness Matter's fall in profit was 10% compared with a 29% fall for Jump). Jump should look into its pricing policy since it may have been buying sales by offering heavy discounts and these may not be sustainable in the long-term.

Active Matters drop in profit is greatest of all but this may be explained by problems in the range and quality of its services. Active matters opened nine new health clubs in the period but there has been an overall fall in revenue of 2%. Jump could analyse Active Matter's offerings to its customers in order to avoid making the same mistakes.

In terms of market share, Jump has maintained its position against slight falls in its competitors.

In revenue per health club, Jump has outperformed its competitors. However, this may be due to Jump having a larger average health club. The average club area for the three companies should be investigated.

Conclusion

In conclusion, Jump seems to be performing well with increased revenues and the maintenance of market share during the decline. The company must guard against the danger of eroding margins too far.

Professional skills marks

Communication:

- Report format and structure (requirement (c)) – use of headings, sub-headings and introduction

- Style, language and clarity – appropriate tone of response, easy to follow and understand, more than a negligible amount of content.

Analysis and Evaluation:

- Appropriate use of data to perform suitable calculations to support discussion on performance

- Balanced and reasoned description of the balanced scorecard perspectives and suggested performance measures

- Comprehensive evaluation of the benchmarking exercise using the information given.

Scepticism:

- Recognition of the limitations of the existing metrics of EPS and share price and of the challenges of benchmarking.

Commercial acumen:

- Effective use of examples drawn from across the scenario information and other practical considerations related to the context to illustrate the points being made

- Recommended performance measures are practical and plausible in the context of the company situation.

Test your understanding 4

Possible measures include:

Financial performance

- Fee levels

- Material sales

- Costs, e.g. course lecturer costs

- Net profit

Competitiveness

- Market share

- Sales growth

- Success rate on proposals

Quality of service

- Repeat business levels

- Number of customer complaints

- Helpline use may be related to tuition quality

Flexibility

- Availability and use of freelance staff

- Breadth of skills and experience of lecturers

Resource utilisation

- Use of freelance lecturers

- Levels of non-chargeable staff time

Innovation

- Number of new in-company courses

- Time to develop new courses

- New course formats

Note: only one measure was required for each dimension.

Test your understanding 5

Report:

To: The Directors of TSC

From: Management Accountant

Subject: The performance of our depots

Date: 5 December 20X1

(a)   **Summary analysis of points gained (1) or forfeited (0) for quarter ended 31 October 20X1**

Revenue and Profit Statistics:	D	L	M	R
Revenue	0	1	1	1
Profit (see note below)	1	0	1	0
Customer Care and Service Delivery Statistics:				
Late collection of consignments	1	0	1	0
Misdirected consignments	0	1	1	0
Delayed response to complaints	1	1	1	0
Delays due to vehicle breakdown	0	0	1	0
Lost items	1	1	1	0
Damaged items	1	0	1	1
Credit Control & Administration Efficiency Statistics:				
Average debtor weeks	0	1	1	0
Debtors in excess of 60 days	1	1	1	1
Invoice queries (% of total)	1	1	1	1
Credit notes as a % of revenue	1	1	1	0
Total points gained	**8**	**8**	**12**	**4**

Workings:

(i) **Profit point calculation:**

Actual results, e.g. Donatellotown = 2.3/15 = 15.3% (1 point) and Leonardotown = 2.4/18 = 13.3% (0 point)

(ii) **Debtors in excess of 60 days (% of total)**

	D	L	M	R
Revenue ($000)	15,000	18,000	14,000	22,000
Debtor weeks	5.8	4.9	5.1	6.2
Therefore debtors	1,673	1,696	1,373	2,623
Less than 30 days	(1,300)	(1,500)	(1,180)	(2,000)
31–60 days	(321)	(133)	(153)	(552)
More than 60 days	52	63	40	71
Debtors in excess of 60 days (% of total)	3.1	3.7	2.9	2.7

(iii) **Value of credit notes raised as a % of revenue**

e.g. Donatellotown = $45,000/$15,000,000 = 0.3%

(b) The summary analysis in (a)(i) shows that using overall points gained, Michaelangelotown has achieved the best performance with 12 points. Donatellotown and Leonardotown have achieved a reasonable level of performance with eight points each. Raphaeltown has underperformed, however, gaining only four out of the available 12 points.

Michaelangelotown is the only depot to have achieved both an increase in revenue over budget and an increased profit revenue percentage.

In the customer care and service delivery statistics, Michaelangelotown has achieved all six of the target standards, Donatellotown four; Leonardotown three. The Raphaeltown statistic of achieving only one out of six targets indicates the need for investigation.

With regard to the credit control and administrative efficiency statistics, Leonardotown and Michaelangelotown achieved all four standards and Donatellotown achieved three of the four standards. Once again, Raphaeltown is the 'poor performer' achieving only two of the four standards.

(c)   The terms listed may be seen as representative of the dimensions of performance. The dimensions may be analysed into results and determinants. The results may be measured by focusing on financial performance and competitiveness. **Financial performance** may be measured in terms of revenue and profit as shown in the data in the appendix of the question in respect of TSC. The points system in part (a) of the answer shows which depots have achieved or exceeded the target set. In addition, liquidity is another aspect of the measurement of financial performance. The points total in part (a) showed that Leonardotown and Michaelangelotown depots appear to have the best current record in aspects of credit control.

Competitiveness may be measured in terms of sales growth but also in terms of market share, number of new customers, etc. In the TSC statistics available we only have data for the current quarter. This shows that three of the four depots listed have achieved increased revenue compared to target.

The **determinants** are the factors which may be seen to contribute to the achievement of the results. Quality, resource utilisation, flexibility and innovation are cited by Fitzgerald and Moon as examples of factors that should contribute to the achievement of the results in terms of financial performance and competitiveness. In TSC a main **quality** issue appears to be customer care and service delivery. The statistics in the points table in part (a) of the answer show that the Raphaeltown depot appears to have a major problem in this area. It has only achieved one point out of the six available in this particular segment of the statistics.

Resource utilisation for TSC may be measured by the level of effective use of drivers and vehicles. To some extent, this is highlighted by the statistics relating to customer care and service delivery. For example, late collection of consignments from customers may be caused by a shortage of vehicles and/or drivers. Such shortages could be due to staff turnover, sickness, etc. or problems with vehicle maintenance.

Flexibility may be an issue. There may, for example, be a problem with vehicle availability. Possibly an increased focus on sources for short-term sub-contracting of vehicles/collections/ deliveries might help overcome delay problems.

The 'target v actual points system' may be seen as an example of **innovation** by the company. This gives a detailed set of measures that should provide an incentive for improvement at all depots. The points system may illustrate the extent of achievement/non-achievement of company strategies for success. For example TSC may have a customer care commitment policy which identifies factors that should be achieved on a continuing basis. For example, timely collection of consignments, misdirected consignments redelivered at no extra charge, prompt responses to customer claims and compensation for customers.

(d) The performance measurement system used by TSC appears simplistic. However, it may be considered to be measuring the right things since the specific measures used cover a range of dimensions designed to focus the organisation on factors thought to be central to corporate success, and not confined to traditional financial measures.

Internal benchmarking is used at TSC in order to provide sets of absolute standards that all depots are expected to attain. This should help to ensure that there is a continual focus upon the adoption of 'best practice' at all depots. Benchmarks on delivery performance place an emphasis upon quality of service whereas benchmarks on profitability are focused solely upon profitability!

Incentive schemes are used throughout the business, linking the achievement of company targets with financial rewards. It might well be the case that the profit incentive would act as a powerful motivator to each depot management team. However, what is required for the prosperity of TSC is a focus of management on the determinants of success as opposed to the results of success.

(**Note**: Alternative relevant discussion would be acceptable)

Test your understanding 6

Customer satisfaction KPIs

- Repeat purchases
- Numbers of complaints
- Value of refunds
- Sales growth by market segment

Flexibility KPIs

- Product/service introduction time
- Product/service mix flexibility
- Internal setup times – the time taken to switch production from one product to another
- Delivery response time – the time taken to meet customer delivery requests

Productivity KPIs

- Revenue per employee
- Sales and administration costs as a percentage of sales revenue
- Units of output per unit of resource
- Capital asset utilisation

Note: only two measures were required for each category.

The role of quality in performance measurement

Chapter learning objectives

Upon completion of this chapter you will be able to:

- evaluate whether the management information systems are lean and the value of the information that they provide (e.g. using the 5 Ss)

- discuss and evaluate the application of Japanese business practices and management accounting techniques, including:

  - Kaizen costing

  - Target costing

  - Just-in-time, and

  - Total Quality Management

- assess the relationship of quality management to the performance management strategy of an organisation including the costs of quality

- discuss and apply Six Sigma as a quality improvement method using tools such as DMAIC for implementation.

PER

One of the PER performance objectives (PO13) is to plan business activities and control performance, making recommendations for improvement. Working through this chapter should help you understand how to demonstrate that objective.

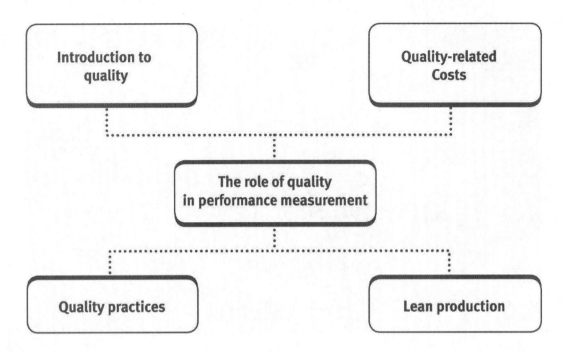

1 Introduction

Quality can be defined in a number of ways:

- Is the product/service free from errors and does it adhere to design specifications?

- Is the product/service fit for use?

- Does the product/service meet customers' needs?

Test your understanding 1
Required:
Explain the reasons why quality may be important to an organisation?

In today's competitive global business environment, quality is one of the key ways in which a business can differentiate its product or service, improve performance and gain competitive advantage. Quality can form a key part of a strategy.

A **quality management system** (**QMS**) is a set of co-ordinated planning and control activities. These activities should be aligned to the organisation's quality objectives and complement the organisation's strategy. An effective QMS should:

- minimise the overall costs of quality

- improve customer satisfaction due to higher levels of quality

- improve staff morale and productivity due to the involvement and pride taken in the work done.

Quality certification

The International Organisation for Standardisation (**ISO**) is one of the major bodies responsible for producing quality standards that can be applied to a variety of organisations.

The ISO quality standards have been adopted by many organisations. An ISO registered company must:

- submit its quality procedures for external inspection
- keep adequate records
- check outputs for differences
- facilitate continuous improvement.

A certified company will be subject to continuous audit.

There are a number of advantages and disadvantages for a company of becoming ISO certified:

Advantages

- Recognised standard – the company's reputation for quality will be enhanced since ISO is a recognised international standard of quality.

- Marketing – ISO certification will act as an excellent marketing tool. It will help to differentiate the company, on the grounds of quality, in the customers' eyes.

- Improved profitability – fulfilment of the ISO criteria should help the company to improve quality and should act as a framework for continuous improvement of the organisation's activities. This, in turn, should reduce costs and improve quality.

- International competitiveness – ISO certification is becoming increasingly useful in international markets and may help the company to compete on a world stage.

Disadvantages

- Cost – fees are upward of $1,500 depending on the size of the company.

- Time – documentation can be time consuming to produce.

- Bureaucracy – the scheme encourages bureaucracy with lots of form filling and filing rather than positive actions.

- Rigid policies – these might discourage initiative and innovation and may therefore hinder the quality process.

- Not all embracing – ISO certification will form a small part of a quality practice such as TQM.

There are a range of ISO standards. One example relates to our discussion of ESG factors, sustainability and EMA (Chapter 4). The ISO 14000 is a series of standards dealing with environmental management. To gain accreditation and provide assurance to stakeholders, an organisation must meet a number of requirements regarding environmental management.

2 Quality-related costs

- As discussed, quality management can form a significant part of the performance management strategy of the organisation. **Monitoring** the costs of quality will be central to the operation of any quality management improvement programme.

- The aim should be to minimise the overall costs of quality.

- Appropriate **measures** and **targets** should be developed based on the costs of quality and these can be used as a basis for staff **rewards**.

There are a number of **types of quality-related costs**:

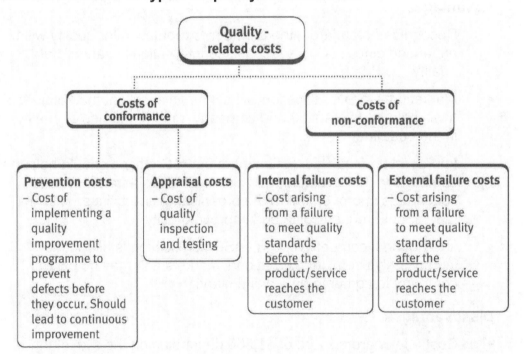

- The **more rigorous conformance is, the lower the costs of non-conformance** will be.

- The organisation's **information systems** should be capable of identifying and collecting these costs. This will lead to a greater management focus on quality since 'what gets measured, gets done'.

Test your understanding 2

Required:

Provide an example for each of the four sub-categories of quality cost.

Test your understanding 3

The following information has been supplied for Company X.

	$000
Revenue	320,000
Costs:	
Design engineering	5,000
Warranty	8,950
Estimated lost contribution from public knowledge of poor quality	9,561
Training	560
Process engineering	3,450
Rework	7,545
Customer support per repaired unit	645
Product testing	65
Transportation costs per repaired unit	546
Inspection	13,800

Required:

Prepare a cost analysis that shows the prevention, appraisal, internal failure and external failure costs for Company X. Any opportunity costs should be included as a separate cost category. Your statement should show each cost heading as a % of turnover and clearly show the total cost of quality.

Note: There is some subjective judgement in classifying costs under the different sub-categories. In the exam, you will be given credit for any reasonable classification and/or justification.

3 Quality practices

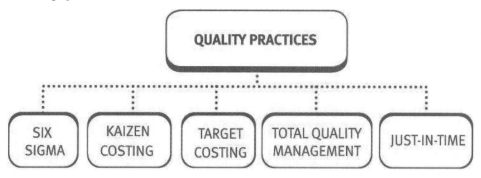

The practices may be used individually but are often used in conjunction with one another.

Note: All of these practices, with the exception of Six Sigma, are Japanese practices (Six Sigma has its origins in America).

3.1 Six Sigma

- Six Sigma is a quality management programme that was pioneered by Motorola in the 1980s.

- The aim of the approach is to achieve a reduction in the number of faults that go beyond an accepted tolerance level. It tends to be used for individual processes.

- The sigma stands for the standard deviation. For reasons that need not be explained here, it can be demonstrated that, if the error rate lies beyond the sixth sigma of probability there will be **fewer than 3.4 defects in every one million units** produced.

- This is the tolerance level set. It is almost perfection since customers will have room to complain fewer than four times in a million.

Illustration 1 – The Six Sigma approach

A hospital is using the Six Sigma process to improve patient waiting times. An investigation of the views of patients has revealed the following:

- Patients do not want to be called before their appointment time as they do not want to feel that they have to be at the hospital early to avoid missing an appointment

- The maximum length of time they are prepared to wait after the appointment time is 30 minutes.

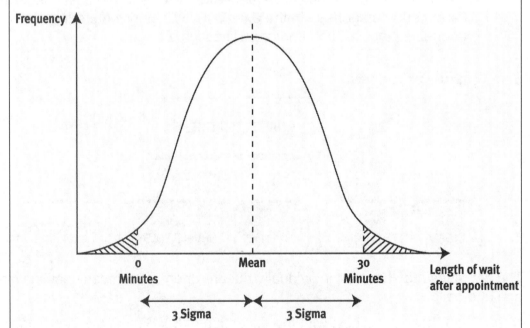

The aim of the Six Sigma programme will be to ensure that no more than 3.4 waits in every million occurrences exceed 30 minutes or are less than 0 minutes.

The five steps of the Six Sigma process (DMAIC)

Step 1: Define customer requirements/problem
- customer requirements can be divided into those that are the minimum that is acceptable, those that improve the customer's experience and those that go beyond the customer's expectations
- quality problem defined in specific, quantifiable terms
- a mission statement is prepared explaining what will be done about the problem. This should also be in specific, quantifiable terms
- a project team is set up from across the organisation and is given the resources to address the problem.

Step 2: Measure existing performance
- the project team does some preliminary work to measure how the current process is working and identifies what is causing the quality problem
- measures should focus on areas where customers will value improvement
- the performance measurement system must be reliable (redesign may be required).

Step 3: Analysis of the existing process
- the project team investigates their preliminary concerns and test different theories to get to the root cause of the problem
- techniques such as Pareto analysis will improve the focus of action on the issues that give rise to the majority of quality problems (i.e. 20% of the causes will give rise to 80% of the problems).

Step 4: Improve the process
- Potential solutions are developed for process re-design. The most appropriate solution will be one that achieves the mission statement within the cost and resource constraints of the organisation.

Step 5: Control the process
New controls are designed to compare actual performance with targeted performance to make sure the improvements to the process are being sustained

How does Six Sigma improve the quality of performance?

Six Sigma improves quality in a number of ways:

- It sets tight targets but accepts some failure (100% perfection may be viewed as impossible to achieve).

- The identification of business process improvements as key to success.

- Management decision making is driven by data and facts, for example the number of customer complaints as a key performance measure.

- The proactive involvement of management and effective leadership to co-ordinate the different Six Sigma projects.

- It involves collaboration across functional and divisional boundaries focusing the whole organisation on quality issues. Training and education about the process will be critical to its success.

- The increased profile of quality issues and the increased knowledge of quality management that comes from the use of different layers of trained experts.

Test your understanding 4

Required:

Explain some of the possible limitations of the Six Sigma process.

3.2 Kaizen Costing

What is Kaizen?

Kaizen is a Japanese term for the philosophy of continuous improvement in performance via small, incremental steps.

Continuous improvement is the continual examination and improvement of existing processes and is very different from approaches such as business process re-engineering (BPR), which seeks to make radical one-off changes to improve an organisation's operations and processes.

Characteristics:

*   Kaizen involves setting standards and then continually improving these standards to achieve long-term sustainable improvements.

*   The focus is on eliminating waste, improving processes and systems and improving productivity.

*   Involves all areas of the business.

*   Employees often work in teams and are empowered to make changes. Rather than viewing employees as the source of high costs, Kaizen views the employees as a source of ideas on how to reduce costs. A change of culture will be required, encouraging employees to suggest ideas (perhaps using quality circles) to reduce costs.

*   Allows the organisation to respond quickly to changes in the competitive environment.

Illustration 2 – Kaizen

Many Japanese companies have introduced a Kaizen approach. In companies such as Toyota, a total of 60–70 suggestions per employee are written down and shared every year. It is not unusual for over 90% of those suggestions to be implemented.

Illustration 3 – British cycling

British cycling's revolution through small, incremental improvements

When Sir David Brailsford became performance director of British cycling, he believed that if it were possible to make a 1% improvement in a whole host of areas, the cumulative gains would end up being hugely significant. His aim was to identify all of the weaknesses in the team's assumptions, viewing these as opportunities to adapt and make marginal gains. For example:

- By experimenting in a wind tunnel, he noted that the bike was not sufficiently aerodynamic. Then by analysing the mechanics area in the team truck, he discovered that dust was accumulating on the floor, undermining bike maintenance. So he had the floor painted pristine white, in order to spot any impurities.

- The team started using antibacterial hand gel to cut down on any infections.

- The team bus was redesigned to improve comfort and recuperation.

Many critiqued the approach and saw David Brailsford as laughing stock. However, the last three Olympics have seen the team win an unprecedented host of gold medals and, never having previously secured a win in over 100 years, British riders have won the Tour de France a number of times since 2012.

What is Kaizen costing?

 Kaizen costing focuses on producing small, incremental cost reductions throughout the production process through the product's life.

The **steps** in Kaizen costing are as follows:

> During the design phase, a target cost is set for each production function.

> The target costs are totalled to give a total target cost for the product. This becomes the baseline for the first year of production.

> As the production process improves, cost reductions reduce the baseline cost.

> Cost reduction targets are set on a regular (e.g. monthly) basis and variance analysis is carried out at the end of each period to compare the target cost reduction with the actual cost.

One of the main ways to reduce costs is through the **elimination of waste**.

Impact of Kaizen on traditional management accounting techniques

There is a marked distinction between a traditional standard costing system and a modern Kaizen costing approach. A traditional standard costing system would not be suitable in a Kaizen environment.

- In a standard costing system, employees are often seen as the source of problems where as in a Kaizen system, employees often work in teams and are empowered and trusted to make positive changes.

- Workers who are used to a command and control structure will have to change their behaviour and speak out about possible improvements.

- Standard costing is used to control costs whereas Kaizen costing has the advantage of focusing on cost reductions.

- Standard costs will have much less value as they are fixed over a relevant period where as Kaizen costing can respond more easily in a dynamic environment.

3.3 Target costing

 Target costing involves setting a target cost by subtracting a desired profit from a competitive market price.

It is an alternative to conventional **cost-plus pricing** which arrives at a selling price by adding the standard cost to the desired profit. Although cost-plus pricing is straightforward, it ignores the price that customers are willing to pay, how much competitors charge for similar products and (the use of a standard cost) does not incentivise cost control.

The **steps** in target costing are as follows:

1   A competitive market price is set based on what customers are willing to pay and how much competitors are charging for similar products.

2   The desired profit margin is deducted from this price to arrive at a target cost.

3   The difference between the estimated cost for the product and the target cost is the cost gap.

4   Techniques are used to close the gap.

Illustration 4 – Closing the cost gap

Examples of techniques to close an identified cost gap:

- Can any materials be eliminated or can a cheaper material be substituted without affecting quality?

- Can productivity be improved, for example by providing additional training?

- Can a cheaper source of labour be used, for example lower skilled labour, without compromising quality?

- Can the layout of the factory be redesigned, for example by reorganising production into teams and ensuring all production is done at a single site?

- Can a move to a just-in-time production system be considered?

- Can the incidence of cost drivers be reduced?

- Can production volumes be increased to improve economies of scale?

Many of the technique for closing the cost gap will be employed at the **design** stage.

Attention should be focused on reducing the cost of features perceived by the customer not to add value; this is called **value analysis**.

Note: Target costing can also be applied to the **service sector**.

Key features of target costing

- **Target costing forces a focus on the customer:** Product decisions and cost analysis have to take account of customer requirements such as quality, features and price. This is not always the case with other cost management methods.

- **Successful target costing considers all costs** related to production and distribution of the products and involves the whole supply chain. This may even include joint working between suppliers and manufacturers to share information and enable cost reductions, particularly for products for which raw materials contribute a high proportion of the manufactured cost.

- **Target costing considers the entire life-cycle** of the product, so that total costs to the manufacturer are minimised.

- **Target costing begins very early in the development** phase of new products, so that changes are made before production begins. Decisions made at this stage generally determine a high proportion of the costs of any product.

- **Target costing is a multi-disciplinary approach** which involves staff from all functions in the analysis and decision making.

- **Target costing is an iterative process** in which teams are making judgements and trade-offs between product features, price, sales volumes, costs and investment requirements.

- **Target costing provides cost targets** for individual inputs and processes which can be used for performance monitoring.

Test your understanding 5

Edward Electronics assembles and sells many types of radio. It is considering extending its product range to include digital radios. These radios produce a better sound quality than traditional radios and have a large number of potential additional features not possible with the previous technologies (station scanning, more choice, one touch tuning, station identification text and song identification text etc.).

A radio is produced by assembly workers assembling a variety of components. Production overheads are currently absorbed into product costs on an assembly labour hour basis.

Edward Electronics is considering a target costing approach for its new digital radio product.

Required:

(a) Briefly describe the target costing process that Edward Electronics should undertake.   **(3 marks)**

(b) Explain the benefits to Edward Electronics of adopting a target costing approach at such an early stage in the product development process.   **(4 marks)**

A selling price of $44 has been set in order to compete with a similar radio on the market that has comparable features to Edward Electronics' intended product. The board have agreed that the acceptable margin (after allowing for all production costs) should be 20%.

Cost information for the new radio is as follows:

Component 1 (Circuit board) – these are bought in and cost $4.10 each. They are bought in batches of 4,000 and additional delivery costs are $2,400 per batch.

Component 2 (Wiring) – in an ideal situation 25 cm of wiring is needed for each completed radio. However, there is some waste involved in the process as wire is occasionally cut to the wrong length or is damaged in the assembly process. Edward Electronics estimates that 2% of the purchased wire is lost in the assembly process. Wire costs $0.50 per metre to buy.

Other material – other materials cost $8.10 per radio.

Assembly labour – these are skilled people who are difficult to recruit and retain. Edward Electronics has more staff of this type than needed but is prepared to carry this extra cost in return for the security it gives the business. It takes 30 minutes to assemble a radio and the assembly workers are paid $12.60 per hour. It is estimated that 10% of hours paid to the assembly workers is for idle time.

> **Production Overheads** – recent historic cost analysis has revealed the following production overhead data:
>
> | | Total production overhead ($) | Total assembly labour hours |
> |---|---|---|
> | Month 1 | 620,000 | 19,000 |
> | Month 2 | 700,000 | 23,000 |
>
> Fixed production overheads are absorbed on an assembly hour basis based on normal annual activity levels. In a typical year 240,000 assembly hours will be worked by Edward Electronics.
>
> **Required:**
>
> (c)   Calculate the expected cost per unit for the radio and identify any cost gap that might exist.   **(13 marks)**
>
> **(Total: 20 marks)**

The distinction between Kaizen costing and target costing

It is important to draw the distinction between Kaizen costing and target costing:

- Target costing occurs at the beginning of a product's life. It can achieve large cost reductions at the design stage of the product.

- Kaizen costing is the process of long-term continuous improvement by small, incremental cost reductions throughout the life of the product. It is used over longer periods than target costing since the full benefits of this approach will not be achieved in a short timescale.

- The target cost is the starting point for Kaizen costing, incorporating the idea of only producing what the customer values. With Kaizen costing, after production begins, each period's target is based on the previous period's reduced costs. Performance is monitored against these targets using variances.

3.4   Total Quality Management

What is total quality management?

Total Quality Management (TQM) is a philosophy of quality management that that is applied to the whole organization and aims for continuous improvement and prevention of all errors. It originated in Japan in the 1950s.

Fundamental **features** of TQM:

- **Prevention of errors before they occur:** The aim of TQM is to get thing's right first time. This contrasts with the traditional approach that less than 100% quality is acceptable. TQM will result in increased investment in prevention costs, e.g. quality design of systems and products. The other quality-related costs i.e. appraisal, internal and external failure costs should fall to a greater extent.

- **Continual improvement:** Quality management is not a one-off process, but is the continuous examination and improvement of processes.

- **Real participation by all:** The 'total' in TQM means that everyone in the value chain is involved in the process, including:

  - **Employees:** they are expected to seek out, identify and correct quality problems. Teamwork will be vital.

  - **Suppliers:** quality and reliability of suppliers will play a vital role.

  - **Customers:** the goal is to identify and meet the needs of customers.

- **Management commitment:** Managers must be committed and encourage everyone else to be quality conscious.

TQM will often be used in conjunction with other continuous improvement practices.

Illustration 5 – TQM success/failure

A TQM success story

Corning in one of the world's leading innovators in materials science. This is partly due to the implementation of a TQM approach, the leadership stamp of the, then, CEO James Houghton. Houghton announced a $1.6 billion investment in TQM. After several years of intensive training and a decade of applying the TQM approach, all of Corning's employees had bought into the quality concept. They knew the lingo – continuous improvement, empowerment, customer focus, management by prevention and they witnessed the impact of the firm's techniques as profits soared.

An example of TQM failure

The communication and services company British Telecom (BT) launched a total quality program in the late 1980s. This resulted in the company getting bogged down by quality processes and bureaucracy. The company failed to focus on its customers and later decided to dismantle its TQM programme. This was at great cost to the company and they have failed to make a full recovery.

Performance measures in a TQM environment

Measuring performance is a key part of a TQM programme. The cost of implementing TQM and measuring performance can often be offset by the costs saved through increased efficiency, improved product quality and higher levels of customer service.

Performance measures must be linked to the TQM programme's CSFs, be widely understood, be based on correct data and data should be easy to collect and be presented in an accessible and understandable way.

Rewards should be aligned to the achievement of the performance measures.

Each organisation will develop its own way of measuring TQM performance but key areas to investigate may be the 3 Es (these were discussed in Chapter 12 but in relation to public sector organisations):

- **Effectiveness**, i.e. the extent to which goals are achieved. Examples include comparing actual and expected figures for:

  - quality of product or service (may be gauged through customer feedback)

  - quantity of units sold

  - number of on-time deliveries

  - speed of response, and

  - unit cost.

- **Efficiency** will compare actual with planned use of resources such as labour, staff, equipment and materials.

- **Economy** will compare the actual costs of TQM with the planned cost, i.e. cost of prevention, detection, internal failure and external failure.

3.5 Just-in-time

What is just-in-time?

 Just-in-time (JIT) is a demand-pull system of ordering from suppliers which aims to reduce inventory levels to zero.

JIT applies to both production within an organisation and to purchasing from external suppliers:

 JIT purchasing is a method of purchasing that involves ordering materials only when customers place an order. When the goods are received they go straight into production.

 JIT production is a production system that is driven by demand for the finished products (a 'pull' system), whereby each component on a production line is produced only when needed for the next stage.

As with TQM, JIT is often used in conjunction with other continuous improvement methods.

 Illustration 6 – Toyota

Toyota pioneered the JIT manufacturing system, in which suppliers send parts daily or several times a day and are notified electronically when the production line is running out. More than 400 trucks a day come in and out of Toyota's Georgetown plant in the USA, with a separate logistics company organising shipment from Toyota's 300 suppliers – most located in neighbouring state within half a day's drive of the plant. Toyota aims to build long-term relationships with suppliers, many of whom it has a stake in, and says it now produces 80% of its parts within North America.

Illustration 7 – JIT and service operations

Although it originated with manufacturing systems, the JIT philosophy can also be applied to some service operations. Whereas JIT in manufacturing seeks to eliminate inventories, JIT in service operations will seek to eliminate, for example, internal or external queues of customers or wasteful motion.

Requirements for successful operation of a JIT system

- **High quality and reliability** – disruptions cause hold ups in the entire system and must be avoided. The emphasis is on getting the work right first time:

    – Highly skilled and well trained staff should be used.

    – Machinery must be high quality and fully maintained.

    – Long-term links should be established with a small number of suppliers, who act as collaborative partners, in order to ensure a reliable and high quality service and to minimise any stoppages in production.

  This will increase prevention costs but other quality-related costs should reduce (hopefully to a greater extent).

- **Elimination of non-value added activities** – for example, value is not added whilst storing the products and therefore inventory levels should be minimised.

- **Speed of throughput** – the speed of production should match the rate at which customers demand the product. Production runs should be shorter with smaller stocks of finished goods.

- **Flexibility** – a flexible production system and workforce is needed in order to be able to respond immediately to customers' orders.

- **Lower costs** – another objective of JIT is to reduce costs by:

    – Raising quality and eliminating waste.

    – Achieving faster throughput.

    – Minimising inventory levels.

JIT and supplier relationships

A company is a long way towards JIT if its suppliers will guarantee the quality of the material they deliver and will give it shorter lead-times, deliver smaller quantities more often, guarantee a low reject rate and perform quality-assurance inspection at source. Frequent deliveries of small quantities of material to the company can ensure that each delivery is just enough to meet its immediate production schedule. This will keep its inventory as low as possible. Materials handling time will be saved because as there is no need to move the stock into a store, the goods can be delivered directly to a workstation on the shop floor. Inspection time and costs can be eliminated and the labour required for reworking defective material or returning goods to the supplier can be saved.

The successful JIT manufacturer deliberately sets out to cultivate good relationships with a small number of suppliers and these suppliers will often be situated close to the manufacturing plant. It is usual for a large manufacturer that does not use the JIT approach to have multiple suppliers. When a new part is to be produced, various suppliers will bid for the contract and the business will be given to the two or three most attractive bids.

A JIT manufacturer is looking for a single supplier that can provide high quality and reliable deliveries, rather than the lowest price. This supplier will often be located in close proximity to the manufacturing plant.

There is much to be gained by both the company and its suppliers from this mutual dependence. The supplier is guaranteed a demand for the products as the sole supplier and is able to plan to meet the customer's production schedules. If an organisation has confidence that suppliers will deliver material of 100% quality, on time, so that there will be no rejects, returns and hence no consequent production delays, usage of materials can be matched with delivery of materials and stocks can be kept at near zero levels.

Jaguar, when it analysed the causes of customer complaints, compiled a list of 150 areas of faults. Some 60% of them turned out to be faulty components from suppliers. One month the company returned 22,000 components to different suppliers. Suppliers were brought on to the multidisciplinary task forces the company established to tackle each of the common faults. The task force had the simple objective of finding the fault, establishing and testing a cure, and implementing it as fast as possible. Jaguar directors chaired the task forces of the 12 most serious faults, but in one case the task force was chaired by the supplier's representative.

JIT evaluation

It is important that you can evaluate JIT. Consider the question below.

The role of quality in performance measurement

Test your understanding 6

Required:

Explain the advantages and disadvantages to an organisation of operating a JIT system.

The impact of JIT on management accounting

The introduction of a JIT system will have a number of effects on the costing system and performance management.

- Allowances for waste, scrap and rework are moved to the ideal standard, rather than an achievable standard.

- Costs are only allowed to accumulate when the product is finished.

- The inevitable reduction in inventory levels will reduce the time taken to count inventory and the clerical cost.

- Minimal inventory makes it easier for a firm to switch to backflush accounting (a simplified method of cost bookkeeping).

- Traditional performance measures such as inventory turnover and individual incentives are replaced by more appropriate performance measures, such as:

  - total head count productivity

  - inventory days

  - ideas generated and implemented

  - customer complaints

  - bottlenecks in production

  - the amount and effectiveness of staff training.

The **management accounting system** will need to be capable of producing performance and control information consistent with the JIT philosophy.

Additional question on quality

Required:

Explain how management accounting/management techniques such as total quality management, just in time, value analysis, activity based costing and the balanced scorecard could contribute towards the analysis of the relationship between costs and quality.

Answer:

Total Quality Management (TQM)

TQM is an approach that seeks to ensure that all aspects of providing goods and services are delivered at the highest possible standard, and that standards keep improving. The underlying principle is that the cost of preventing deficient quality is less than the costs of correcting poor quality.

Quality related costs are concerned with both achieving quality and failure to achieve quality. Quality costs can categorised as:

- **Prevention costs** – communicating the concept, training, establishing systems to deliver quality services

- **Appraisal costs** – e.g. inspection and testing

- **Internal failure costs** – wasted materials used in rejects, down time resulting from internal service quality failures, resources devoted to dealing with complaints

- **External failure costs** – loss of goodwill and future business, compensation paid to customers and rectification costs.

The TQM view is that by getting it right first time and every time, the prevention and appraisal costs will be outweighed by the savings in failure costs, hence lower costs and improved quality are congruent goals. TQM requires everyone in the organisation to have identified customers, whether external or internal, so that a continuous service quality chain is maintained all the way through the organisation to the final customer.

Just In Time (JIT)

JIT is a manufacturing and supply chain process that is intended to reduce inventory levels and improve customer service by ensuring that customers receive their orders at the right time and in the right quantity. The system should facilitate a smooth workflow throughout the business and reduce waste. Goods are produced to meet customer needs directly, not for inventory.

Cost reductions should arise from:

- Lower raw material and finished goods inventory levels, therefore reduced holding costs.

- Reduced material handling.

- Often a reduction in the number of suppliers and lower administration and communication costs.

- Guaranteed quality of supplies reduces inspection and rectification costs.

Quality improvements should arise from:

- Fewer or even single sourcing of supplies strengthens the buyer–supplier relationship and is likely to improve the quality.

- The absence of customer stockholding compels the supplier to guarantee the quality of the material that they deliver.

- The necessity to work regularly and closer with hauliers strengthens the relationship with them. The deliveries become high priority and more reliable.

- Customers are not faced with the traditional problems of having to wait until their supplier's inventories are replenished. The system is designed to respond to customers' needs rapidly.

- Direct focus on meeting an identified customer's need.

Value analysis

Value analysis is concerned with concentrating on activities that add value to the product/service as perceived by the customer. It examines business activities and questions why they are being undertaken and what contribution do they make to customer satisfaction. Value added activities include designing products, producing output and developing customer relationships. Non-value added activities include returning goods, inventory holding, and checking on the quality of supplies received. Wherever possible eliminate the non-value added activities.

Value analysis commences with a focus on customers. What do they regard as significant in the buying decision: function, appearance, longevity or disposal value? This is concerned with identifying what customers regard as quality and then providing it: do not expend effort on what they regard as unimportant.

It is about clarifying what the constituents of quality are on the Costs and Quality diagram. Having decided this there is a need to develop alternative designs, estimate costs and evaluate alternatives.

Activity Based Costing (ABC)

ABC is concerned with attributing/assigning costs to cost units on the basis of the service received from indirect activities e.g. public relations, recruitment, quality assurance general meetings. The organisation needs to identify cost drivers – the specific activities that cause costs to arise e.g. number of orders taken, telephone calls made, number of breakdowns or the number of visitors to an attraction.

ABC intends to avoid the arbitrary allocation of overheads to products/services by identifying a causal link between costs, activities and outputs. Because of higher degrees of automation, the increasing significance of overheads in the cost make up of output intensifies the need to improve the apportionment of them. Accountants can contribute towards providing better cost information to the value analysis referred to above. Product managers need to know what is the real cost of quality? What are the cost driving activities that do not impact on quality? What activities that generate minimal costs have a significantly favourable impact on quality?

The balanced scorecard

The balanced scorecard provides a framework for a business to achieve its strategic objectives include both financial and non-financial objectives. The approach claims that performance has four dimensions: financial, customer, internal business, and innovation and learning. The customer perspective asks: How does the business appear to the customers? The internal business perspective asks: What do we need to do to satisfy shareholders and customers, including the monitoring of unit costs? The innovation and learning perspective looks at how products and processes should be changed and improved.

The scorecard is concerned with monitoring and measuring the critical variables that comprise the customer and internal perspective. The choice of variables for inclusion in the scorecard is significant because the scorecard report is a design for action. Inappropriate indicators will trigger damaging responses. For example, the organisation needs to monitor what factors customers regard as contributing to improved quality, not what the business thinks it should provide. Therefore the scorecards would be suitable for inclusion as quantifiable indicators on the axis on the Costs and Quality diagram. The balanced scorecard attempts to improve the range and relationship between alternative performance measures, in the case under discussion, costs and quality.

4 Lean production

4.1 What is lean production?

The 'lean' concept was introduced in the discussion of lean MIS in Chapter 7, section 4.3.

Lean production is a philosophy of management based on **cutting out waste** and unnecessary activities including:

- **Over-production** – produce more than customers have ordered.

- **Inventory** – holding or purchasing unnecessary inventory.

- **Waiting** – production delays/idle time when value is not added to the product.

- **Defective units** – production of a part that is scrapped or requires rework.

- **Motion** – actions of people/equipment that do not add value.

- **Transportation** – poor planning or factory layout results in unnecessary transportation of materials/work-in-progress.

- **Over-processing** – unnecessary steps that do not add value.

Lean production is closely related to quality practices such as Kaizen, JIT and TQM.

	Illustration 8 – Comparison of non-lean versus lean production	
	Non-Lean manufacturer	**Lean pioneer – Toyota**
Production	Mass production requiring: • time to set up machinery and • skilled engineers	Production in smaller batches leading to: • quick set up • flexibility • production line staff trained to do set ups
Human resources	Cyclical nature of industry resulting in: • staff layoffs • unmotivated staff	• Job for life • Defined career path • Empowered staff
Employee roles	• Assembly worker • Foreman • Housekeeper • Engineer	Eliminates non-value adding activities so all workers trained on all aspects hence no indirect wages
Production problems	• Couldn't stop the production line • 20–25% defects	• Stops the production line and then the team works to solve issues quickly • Zero defects
Suppliers	Chosen on cost	• Use supplier expertise • Fair price • JIT
Sales	• Sell through dealers • Narrow product range	• Sell direct to customers • Customer feedback valued • Flexibility resulting in wide product range

Test your understanding 7

Although the lean approach was developed in the manufacturing industry it can also be applied in the service sector.

Required:

Identify some possible sources of waste in a restaurant business and categorise them according to the seven main types of waste described above.

4.2 The 5 Ss concept

As covered in Chapter 7, the 5 Ss concept is often associated with lean principles and has the aim of creating a workplace which is in order.

5 Ss	Explanation
Structure (sometimes called **sort**)	Introduce order where possible, for example by ensuring that items are arranged so that they are easy to find.
Systemise(sometimes called **simplify**)	Arrange and identify items for ease of use and approach tasks systematically. For example, by arranging items so that they can be accurately picked in the shortest time.
Sanitise (sometimes called **scan**)	Be tidy, avoid clutter. This makes things easier to find, makes access more efficient and may improve safety.
Standardise	This involves finding the best way of undertaking a process or task and applying it consistently.
Self-discipline (sometimes called **sustain**)	This relates to sustaining the other S's by motivating employees to do the above daily.

Student accountant article: visit the ACCA website, www.accaglobal.com, to review the article on 'Lean enterprises and lean information systems'.

Chapter summary

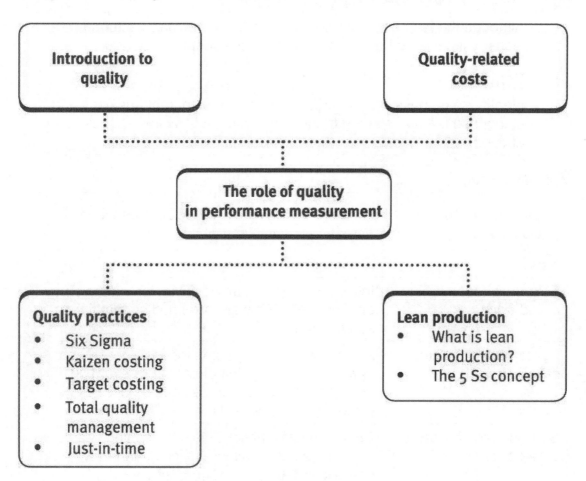

Test your understanding answers

Test your understanding 1

Higher quality can help to increase revenue and reduce costs:

- Higher quality improves the perceived image of a product or service. As a result, more customers will be willing to purchase the product/service and may also be willing to pay a higher price.

- A higher volume of sales may result in lower unit costs due to economies of scale.

- Higher quality in manufacturing should result in lower waste and defective rates, which will reduce production costs.

- The need for inspection and testing should be reduced, also reducing costs.

- The level of customer complaints should fall and warranty claims should be lower. This will reduce costs.

- Better quality in production should lead to shorter processing times. This will reduce costs.

Test your understanding 2

Prevention costs

- Cost of designing products and services with built in quality.

- Cost of training employees in the best way to do their job.

- Cost of equipment testing to ensure it conforms to quality standards required.

Appraisal costs

- Inspection and testing, for example of a purchased material or service.

Internal failure costs

- Cost of scrapped material due to poor quality.

- Cost of re-working parts.

- Re-inspection costs.

- Lower selling prices for sub-quality products.

External failure costs

- Cost of recalling and correcting products.

- Cost of lost goodwill.

Test your understanding 3

	$000	% of turnover
Prevention costs:		
Design engineering	5,000	1.56
Process engineering	3,450	1.08
Training	560	0.18
Total	**9,010**	**2.82**
Appraisal costs:		
Inspection	13,800	4.31
Product testing	65	0.02
Total	**13,865**	**4.33**
Internal failure costs	7,545	2.36
Total	**7,545**	**2.36**
External failure costs:		
Warranty	8,950	2.80
Customer support	645	0.20
Transportation	546	0.17
Total	**10,141**	**3.17**
Sub-total	**40,561**	**12.68**
Opportunity costs	9,561	2.99
Total quality costs	**50,112**	**15.66**

Test your understanding 4

(a) The target costing process should be undertaken as follows:

Step 1: Establish the selling price by considering how much customers will be willing to pay and how much competitors charge for similar products.

Step 2: Deduct the required profit from the selling price.

Step 3: Calculate the target cost, i.e. selling price minus profit.

Step 4: Find ways to reduce the cost gap, e.g. cheaper materials, cheaper labour, increased productivity or reduced waste.

(b) The benefits are as follows:

- Target costing has an external focus, i.e. it considers how much customers will pay/competitors will charge.

- Cost control can occur earlier in the design process and the required steps can be taken to reduce the cost gap.

- The performance of the business should be enhanced due to better management of costs.

- The focus will be on getting things right first time which should reduce the development time.

(c)   (W1) **Production overhead** (using high low method)

	Production overhead $	Labour hours
High	700,000	23,000
Low	620,000	19,000
Difference	80,000	4,000

- Variable overhead = $80,000 ÷ 4,000 = $20 per hour

- Total cost $700,000 = fixed cost + variable cost ($20/hour × 23,000). This gives a monthly fixed cost of $240,000. (Note: the total cost at the low level of production could also be used to find the fixed cost).

- Annual fixed cost = $240,000 × 12 = $2,880,000

- Overhead absorption rate (OAR) = $2,880,000 ÷ 240,000 hours = $12 per hour

Cost card and cost gap calculation

	$ per radio
Component 1	4.10
Component 1 delivery = $2,400 ÷ 4,000	0.60
Component 2 wiring = $0.50 × 0.25 metres × 100/98	0.128
Other material	8.10
Assembly labour = $12.60 × 0.5 hours × 100/90	7.00
Variable production overhead = $20/hour (W1) × 0.5 hours	10.00
Fixed production overhead = $12/hour (W1) × 0.5 hours	6.00
Total cost	**35.928**
Desired cost	35.20
Cost gap	**0.728**

Test your understanding 5

Advantages of JIT

- Lower stock holding costs means a reduction in storage space which saves rent and insurance costs.

- As stock is only obtained when needed, less working capital is tied up in stock.

- There is less likelihood of stock perishing, becoming obsolete or out of date.

- Avoids the build-up of unsold finished products that occur with sudden changes in demand.

- Less time is spent checking and re-working the products as the emphasis is on getting the work right first time.

- Increased flexibility in meeting the customer's individual needs.

The result is that costs should fall and quality should increase. This should improve the company's competitive advantage.

Disadvantages of JIT

- There is little room for mistakes as little stock is kept for re-working a faulty product.

- Production is very reliant on suppliers and if stock is not delivered on time or is not of a high enough quality, the whole production schedule can be delayed.

- There is no spare finished product available to meet unexpected orders, because all products are made to meet actual orders.

- It may be difficult for managers to empower employees to embrace the concept and culture.

- It won't be suitable for all companies. For example, supermarkets must have a supply of inventory.

- It can be difficult to apply to the service industry. However, in the service industry a JIT approach may focus on eliminating queues, which are wasteful of customers' time.

Test your understanding 6

Six Sigma contains has number of limitations:

- Six Sigma has been criticised for its focus on current processes and reliance on data. It is suggested that this could become too rigid and limit process innovation.

- Six Sigma is based on the use of models which are by their nature simplifications of real life. Judgement needs to be used in applying the models in the context of business objectives.

- The approach can be very time consuming and expensive. Organisations need to be prepared to put time and effort into its implementation.

- The culture of the organisation must be supportive – not all organisations are ready for such a scientific process.

- The process is heavily data-driven. This can be a strength, but can become over-bureaucratic.

- Six Sigma can give all parts of the organisation a common language for process improvement, but it is important to ensure that this does not become jargon but is expressed in terms specific to the organisation and its business.

- There is an underlying assumption in Six Sigma that the existing business processes meet customers' expectations. It does not ask whether it is the right process.

Test your understanding 7

Suggestions could include:

- Pre-preparing plated servings of perishable desserts which are not ordered and need to be thrown away – over-production.

- Poor kitchen layout which could lead to unnecessary movement of staff and result in waste from motion and from transportation of material or lead to accidents and spillages and waste in processes and methods.

- Poorly trained cooking staff who produce sub-standard meals which cannot be served – product defects.

- Producing too many pre-prepared components such as sauces to be incorporated in dishes which are then not needed – waste from inventory.

- Poor scheduling in the kitchen leading to serving staff waiting for meals to be ready – waste from waiting time.

Professional skills

Chapter learning objectives

This chapter contains an overview of the professional skills syllabus area. This is relevant for all ACCA Strategic Professional Options Exams (AFM, APM, AAA and ATX-UK).

1 Purpose of chapter

This chapter explains the content included within the professional skills syllabus area. This syllabus section is included in all Strategic Professional Options Exams syllabi.

The inclusion of this syllabus area reflects ACCA's continued focus on ensuring that the professional accountants of the future have the right blend of technical and professional skills, coupled with an ethical mindset. These professional skills will make candidates more employable, or if already in work, will enhance their opportunities for advancement.

More details can also be found in the professional skills section on the ACCA website.

2 Content of the professional skills syllabus area

The Strategic Professional Options Exams will expect candidates to demonstrate the following Professional Skills:

- Communication

- Analysis and Evaluation*

- Scepticism (and Judgement)**

- Commercial Acumen

*Analysis and Evaluation have been combined into one overall skill, as it has been deemed that for the Options exams, analysis is done in order to arrive at a thorough and comprehensive evaluation of a matter.

** Judgement is added to the Scepticism descriptor for Advanced Audit and Assurance (AAA) only, as it is a defined requirement for auditors.

Each of the four professional skills has a number of leadership capabilities associated with it. The Strategic Professional Options Exams will use these capabilities to allocate marks in each exam question as appropriate.

More detail on the capabilities associated with these professional skills are given in section 4 below.

3 Format of the exam, including professional skills

	Total marks	Technical marks	Professional skills marks
Section A: One compulsory question	50	40	10
Section B: Two compulsory questions	50 (25 per question)	40 (20 per question)	10 (5 per question)
Overall	**100**	**80**	**20**

- The syllabus is assessed by a 3 hour 15 minutes computer based examination (CBE).

- The pass mark for all ACCA Qualification examinations is 50%.

- The technical syllabus sections are A, B, C and D.

- Syllabus section E is professional skills:

  - In terms of earning professional skills marks, the examining team will be looking for that skill to be evident in the technical points you make.

  - The professional skills marks will be attached to the overall question, rather than individual requirements.

  - Candidates are expected to think professionally across the whole of their response as the professional skills are interconnected and tied to the technical requirements. For example, a thorough evaluation of a matter may require challenges of assumptions/data to be made and also evidence from the organisational context to be used to support a recommendation which has to be commercially sound.

- For both technical and professional skills marks there will be slightly more marks available than the set amount for students to score, for example in a Section B question there are five professional skills marks, however those five marks could be scored from a possible seven marks.

- Syllabus section F is employability and technology skills (discussed in Chapter 16).

Section A

Section A will always be a single 50-mark case study. The 50 marks will comprise of 40 technical marks and 10 professional skills marks.

Technical syllabus sections A, B and C are examinable is Section A.

All four of the professional skills will be examined in Section A. The professional skill "Communication" will only appear in the Section A question, because that is where a request for a specific format for the answer (i.e. a report format) will be made.

Section B

Section B will consist of two compulsory 25-mark questions. The 25 marks in each question will comprise of 20 technical marks and 5 professional skills marks.

In Section B, one question will include technical marks mainly from Syllabus section D. The other question will include technical marks from any other technical syllabus section(s).

Section B questions will contain a combination of professional skills appropriate to the question and the marks will not necessarily be an even split across the skills being tested. Each question will contain a minimum of two professional skills from Analysis and Evaluation, Scepticism and Commercial Acumen. Analysis and evaluation will be included in all APM questions.

Question presentation

The wording for the Professional Skills at the end the Section A question will be:

Professional marks will be awarded for the demonstration of skill in communication, analysis and evaluation, scepticism and commercial acumen in your answer. **(10 marks)**

For Section B questions, only the Professional Skills being tested in that question will appear, so for example:

Professional marks will be awarded for the demonstration of skill in analysis and evaluation and commercial acumen in your answer.

(5 marks)

4 Details of the professional skills for APM

In the ACCA's detailed APM study guide, the professional skills are fully explained. This explanation is included and built upon below.

Communication

Detailed study guide explanation of "Communication"	
Leadership capability	**Explanation**
Inform	Inform concisely, objectively and unambiguously, adopting a suitable style and format, using appropriate technology.
Persuade	Advise using compelling and logical arguments, demonstrating the ability to counter argue where appropriate.
Clarify and simplify	Clarify and simplify complex issues to convey relevant information in a way that adopts an appropriate tone and is easily understood by and reflects the requirements of the intended audience.

In summary, this means you have to express yourself clearly and convincingly through the appropriate medium while being sensitive to the needs of the intended audience. This means responding in a professional manner and adhering to any specific instructions made.

Illustration 1 – Communication skills marks in APM

In the APM exam, some examples of how communication skills marks could be awarded in Section A are as follows:

- Producing an answer in the **correct report format**. For example, Section A questions always ask for a report, requested by the organisation's senior management, to address key matters facing the organisation. In terms of **structure**, this report should have appropriate report headings (i.e. include four lines at the start indicating each of the following – who the report is to, who it is from, the date and the subject), sub-headings and an introduction which explains the content of the report to follow.

- **Style, language and clarity** – Your response should look professional, use appropriate language and be clear and effective. For example, appropriate tone of report response for the audience, appropriate presentation of calculations, appropriate use of CBE tools, answer is easy to follow and understand, more than a negligible amount of content.

- **Effectiveness of communication** – Content of the report is relevant and tailored to the question scenario.

- **Adherence to a specific request** – For example, to the CEO's request to not provide more than two additional KPIs.

Analysis and Evaluation

Detailed study guide explanation of "Analysis and Evaluation"

Leadership capability	Explanation
Investigate	Investigate relevant information from a range of sources, using appropriate analytical techniques to estimate reasons and causes of issues, assist in decision-making and to identify opportunities or solutions.
Consider	Consider information, evidence and findings carefully, reflecting on their implications and how they can be used in the interests of the individual, business function, division and the wider organisational goals.
Assess and apply	Assess and apply appropriate judgement when considering organisational plans, initiatives or issues when making decisions; taking into account the implications of such decisions on the organisation and those affected.
Appraise	Appraise information objectively with a view to balancing the costs, risks, benefits and opportunities, before advising on or recommending appropriate solutions or decisions.

In summary, this means you firstly have to thoroughly investigate and research information from a variety of sources and logically process it with a view to prioritising activities and arriving at an appropriate conclusion or recommendation ("Analysis").

This analysis should form part of a comprehensive evaluation of a matter where you have to carefully assess situations, proposals and arguments in a balanced and cogent way, using professional and ethical judgement to predict future outcomes and consequences as a basis for sound decision-making ("Evaluation").

All APM questions will include this professional skill, as it is fundamental to performance management. It is common for APM questions to focus on the evaluation of a report, method, model, system, or technique, of which part may be the analysis of some data or information. It is important in APM to remember that any analysis or evaluation is contextual and must take into account the situation in which the organisation in the question operates.

Illustration 2 – Analysis and evaluation skills marks in APM

In the APM exam, some examples of how analysis and evaluation skills marks could be awarded are as follows:

- **Appropriate use of data to:**
  - perform suitable calculations, i.e. analysis (for example, for the financial perspective of the balanced scorecard) to support your evaluation
  - support discussion and draw conclusions from the data/information analysed so that appropriate responses can be designed and advice given, including recognition of areas where data appears to have been omitted or where further analysis could be carried out to enable a full evaluation
  - perform suitable calculations to complete the work started (for example, by the junior accountant)
  - determine relevant calculations (for example, to analyse the outsourcing proposal)
  - provide relevant calculations, support discussion and draw a conclusion (for example, as to whether the report given presents a manipulated picture).

- **Balanced and reasoned appraisal** to determine the impact of a course of action and to, perhaps, make a recommendation, demonstrating reasoned judgement to consider all relevant factors applicable, decide what to prioritise and then come to a suitable and justified conclusion.

- **Balanced and reasoned assessment** to determine the impact of a course of action (for example, the changes that will be required as a result of introducing JIT).

- **Problems** (of, for example NFPIs) **are clearly supported with examples** from the scenario information given.

- **Comprehensive evaluation** (of how, for example, the BPR proposal could improve performance).

Scepticism

Detailed study guide explanation of "Scepticism"	
Leadership capability	**Explanation**
Explore	Explore the underlying reasons for key organisational plans, issues and decisions, applying the attitude of an enquiring mind, beyond what is immediately apparent.
Question	Question opinions, assertions and assumptions, by seeking justifications and obtaining sufficient evidence for either their support and acceptance or rejection.
Challenge and critically assess	Challenge and critically assess the information presented or decisions made, where this is clearly justified, in the wider professional, ethical, organisational, or public interest.

In summary, this means you have to explore, question and challenge information and views presented to you, recognising that all information is available or that there may be underlying bias, to fully understand business issues and to establish facts objectively, based on ethical and professional values.

In the APM exam, having a questioning approach is key for this skill.

Illustration 3 – Scepticism skills marks in APM

Some examples of how scepticism skills marks could be awarded are as follows:

- **Demonstration of effective challenge of information, of evidence and assumptions** of, for example both the CEO and the production manager. This includes the ability to provide contradictory evidence and remain sceptical about the information provided in the scenario. APM often bases questions on theoretical performance management models, which include assumptions and therefore may not perfectly fit an organisation's situation and you need to be prepared to raise such issues.

- **Demonstration of the ability to probe into why** a particular action was taken.

- **Recognition that the data provided does not allow adequate measurement**, for example of some of the CSFs/KPIs.

- **Identification that some information is missing or is difficult to obtain.**

- **Recognition that the use of, for example ROCE, is not appropriate or should not be used in isolation.**

- **Recognition of the limitations or challenges of a possible course of action**, rather than a sole focus on the potential benefits. APM often has stakeholders in question scenarios making statements about their beliefs and perceptions of a matter and you may be required to challenge those statements. Importantly, reasons for issues and problems are needed before challenges can be upheld and deemed appropriate.

All of this means that you need to apply professional judgment to draw conclusions and make properly informed decisions which are appropriate to the business.

Commercial Acumen

 Detailed study guide explanation of "Commercial Acumen"

Leadership capability	Explanation
Demonstrate awareness	Demonstrate awareness of organisational and external factors, which will affect the measurement and management of an organisation's strategic objectives and operational activities.
Recognise key issues and use judgement	Recognise key issues in determining how to address or resolve problems and use judgement in proposing and recommending commercially viable solutions.
Show insight	Show insight and perception in understanding behavioural responses, process and system-related issues and wider organisational matters, demonstrating acumen in arriving at appropriate recommendations.

In summary, this means you have to show awareness of the wider business environment and external factors affecting business and use commercially sound judgement and insight to resolve issues, exploit opportunities and offer valid advice and realistic recommendations.

Illustration 4 – Commercial acumen skills marks in APM

In the APM exam, some examples of how commercial acumen skills marks could be awarded are as follows:

- **Recommendations are practical and plausible** in the context of the organisation's situation. All APM questions are set in commercially realistic scenarios. These can range from private to public sector organisations to not-for-profit organisations and to regulated industries. This requires candidates to understand what does and does not work in an organisational context, therefore any advice or recommendations have to be practical and plausible in the given situation.

- **Effective use of examples drawn from the scenario** information **and other practical considerations** related to the context to illustrate points made. Organisations do not operate in a vacuum so, in addition to considering internal constraints, you need to look at external constraints and opportunities where relevant and also consider the validity or reasonableness of any assumptions that the organisation may be working under, given the external environment.

- **Recognition of the possible consequences of past and future actions** to ensure a considered and forward-looking approach and so that the right choices can be exercised.

- **Recommendations clearly demonstrate an understanding of the issues and are commercially sound.**

- **Comprehensive assessment of the possible ethical consequences** of, for example the BPR proposal.

5 General advice from the ACCA examining team

- Make sure you include the most important, relevant, and crucial points relating to the requirement. Use your judgment to consider which points are the most convincing and compelling and only include additional less important points if you are not sure you have made enough valid points to achieve all the technical marks available for the requirement.

- Show deep/clear understanding of underlying or causal issues and integrate or link information from various parts of the scenario or different exhibits.

- Only make relevant points and try not to include superfluous information or make unsupported points. Bland statements with no application do not demonstrate professionalism nor does including information which does not address the requirements.

- Avoid repeating points already made. Professionally competent candidates do not needlessly repeat information. They may reinforce a previous point, but this is usually made as a development of a point rather than repetition.

- Address the requirements as written, taking particular notice of the verb used. Answering the question asked is an indication of your ability to read and comprehend instructions appropriately as is a demonstration of professionalism expected in the workplace.

- Show your ability to prioritise and make points in a logical and progressive way, building your response to a question.

- Structure and present your answers in a professional manner through faithfully simulating the task as would be expected of a professional accountant.

- Demonstrate evidence of your knowledge from previous learning or wider reading and apply this knowledge appropriately to strengthen arguments and make points more convincing.

- Demonstrating professionalism is not about linguistic eloquence or having an extensive vocabulary or having perfect grammar, it is about the ability to express points clearly, factually, and concisely and show credibility in what you are saying.

6 Time management and planning

For time management purposes, candidates should allocate time based on the technical marks available, as the professional skills marks should not be thought of as separate requirements. Remember professional skills marks are earned as you work through the technical marks by providing comprehensive and relevant responses to the technical requirements.

In terms of time management, it is important to use the approach that will suit you best:

- If 15 minutes are spent reading the examination requirements (it may be sensible to allocate time to this), your time allocation should be 2.25 minutes per mark (180/80). This gives 90 minutes for section A and 45 minutes for each section B question.

- If you do not allow a specific amount of time for reading and planning (a more straightforward approach but the risk is that you run out of time) your time allocation will be 2.4 minutes per mark (195/80). This gives 97 minutes for section A and 49 minutes for each section B question.

- If you plan to spend more or less time on reading and planning, your time allocation per mark will be different.

In terms of the technical requirements, you should consider how many marks there are for the requirement and then decide how many different points need to be made to achieve these marks. For the Strategic Professional Options examinations this is normally on the basis of one mark per point, possibly with an extra mark for more fully developing the same point.

Chapter summary

The professional skills will be worth 20 marks out of the total 100 in the exam.

Make sure you practise plenty of questions before the exam date, and focus on developing your professional skills as well as your technical skills.

Communication
- Report format and structure
- Style, language and clarity
- Effectiveness of communication
- Adherence to a specific request

Analysis and Evaluation
- Appropriate use of data
- Balanced and reasoned appraisal
- Balanced and reasoned assessment
- Problems clearly supported with examples
- Comprehensive evaluation

PROFESSIONAL SKILLS

Scepticism
- Challenge of information, evidence and assumptions
- Ability to probe into why
- Recognition that data is inadequate
- Recognition that information is missing or difficult to obtain
- Recognition that the use of information is inappropriate or that information should not be used in isolation
- Recognition of limitations or challenges of a course of action

Commercial acumen
- Recommendations are practical and plausible
- Effective use of examples and other practical considerations
- Recognition of possible consequences of past and future actions
- Recommendations demonstrate understanding of issues and are commercially sound
- Comprehensive assessment of possible ethical consequences

Employability and technology skills

Chapter learning objectives

This chapter contains an overview of the employability and technology skills syllabus area. This is relevant for all ACCA Applied Skills (except LW) and Strategic Professional exams.

1 Purpose of chapter

This chapter explains the content included within the employability and technology skills syllabus area. A similar syllabus area is included in all Applied Skills (except LW) and Strategic Professional level syllabi.

ACCA exams utilise software and technology similar to those used in the modern workplace. By studying ACCA exams, candidates will be equipped with not only technical syllabus knowledge and professional skills, but also practical, applied software skills. The employability and technology skills syllabus area is included within the syllabus to acknowledge this acquired skillset.

2 Content of the employability and technology skills syllabus area

The employability and technology skills syllabus area is outlined in the syllabus and study guide. It consists of the following:

1   Use computer technology to efficiently access and manipulate relevant information.

2   Work on relevant response options, using available functions and technology, as would be required in the workplace.

3   Navigate windows and computer screens to create and amend responses to exam requirements, using the appropriate tools.

4   Present data and information effectively, using the appropriate tools.

By using a computer-based examination (CBE), the ACCA has enabled the use of word processing, spreadsheet, screen navigation and data processing functionalities to become part of their assessment range. This replicates the skills used in the modern workplace, whether in accounting practice, in industry or outside of accountancy altogether.

Whilst sitting an exam, candidates will be using the functionality of the CBE software in a variety of ways e.g. to prioritise information within the question data provided, to organise and present their answers in a manageable fashion, to use shortcuts and software functionality to increase efficiency. Skills garnered in the workplace can be used in the examination and vice versa.

This reflects that exams offered at Applied Skills and Strategic Professional are designed to be relevant and accessible to all students. The delivery mode and assessment types require students to demonstrate similar skills to those required in the modern workplace. Offering computer-based exams (CBE) at all levels gives students the opportunity to focus on the application of knowledge to scenarios, using a range of tools – spreadsheets, word processing and presentations. This not only allows students to demonstrate their technical and professional skills, but also their use of the technology relevant to the modern workplace. CBEs, therefore, offers the candidate an examination delivery method that allows them to demonstrate their knowledge and skills with the technology they are most familiar with, in the classroom or at work.

3 CBE support and the ACCA Exam Practice Platform

ACCA candidates can access the ACCA's Exam Practice Platform to practice attempting questions using the CBE software. It is imperative that candidates are familiar with the software before attempting the exam.

The link to the APM Exam Practice Platform access gateway can be found here:

APM Exam Practice Platform

This requires a MyACCA login to access the platform.

Support, access to other exams, tutorial videos and CBE advice can be found here:

ACCA website CBE preparation resources

4 Contents of the CBE and Exam Practice Platform

On entering the Exam Practice Platform, candidates will access their dashboard, as follows:

Candidates should click their appropriate exam in the right hand side menu. There they will be able to 'assign' content to their workspace. Candidates can assign a blank workspace or ACCA official resources (which include past exams presented using the CBE software for the candidates to attempt) to their workspace.

This will be added to the candidate's 'Self-Assigned Material' listing as below:

When working within the assignment the candidate will use response options to provide their answer.

The **Response Options** are where the candidate will attempt their answers.

There are up to three types of response option provided, dependent upon the specific syllabus a candidate is studying. Not every option will appear in each exam. Check the exam practice platform for examples of the responses that are commonplace within your exam.

The response options are:

- the word processor,

- the spreadsheet, and

- the slides (not relevant for APM).

The candidate must determine which of the response options is the most suitable for their specific answer.

These replicate the functionality of widely used software packages. The ACCA has developed this software, for use during home question practice and under exam conditions, to replicate the practical skill sets and work-based behaviours adopted by various industries throughout the world. By studying the ACCA qualification, candidates will improve, not only on their technical knowledge and understanding, but also on skills applied on a daily basis within their work environments. Candidates should practise questions using the CBE platform to ensure they are familiar with the various functions available within their specific examination.

Word Processor

The word processor response option, when relevant, will appear as follows:

This resource has the following advantages and disadvantages:

Advantages	Disadvantages
It is easier to continue typing without entering new cells or becoming concerned about cell width	It cannot automatically perform calculations
Answers can be more easily split into paragraphs to make them more visually appealing and easier to mark	Numerical tables can be difficult to label and align
Bullet points can be used to present lists	
Text can be easily aligned and justified	
Superscript and subscript can be easily added to express terms such as 4^2, for example	

It is, therefore, best suited to discursive answers where candidates are asked, for example, to discuss, analyse or evaluate issues from a scenario or calculation.

The word processing software application could be used in the workplace within the writing of meeting agendas, meeting minutes, external letters, marketing output, briefings, audit reports, textbooks and instructional documentation.

Spreadsheet

The spreadsheet response option, when relevant, will appear as follows:

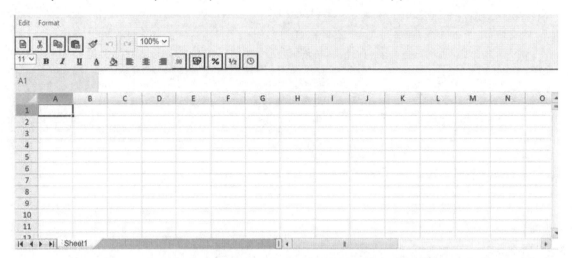

The spreadsheet software uses the same functionality as other commonly used spreadsheet software. Basic formulae functionality, such as SUM, power functions (e.g. SQRT) and the use of brackets are all reproduced within the ACCA software. Candidates are advised to practise questions using the software so that they are familiar with the functions available and how they can be utilised to the candidate's advantage through improved efficiency.

This resource has the following advantages and disadvantages:

Advantages	Disadvantages
This can quickly and easily perform calculations (e.g. using sums for totals or formulae for calculations)	Text will carry over beyond one cell and may go across and beyond the page width making answers difficult to follow (and mark)
Data within tables can be easily aligned	Bullet points are difficult to use
Shortcut icons can be used to quickly round figures, change numbers to percentages etc.	
Tables can easily and quickly be copied when calculations need to be reperformed (e.g. for sensitivity analysis, tax calculations for more than one person, financial statements for more than one company etc.)	
Column width can be adjusted to label length	

It is, therefore, best suited for performing calculations within the examination e.g. NPVs, tax computations, goodwill calculations.

Spreadsheet software is ubiquitous in the modern workplace. It has the capacity to record, store and organise huge swathes of data and information relating to all aspects of a business. Examples of only a few of its possible practical applications include the preparation of management and financial accounts, operational controls and record-keeping e.g. expense claims, data analytics, project appraisals, sample size selection and tax computations.

5 Chapter summary

The CBE software will replicate the work that is performed by accountants in a typical workplace. It will be used across the syllabus to support a candidate's answer by providing suitable response options for different types of answers.

These response options will be most suitable in the following instances (when available):

- For discursive answers: it is best to use the word processing option

- For calculations: it is best to use the spreadsheet option.

Index

KAPLAN PUBLISHING